Is Jesus Unique?

A Study of Recent Christology

Scott Cowdell

PAULIST PRESS
New York • Mahwah, N.J.

Library of Congress Cataloging-in-Publication Data

Cowdell, Scott.
     Is Jesus unique? : a study of recent christology / by Scott
Cowdell
        p.   cm. -- (Theological inquiries)
     Includes bibliographical references and index.
     ISBN 0-8091-3628-7 (alk. paper)
     1. Jesus Christ--History of doctrines--20th century.   I. Title
II. Series.
     BT198.C62   1996
     232'.09'045--dc20   95-47055
                                              CIP

Published by Paulist Press
997 Macarthur Boulevard
Mahwah, New Jersey 07430

Printed and bound in the United States of America

CONTENTS

iii

*This study is dedicated
to my wife, Lisa Carley*

Flaunt out, O sea, your separate flags of nations!
Flaunt out visible as ever the various flags and ship-
    signals!
But do you reserve especially for yourself and for the
    soul of man one flag above all the rest,
A spiritual woven signal for all nations, emblem of
    man elate above death,
Token of all brave captains and of all intrepid sailors
    and mates,
And of all that went down doing their duty,
Reminiscent of them, twined from all intrepid cap-
    tains young or old,
A pennant universal, subtly waving all time, o'er all
    brave sailors,
All seas, all ships.

Walt Whitman,
from "A Song For All Seas, All Ships"

Theological Inquiries

Studies in Contemporary Biblical and Theological Problems

General Editor
Lawrence Boadt, C. S. P.

PAULIST PRESS
New York ● Mahwah

PREFACE

I commenced work on recent Christology in 1988 when as a newly ordained deacon I began four years as a graduate student and tutor at the University of Queensland. The issue of Jesus' uniqueness and finality captured my imagination and preoccupied me from the latter part of 1989.

I wish to thank the Department of Studies in Religion at the University of Queensland for the support and the working environment provided there. Among the staff my thanks goes to Prof. Michael Lattke, Dr. Edgar Conrad, Rev. Dr. Ian Gillman and Dr. Richard Hutch for their kindness and friendship. Especially, however, I thank my supervisor, Dr. Philip Almond, who helped introduce me to the study of religion and theology as a first-year undergraduate in 1983 and has been helpful and encouraging ever since. Thanks are due to the Inter-Library Loan staff of Main Library who obtained the numerous journal articles I ordered. For financial assistance I am grateful to the Federal Government for an Australian Postgraduate Research Award.

During the period of my full-time work on this project I was also Honorary Assistant Curate of Holy Trinity Anglican Church at Fortitude Valley in Brisbane's inner-city. This was a wonderfully encouraging experience and a good counterfoil to work in the secular university. I express my gratitude to the parish, but in particular to the then rector, Canon Lyall Turley, who helped me through diaconate into priesthood, assisted me in every way, and taught me much by word and example. I greatly value his continuing friendship.

In the two years from mid-1992 the second half of this study was written in the midst of my newfound responsibilities as Rector of All Saints' Anglican Church in Chermside, a suburb of Brisbane.

To the then Regional Bishop, Rt. Rev'd. George Browning, and the parochial nominators who wanted to have me in spite of my urgent need to finish a Ph.D., I extend my thanks, and to the parishioners at large who are helping continue my education both theologically and practically. I am particularly grateful to my secretary, Mrs. Lyn Gregory, who eased my parish duties to allow me sufficient time to read and write, and to the memory of our honorary assistant, Deacon Brian Spry, who gladly took on extra pastoral work while I brought this study to a close but whose untimely death from cancer prevented him seeing its eventual publication.

I am thankful to my friend Fr. Howard Munro for his moral support through a long project, for reading the text as it appeared bit by bit then again in full, and for valuable discussions. The examiners of this work in its first incarnation as my doctoral thesis deserve thanks for their encouraging assessments and thoughtful critiques: Rev. Dr. James Haire (Head, School of Theology, Griffith University, Brisbane), Rev'd. Dr. Dennis Nineham (former Warden of Keble College, Oxford) and Rt. Rev'd. Dr. Rowan Williams (formerly Lady Margaret Professor at Oxford; now Bishop of Monmouth, Wales). Weaknesses in the finished product are not for want of any effort or perceptiveness on their part. Thanks are also due to Fr. Lawrence Boadt, C.S.P. and the team at Paulist Press in far-off New Jersey for kindnesses rendered and editorial expertise displayed.

To my wife Lisa Carley goes my deepest thanks, however. She has helped more than I can say—not only by proofreading the text, compiling the Bibliography and obtaining copyright permissions, but by her cheerful and wholehearted (albeit occasionally bemused) support through all my ups and downs as a fledgling priest and embryonic theologian, and despite the constraints this project has placed on our living "a normal life." To Lisa this study is dedicated, from a full heart.

Brisbane   SC
All Saints' Day, 1995

INTRODUCTION

Jesus' uniqueness and finality can no longer be taken for granted. Nowadays it is abandoned by a small but growing number of theologians; it is among the last crown jewels sold off by "the queen of
the sciences," lately fallen on hard times.[1] "Orthodox" writers of
Christology now find themselves defending the doctrine, whether explicitly or implicitly, well or badly, in a range of ways often as new
as the challenges they are answering. To date no thorough study of
these matters has appeared, though the last three decades have been
marked by an explosion of Christological writing expressing a variety of fundamental orientations, in response to deepening seculariza-
tion and to quite new theological conditions: globalization, skepticism, pluralism.[2]

This is a study in the Christological trends of a quarter-century,
beginning from the mid-1960s. In particular, it is a study of how
Jesus' uniqueness and finality has been treated by theologians of
every complexion during this period of convulsive change—for the
western world in general and its theology in particular.

While this study seeks to deal comprehensively with a specific
Christological matter, however, I venture that (in the light of many
wider issues involved) it might also serve as a general introduction to
Christology and even theology as a whole in the late twentieth century. In a time of methodological ferment, adequate comprehension of
a writer's thoughts about Jesus' uniqueness and finality calls for
careful attention to things touching not only on Jesus but on broader
areas within philosophical (or "fundamental") theology concerning
the nature of revelation, authority, creation and history, language and
society, the human person and the world religions. There can be no
doubt that the current quest for an adequate theological method is

1

fully represented in Christology, which could once remain aloof from such considerations, "safe" in the realm of systematic theology.

It is also important to note that these waters are frequently found muddied. Because discussion of Jesus' uniqueness and finality has of late taken some quite new directions, not all the reflections investigated here are as mature and considered as they might be, nor is the amount of unargued fundamental conviction always recognized. This makes for interesting encounters with theologians who have yet to fully assimilate the new conditions, so that to investigate their views on Jesus' uniqueness and finality is to approach their Christology, and even their theology as a whole, from a blindspot. As a result, and to mix a metaphor, normally poised and impressive theologians are occasionally encountered off-balance in the investigations which follow.

All this is offered to explain and justify the method employed in this study, which involves a critical overview of major contributions to recent Christology with the help of a new typology I have devised. This calls for a "close reading" of many key Christological texts of recent vintage, and often a reading of them "between the lines."

The original typology employed in this study identifies and explicates a fourfold pattern of Christological styles. The various methods and thinkers are examined according to their reliance on revelation, or else upon ontological structures determining the nature of reality, history and human existence; they are also sorted from one another according to how they utilize the historical Jesus in their systems, along with the human condition (whether anthropological constants provide a foundation for their theology). As a result, four positions emerge in which major contributors and approaches from the period of interest can be identified, while the advantages and disadvantages of their positions are brought all the better to light. These positions are "Conservative," "Idealist," "Liberal" and "Radical"; the last of these incorporates those who abandon the uniqueness and finality of Jesus, while the first three positions embrace those who maintain the doctrine in various ways.

To each of the four positions a chapter is devoted, with major sections considering each of today's prominent theologians. Other figures with something important to say are mentioned either in the text or in footnotes, as appropriate. While the study is not exhaustive, it is believed that the figures and the ideas considered are truly representative of late twentieth century Christology, its twists and turns, its strengths and weaknesses. None of these positions will ultimately be seen to provide an entirely satisfactory case, however, and some promising new directions will be considered in the Conclusion of this study.

In ending these preliminary comments, I express my hope that the comprehensive expositions, the sustained methodological questionings and the many critical evaluations undertaken in what follows will commend this study to the widest possible reading audience—to those interested in any aspect of recent Christology or theology in general, or in any of today's key theologians, as well as those readers with a particular interest in the uniqueness and finality of Jesus.

Before introducing the typology in detail, it is important to demarcate more fully the period of interest which will be covered. The mid-1960s saw the end of an era in theology and the birth of a new one. In Protestantism the great creative geniuses of modern theology were vacating the stage—Barth, Bultmann, Bonhoeffer and Tillich. The neo-orthodox tradition, begun with Barth and reaching forward through the work of Bonhoeffer, finally volatilized in the secular theology of early 1960s' America. While this was happening, Roman Catholicism was throwing open its windows to modernity after a long period of pre-critical, neo-scholastic theology. And Anglicanism had begun at last to learn the lessons of nineteenth century biblical criticism. All of this took place against the backdrop of a world reconstructing itself after war and settling into a half-century during which society was reinvented from top to bottom, with hitherto unimagined depths of uncertainty encountered.

The climate in this period of interest is well drawn by Edward Schillebeeckx. He speaks of the emergence of a global sense of our "co-humanity" since the 1950s, initially buoyant in the euphoria of peace after World War II but increasingly pessimistic since the 1970s. He points out

that only since 1965 has there been a call in our world for more democratizing of all relationships, individual and structural. Only then did major world problems with

deeply human connotations come to the attention of all of
us, a development also encouraged by the obvious attention paid to them by the media: nuclear energy, nuclear
armament, the pollution of the environment, the exhaus-
tion of our natural resources, the oil crisis and the shifting of the East-West conflict to the North-South conflict.
Moreover the Eurocentric place of the West European
Churches has been weakened, and Europeans are more
than ever aware of their regional and thus one-sided self-
understanding. The 1970s also brought great alarm about
Western prosperity. This led to mistrust, helplessness and
anxiety; people saw the fragility of the political and economic world situation. Periods of crisis always provoke
radicalizing, conflicting trends which lead to polariza-
tion. Many people then become apolitical, escaping into
free inwardness, and others escape into external wanton-
ness and grim vandalism—often without any soul or inwardness, without the concern to help humanity to survive in ourselves and others.[3]

This evocation of the 1960s through the 1980s mentions the kind of
historical and social forces which have helped shape theology in
these times. The main issue arising is that of the loss of absolutes.

One aspect mentioned by Schillebeeckx is the collapse of Eurocentrism. This is further explicated by Langdon Gilkey.

The West has been dominant in almost every sphere, at
almost every level, for four centuries: militarily, scientifically, industrially, politically, sociologically, morally, and
religiously—or at least the West had no doubt of that
dominance.... After 1945, this began to collapse, and to
collapse on all levels—military, political, moral and religious. Colonies vanished, Europe disappeared as a major
power, other non-Western power centers appeared representing other ways of life and other religions. The West
no longer ruled the world; Western ways were no longer
unassailable; Western religion became one among the
other world religions; and (not insignificantly) the Christ-

ian faith became the one now most morally culpable, the chief imperialistic, nonspiritual and in fact barely moral faith! Correspondingly, Western culture became radically open to non-Western religions; missionary influence flowed in the opposite direction; and the spiritual power of other faiths began to assert itself on Christian turf.[4]

As a result of this collapsed Eurocentrism, and all of a sudden, theology was forced to reckon with an entirely new situation. Wilfred Cantwell Smith relates an incident in which an undergraduate writing in the Harvard student newspaper was able to show up a major misunderstanding in something Paul Tillich had concluded about the religious traditions of Asia. For Cantwell Smith an incident like this shows that the days are over when someone could be a major spokesperson for his or her own religious tradition with little real awareness of other traditions—less than that of an undergraduate. "Looking at the matter historically," he writes, "one may perhaps put it thus: probably Tillich belongs to the last generation of theologians who can formulate their conceptual system as religiously isolationist.... The new generation of the Church, unless it is content with a ghetto, will live in a cosmopolitan environment, which will make the work of even a Tillich appear parochial."[5] Since this prophetic statement of 1961, theology has indeed been forced to deal with these challenges. One of the characteristics of every major figure dealt with in this study is that they have given conscious attention to the problem of Christianity and the world religions.

Alongside this is a new sense of the relativity of all our ideas, contributing to our loss of absolutes in the west and resulting in a serious crisis of confidence. George Lindbeck points out, again with regard to Paul Tillich, that a great liberal theologian could command a wide audience from across the board in the humanities in the 1950s, trading on shared assumptions in many disciplines about the nature of humanity as illuminated by existentialism. But those days are gone, with no dominant "philosophical anthropology" to be found in today's world and certainly no agreement about the place of human experience in theology.[6]

This state of affairs was brewing in the nineteenth century when sociology and cultural anthropology were born, with their dawning understanding of human behavior in terms of cultural wholes.[7] There followed, early this century, the so-called "linguistic turn" in philosophy of language, which bore mature fruit in the "linguistic naturalism" of the later Wittgenstein, for whom language had become an intra-cultural thing, the meaning of which was found in its use rather than in reference to things.[8] This development was paralleled in the field of linguistics, in which structuralists sought meaning in the interplay of signs (signifiers) rather than in any "referent" in the world, or any "signified" pre-linguistic idea in the mind (thus severing the link between meaning and human interiority, so beloved of Romantics and of theologians like Schleiermacher). Attention to this play of linguistic signs is denied any metaphysical weight whatever in the work of Jacques Derrida. In turn, the post-structuralist movement in literary theory sees meaning in terms of various readings of a text only, an entirely relativistic theory.[9]

In addition the neo-Marxist challenge to our western sense of moral rectitude began to be felt with the worldwide student protests of 1968. Thus the suspicions of Marx and Nietzsche about corruption of truth by the powerful have lent a political edge to these relativizing and skeptical cultural forces which are now normally called "post-modernity." In the radical French historian of ideas Michel Foucault we have perhaps the "compleat" post-modern intellectual, combining a deconstructive reading of historical continuities, according to which different historical epochs represent completely different (and essentially exclusive) cultural totalities, on the one hand, and an anarchic spirit on the other—Foucault is eager to undermine societal authority structures which underlie much of what we would call "civilization." This he does by seeking to expose their origins, which he usually finds to have involved a drive toward power and social control.[10]

Through all of this the cumulative thrust is toward an unseating of the individual, and its replacement by collective realities like language and society. This includes the undermining of human interiority, reason and feeling as of no epistemological importance, contrary to the way they have functioned for empiricists, rationalists and romantics, in favor of radically non-realist, constructivist epistemologies. Thus the "turn to the individual" which began at least with Descartes and his *cogito* has become, in the second half of the twen-

tieth century, a "turn to the collective." As a result a radically destabilizing force has been unleashed on the humanities and the social
sciences, echoing the cultural and social upheaval more generally experienced in the west today.[11]

In the same way that neo-Marxist currents, via critical theory
and the theology of hope, have influenced the rise of liberation theology in the third world, so this new methodological anti-foundationalism has influenced theology in the west. Liberal theology, confident
of the religious disclosivity of human experience and the purposive-
ness of history (both of which have nineteenth century roots in romanticism and German idealism), has faced an onslaught under these
new conditions, in which the whole long tradition of natural theology
in western Christianity has been impugned—essentially because this
newfound relativism denies nature any self-same foundations apart
from culture's variegate construal of nature.[12]

All these post-modern challenges, of historical and "political"
skepticism as well as those involving cultural relativism, are faced
by the major figures discussed in this study (with varying degrees of
seriousness and effectiveness to be sure, but confront them they do).
The credibility of any theology today, not to mention any case for
Jesus' uniqueness and finality, depends on the seriousness of its engagement with the period's special challenges.

In this period, then, theological foundations formerly thought to
be certain are regularly questioned, such as the scriptures, the inner
witness of the spirit for pietists, and the various Protestant confes-
sions.[13] In 1966 John McIntyre realized that Christology had moved to
the center of this newfound void, providing a focus for talking about
revelation in theology: "beyond its usual reach Christology picked-up
exegetical, expository and hermeneutical functions as well as normative and critical ones."[14] In the Roman Catholic world it has also been
a fertile period for Christology, with the authorization of critical biblical studies in the 1943 papal encyclical *Divino Afflanté Spiritu* (reiterated in Vatican II's Dogmatic Constitution on Divine Revelation, *Dei
Verbum*, of 1965),[15] and with the 1500th anniversary of the Council of
Chalcedon in 1951, issuing in a re-emphasis on the humanity of Jesus
after a long neo-scholastic period in which his divinity was much to
the fore.[16] The result, according to Francis Fiorenza, has been a
change in Roman Catholic theological methodology so that dogmatic

definition becomes the end point rather than the starting point, with New Testament Christology and present human experience in both world and Church coming first—a process sufficiently diverse for Fiorenza to conclude that "Contemporary Christology is in general characterized by a pluralism of theological method that was previously unknown in Catholic theology."[17] Anglicanism, too, began at last to take aboard the insights and challenges of modern biblical studies. For Robert Morgan, writing in 1982,

> As the Orontes once flowed into the Tiber, so it seems today that the Neckar has flowed into the Isis. English theology over the past fifteen years, like Roman Catholic theology on the Continent and in the United States, has quite suddenly come to terms with relatively sceptical conclusions in the historical study of the gospels. After more than a century of polemic and resistance, the methods pioneered in Germany by Strauss and Baur have become broadly accepted in academic theology, even if the debt is rarely acknowledged, and non-specialists remain angry or perplexed.[18]

Another distinguishing feature of this period is that the historical Jesus has returned from the theological exile to which he was banished from roughly 1906 to 1953. Schweitzer had finally sounded the death-knell for the nineteenth century quest of the historical Jesus when he showed just how little history and just how much projection of religious ideals from that century went into the various nineteenth century "lives."[19] As a result, the historical Jesus was not important for Bultmann and Tillich in early to mid-twentieth century theology. They emphasised the Christ of the kerygma who changed lives in the present, or the "New Being" in which Christians could participate as they claimed the benefits of Christ; these leading figures of early to mid-twentieth century theology did not appreciate the strange apocalyptic figure from the first century to which Schweitzer had introduced the theological world.[20]

In 1953, however, Ernst Käsemann, a student of Bultmann, cleared the way for the so-called "new quest of the historical Jesus," advocating a quite different historical strategy from that used in the original quest. He abandoned the attempt to pare away later interpretations of Jesus as championed by Harnack, who believed that the corruption of Jesus' message had begun with Paul and that the bare historical figure, the "brief Galilean vision of humanity," alone had credibility. Instead of this discredited option, Käsemann followed the existential historiography of the British philosopher of history R.G. Collingwood[21] in seeking the history of Jesus *through* rather than *behind* (and "thanks to," rather than "in spite of") the faith-testimony of Jesus' interpreters in the New Testament.[22]

So, riding on the new quest, the historical Jesus made a "triumphal entry" to the holy city of mainstream theology, arriving in the mid-1960s. This reappearance of the historical Jesus has influenced all the Christology done since that time. Concerning the figures to be discussed in this study, the historical Jesus of the new quest is soundly employed by a few of them, invoked with varying degrees of success by some of them, rejected by a few of them, but ignored by none of them.

Having thus considered the major influences on Christology in our period of interest, the parameters of the study must be set out and the typology introduced more fully before the investigation can begin.

Obviously, criteria for inclusion and exclusion must be stated in a study of this sort. Those theologians considered in what follows have been selected for their attention to crucial theological issues characterizing the period of interest, as set out in the preceding discussion. It goes without saying that they are also those who have written on the subject of Christology.

Very important is their engagement with the world of serious, critical biblical study. For this reason, conservative evangelical writers who insist on a literal reading of scripture are not considered— for such persons Jesus' uniqueness and finality is simply not an issue for discussion. In the same vein, those committed merely to a reiteration of traditional dogmatic formulae, whether or not this is done with any methodological sophistication, are not considered (those called "Conservative" in this study accept the challenges of liberal theology as valid and engage with these challenges at some depth— they are not like those content to issue pronouncements secure within their dogmatic edifice).

So, for instance, writers offering updated versions of nine-teenth century kenotic theories of the incarnation are not considered. To be sure, David Brown is right in calling this important movement "the first serious attempt of orthodoxy to come to terms with modern critical scholarship,"[23] because it allowed Jesus' human limitedness, as brought to light by historical critical studies of the gospels, to be incorporated into the traditional understanding of his divine person-hood. This was achieved by describing his incarnate life as that of God in kenosis, doffing his attributes of power, perfection etc. But there are many faults with this theory, not least that it leaves us with the God of theism whose essence is power—the very God which ad-vocates of panentheism and process theology are quick to offload nowadays as a liability in the face of scientific and moral critiques, the problem of evil etc. For our purposes, however, the kenotic vi-sion is inadequate because Chalcedonian orthodoxy is simply pre-supposed,[24] whereupon ways are sought to make the dogma more palatable in the atmosphere of modern thought.[25] This is not the sort of serious engagement with modernity and post-modernity we find in the major theologians studied here, however. Even if they do end up with a dependence upon revelation to the exclusion of any attempt at establishing a human meeting point, as Moltmann does, for instance, nevertheless they do so in confrontation with the tenets of liberal the-ology at every step, making a case for their starting point rather than merely assuming it.[26]

Before discussing the typology to be employed here, it is fit-ting to say something in general about the importance of typologies as used in recent theology. Such tools have proved very useful in clarifying debates and furthering discussions.

Well known, for instance, is Gustav Aulén's now classic typo-logical arrangement of atonement theories into "objective" (or "Latin," Anselmian), "subjective" (or "humanistic," pietistic) and "classic" (as in St. Paul, the fathers and Luther—"Christus Victor"). This exercise certainly helped revive the fortunes of the "classic" the-ory, which Aulén favored.[27] Also important for both Christian theolo-gy and Christian action was the famous typology of H. Richard Niebuhr, in which the relationship of Church and gospel with world and culture was found to have five typical expressions: "Christ against Culture," "the Christ of Culture," "Christ above Culture,"

"Christ and Culture in Paradox" and (the favored option, as in Augustine and F.D. Maurice) "Christ the Transformer of Culture."[28]

Regarding theological method, there are a number of important typological statements. Looking at options available at the end of the theological era preceding the period under investigation here (the era of Barth, Bultmann and Tillich), the sociologist and theologian Peter Berger offers a typology of options: theology is either "deductive" (conservative, reliant upon authority), "reductive" (as in Bultmann and the secular theology which Berger finds distasteful) or "inductive" (Berger's favored option, as in Schleiermacher). Thus Berger sees theology as either reaffirming the tradition in spite of challenges to it, secularizing the tradition, or else reinvigorating and renewing the tradition by recovering the experiences embodied in it.[29] A variant of this is the currently very influential typology of George Lindbeck, in which the second and the third of Berger's options are, essentially, reversed. For Lindbeck, theology today is either "cognitive-propositional" (conservative, basically), "subjective-expressivist" (essentially liberal theology in the Schleiermacher tradition) or "cultural-linguistic," a new category expressing the post-liberal position which Lindbeck names and advocates in his influential book.[30] Lindbeck's typology proved helpful in conceiving my own for this study, as did the similar but rather simpler division of theology into "Conservative," "Liberal" and "Radical" championed by Don Cupitt.[31] More aware of the variety and sophistication of current options in liberal theology, however, is David Tracy, who offers a fivefold typological arrangement of current theology into "Orthodox," "Liberal," "Neo-Orthodox," "Radical" and "Revisionist." The first four options are basically those we have met in Berger, Lindbeck, and Cupitt, though the conservative camp is split into "Orthodox" and "Neo-Orthodox." The "Revisionist" option is new, however, representing the re-emergence of a method of correlation in more attenuated, post-modern times—this is Tracy's position, which he also calls "critical correlation."[32]

Another area where typologies have proved helpful is in the Christian theology of non-Christian religions. Niebuhr's schema is taken up and modified in this context by Charles Davis.[33] Alan Race offers another, with a division of the field that has proved very powerful in his simple schema of "Exclusivism" (no salvation, though perhaps some revelation, in other religions), "Inclusivism" (salvation through Christ available in all religions, as in Karl Rahner's "Anonymous Christians" idea) and "Pluralism" (that salvation is present apart from Christ *through* all the religions—the view we will encounter with Hick and Cantwell Smith in Chapter 10, below).[34] A variant typology belongs to Paul Knitter, with "Exclusivism," "Christ Within the Religions," "Christ Above the Religions" and "Christ Alongside the Religions." Knitter's second and third options divide the position which Race termed "Inclusivism," allowing the view of Hans Küng to be included—that Christ is norm and critical standard among the religions (an improvement on the views of Rahner, Küng believes). The fourth option, "Christ Alongside the Religions," represents Knitter's own solution, also called "complimentary uniqueness," which will be discussed in Chapter 10, below.[35]

In the field of Christology today there is not much typological assistance. Avery Dulles offers a grouping of approaches under the headings "The Dogmatic Approach" (conservative, including neo-orthodoxy), "The Historical Approach" (interested in the historical Jesus through the new quest), "The Biblical-Kerygmatic Approach" (Bultmann *et al.*), "The Liturgical-Sacramental Approach" (emphasising the ongoing presence of Christ in church experience as important for Christology) and "The Secular-Dialogic approach" (basically Paul Tillich and his method of correlation).[36] While Dulles has correctly identified a number of important emphases in recent Christology, such as the historical Jesus and the role of contemporary experience, nevertheless other emphases which he highlights are now either on the wane (such as the confident Tillichian synthesis fatally mauled by post-modern challenges) or else completely absent from the field (such as a Bultmannian kerygmatic approach in isolation from any discussion of the historical Jesus). A more powerful instrument is required which picks out key issues from the current crop of writers who have risen to prominence while the generation of post-war theologians has declined.

The sort of instrument which appeals to me is the type which goes beyond merely listing options and employs a genuine typology which can be visualized with a grid. The priest/sociologist Andrew M. Greeley offers such a tool in his discussion of the varying attitudes toward God in western society, with a vertical axis ranging from "warm" (top) to "cool" (bottom), and a horizontal axis ranging from "impersonal" (left) to "personal" (right). Thus a fourfold grid is established, with (proceeding clockwise from the top left): 1) a "Warm-Impersonal" idea of God (the absolute good); 2) a "Warm-Personal" notion (God as ever-present helper, friend and comforter); 3) "Cool-Personal" (with God as creator, personal spiritual power or judge); and 4) "Cool-Impersonal" (God as an indefinable spirit, or even beyond description).[37] Our understanding of "folk Christianity" is certainly enhanced by such an instrument.

In the area of Christology there is an immensely attractive and powerful "grid typology" offered by George Rupp, linking theories of the atonement with the metaphysics of divine action in the world (directly) and even the history of western culture (indirectly).[38] Both of the grid's axes deal with the scope of the atonement and the sphere of its impact: the vertical axis, dealing with "space," has "Realist" (focusing upon the whole universe) at the top, and "Nominalist" (focusing upon the individual) at the bottom; the horizontal axis, dealing with "time," has "Transactional" on the left (the atonement focused at one point in history) and "Processive" on the right (the atonement accessible throughout all of time and history). So (again, proceeding clockwise from the top left) a "Realist-Transactional" theory would emphasise a once-for-all change for the whole world, as in Anselm or Barth; a "Realist-Processive" view would conceive the atonement as an ongoing process through history, as in Irenaeus and Schleiermacher; a "Nominalist-Processive" perspective would be a psychological one, understanding the atonement as a *process* of individual transformation in personal spiritual life; while a "Nominalist-Transactional" approach would focus on a *single event* of transformation for the individual, as in Bultmann's understanding of the kerygma's "saving" impact.

Addressing a theological issue using such a "grid typology" allows far more nuance and subtlety in disclosure than a mere list of the various features or styles of argument—while Aulén's division of atonement theories into three types was most instructive, nevertheless Rupp's typology adds life to these categories, showing how they differ from one another in basic ways, pointing out where far-from-obvious affinities are to be found, and so allowing keener distinctions to be made.[39]

It is now apposite that I introduce my own typology. It uses this "grid method," rather than a "list method," so allowing a significant insight into the way Jesus' uniqueness and finality has been approached in this new theological period—from the mid-1960s to the start of the 1990s. My typology is reproduced in diagram form in the accompanying chart.

The vertical axis of my typology shows reliance on overarching structures of meaning, whether they be understood by those under consideration as either revelation or as metaphysics—a high dependence is found among those on the high side, and a low dependence among those on the low side (top and bottom). We might label this vertical axis the axis of "revelation and/or ontology." The horizontal axis intersecting it shows reliance on evidence from human experience in history—*in particular the historical Jesus and conceptions of a uniform "human condition."* Low dependence is found on the left side and high dependence on the right side. We might label this horizontal axis the axis of "history."

Thus a fourfold grid is established, with positions (again, commencing clockwise from the top left) numbered 1 through to 4, each of which has a section devoted to it, from Part I through to Part IV. Those in Positions 1 to 3 all continue to maintain the uniqueness and finality of Jesus, each in his own way. Those in Position 4 do not, for various but related reasons—their Jesus is *not* unique and final.[40]

Position 1 contains the theologians I am calling "conservative." They have a high dependence on "revelation and/or ontology," and a low dependence on "history," by which I mean their work does not rely on conclusions about the historical Jesus or any universal human condition. There are three current approaches identified within the "conservative" conception of Jesus' uniqueness and finality, each of which is awarded a chapter in Part I.

The "Theology of the Cross" position, as exemplified by Jürgen Moltmann, centers on the revealing in Jesus' cross of a God otherwise hidden in the world and in history (hence a high dependence on revelation and no real dependence at all on what can be known of Jesus historically, nor on any universal human experience—indeed, Moltmann denies any such experience in post-modern fashion).

TYPOLOGY OF APPROACHES
TO THE UNIQUENESS AND FINALITY OF JESUS
IN LATE TWENTIETH CENTURY THEOLOGY

1. CONSERVATIVE

Revelation
and/or
Ontology
(HIGH)

2. IDEALIST

Theology of the Cross
— Jürgen Moltmann

Theology and
the Pressure of Reality
— Thomas F. Torrance
— D. M. MacKinnon, Colin Gunton

Theology and
the *Christus Praesens*
— Hans Frei
— Dietrich Ritschl

Transcendental Anthropology
— Karl Rahner, S.J.

Proleptic Eschatology
— Wolfhart Pannenberg

A Bridging Figure
— Walter Kasper

History (LOW) ——————————————— *History (HIGH)*

Historical Skeptics
— Dennis Nineham, John Bowden
— Maurice Wiles, Frances Young

Religious Pluralists
— John Hick
— Wilfred Cantwell Smith
— Paul F. Knitter

Complete Relativists
— Don Cupitt
— George A. Lindbeck

Logos Christology
— Piet Schoonenberg, S.J.
— John A.T. Robinson

Christology "From Below"
— Edward Schillebeeckx, O.P.
— Hans Küng

Revelation
and/or
Ontology
(LOW)

4. RADICAL

3. LIBERAL

The next group are gathered under the heading "Theology and the Pressure of Reality," with Thomas F. Torrance as the major exponent (his views are tempered somewhat by D.M. MacKinnon and Colin Gunton, two other British theologians also considered there). Torrance rejects the Kantian epistemology underlying liberal theology, with its interjection of human interiority between the object and subject of revelation. For Torrance any *object* of knowing provides the *subject* with an appropriate means of knowing, in theology as (allegedly) in science. So he shows a high reliance on revelation (as quite unmediated) and a low reliance on human experience, which is not allowed to intrude. Nor does Torrance depend at all on the historical Jesus to establish his case, though like all the writers considered in this study he does take critical biblical studies into account.

The third group in Part I appear under the heading "Theology and the *Christus Praesens*"—the present Christ. Hans Frei and Dietrich Ritschl introduce a theme which will prove unavoidable in this study, and that is the role of participation in Christian worship and praxis for all Christology (understood as opening a cognitive world of its own within the wider world of meaning and experience). For Frei this means entering into the world of biblical narrative, the "story of Jesus Christ," rather than trying to translate that story into something which modern western people can integrate with the values and priorities of their culture (an assimilation which he identifies at the heart of liberal theology, and as fundamentally wrongheaded). Ritschl is similar, though he understands "the story" more broadly in terms of ongoing Christian tradition and worship. He follows Torrance in rejecting an individual focus, which he traces from Augustine through Kant and the enlightenment to Christianity today. For both these writers, revelation is very prominent—one must enter an authoritative world to share their perspectives. The historical Jesus does not feature, for the historical Jesus is excerpted from "the story" in the gospels and the tradition and it is this story inviolate which stands centrally for both Frei and Ritschl. Nor is the human condition important—it is seen as a bulwark of liberal theology impeding access to the true place of encounter with God, which is found by looking away from "the world" and into "the story."

Thus in Position 1 we have a variety of related approaches which all place a high premium on "revelation" and a low premium on both the historical Jesus and the human condition.

Position 2 covers those who in Part II are called "idealist." Rather than revelation pure and simple, it is an idealist view of history which calls the tune in their theology; an overarching understanding of the meaning of all history and human experience, seen as the process of divine action and disclosure, determines everything else. These writers believe in the importance of historical experience, and the life of Jesus within it—after all, they see history and human experience as the realm of God's action and revelation. Their Jesus remains quite definitely unique and final as the meeting point of God and humanity in revelation, or else as the revelatory centerpiece of history.

The "transcendental anthropology" of Karl Rahner is a vision of the human person in the divine economy, with the human condition disclosing an active, in-built disposition toward revelation which is answered by God in the person of Jesus; so revelation, ontology, human condition and historical Jesus are blended together by this quintessential "idealist." The "proleptic eschatology" of Wolfhart Pannenberg is a different type of "idealist" case, in which the meaning of all history is disclosed in advance in the resurrection of Jesus, understood as a publicly accessible event within that history. Pannenberg subsumes the human condition and the events of Jesus' life within a meaningful whole, leading me to locate him on the upper side of my typology, and on the right, as very definitely an "idealist." Walter Kasper is mentioned as a bridging figure—between Rahner and Pannenberg, but also between the "idealist" and "liberal" positions.

Position 3 gathers together those who in Part III are called "liberal" theologians. They have a low dependence on revelation and grand historical schemas, preferring to start their theological exploration from the (supposed) facts of human experience and the historical facts which can (allegedly) be known about Jesus. It ought to be mentioned that the "historical Jesus dependence" of those in Part II, while serious, is not as pivotal for the cases addressed there as it is for those in Part III. Because these "liberal" theologians are not beginning from a broader conception of revelation or ontology into which "the facts" of history are fitted, but from the facts themselves, theirs tends more toward a theology "from below," as distinct from the theologies "from above" found above the horizontal axis in my typology.[41]

Two groups are discussed in Part III. The "logos theology" of Piet Schoonenberg, and that of John Robinson, are liberal theologies which understand human experience, insight and life in the world as the realm of revelation. The focus of that revelation is found in the life of Jesus, which they deem to be historically accessible. To be sure, they go on to draw metaphysical implications from the strong correlation they identify between the person of Jesus and the human condition, extolling him as the logos incarnate. But this "ontological" discussion follows upon "the facts" of history and experience, rather than preceding them; while the "idealist" writers inserted the facts into their overarching frameworks, Robinson and Schoonenberg tend to invoke these framework in response to "the facts." So while there are similarities between them and some in Part II, Rahner and Kasper especially, nevertheless the limited place of metaphysics in their programs and their understanding of revelation as entirely "from below" suffice to distinguish Schoonenberg and Robinson from the "idealist" position.

Under the heading "Christology 'From Below'" Edward Schillebeeckx and Hans Küng emerge among those treated in this study as the theologians most attentive to the historical Jesus and to the yearnings of our human condition—and as the least interested in any overarching framework of revelation and ontology apart from human experience with Jesus. In Jesus, as the new quest reveals him, they find a unique answer to the human dilemma, which they think constitutes a sufficient claim—their theologies are truly "from below."

Lastly, in Position 4 there are the "radical" theologians, labeled thus in Part IV because they deny Jesus any uniqueness and finality. With those in Position 3 they avoid any grand conception of the world and God's revelation to it, just as they share with those in Position 1 an avoidance of the human condition and the historical Jesus. Put these convictions together and there are no grounds left to them for asserting that Jesus is unique or final.

The rejection of the historical Jesus provides a theological foundation by these "radicals" because of a combination of historical skepticism and cultural relativism, which also explains their (post-modern) denial that any transcultural human condition exists at all. The denial of both these elements is central for Dennis Nineham, John Bowden, Maurice Wiles and Frances Young, the British theologians here named as "historical skeptics." John Hick and Wilfred Cantwell Smith, old campaigners in the cause of breaking-down Christian exclusivism vis à vis the world religions, retain some liberal elements in their cases, however. Along with their fellow "religious pluralist" Paul F. Knitter, though, they differ from the "liberal" writers in denying Jesus any uniqueness and finality. The "complete relativists," also found there, are entirely post-modern, abandoning any foundations for theology whatever: not human experience, not the historical Jesus (who, even if he were historically reliable, could not be universally relevant)—there being no way from particularity to universality according to these writers, for whom diversity is everything. In Don Cupitt we have the most radical position of all—a full-blown Christian atheism which is grateful to Jesus certainly, while finding him to be nothing more than a personal favorite.

Having set out the details of my typology and addressed the material to be covered in this study at some length, it is important to state that typologies are only tools, and not overly interesting for their own sakes. Nor are they necessarily most interesting in what they manage to include—often, the fact that some aspect of someone's otherwise "well-behaved" position manages to escape its allocated place in my typology proves more interesting than an exact fit (as is the case, for instance, with the liberal trends identified in all the non-"liberal" positions). What is more, it will become clear that there are *additional* factors affecting those grouped into the first three positions, those "from below" as well as "from above," such as the resurrection of Jesus and the experience of the impact of his life on the church and on individual Christians.

Nevertheless, a typology such as this does allow certain strengths and weaknesses in the various styles of argument to be discerned—indeed, the weaknesses of each position will be put as questions to those considered in the subsequent part, and so on down the line. One hopes that significant clarification and a goad to further investigation is provided by such an undertaking, apart from which there could be no moral justification whatever for inflicting yet another typology on the undeserving reader.

PART I

CONSERVATIVE

The study begins with a group of theologians here deemed to be "conservative." Their conservatism is shown in strategic biblical literalism or else in Barth-style revelational positivism, though by no means in any simple regurgitation of Chalcedonian (or any other) orthodoxy. They are also "conservative" rather than "idealist" (i.e. as in Part II, below) in their refusal to link Christ with any process of historical coming-to-be, whether it be Hegelian or Teilhardian. They are distinct from those on the right side of my typology in carefully avoiding explicit dependence on any "human condition" and on the historical Jesus as mainstays of their theology. But theirs is, nevertheless, a conservatism hammered out on the anvil of liberal trends in Christology.

Nearly every approach considered here represents some variation on the neo-orthodox theme. Yet a wide range of recent thought and experience is invoked in its articulation—from the influence of biblical theology, neo-Marxist critique and the memory of wartime rigors upon Moltmann's *theologia crucis*, to that of Polanyi's severely realist philosophy of science upon the Reformed theology of Torrance, to that of literary theory on Frei.

Whether the ghost of liberal theology has been thoroughly exorcised, however, looms as a major concern. Occasional "lapses" will be identified throughout these chapters. These are offset by what amounts to a resolute fideism, with insufficient attention given to questions of religious knowing. So while the largely anti-idealist and anti-liberal campaign of these "conservative" writers is frequently heady in its insights, it is not always hermeneutically satisfying in its arguments nor, therefore, is it overwhelmingly compelling in its conclusions.

21

Chapter One

THEOLOGY OF THE CROSS

Christian "theology of the cross" began with St. Paul and flowered with Martin Luther.

For Paul the cross of Jesus Christ offered the only true knowledge of God, declaring spiritually bankrupt those who boasted of knowing God otherwise. Paul's God acted in the darkness of Jesus' cross to exalt the humble who pin their hopes there, and all this at the expense of those clinging either to private gnostic revelations or else to the supposed privileges of Israel's old covenant and its law.

For his part, Martin Luther countered the medieval church's "bureaucracy of salvation" with the same vision: knowing God was not the preserve of popes nor were God's workings open to the syllogisms of schoolmen (with their *theologia naturalis*). Only in the cross of Jesus Christ is God known aright as a savior who justifies the unrighteous on the basis of his own righteousness through grace alone. Any such *theologia crucis* is thus opposed to any *theologia gloriae*, with its "obvious" God and its spirit of triumphalism. For Luther, as for St. Paul at its inception, it was in this theology alone that sinners could find a true theology of freedom.[1] Jürgen Moltmann is an inheritor of and a major contributor to this venerable tradition.

JÜRGEN MOLTMANN

Jürgen Moltmann is a professor of systematic theology at the University of Tübingen and an ordained minister in the German Reformed Church. He is arguably the most important and influential contemporary theologian, clearly occupying center stage in current Christology alongside Edward Schillebeeckx.

It is surely correct to label Moltmann a theological "conservative" according to the terms of this study, though by no means is he either reactionary or hidebound. To call him conservative does not mean that all liberal alternatives are, by definition, more hermeneutically self-conscious and sophisticated. On the contrary Moltmann has worked up his program from the beginning as a challenge to liberal theology. Nor is Moltmann a conservative in the sense of one who will not question credal orthodoxy. He offers ecclesiastical surprises, too, challenging "culture Protestantism" with some rather sectarian ideas, including a repudiation of infant baptism.[2] And Moltmann is no social conservative; he writes increasingly as a political activist embracing feminist and ecological issues (his wife, Elisabeth Moltmann-Wendel, is a feminist theologian).

Moltmann is accredited as founder of "the theology of hope school," which also includes Wolfhart Pannenberg. From this movement came some of the inspiration for Latin American liberation theology.[3] "Theology of hope" restores a full-blown "biblical" doctrine of eschatology to centrality in Christian theology in the face of all attempts by liberal theology to see it historically actualized through human effort, or else to personalize and demythologize it. This hope then becomes a catalyst for subverting unjust structures of every kind in the present for the sake of God's coming kingdom. So Moltmann, as was also said of Barth ("the red pastor of Safenwil"), is quite radical for a conservative.

According to Moltmann's future-oriented theology, full revelation, along with "proof" of God and of Christian hope, will only be granted in the eschaton. Thus Christianity and Judaism can continue serving as joint witnesses in the meantime. To this extent Moltmann's Jesus is *not as yet* unique and final—this could only be declared true in the *parousia*. But, nevertheless, Moltmann leaves no doubt that Jesus Christ is the one he expects will fulfill the role of God's final revealer and savior and that he is knowable as such *proleptically* with the eyes of faith. Perhaps we could say that for Moltmann Jesus Christ is the unique and final pointer toward, and to that extent the present embodiment of, God's coming messiah, though his later work tends more toward an understanding of Jesus as God's present incarnation.[4]

We can better understand Moltmann's program by examining some of its formative influences. According to Calvin and Barth[5] our minds share in the general fallenness of human nature, and so too for Moltmann—the "natural man" cannot know God unaided. Moltmann learned this lesson, and discovered the Christian hope which enabled him to deal with it, in the aftermath of World War II and particularly as a prisoner of the British in Scotland and in the north of England. He returned to Germany and took up the study of theology at Göttingen, unable to stomach any liberal Protestant *theologia gloriae*; all he and his friends could understand in dark days of God's absence was Luther's *theologia crucis*.[6] Moltmann was also among the first to undertake serious study of Dietrich Bonhoeffer,[7] and Hans Küng points out the influence of death of God ideas in Hegel and Bonhoeffer on Moltmann's own.[8]

Biblical theology also has a place. Moltmann took up the prophets' emphasis on eschatology and judgment, along with Old Testament notions of covenant, through the work of Gerhard von Rad, Walter Zimmerli and Rolf Rendtdorf. Apocalyptic in the New Testament, and synoptic teaching on the kingdom of God and Pauline *theologia crucis*, have also made their impact through the work of Ernst Käsemann and Ulrich Wilckens.[9] Thus the biblical hermeneutic Moltmann prefers is one of promise.[10]

Moltmann rejects tendencies in modern historiography and theology which amplify historical reason but fail to note that perpetual revolutionary character to which the modern, enlightenment period also gave rise—the age of revolution.[11] Instead he pursues "the Hegel-Marx-Bloch line, considered as an alternative to existentialism."[12] According to Meeks the widespread 1960s theme of hope for a better future was more accurately tapped by Moltmann's theology of hope than by then influential secular theologies. So Moltmann was able to offer biblical thinking, with its eschatological bias, as more "relevant" than various liberal alternatives intent on demythologizing eschatology.[13]

The major works of Moltmann to be considered here are his *Theology of Hope: On the Ground and Implications of a Christian Eschatology* (1965, ET 1967), *The Crucified God: The Cross of Christ as the Foundation and Criticism of Christian Theology* (1973,

ET 1974), *The Trinity and the Kingdom of God: The Doctrine of God* (1980, ET 1981) and his recent full-blown Christology *The Way of Jesus Christ: Christology in Messianic Dimensions* (1989, ET 1990). This last work will call for systematic exposition, but the earlier ones can, for present purposes, be more profitably considered according to recurring themes of particular relevance to this study. As *Theology of Hope* sets the scene for all that follows, however, it will receive primary attention.

In *Theology of Hope*, Moltmann rejects aspects of both "traditionally orthodox" as well as modern liberal Christology.[14] Preferring the God of Jesus' cross and resurrection to the unchangeable, immutable and impassable metaphysical deity of much conservative theology, Moltmann also has little time for the liberals' gods and christs. It is chiefly modern theology's turn away from "the transcendental subjectivity of God" to "the transcendental subjectivity of man" which he opposes.

Tellingly and accurately, Moltmann identifies Prometheus and Sisyphus as the patron saints of nineteenth century liberal theology and twentieth century existential-liberal theology respectively (24). The former was challenged by Barth's neo-orthodoxy, and Moltmann has more to say on theodicy questions begged by such liberal optimism in *The Crucified God*. In *Theology of Hope*, however, his attention is centered on the "Sisyphus theology" of Bultmann, ministering as it does to the anxious interiority of existentialism.[15] For Moltmann any such dependence on what amounts to the human condition breaks down; his epistemological foundations are in opposition to the "modern" style of Bultmann and other liberals considered in this study: "To be sure," Moltmann writes, "there is no hard and fast nature of man which exists as a self-identical factor anterior to history and independent of it" (176). Bultmann is accused by Moltmann of isolating the individual from that wider nexus of persons, their history and their natural environment apart from which true personhood is inconceivable (67)—and any such dethroning of "the individual" is characteristically post-modern. Nor should the Christian welcome any salvation for the individual simply in terms of "coming to oneself" (125), apart from salvation for the world as a whole (69)—of such an individualized approach to salvation, Moltmann observes that "In Heidegger and Bultmann it was...addressed only to the cultured classes for whom 'existence' was experience of the self and not economic, social and political survival."[16] Similarly, Moltmann is critical of Paul Tillich for conceiving justification solely in terms of the justified individual, who then changes the world, without recognizing the social and political determinants which shape the deepest interiority of that individual.[17] Existentialism, for Moltmann as for his guiding lights in the Frankfurt school, is thus unable to make anything of the world of objects, nor properly of persons: "Our 'neighbor' comes on the scene only in personal encounter," he writes, commenting upon the truncated vision of existentialism, "but not in his social reality" (314).

Moltmann deplores the contempt for past traditions (121) as well as the typical disregard for present social factors (122) shown by the enlightenment mind in its approach to defining the human, whereby variegate humanity is replaced by an ahistorical unity (291ff). Thus he rejects both traditional and liberal doctrines of analogy, having perceived their similarity: "The place of the substantio-metaphysically conceived common core of similarity in all events, which makes analogical understanding possible, is taken by a similarity in the historic character of human existence, which is conceived in terms of fundamental ontology and makes understanding possible between one existence and another in encounter" (185). So, for Moltmann, the Christ event is not discerned as unique on the basis of any pre-existing sense of ideal humanity. Rather, it produces the conditions under which authentic humanity can emerge in the first place; it is "this event which makes man, theologically speaking, true man" (143).[18]

As for natural theology, and the deep human longings to which liberal theology appeals, Moltmann sees these as *produced* by the Christian hope, and not vice versa:

> The openness of Christian existence is not a special case of general human openness. It is not a special form of the *cor inquietum*, the restless heart that is part of man's created makeup. Rather, the historic and history-making *cor inquietum* of man arises from the *promissio inquieta*, and clings

to it and is dependent on it. The resurrection of Christ goes
on being a *promissio inquieta* until it finds rest in the resurrection of the dead and a totality of new being (196).

And, "'natural theology'—theology of existence and theology of history—is a halo, a reflection of the future light of God upon the inadequate material of present reality, a foretaste and advance intimation
of the promised universal glory of God" (90). Hope and promise thus
supply the missing link in modern theology, says Moltmann: "This
world is not the heaven of self realization, as it was to be in Idealism.
This world is not the hell of self-estrangement, as it is said to be in
romanticist and existentialist writing. The world is not yet finished"
(338). Just what are the hope and promise so central to Moltmann's
thought, and how do they arise?

The realm of promise is not that of natural human yearnings;
hope is something quite specific for Moltmann—it is the expectation
of what God has promised in the resurrection of Christ: "Without
faith's knowledge of Christ, hope becomes a utopia and remains
hanging in the air" (20). Moltmann does not see this promise as reducible to human dimensions—it is cosmic and has not lost the apocalyptic element present at its inception (138). But his God of promise
is not a God given to epiphanies, the God of Parmenides (43, 84-85).
Instead the knowledge of this God can only be anticipatory, "upheld
by the hopes that are called to life by his promises" (118). Thus
Moltmann shows himself to be no "traditional theist" in the philosophical sense of being concerned with proofs of God's existence.
Nor is Moltmann an apologist—his God will establish his own existence apart from any human religious insights. He sees all alleged
proofs of God as "back-projections," if you like, of the eschaton:
"All proofs of God are at bottom anticipations of that eschatological
reality in which God is revealed in all things to all" (281). So for
Moltmann this hope and promise, rather than stabilizing and calming
the believer in the face of life's inconsistencies and sufferings, actually *destabilizes* and agitates the believer, bringing unfulfillment and
disharmony where religion is normally thought to relieve them (105,
214 n.). This is very Barthian.

The roots of such a promise, for Moltmann, are not to be found
within the generality of human religiosity. On the contrary, they are

in the Old Testament as what amounts to revealed truth. The promise Paul rediscovers in the New Testament is none other than that to Abraham (152): "The gospel has its inabrogable presupposition in the Old Testament history of promise" (147). And, viewed eschatologically, this promise is the same for Jews and Christians (147-48). According to Moltmann, this religion of promise issues from a God of nomads rather than from a deity of the more settled nature religions encountered by Israel in the ancient near east (96). So it is that Yahweh's appearances do not hallow a place so much as point to a promise; they do not bring the present into congruence with eternity, but disrupt the present in light of the promise (99-100). In such religion are found seeds of dissolution for a mythical and magical worldview (102).

According to Moltmann, Israel developed a unique perception of history based on this promise, seen stretching ahead to its fulfillment. Disregarding historico-sociological questions about how such views might have arisen, and without the benefit of more recent Old Testament historiography which is increasingly suspicious about what we can know of ancient Israelite history apart from the biblical text itself,[19] Moltmann appears to ground the sense of hope he identifies in an actual divine revelation, with Yahweh's promise to Abraham genuinely thought to have taken place.[20]

But that promise, in itself, is not enough; according to Moltmann, "Christianity stands or falls with the reality of the raising of Christ from the dead by God" (165). This resurrection does not illustrate a general truth or mirror conventional reality; on the contrary it is a "concrete, unique, historic event" effected by Yahweh, grounded in his promise to Israel and expected by Moltmann to become "general through the universal eschatological horizon it anticipates" (142).

Now, this approach will inevitably run into trouble with modern historiography. Troeltsch recognizes that postulating analogy between events is what enables us to reconstruct historical happenings and actions at a distance, by analogy with our own experience, motivations, understandings etc. Such deep historical sameness Moltmann identifies with Greek cosmology in which a fundamental constancy belies the diversity of events, with historical occurrences seen merely as *accidental*, as expressing a more deeply rooted similarity (175-76). But this is precisely what Moltmann denies about the res-

urrection; it is not "a possible process in world history, but the eschatological process to which world history is subjected" (179-80). It is,
then, a "history making event" by which "all other history is illu-
mined, called in question and transformed...the resurrection of
Christ does not offer itself as an analogy to that which can be experienced any time and anywhere, but as an analogy to what is to come
to all" (180). Thus Moltmann would claim for Christian theology a
privileged perspective on history, and a method of doing history,
based on the raising of Jesus by God: "It is unique, a *novum*, so one
must reject views of history that cannot find room for resurrection,
and look for a new conception of history that will not be positivis-
tic."[21] For all of that, however, Moltmann does not see the resurrection providing any historical proof, as is the case for Pannenberg
(82). Faith is still required and indeed Moltmann locates a basis for
resurrection belief in the faith of New Testament Christians—a faith
which drove their gospel memories of Jesus and was central to their
missionary proclamation (166). But not for Moltmann the content-
ment of a Bultmann, say, to leave the matter at that, happy to see the
resurrection as no more than ongoing power in the word of Jesus'
cross for Christian life. For Moltmann, faith asks "how" and not just
"why" the earliest church began this proclamation, leading him to
ask about the event grounding it (188).

Is there a hint of confusion in all of this, however? Moltmann
turns to the eschatological promise as basis for our certainty about
the resurrection—an epistemological "back to the future" (189ff).
But, then, there is also his claim to find primary evidence for the resurrection in the early church's experience (186), as if it were a fact of
history already. There is little doubt that belief in revealed truth is the
bottom line for Moltmann here, resting in turn on a literal reading of
scripture. "The promise" emerges not from a "faith-interpretation"
by Israel of its history, then, with the resurrection of Jesus similarly
understood with reference to Jesus' ongoing reality for Christians, as
a not untypical liberal interpretation would have it; rather, promise
and resurrection are divinely guaranteed things, appropriated by faith
and *confirmable,* in principle, by their eschatological outworking. So
while at the level of ordinary history the faith of early Christians is
all we have, on the basis of his preferred way of reading the bible
Moltmann makes more fulsome claims.[22]

If one expects the historical Jesus or even the ministry of Jesus as presented in the gospels to rate little mention in *Theology of Hope*, then one will not be disappointed. The important things are the death and resurrection of Jesus and not so much what he taught and did prior to these. In fact, Moltmann is not dissimilar in emphasis from the church's ancient creeds at this point. I hasten to add that he increasingly redresses this imbalance in subsequent books, eventually placing great importance on gospel accounts of Jesus' ministry in *The Way of Jesus Christ* (1990). But the historical Jesus, the figure behind the gospels sought by liberal theology through various methods of critical biblical studies, features barely at all in Moltmann's program, then or now.

Moltmann declares that God must have been present in the crucified one by looking retrospectively from the resurrection (198), and that this continuity "must repeatedly be sought and formulated anew and must never be surrendered" (199). But Moltmann never seeks in the early writings to work this up into a doctrine of the incarnation—the *full* presence of God in Jesus would be incompatible with his ideas about promise. And it is doctrinally important for him to deny that idealism abstracted from Jesus' concrete, historical person which the "idealist" writers or those in the "liberal" group with a "logos Christology" will be seen to exhibit in the subsequent parts. Nor will Moltmann countenance any mythical talk about a heavenly being nor anything docetic and disembodied: "Historical knowledge of Jesus must therefore be constitutive for the faith which awaits the presence and future of God in the name of Jesus" (300). But in all of this it is the *fact* of Jesus' actual existence rather than the likely and historically accessible *details* of that existence which matters. What concerns Moltmann at this stage is not Jesus' self-consciousness—the liberal theologian's recourse for establishing Jesus' divinity from Schleiermacher's "uniquely potent God-consciousness" through to Schillebeeckx's "abba relationship." Instead, Moltmann is content with the testimony of scripture to establish who Jesus is; he is simply declared to be "the last prophet of the coming kingdom" (218).

Moltmann's next work, *The Crucified God* (1974), "would have a good claim," John Macquarrie suggests, "to be regarded as possibly the most important theological book to be published in the second half of the twentieth century."[23] Moltmann's antipathy toward incarnational Christologies, met in the first book, perseveres. Particular aversion is, however, exhibited toward two types of liberal approach.

Idealist incarnational Christology, as considered in the discussion of "idealist" writers, below, is rejected by Moltmann as inadequate to the historical particularity of Jesus' life and ministry, the features of which become inessential (89ff). The Hegelian D.F Strauss provides a representative illustration, in his refusal to confine the ideal met in Jesus to only one instantiation (97).

But Moltmann is chiefly opposed to certain approaches "from below," such as some "liberal" positions to be considered later in this study, wherein Jesus and his inner life are fixed upon as "archetypally human" (93). Moltmann identifies the spirit of Kant's "practical reason" here, with Jesus fitted to a prior moral ideal of human perfection and seen to empower our consciousness by the spiritual power of his own consciousness. Claims for the uniqueness and finality of Jesus in such an understanding hinge on the assertion that no better human being has ever appeared (96), which Moltmann counters by denying any publicly accessible basis for such a claim—a claim "which is accepted within its own circle, but has virtually nothing to say to non-believers, unbelievers or those who hold a different faith" (97). Instead, Moltmann reiterates the revelatory basis of his own faith in Jesus, rooted in the promise, as providing a firmer foundation: "His office is upheld not by the incarnation of the eternal son of God nor by the archetype of true humanity, but by the future of the kingdom which is inaugurated in him and around him" (98).[24]

Questions arise, however, as to whether Moltmann's preferred starting point offers any greater surety. To accept the historical facticity of gospel miracles and echo New Testament claims for Jesus without too much critical analysis appears to be Moltmann's alternative. Modern biblical studies leave no reasonable doubt, however, that forms of community life and understanding, including the particular theological peccadilloes of redactors and structural traces of prevailing attitudes from the first century, indelibly color gospel portraits of Jesus. Faith cannot be excised from the portrayal of Jesus, then, as the so-called "new questers" have learned. Exempting oneself from such publicly acknowledged concerns cannot further the cause of publicly meaningful theology, according to Moltmann. So although he may be right in prophesying a decline in liberal theological fortunes through these epistemologically dark times of thorough-going pluralism and skepticism, nevertheless his alternative really is just a fideism no more compelling than the liberalism he censures.[25]

Once again, the resurrection of Jesus emerges as the lynchpin of Christian hope for Moltmann. And, once again, it is not cast in the language of facts; faith and hope remain indispensable (173). It is the resurrection that provides a basis for Moltmann's immanent notions of God's presence. But this is the extent of his interest in the notion of an immanent, incarnational understanding of God. In terms of Moltmann's explicit claims all we have is at best a *de facto* incarnation, with the resurrection constituting "the incarnation of the coming God" (169). Or, if you prefer, Moltmann believes that "the crucified Jesus is the incarnation of the risen Christ" (185).[26] Nevertheless, for Moltmann, such faith knows "the cross of Christ as the *unique* and *once-for-all* anticipation of the great world judgement in the favour of those who could not survive at it" (176) (italics mine).

The implications for reconceiving God are close to the surface here. Rejecting H. Richard Niebuhr's much-quoted notion, Carl Braaten (in a discussion of Moltmann's theism) has written that "Christian faith is *not* radical monotheism."[27] Moltmann would agree, calling his view of God panentheistic rather than theistic, but not in the way "liberal" writers like John A.T. Robinson use the term. Where Robinson would speak of God as immanent within the natural process as well as transcending it, Moltmann avoids any such speculative metaphysics and appears to content himself with talking about panentheism at the level of epistemology; that is to say, he sees that "a Trinitarian theology of the cross perceives God in the negative element and therefore the negative element in God, and in this dialectical way is panentheistic" (277).

For the sake of the cross, then, and for the Godforsaken, Moltmann bids us dispense with the inhuman God of theism—the remote God of Parmenides, if you like. Here Moltmann believes Christian atheism, of the 1960s variety, to be in the right (251). Beyond theism and atheism therefore, and particularly beyond the typical conclusions of "protest atheism," Moltmann bids us reconceive God in a Trinitarian pattern as the God disclosed in Christ crucified: "He is no "cold heavenly power," nor does he "tread his way over corpses," but is known as the human God in the crucified Son of Man" (227).[28] Only thus can Moltmann see an answer to "the problem of evil," for he flatly denies there can be any theistic answer.[29] But neither can he bear the atheistic possibility of "avoiding this question and being content with the world" (224).

Lastly, what of the historical Jesus in *The Crucified God*? On the face of it, Moltmann appears firmly committed to his importance: "The first task of christology," he writes, "is the critical verification of the Christian faith in its origin in Jesus and his history" (83). But is it to the historical Jesus, the Jesus of history, or merely to aspects of the various New Testament "Jesus-portraits" that Moltmann really refers? There is not much evidence here of engagement with the niceties of historical criticism, or even awareness of their necessity.[30] In the light of Moltmann's distaste for idealist Christology, however, which he sees as surrendering Jesus' historical particularity, is it obvious that his recourse to the kerygmatic Christ, often with only slight historical backing, is noticeably better? Is Moltmann's Jesus any more a *truly* historical figure and any less the mere linchpin of a theological system, any less a soteriologically motivated construct than "the idealist Jesus" he criticizes?

One would have to say, once again, that the *really* important historical fact about Jesus, for Moltmann, is his death on the cross; while Moltmann declares "Jesus' individuality" important, it is "his concrete historical death upon the cross" which is central (103). The details of Jesus' ministry, however, albeit as portrayed in the gospels and not as they might be reconstructed (deconstructed?) by historical Jesus research, *do* eventually become more consequential for Moltmann. This involves an important realization, for, as Zimany avers, "We don't have to wait until Jesus is on the cross to find the unexpected. His life is filled with the unexpected."[31] Indeed, many features of Jesus' public ministry which Zimany identifies as new and distinctive are also recognized by Moltmann (121). Thus Moltmann is beginning to acknowledge not merely the death of God's Son in abandonment as revealing God's salvific suffering among the Godforsaken, but that "*In his ministry* Jesus ... demonstrated God's eschatological law of grace towards those without the law and the transgressors of the law" (128) (italics mine). This becomes a pre-eminent feature of Moltmann's program in *The Way of Jesus Christ* (1990).

Before considering that work, however, *The Trinity and the Kingdom of God* (1981) bears mention. It consolidates a move beyond the opening of biblical categories to today's world, which exercised Moltmann in earlier works, to a reconceiving of God in line with (post-biblical) Trinitarian dogma.[32] And so, too, it moves beyond theology of hope and its thoroughgoing futurity toward a sense of God's incarnate suffering in the present. This reflects Moltmann's growing concern, since his short book *Theology and Joy* (1971), to balance his prophetic praxis and perennial discontent with the present against celebration and doxology,[33] therein recalling eschatologies more proleptic than his own.

Moltmann makes much of Andrei Rublev's famous fifteenth century Russian icon of the Trinity, with the three persons of Godhead deployed about a central chalice denoting Jesus' cross (xvi). Thus, as Michael Cook observes, Moltmann's Trinity concerns the cross and is not about "thinking";[34] it is not a matter of speculative metaphysics.[35]

The notion of divine suffering (*theopathy*) is then traced from Origen through to the Anglican theologian G.A. Studdert Kennedy (England's famous World War I padre, "Woodbine Willy"), with the Spanish passion mysticism of Miguel de Unamuno opening for Moltmann a universal, mystically conceived theology of pain centered on the cross (yet free of any grounding in natural theology) (23-38). But there is no corresponding anomie or stoic resignation;[36] Moltmann maintains that "theology of the cross without the resurrection is hell itself" (41-42). Nevertheless suffering love is declared ever to abide in the heart of God, as Moltmann reads in biblical verses such as Revelation 5:12 with its lamb slain from the foundation of the world, and in keeping with his long-standing commitment to understanding Jesus as abandoned by God. So: "The Father is crucifying love," he writes, "the Son is crucified love, and the Holy Spirit is the unvanquishable power of the cross" (83).

Moltmann maintains the eschatological tension of his earlier work, however, by declaring the Trinitarian process of creation and redemption to be incomplete, albeit well underway in the Christ event. As he tabulates it (94):

In the sending, delivering up and resurrection of Christ
we find this sequence:

Father—Spirit—Son

In the lordship of Christ and the sending of the Spirit the
sequence is:

Father—Son—Spirit

But when we are considering the eschatological con-
sumation and glorification, the sequence has to be:

Spirit—Son—Father

The second term here obviously embodies the *filioque* clause,
to which Moltmann remains dedicated despite his obvious sympathy
for the Eastern Orthodox and their commitment to a "single procession." But while he would agree that the Spirit proceeds from the Father, nevertheless it receives its relational form from the Son (186) so
that "The Son is the logical presupposition and the actual condition
for the procession of the Spirit from the Father" (184). It appears,
then, that Moltmann would support the compromise formula which
has been suggested as best likely to resolve this impasse of a millennium: the Spirit "proceeds from the Father *through* the Son."[37]
It can at last be said that Moltmann has embraced the incarnation, though, again, it is not without qualification. His God is eternally related to the world through "the eternal Son/Logos" (108), but the
Son is *not* the Logos. Rather, it is all a matter of perspective: "The
Son is *the Logos* in relation to the world. The Logos is *the Son* in relation to the Father" (108, cf. 117). Indeed, Moltmann goes as far as to
adopt an Irenaean view of incarnation completing creation, and preceding it in intention (117). But that is not all; he goes further along
this line, beloved among the "idealist" (and some "liberal") writers to
be considered below, in openly alluding to Jesus as the appearance of
"true man, the person corresponding to God" (117). But an element of
eschatological distance, of "not yet," is preserved by Moltmann to
qualify such unfamiliar assertions. He declares that while the Son *is*
the fulfillment of creation, nevertheless this will only be completely
the case in creation's eschatological climax, when *all* are reconciled
and liberated through participation in him (118). Herein Moltmann

establishes his position on the two-natures doctrine of Chalcedonian incarnational orthodoxy, quick to abjure any impression that the two natures are metaphysically distinct entities. Instead he employs this doctrine to speak of the Son's unique, once-for-all relationship to the Father on the one hand and his representative, inclusive role toward humanity on the other: "It is an expression of his exclusive relationship to the Father, by reason of his origin, and his inclusive relationship of fellowship to his many brothers and sisters" (120). And so it is that the Son is first-born, *eikon*, but also leader and, very importantly, it is not just the *person* of the Son, but his *way* that matters—believers are to follow his *way* into passion and thence to glory at the leading edge of a cosmos which is taken up into the glory of God thereby. But this is the "flip-side" of God's first having entered the world entirely in the Son: "In the incarnation of the Son God humiliates himself, accepting and adopting threatened and perverted human nature in its entirety, making it part of his eternal life" (121). This entry and return echoes Hegel's dialectic of history and his conception of the Trinity as a process of exile and return, recalling also an Eastern Orthodox doctrine of deification.[38]

As for the historical Jesus, Moltmann continues his literal reading of the gospel accounts to establish Jesus' claim to divine sonship, both in terms of the revelation "to us" in scripture and of God's direct revelation to Jesus which scripture attests: "This is where his unique authority is to be found. The content of the revelation bestowed on Jesus through his baptism and call must lie in the name for God which he used uniquely, and exclusively: Abba, my Father" (69). Actually, however, along with a statement that "The liberty of his prayer to the Father reveals his sonship" (73), such claims veer Moltmann uncharacteristically close to the liberals, and Schleiermacher in particular. By invoking such liberal-style evidence, however, Moltmann cannot escape liberal-style conclusions about Jesus' consciousness of his special relationship to God.[39] And then, of course, skeptics such as Dennis Nineham quite properly descend, asking awkward questions about historical verification.[40] Still, at the end of the day, Moltmann takes his stand on a decidedly non-liberal recourse to the revealed truth of scripture, therein mitigating this challenge somewhat. But the epistemological waters have been rather muddied nonetheless.

Thus, finally, to *The Way of Jesus Christ: Christology in Messianic Dimensions* (1990). An overview will show all of Moltmann's key ideas gathered, with old ambiguities repeated and new conclusions offered.

Moltmann begins by treating messianism as a Jewish vision yet to be fully realized in Jesus: "He is the Lamb of God, not yet the lion of Judah" (32); that is to say, Jesus is open toward messiahship and grows into it while yet awaiting its eschatological completion (139). Again, however, Moltmann admits no other "contender for the title" (his views on Christianity as the fulfillment of Judaism will be considered subsequently).

Despite reiterating his opposition to Schleiermacher and Rahner (55-69), trusting resurrection and eschatological hope to better establish claims for Jesus' uniqueness and finality than could historical concern over what he sees to be irrelevant and uninteresting aspects of "an ancient private life" (41), nevertheless Moltmann's newer (alleged) commitment to the historical Jesus perseveres. He again invokes Jesus' sense of God as "abba," "in order to elicit from this mutual relationship between the messianic child and the divine Father what is truly divine and what is truly human" (53; cf. 142-43), but Trinitarian dogma is then immediately invoked for support. This inconsistent recourse to the Jesus of history (never the scholars' historical Jesus, however) is then defended as constituting dialectical theology:

> Anyone who resolves this dialectical process of perception into dogmatic alternatives, is resolving—or dissolving—christology altogether. That person will end up with a theological christology without Jesus, or with an anthropological Jesuology without God. It is therefore high time that we abandoned the infelicitous phraseology 'from above' and 'from below' in christology, in order to turn to the more complex processes of coming to know Jesus Christ (69).

Worthwhile or not, however, we can be quite confident Moltmann does not take his own medicine as here prescribed. Anti-idealist commitment to the concrete particulars of history and pseudo-historical resort to gospel stories do not a dialectician make, and especially when they constitute half-measures which are hopelessly overbalanced by Moltmann's fideism—his biblical literalism over Jesus, his dogmatic literalism over the Trinity. All his contrary protestations aside, therefore, Moltmann's work remains "theology from above" with a vengeance.[41]

Moltmann's discussion of Jesus' messianic mission in *The Way of Jesus Christ* begins with an account of pre-existence ideas. They represent, for him, the last step in retrojecting Jesus' current presence in the spirit back into his life-history and before, whereby his being is known in the light of its end (77-78). But interestingly Moltmann does not question this pre-existence, despite his account of the idea's origin. Indeed, he declares elsewhere that the "abba relationship" means God and Jesus are related in a way that *must* be pre-existent (142-43).

He proceeds to discuss Jesus' birth in terms of pneumatology, and at the expense of traditional claims concerning Mary's gynecology—Moltmann rejects the doctrine of Jesus' virginal conception as unimportant in New Testament testimony, as based on legend, as hindering belief in Jesus' humanity (where once, for the fathers, it underpinned it) and as contemptibly patriarchal (79-84): "The Mary who in human and temporal terms is 'a virgin' must then be seen as a symbolic embodiment and as the human form of the Holy Spirit, who is the eternally virginal and divine mother of Christ" (84). Standard exegesis might prefer Mary as a figure for faithful Israel and a link to the Davidic line, with the Holy Spirit as the equation's "other term."[42] But Moltmann is as uninterested in mainstream biblical studies here as he is in being consistent about the literal truth of scripture, which he is apparently willing to sacrifice when, as here, it is incompatible with his program.

Moltmann speaks of Jesus' baptism as "a *kenosis of the Holy Spirit* which emptied itself and descended from the eternity of God, taking up its dwelling in this vulnerable and mortal human being Jesus" (93). Liberals who might question the exclusiveness of this endowment are simply given a dogmatic reminder of "the unique character of Jesus' imbuement with the Spirit, which led to his divine Sonship and his special mission" (94). Jesus is not yet messiah, then, but nevertheless he is divine Son and, uniquely, man of the Spirit.

This is, however, understood *qualitatively* in terms of unique "character" and not in terms of unique extent, as it would be in any necessarily *quantitative* "Christology of inspiration."

As for Jesus' miracles, they represent not the "supernatural" but the "natural" world, where that means the world as it should be (and "will be" in the eschaton), though prefigured now through liberation of those under the sway of "powers and principalities." This is discussed in quasi-political, liberation theology terms, with the same carelessness liberation theologians often show over historical-critical biblical issues. Nevertheless, Moltmann has come to a high valuation of Jesus' praxis as portrayed in the gospels, far from his early emphasis on passion, death and resurrection alone. But this is *not* the historical Jesus; reliance on revealed truth is never far away with Moltmann, who declares Jesus' miracles unique because their context is unique: "this context is the dawn of the Lordship of the divine life in the era of Godless death" (104). Similarly, the compassion of Jesus for the outcast and downtrodden "is not charitable condescension. It is the form which the divine justice takes in an unjust world" (149).

In sum, Moltmann now wishes to understand Jesus as a "social person" in terms of his liberating praxis, in addition to the "eschatological person" to which he has long accustomed us and to the "theological person" (the one intimately related to God in his life, the divine child) Moltmann has been struggling to embrace in recent books under a redefined rubric of "dialectical theology."[43] All this he calls the "three-dimensional person of Jesus Christ" (149). The desire to reinstate the liberating mission of Jesus, the "social person," alongside the other dimensions, leads Moltmann to envisage an appropriate extension of the Nicene Creed, conceived as a "mental addition" to follow "and was made man"; viz:

> Baptized by John the Baptist,
> filled with the Holy Spirit:
> to preach the kingdom of God to the poor,
> to heal the sick,
> to receive those who have been cast out,
> to revive Israel for the salvation of the nations, and
> to have mercy upon all people (150).

But while all of this (the history of Jesus' life) now determines for Moltmann the *content* of his belief in Jesus Christ, nevertheless Easter faith still determines the *form* of that belief, making explicit what was implicit before Easter (140).[44] We are thus left with what others would call "the mystery of faith," and Moltmann leaves no doubt that he thinks it best left alone: "The uniqueness of what may have taken place between Jesus and his God on Golgotha is therefore something we do well to accept and respect as his secret, while we ourselves hold fast to the paradox that Jesus died the death of God's son in forsakenness" (167). Moltmann thus appears more coy about probing the "divine mystery" than he was in *The Trinity and the Kingdom of God*, discussed above, where the divine life was conceived as a more open and visible process.

But such reservations do not extend to the outworking of this mystery. Moltmann expands his discussion of resurrection beyond history to include nature, so exhibiting another post-modern tendency—away from anthropocentrism and individualism, toward holism and ecological sensibility. And the resurrection ceases to be "event" and becomes "process," in the sense that it will not be complete until the whole of history and the whole of the cosmos are taken up with the risen one into "the new creation." This *process* is at the same time a "universal theodicy trial" for God, which will only be complete when the whole history of human and natural death, suffering and meaninglessness is put right in the eschaton—the "cosmic doxology" awaits (183).[45]

But if physical resurrection means the empty tomb interpreted as a miracle, then Moltmann is having none of it, and this is most interesting: "The proclamation that Jesus had been raised from the dead is not an interpretation of the empty tomb. The empty tomb was passed down by tradition only as an external sign of Jesus' resurrection" (222). The physicality of the resurrection, for Moltmann, is adequately accounted for if seen to inhere in the resurrection appearances. Because they are identifiably appearances of Jesus, then they, and hence Jesus' resurrection overall, can be called "physical."[46]

Lastly, we consider Moltmann and the cosmic Christ. He rejects both a full-blown fall-redemption theology which devalues created goodness in the cosmos (confirmed in God's plan's for redeeming it) (285-86), and the downplaying of evil and false harmony that "creation theology" is inclined to claim (278) (and here one thinks of Matthew Fox and his views, noted in Part III). In particular, Moltmann takes issue with evolutionary Christology such as that of Teilhard de Chardin (292-97) and Karl Rahner (297-301), but particularly the former. Moltmann affirms the vision of a world growing up into the fullness of God which is found in both thinkers, but while the Christ of Rahner's "Christology Within an Evolutionary View of the World" (1966) is the summit of development, he is not the redeemer of that development from its ambiguities (300). This point is made with particular poignancy concerning Teilhard's outlook: "A *Christus evolutor* without *Christus redemptor* is nothing other than a cruel, unfeeling *Christus selector*, a historical world-judge without compassion for the weak, and a breeder of life uninterested in the victims" (296). Instead, Moltmann hopes for the redemption of evolution, the raising of history's victims and the resurrection of nature (297).[47]

Nevertheless, he now welcomes a vision of Christ as Lord of original nature (cosmic wisdom), of evolving nature and of perfected nature if all are taken together, and thus he redefines the traditional *munus triplex* of Reformed orthodoxy—Jesus as prophet, priest and king. This Moltmann expresses in a way which improves on both the romanticism of creation theology and what he would now see as the undue pessimism of his earlier fall/redemption emphasis:

> If Christ is described only as the ground of creation, this world which is often so chaotic, is enhanced in an illusory way, and transfigured into a harmony and a home. If Christ is described solely as the 'evolutor'...the evolutionary process itself takes on a redemptive meaning for the initial creation; but the myriads of faulty developments and the victims of this process fall hopelessly by the wayside. If, finally, we look simply at the coming Christ who is to redeem the world, we see only this world in its need of redemption, and nothing of the goodness of the Creator and the traces of his beauty in all things (287).

Prior to concluding this discussion of Jürgen Moltmann, a consideration of his views on Christianity among the world religions, and in relation to Judaism in particular, will help complete our picture of his attitude to Jesus' uniqueness and finality.

While his fullest opinion on the issue, in *The Church in the Power of the Spirit* (1977, ET 1981), contains no *extra ecclesiam nulla salus* view, nevertheless it does entail one of "Outside Christ no salvation" according to which "Christ has come and was sacrificed for the reconciliation of the whole world" (153). Christians have much to learn from the other religions, though, and not least in fostering indigenous Christian expressions (160, 162). But if Moltmann's church is not the ark of salvation, so that "it is not necessary for one to acknowledge the Christ event in order for one to be included in it,"[48] nevertheless the Church's task is to "prepare the way of the Lord" in the midst of other religions which "will not be ecclesiasticalized in the process, nor will they be Christianized either; but they will be given a messianic direction towards the kingdom" (163).

In Moltmann's recent essay "Is 'Pluralistic Theology' Useful for the Dialogue of World Religions?" (1990), as part of a volume challenging the John Hick and Paul F. Knitter symposium entitled *The Myth of Christian Uniqueness* (1987), he rejects such pluralistic approaches to the truth of religion as we shall meet in Chapter 10 below. Moltmann sees these approaches as implicated in what Herbert Marcuse has called the "repressive tolerance" of western consumer society, sanitizing the religions by robbing their various claims of any forcefulness (152). In the light of his own experience with Christian-Marxist dialogue in the 1960s, Moltmann is convinced that pressing global and social issues have provided necessary catalysts for the truest dialogue, and that dialogue partners will not respect Christians if they surrender their truth claims as readily as the pluralists will, and in advance of the actual dialogue—"A religion which has given up claiming uniqueness, one might fairly say, is of no special interest" (155). So Moltmann sees strong adherence to Christianity's uniqueness claims as compatible with the "right sort" of pluralistic tolerance among religions—not the relativistic sort but, rather, tolerance which serves the causes of justice, peace and sustainability (155).[49]

Moltmann has a distinctive attitude to the place and ongoing validity of Judaism in the divine dispensation. John Pawlikowski identifies him as the first major theologian to grapple profoundly with the holocaust. Pawlikowski recognizes Moltmann's support for the continuing value of Judaism, he highlights Moltmann's refusal to distinguish Christianity as a religion of love from Judaism as a religion of law, and he denies that Moltmann's Christianity supersedes Judaism—the eschaton being awaited in both religions and set to supersede them both.[50]

Moltmann's primary discussion of the matter is found in *The Way of Jesus Christ*. He reaffirms that Christian hope is based in the election of Israel (36), but that ancient Israel's hope is given new direction and strengthened in Christ.[51] But there *does* appear to be a supercessionist thrust in this suggestion that Christianity represents the universalizing of ancient Israel's religion. Moltmann does not want the Jews blamed for their unbelief; indeed, on the basis of Romans 9–11 he designates the Jewish "no" to Jesus as the necessary "hardening of Israel's heart" which gave Christianity access into the Gentile world. So it is that Moltmann can envisage a possible end to antisemitism in this capacity to make something theologically positive out of Israel's one-time "no" to Jesus (34). Moltmann, again following Paul, believes that Israel's salvation will come once the full measure of Gentiles are brought in by Christ at the parousia (35).

Christians, in consequence, are challenged to stop viewing ancient Israel's religion as a *praeparatio evangelica*, as if they carry a surety of divine favor which Israel lacks. But, in the same spirit, today's Jews are invited to view Christianity as a necessary extension of their own mission to the world in anticipation of the eschaton awaited by both—viewing Jewish religion not as a *praeparatio evangelica*, then, but as a *praeparatio messianica* (37).[52]

To conclude this discussion of Jürgen Moltmann, we recall his relatively consistent view that Jesus is *provisionally unique and final*, until the eschaton. But we recall, too, how Moltmann has latterly moved toward the incarnationalism repudiated in his early books, linking Jesus uniquely to the Spirit, and identifying him with the divine Son of God the Father. We have noted Moltmann's lack of liberal dependence on either historical Jesus or "human condition," the former by uncritically confusing the Jesus of history with the various gospel figures of Jesus, and the latter by preferring a more fluid, post-modern conception of humanity as a cultural-linguistic and socio-economic product rather than a pristine, universal ahistorical entity.

Moltmann has been criticized, above, for his uncritical biblical literalism.[53] He certainly ignores many critical issues raised in current Christological debates,[54] too—his difficulties over the incarnation being intra-dogmatic rather than concerned with any possible contemporary meaningfulness the dogma might have, as in the case of English theology's myth debate. In short, Moltmann's radicalism, in his "anti-theistic God-talk" as elsewhere, is a radicalism thoroughly undergirded by unquestioned divine revelation. It is as a conservative that Moltmann disagrees with other conservatives.[55]

Moltmann has also been accused of confusion. Bauckham and McGrath, both operating in the Anglo-American atmosphere of English theological thought, would support suggestions, as expressed earlier (especially over the unclear distinction between divine persons and actions in *The Trinity and the Kingdom of God*), that Moltmann is not careful enough or systematic enough;[56] Moltmann is a dialectician as prone to identifying mythological and doxological talk with revealed fact as he is vulnerable to confusing history with faith in his assessment of Jesus' person.

Also, Moltmann is rather prone to a circularity of argument (which he calls dialectical). He looks to the gospel records to establish Jesus' specialness, as in more recent mentions of the "abba relationship," while at the same time introducing that relationship and Jesus' specialness overall as a *fait accompli* of revelation—a revelation Jesus himself receives, as does the reader of scripture. In all of this it is not obvious that Moltmann has accomplished his recent shift to considering Jesus' person and work, and especially his "God-consciousness," while remaining entirely untouched by the liberal perspectives he cannot help but court thereby. One must ask, then, that if theology "from above" and theology "from below" no longer represent a necessary distinction, as Moltmann would have it, is there no better alternative than simply to invoke both together? A truly dialectical solution would look for an alternative emerging from and surpassing both,[57] such as the "revisionist" option of David Tracy.

I also doubt that Moltmann has adequately accounted for the origins of those beliefs he deems central. What is one to make of

Moltmann's assertion that hope in God's promise arose by revelation in ancient Israel and all human hope arose subsequently as a result of its historical and cultural dissemination? And what is one to make of his views on the resurrection, with secular historiography acknowledged as allowing no other testimony but that of early disciples and their "resurrection appearances," but with the doctrine guaranteed beyond any methodological doubt nonetheless? What events and experiences led to the birth of such beliefs in eschatological hope and in Jesus' resurrection? Unless some recourse is taken to the experience of ancient faith communities, some inquiry made into the genesis of such new religious ideas against the background of their time; that is, unless something like a liberal position is adopted, with belief arising within communal reflection fully conditioned by historical conditions and limitations, then the only recourse remaining is to a biblical literalism and fideism scarcely more sophisticated at bottom than that of the crassest fundamentalism.

For all his restoring of hope to centrality in defining the human, then, for all the dialectical bite of his revised theism, for all the perennial worth of the cross as "a bomb in the playground of the theologians," for all his refreshing skepticism about realized eschatology in the poor light of actual historical and ecclesiastical conditions, for all the holistic appeal of his cosmic vision, for all the eirenic good will of his attitude to Judaism and the world religions as a whole, for all the timeliness of his post-modern reservations about bourgeois liberal theological subjectivism, nevertheless Moltmann is one too often beset by inconsistency and a disregard for critical theology, one who is at heart a fideist, a literalist, whose work will only offer, for many readers, a suggestive clutch of correctives to liberal theology.[58]

Chapter Two

THEOLOGY AND THE PRESSURE OF REALITY

Theologians considered in this section believe the revelation supporting their convictions about Jesus' uniqueness and finality has a natural corollary. These thinkers claim that *all* true knowledge is imposed upon us by what we might call "the pressure of reality," so that all true knowledge is "revelatory."

Whereas since Kant western thought has declared all empirical knowledge to be filtered, contingent, and second-hand, these thinkers oppose every such dualism. Michael Polanyi's philosophy of science has emphasized just this power of the "object" of knowledge to impose its own reality on the inquiring "subject" (of which more throughout). Thomas Torrance is the chief matchmaker between the theology of Barth and the philosophy of Polanyi to be considered here. Torrance's views are tempered somewhat in the Anglo-American philosophical environment inhabited (at least partially) by D.M. MacKinnon and Colin Gunton, also to receive consideration here, though their message is much the same as his.

THOMAS F. TORRANCE

Thomas Torrance, Professor Emeritus of Dogmatics at the University of Edinburgh and former Moderator of the Church of Scotland, is a Reformed thinker whose learned contributions at the interface between theological method and philosophy of science once earned him the Templeton Prize in Religion. Torrance's is a theology of the incarnation, while Moltmann has only latterly moved in that direction. It is for dogmatic, intra-Trinitarian reasons that Torrance's

Jesus is the unique and final instrument of God, the Son of God, to the exclusion of all other religions and their claims. Torrance sees such dogmatic claims as *inevitable,* given his understanding of revelation and science, denying more "subjective" alternatives (as will occupy us in subsequent parts).

Torrance is *severely* realist in conceiving the "objects" of both scientific inquiry and Christian theology; reality, he claims, both earthly and divine, *discloses* itself purely and directly (though not necessarily fully) to the correctly disposed seeker, the one attending to the "object" of inquiry in a manner properly befitting it. There is no concession to constructivism, instrumentalism or any other "soft" pragmatist options in Torrance's vision, according to which human subjectivity, cultural constraints, social forces, paradigms or whatever are understood to interpose themselves and so obscure the "object."[59]

So it is that Torrance's theology, like that of Moltmann, carries the attack of Calvin and Barth up to twentieth century liberals who concentrate on humanity's response to God, some of whom have favored subjectivity to the point of courting agnosticism. So both men are sworn theological enemies of Rudolf Bultmann, for instance.[60] Torrance displays none of Moltmann's "reserve" in making his untroubledly fulsome dogmatic claims, however. He follows Calvin and Barth in declaring God to be fully present in Jesus Christ *already*, without that eschatological proviso Moltmann insists upon in his theology of hope.[61]

According to Torrance, "theological science and natural science are a posteriori activities, conditioned by what is given ... wherein reality actively gives itself, together with the appropriate mode of knowing it, and we actively respond by knowing it in the fashion it provides."[62] Torrance thus believes that truly scientific endeavor overcomes any separation of the theoretical and the empirical, and that the object of inquiry will impose upon observers the appropriate rational tools for properly appreciating it. True science thus involves being grasped by the mystery, if you will.[63] Torrance does countenance the (post-modern) realization that language and convention color our perception in all such matters, though he remains convinced nonetheless that true scientific thought pushes past conventional thinking, present paradigms etc. in response to its veiled object.[64] And as nature has different levels only accessible to the right sort of questions (e.g. there are newly emergent realities at the atomic, chemical, biological, and social levels—Torrance is no reductionist) so too the correct sort of questions are necessary to approach God aright—theological questions.[65] But in all such questioning there is ever a clarifying pressure from the object, guiding "the fight of thought with the obtuseness of speech" toward comprehension.[66]

In the matter of theology, too, a similar "objective control" is exercised. It is only in Jesus Christ, says Torrance, that God can be appropriately known and in whom the right "epistemologically humble" form of response can be made:

> it is only through this encounter with Jesus Christ in His implacable objectivity in which we become crucified to the world and to ourselves that we are enabled to know objectively as we are known by Him and so to think appropriately of God in accordance with his nature, and not out of a centre in ourselves in which we impose our own patterns of thought upon Him and then fail to distinguish Him in His reality from our own subjective states and conditions.[67]

How does this revealed knowledge relate to our natural knowledge in the world? Torrance does not find the divine nature communicated to the world in the manner of natural theology, but God nevertheless "confers upon [the world] a created rationality different from, yet dependent on, His own transcendent rationality, and thus gives it an inner law."[68] This created rationality has two levels, number and word ("small-l" *logos*), physical and spiritual—these are united in humanity.[69] Into the created rationality of this *logos* enters the uncreated rationality of God's word, or ("big-L") *Logos*, assimilating the created *logos* to God through the incarnation. But there is no primordial or abiding natural link between the two levels; to suggest otherwise would constitute "a 'category mistake' of the gravest order."[70]

In the light of these convictions, various twentieth century theologians of liberal stamp become the objects of Torrance's censure.[71] Bultmann and existentialist theology are criticized for diverting attention to the dynamics of our own inner spiritual transformation, to our own existential decisions, leaving us thereby with "no really objective

Christ, no vicarious saviour."[72] God's action on behalf of those he justifies is demythologized in such approaches into a way of talking about
an impact of the kerygma, which becomes effectively "software" for
personal religious users imprisoned in their interiority. Torrance thus
sees Bultmann and his kerygma as reducing Christianity to a timeless
message about selfhood and, what is more, to a message *generally accessible* through philosophy.[73] All of this reflects a dualism separating
persons and concrete history, says Torrance, present also in the existentialist bifurcation between *Historie* and *Geschichte*.[74] This effectively restricts "real" history to the confines of "history as it matters to
me," thereby making my own mental events the most important
events.[75] This turn to the self, however, is for Torrance "the antithesis
of the unremitting attack of Jesus upon every form of human self-cen-
tredness."[76] It is characteristic of demythologizing in this existentialist
spirit, too, that divine action retreats from the realm of space and time[77]
to an inner, surer realm. This, for Torrance, represents the dualism he
loathes in its worst form.

   Torrance is severely critical of John A.T. Robinson's *Honest to
God*,[78] and the 1960s death of God theology. All of this he sees as a
dangerous fooling with atheism on the flanks of real theology, as was
the case with Arianism and gnosticism in Christian antiquity (he believes such "popular theology" represents quite the transitional stage
that they did, too).[79] For Torrance God is not dead nor is the "contemporary meaningfulness" of God-talk in question but, rather, God has
been eclipsed by the bloated selfhood of modern liberal theologians
who make such claims—by those he thinks are "unable to break out
of the teenage mentality in which they are engrossed in their own
self-fulfillment."[80] This is the result of theology abandoning any objectivity in favor of "the incoherent flux of existentialism"[81] and
pious individualism, says Torrance, reducing historical, objective
truths of incarnation and atonement to idealist metaphors serving the
end of self-realization—"Is it not Dr. Robinson himself who requires, as it were, to be demythologized?" he asks.[82] The "real theologian," on the other hand, needs to "leave adolescent preoccupation with self-exploration and self-fulfillment behind and to become
man enough to engage in the unrelenting processes of scientific
questioning in which he himself will be questioned down to the very

roots of his existence...[by]...something beyond the echo of his own thought...a Word coming to him from beyond which he could never tell to himself."[83]

Recently, Torrance has criticized similar liberal trends in Edward Schillebeeckx. Whereas Athanasius and Cyril of Alexandria (nobody could be less "Antiochene" and more "Alexandrian" than Torrance) believed God to be knowable on the basis of God's own self-evincing reality, on God's own terms, the Aristotelian-Augustinian tradition reserved this for the *beati*. In this spirit, Aquinas held that no truth can so move the mind that it *demands* assent; rather, the will must also be moved if assent is to be given,[84] which in turn requires an "infused grace" or "light of faith" to prompt it. Torrance sees Schillebeeckx as participating in such a Thomistic "dualism which snapped the subjective pole of conceptuality from its objective pole deep in the being and intelligibility of God."[85] But the collapse of Thomism's "ambiguous realism" in the late middle ages sounds the death knell for all such theologies that rest not on God's own knowability but on what Torrance thinks to be "human choice,"[86] amounting in effect to nothing more than the moral evidence canvassed by a Kantian "practical reason." The consequence foreseen by Torrance is that such theology will remain the second-order discipline we find it to be in Schleiermacher, attending to the interiority of its subject rather than to the priority of its object.[87]

> Thus to posit a non-evidential relation between our minds and God is tantamount to substituting for the Holy Spirit a human and creaturely 'spirit', the dynamism of the human spirit, which in actual effect is what Schillebeeckx does, for the break in evidential relation with God throws his understanding back upon himself and some inner experience in the activity of the human spirit. The whole situation is very different, however, if we take our stand on the non-dualist, unitary basis of the Nicene theology. Then we do not need to resort to the device of bringing in some intermediary element of 'created grace' *which cannot be finally distinguished from human nature.*[88]

And thus we see the point of this discussion for our purposes: Torrance rejects natural theology, "created grace" (though not "created rationality"), in forms of Thomism ancient and modern, *and so he rejects human nature as providing any insight into God whatever*. Schillebeeckx turns to the contours of human nature for his theistic apologetic, as he does to establish the uniqueness of Jesus (as we shall see when discussing this major figure in Chapter 3, below). But Torrance denies all such recourse out of hand, preferring to look for God in God's own revelation and according to the guaranteed certainties he believes can be found there.[89]

What are the revealed certainties which Torrance invokes, delineated apart from anything subjective such as "human nature"? And what of Jesus' uniqueness and finality in this unmediated dispensation?

Concerning the incarnation, which constitutes a revealed truth for Torrance, a kenotic view is explicitly rejected. Kenoticism adopts the Aristotelian notion of space and time as a receptacle, with Christ as the earthen vessel into which God emptied himself.[90] Torrance not only finds that such a view compromises the deity of Christ, however, but that it localizes and "objectifies" the incarnation in an unacceptable way.[91] Favored instead is something less crudely, detachedly spatial and more holistically conceived—more *connected* to the "created rationalities" which link space, time and conceptuality in his thought. So instead of an attenuated appearance at one point, as kenoticism might have it, Torrance conceives the incarnation as God entering and fulfilling the created rationality conferred upon the whole world. His outlook is that of "Word" coming to fulfill "word" and "number," if you like. This *almost* involves a natural theology, but not quite; Torrance's analogies between God and the world are not naturally there for all to see but are, rather, "driven," provisional ones, perpetually needing to be "revealed." "No doubt," Torrance writes, "the created rationalities of word and number are very different... but they go back to the same source in the transcendent rationality of God and they are both brought together in the incarnation of God's word in Jesus Christ, *for they are upheld and sustained by Him.*"[92]

What is more, Torrance sees the world of space and time as forever changed by what has happened to its deepest structures in the event of incarnation.[93] Our existence being formerly grounded *beyond itself* in God's own being, Torrance sees the incarnation as a *new act* grounding our existence *within its own levels* and fulfilling it there.[94] The effects of God's presence in Jesus Christ can be properly sought within the purview of our existence, therefore, which is why Torrance thinks it appropriate to expect correlates of Jesus' resurrection (for instance) within ordinary experience and history. Although it would be inappropriate to bracket the resurrection as one event among many other events at the same natural level, rather than regard it out of the perspective accessible within incarnational belief (from the perspective of all things in heaven and earth already linked in Christ, if you like), nevertheless Torrance considers the resurrection to be nonsensical without the "empirical correlate" of an empty tomb.[95] Others, such as liberal Anglican theologians John Knox and Maurice Wiles, have suggested that an "ontological correlate" at the level of perennial Christian experience alone would suffice to ground Christian resurrection belief,[96] but we have noted Torrance's contempt for talk of human interiority involving a dualistic concept of reality. And, like Moltmann in *The Crucified God,* he is not content that the atonement wrought by Christ be reduced to a general idealist metaphor of human redemptive suffering. So it is that Torrance corrects what he sees to be Protestant preoccupation with Christ's work (redemption) at the expense of his person (incarnation). As he puts it,

> Everything depends on *who* He was, for the significance of His acts in life and death depends on the nature of His Person. It was *He* who died for us, *He* who made atonement through His one *self*-offering in life and death. Hence we must allow the Person of Christ to determine for us the nature of His saving work, rather than the other way round. The detachment of atonement from incarnation is undoubtedly revealed by history to be one of the most harmful mistakes of Evangelical Churches.[97]

Torrance is also very clear on the place of Jesus as God's Son within a thoroughly orthodox Trinitarianism. And he is far crisper and totally consistent in his setting out of these relations than is Moltmann in *The Trinity and the Kingdom of God.* The Spirit is *not* the Word according to Torrance, as Moltmann was unable effectively to distinguish, but is, rather, "the living Action and Presence of God"[98] making God the Word known to us in the earthly form and life of Jesus. Concerning the intra-Trinitarian relations, Torrance's Holy Spirit is the consubstantial bond between Father and Son, as with Augustine and his *vinculum amoris*.[99]

Not surprisingly, then, Torrance sees the uniqueness and finality of Jesus simply as a given of revelation: "Jesus Christ is Himself the hearing man included in the Word of God, *and He is that in a final and definitive way*."[100] At the same time his Jesus realizes perfect humanity in his life on earth, offering it to the Father.[101] It is a representative, substitutionary humanity, too (which papers over the important theological distinction between these two terms pointed out by Dorothee Sölle in *Christ the Representative* [1967]).[102] But there is no sense that this constitutes a level of human obedience and perfection sufficient to or able to *earn* Jesus divine honors, as liberal Christology allows. Instead, it is a "divinely provided response."[103] After all, to allow that God was at work *the same way* in Jesus as in other humans would court the "paradox of grace" Christology of D.M. Baillie's *God Was in Christ*—a possibility which would *appall* Torrance.[104]

Convictions such as these, regarding Christ as God's unique instrument, require from Torrance the rejection of all religious alternatives. In a thoroughly Barthian fashion he declares Christ sole mediator, and the whole of religion to be a purely human undertaking bereft of worth or truth.[105] This rejection of other religions he justifies with a metaphor based on Fermat's Principle[106] (cast in a form he fails to explain) entailing that a path, once chosen, subsequently excludes all other possibilities.[107] God could have ordered things differently, admits Torrance, "but the actual coming of his eternal word into our contingent existence in Jesus Christ excludes every other way to the Father, and stamps the vicarious humanity of Christ to be the sole norm and law as well as the sole ground of acceptable human response to God."[108]

As regards the religion of ancient Israel, it is to be seen as the womb prepared by God, the matrix of appropriate thought and speech for receiving the incarnation (and especially as regards its prophetic aspect). Judaism is deemed to be fulfilled, transcended and finalized, according to Torrance, "by the final and permanent forms which the Word has taken ... in Jesus Christ."[109]

It is not unexpected that all this talk of revelation hinges, once
again, on a literal reading of scripture. Torrance admits that biblical
interpretation must take the intention of texts into account.[110] But in
so doing it must recall that the ultimate horizon of meaning in scripture is provided by "a dimension of rationality and objectivity that
reaches out far beyond them into the divine being and is backed up
by His creative Word and Spirit."[111]

So it is that uniqueness claims are supported by Torrance with
assertions about the ministry of Jesus, read as history out of the
gospel accounts.[112] He certainly understands the miracle accounts as
establishing the actual historical occurrence of divine acts, finding no
difficulty with this.[113] But it is his attitude to the parables which is
most interesting for present purposes. These Torrance sees as disruptive speech acts ushering the hearer into a new world-view,[114] as we
also find them to be in the existential-narrative readings of Via,
Crossan and other recent students of the parables.[115] But they are then
declared to have their true and only meaning in the interpretation
which Jesus (not the evangelists) gives to them, as signifying the
coming of God's kingdom in Jesus' own person.[116] However, a plain
reading of the parables shows that they are *not* Christ-centered in
themselves. They point, rather, to God's kingdom accessible everywhere and awaiting its opportunity to dawn in human experience.
Moreover, they appeal to human wisdom and draw upon recognizable examples from human life, resonating with experience and
evoking sympathy. Have they no value apart from their use by the
evangelists who insist, whether or not Jesus claimed it, that the kingdom has come near in Jesus? Is the Jewishness of the parables to be
effaced, too, or the former value of that literary genre they represent
denied? Obviously yes, according to Torrance; we have, after all,
seen him declare Judaism to be defunct and other religions as worth-
less in the light of Christian revelation.

Now let us evaluate. Can we accept Torrance's theological
method and his Christology, with the uniqueness and finality of
Christ a datum of revelation, knowing that such a sense contradicts
virtually every major insight of modernity and post-modernity (especially those concerning the omnipresence of historical skepticism,
the subjective component of all observation, cultural relativism and

the plurality of religions)? My conclusion here is that Torrance's views on method, derived from science, and his understanding of theology are not as compelling as he thinks, with the consequence that his understanding of Jesus' uniqueness and finality is thrown into doubt. I offer more criticism here than I offered in the discussion of Moltmann *because Torrance claims more than Moltmann*, attempting to *justify* the literalism and fideism he shares with Moltmann on the basis of links to what is allegedly best in modern scientific thought.

As regards Torrance's purportedly scientific methodology, I have three major apprehensions.

First, are all fields of inquiry equally open to the control of their object as he believes science to be? History, for instance, is a field in which modern researchers have become increasingly chastened, believing that many things will *never* be known with certitude. And, like literary theory, history has learned how inexcisable is the perspective of a writer—written histories from the past are now items of historical interest themselves. So while Torrance might succeed in dismissing (increasingly prevalent) instrumentalist currents in the philosophy of science, and talk of its cultural dependence, this is far harder to achieve with respect to the humanities. Scientific inquiry depends upon a high degree of control being exercised over its object. Extraneous variables can be held constant allowing the phenomenon of interest to emerge, while enormously expensive apparatus are often designed or adapted for single experiments, so that in many ways the inquiry becomes a *simple* matter. But the more complex the object the more difficult it is to simplify in this way, and so the *softer* the form of scientific investigation appropriate to it is regarded.[117] I suggest, therefore, that Torrance cannot justify his assumption that all objects are scientific kinds of objects, and that they will present themselves to us with the same clarity and inevitability achievable by science. As for theology, it is clearly an enormously diverse field in which schools of thought compete for adherents with no foreseeable resolution, this being a feature of the human sciences and the humanities and *not* of the harder sciences upon which Torrance chooses to model theology. Only by claiming incontrovertible evidence, in his resort to clear divine revelation, is Torrance even able to contemplate such a comparison.

My second concern, and one shared by Colin Weightman,[118] is that Torrance's view of science may already be out of date. The sternly realist, "one-answer-only" attitude he takes from Einstein is anything but dependable nowadays. Einstein's determinist interpretation of quantum mechanics, in resolute opposition to the probabilistic reckoning of Niels Bohr and his Copenhagen school, sought "hidden variables" that *must* ground the flux of apparent quantum indeterminacy. This may once have been a sustainable argument, but more recent results such as Bell's Theorem[119] strongly support an understanding of the universe as insubstantial, statistical, multivocal if you like, and *not* so totally deterministic at heart. A similar awareness is developing in the new field of Chaos Theory.[120] One might observe that reality so conceived suits metaphorically a "softer" view of God and theology than the one Torrance advocates. Indeed, insofar as quantum phenomena only declare their nature in the act of observation[121] we might discern a metaphor for theology being open-ended and its conclusions irresolvable in advance of their use (theology and praxis, pragmatism) or, alternatively, in advance of the eschaton (theology of hope). Modern physics is, after all, read variously by its religious interpreters: Fritjof Capra thinks of eastern mysticism when he contemplates the endless flux disclosed at the heart of reality by quantum and sub-atomic physics, while John Polkinghorne (following process theology) conceives links to a plural, broadly non-exclusive Christianity. Clearly the evidence is not compelling, and Torrance's are not the only theological lessons that can be learned from science.[122]

My third point at issue concerns the difference between science and theology in the matter of public accountability.[123] The results of science must be cast in a form that allows them to be checked and, if possible, to be falsified. Anyone suitably trained and qualified can in principle perform such checks, and scientific claims will not stand unless they prove resilient to such *fundamentally public* scrutiny. Liberal theology wishes to make the same sort of claims about its own object—that reason, human experience, etc. can tell for or against the likely truth of doctrines. Such theology avoids sectarian epistemologies in favor of something like the publicness of science. Even though it is recognized, for instance, that not all will have religious experiences or find themselves adhering to religious beliefs of a particular sort, nevertheless liberal theologians have ensured that the phenomena of the religious experiences have been studied,[124] and the nature of religious believing expounded as thoroughly as possible (psychologically, sociologically, etc.).[125] Thus the dynamics of Christian faith and life are rendered publicly accessible, their connections to wider human experience established and even their veracity opened to public criticism. But Torrance seems to restrict theology to a much narrower audience by demanding that his own view of rationality must prevail, so overcoming the criteria of public meaningfulness which liberal theologians seek to apply. This reflects his total denial that theory in any way creatively influences observation in science—a suggestion which need *not* entail complete instrumentalism (there is, rather, a creative *dialogue* between theory and observation[126]). But Torrance does not recognize this; in science (as in theology) he hears only a monologue in which the concerns of the subject are overwhelmed by those of the object.[127]

This leads me to the first of four questions I would put to Torrance regarding his theology.

First, has Torrance let his theology determine his scientific method—an instance of the cultural influence and subjectivism he will not tolerate in others? In particular, consider his understanding of the scientific object as overwhelming the subject.[128] I suggest that there are religious doctrines claiming just this, and Calvinist ones at that. The doctrines of election and irresistible grace[129] thus appear to me to be the silent partners of Torrance's favored scientific method. The God they presuppose imposes himself upon the few apart from any publicly accessible evidence or human will. If the will has no opportunity to accept or reject, then election and irresistible grace may well be at work.[130]

This raises my second point, about the seriousness of our engagement with relativism and subjectivism in the present intellectual climate going unrecognized by Torrance. If Torrance believes that there are different levels of questioning and certainty appropriate to different levels of reality, however, then could it not be possible to recognize and accommodate the doubts that modernity brings at an appropriate level within his system?[131] If Torrance sees all levels of reality as linked, the conceptual with the spatial and the temporal, need he be quite so suspicious about theology which takes human subjectivity into account? Why must theology deal only with objective truths of revelation correlated to objective events in history (such as he claims the resurrection to be) and not look to inner, less objective human realities such as religious experience, moral and aesthetic sensibility, existential categories such as Jaspers' "boundary situations," etc. (the stuff of liberal theology)? Are these of such a different order? Why cannot reality speak through the "created rationalities" of human interiority, or are there no created rationalities in the area of the human? In denying any such possibility, though, Torrance effectively denies that God does take all levels of created rationality seriously. Everything touched by the enlightenment heritage thus constitutes an aspect of worldly rationality that is *not* infused and brought to fulfillment in the incarnation of God's "uncreated rationality," the Word. Is none of God's "created rationality" to be found there, then, but only the sin of pride?

Thus I fear that Torrance adds the doctrine of total depravity to those of election and irresistible grace in the Calvinistic "compound eye" with which he views reality, seeing no prospect that anything touched by human fallenness might attain to knowledge of God. But, then, neither does he attend much to the interiority of investigators in his view of science either, which suggests that total depravity is a guiding principle in his thinking about science too. Thus I suggest that Torrance might once more have allowed the dogmas of his religion to guide his allegedly "objectivity enshrining" philosophy of science.

Third, having vehemently rejected the subjective focus thought typical of liberal theology, has Torrance smuggled subjective religion in through the back door with his emphasis on salvation and justification? To be sure, the objective focus of orthodox Protestantism *was* cashed out at the level of existential decision by Bultmann, and so subjectivized. And liberal theology since Schleiermacher *has* looked to "internal evidence" for religious truth. Torrance is right about all this. But is not declaring the centrality of human salvation in God's purposes, as Torrance's emphasis on justification seems to declare, also a form of subjectivism? This suggestion is based on the insights of recent "creation theology," which exposes the western theological focus on fall and redemption as fostering just the sort of spiritual narcissism which Torrance, for one, is quick to censure. Matthew Fox points to billions of years in earth history preceding the emergence of humanity, let alone "the fall," as challenging our theological presumption that the human drama is, somehow, cosmically "center stage." In the light of all this history of creation before the arrival of human evil, Fox prefers to talk of "original blessing" rather than "original sin."[132] Now, while it is eminently possible to reconcile creation and redemption theologically without the excesses and omissions evident in polarized positions such as those of either Torrance or Fox, in a way doing justice to both Augustinian and Irenaean traditions,[133] nevertheless the creation theologian's charge of anthropocentrism in our fall/redemption theologies is a serious one which must be faced, despite whatever other weaknesses one might find in creation theology. For all his interest in science, then, and in the face of the enormous vistas science has opened during his long life, nevertheless the only "world" for which the allegedly anti-subjective Torrance shows any theological concern is the world of human redemption. This he calls a God-centered world, in focus, intention and operation, but nevertheless all eyes in heaven and earth remain clearly fixed on *us*. Thus subjectivism, of a sort, *can* be seen to have crept in the back door of Torrance's theology.

My fourth and last point of criticism is offered in a more general vein. It concerns Torrance's charge that today's existentially-influenced theology repeats the sin of our "first parents," answering "the old demonic whisper, 'Ye shall be as gods.'"[134] Thus he believes we have eclipsed God with the demands of our own bloated selfhood in an age characterized by the sin of pride. But in his flight from the justifiable concerns of that age into an unassailable positivism of revelation, could it be that Torrance has committed the same sin himself, seeking Godlike certainty? But Torrance is presumably "fallen," too, and so he should expect no more than to eke out his theological existence "east of Eden" alongside the rest of us, without his accustomed epistemological comforts. Or have he, Calvin and select others in fact *returned to Eden,* in their fulsome certainty of revelation, somehow evading the cherubim's fiery sword which mainstream philosophical theology, wisely, has never sought to pass?[135]

As with Moltmann, then, so with Torrance, I find the diagnosis of spiritual and theological ills to be frequently compelling. Torrance's great contribution is to challenge self-serving forms of thought in theology, strengthened by the conviction held dear among scientists that reality confronts our claims with its own. But his thoroughgoing realism in science underrates the undeniable contribution investigators, as individuals and as a scientific community, make in the actual doing of science. Creative dialogue and a moderated "critical realist" epistemology (with theory understood as correlated to reality though not embodying it exactly) better express the working scientist's view.[136]

As for Torrance's theology, having declared his diagnoses good, nevertheless I am convinced that, as with Moltmann, aspects of the proposed cure are as bad as the disease itself! I would far more readily support a "critical realist" approach to theology, as to science, such as we find in the "critical correlation" between reason and tradition/scripture attempted by that "new-generation Tillichian," David Tracy.[137] But neither should we forget substantial alternatives lying far nearer to hand, such as those of D.M. MacKinnon and Colin Gunton.

D.M. MacKinnon and Colin Gunton

D.M. MacKinnon was Norris Hulse Professor of Divinity at Cambridge. He is a metaphysician, an Anglican layman and no neo-orthodox, but he does match key concerns of Torrance, and not least in favoring "control by the object." But the dogmatic assertions of Torrance's neo-orthodoxy are absent from MacKinnon's characteristically English and non-systematic approach to theology.

MacKinnon is critical of modernism—the supplanting of direct access to faith's object by the church's faith itself. Thus the church, made unsure of its historical ground by recent biblical criticism, turned to the history of its own faith. This was supported by Bultmann and his school in form and redaction criticism, with a promise to recreate the faith of early Christians.[138] To this spirit MacKinnon finds added the functionalism of Melancthon's famous dictum *Hoc est Christum cognoscere, eius beneficia cognoscere* ("to know Christ is to know his benefits") according to which Christ's person is reduced to his roles, whereby the claims of the object are firmly supplanted by the needs of the subject in theology.[139]

Like Torrance, however, MacKinnon believes all such functionalism to be an escape from the necessary claims of ontology, denying emphatically that "The proper study of the theologian is ecclesiastical man."[140] Instead, he writes, "it is still Christ's person that raises the issue of the significance of the Church's existence more than that existence which raises and explicitly answers the question of his significance."[141] Like Torrance, MacKinnon believes that "we receive from God through Christ's act the manner in which our relation to him is given form" and that Jesus "gives rather than receives sense."[142] This control by the object is recognized in the doctrines of Trinity and *homoousion*, thinks MacKinnon, which bear relentless witness to the mystery of their object. Without such attention there can be no *necessary* connection between Christian experience and God.[143]

But for all his denial of subjectivism MacKinnon stays far closer to Christian experience and is far less speculative than Torrance, believing that theologians will be "thrust towards the acknowledgement of that which in its inmost essence must remain unknown."[144] MacKinnon even recognizes the inevitability of contradictions in defining faith's object: "If in such effort we often find ourselves reduced to silence by inability to eliminate apparent contradiction from the concepts we invoke, at least we may hope that this silence reflects disturbed movement towards, rather than comforting escape from, the unutterable love."[145] This appears to constitute that very "critical realism" for which I have declared a preference, over against Torrance's strict realism. It illustrates how Torrance's central insights might be embraced without subscribing to his dogmatism and fideism.[146]

Colin Gunton, a United Reformed minister and Professor of Christian Doctrine at King's College in the University of London, also shares a number of concerns with Torrance (and MacKinnon). The burden of his *Yesterday and Today: A Study of Continuities in Christology* (1982) is that patristic Christology remains highly relevant—that pitfalls it faced and solutions it offers remain, and this in the face of recent Christology (especially from England) preferring to cut adrift its classical Christian past and reconceive Christology along exclusively enlightenment lines.

The link to Torrance comes in Gunton's disavowal of dualism. Platonic and Kantian dualism, he argues, have required of theologies ancient and modern the denial of temporality as meaningful and as important to God (110). The Platonic negation of temporality in favor of eternity, the Kantian "view that because the manifold was in itself patternless, the mind must impose rationality upon it," and the immanentist attempt to "redeem temporality" by consigning to it the unfolding of ultimate purpose (Hegel, Marx, various utopianisms, process theology, evolutionary Christology) all "entail conceptions of the world hostile to Christology," writes Gunton, "which is the place where an attempt is made to conceive eternity and time in a positive relation, the one losing its fallenness through the saving presence of the other" (120).

Gunton, like Torrance, aims to out-think dualistic culture as he believes the fathers of credal orthodoxy did. Thus, with Torrance, he turns to modern science, finding therein an alternative to the dualism of Kant's closed world order (108), which is irremediably bifurcated into noumenal (objective) and phenomenal (subjective) realms. Instead, there *can* be an "indwelling" of reality by both human investigator and human language which overcomes that epistemological bias against ontology typical of Kantian agnosticism.[147] So Gunton, with Polanyi and Torrance, denies any fundamental separateness between necessary truths of reason and contingent truths of history. He believes, rather, that "Because we indwell the world knowledge can be contingent, fallible and partial without for that reason losing its claim to be knowledge" (145).[148]

Eternal and temporal are linked by Christology—*this is what it does,* says Gunton. Thus there need be no recourse to "mythology" as a category for talking of the eternal within the temporal (124), as in Bultmann, for the two realms are not separate. Gunton supports this argument with illustrations from the sphere of music.[149] The trouble, he says, is that "visual thinking" conditions us to conceive different things as mutually exclusive, as unable to coinhere according to spatial reckoning. But music allows different tones to coinhere and so to harmonize (115-16), "without confusion, without change, without division, without separation," as it were, in the language of Chalcedon. And so too with Gunton's Christology, where Jesus is "the temporal logic of the eternal love of God."

As for the uniqueness and finality of Jesus, it is again a matter of revealed truth. Yet Gunton's position is nowhere near Torrance's exclusivism. His God is met far more widely—in history, in nature, in political and religious movements apart from Christianity. But Gunton nonetheless chooses to honor the claim found in both New Testament and mainstream tradition that in Jesus God is met in a unique way (163), though he recognizes how offensive to the idealist mind is this "scandal of particularity" (165). For Gunton, recalling Torrance,

> the uniqueness should be seen as the perfection of a pattern of the divine loving, which can be found elsewhere but is only here to be found as present in person. This love can be found especially in the ways of God towards Israel, for it is the Old Testament which enables us to understand both the concreteness of the divine love and the anticipatory form which it took in relation to Israel. If we are able to conceive Jesus as uniquely the presence of God, it is because in this essential context we have a preparatory conception of his presentness which is both corrected and transcended by what happens here. The Old Testament theologies, then, provide what can be called the formal basis for the ascription of uniqueness to Jesus (164).

He also believes, again recalling Torrance, that "only [in Jesus] is authentic humanity understood and given" (164). Note that this arises *a priori*, as in traditional Christology, as an induction from the dogma of incarnation, rather than *a posteriori*, as in much "liberal" Christology, as an alleged deduction from examining the historical Jesus and the human condition. Interestingly, Gunton affirms the historical skepticism of Dennis Nineham's "Epilogue" to *The Myth of God Incarnate* (1977) in this connection, denying the viability of basing Christology on history alone (63).

Gunton's conclusions are far less dogmatically insulated than those of Torrance. Along with a greater openness to recent New Testament scholarship Gunton also recognizes the range of dependencies evident in his own claims, invoking at one point both eschatological verification *and* modernist-style resort to Christian experience in defending them, as is evident when he declares that our christological language is justified if it says what is true about Jesus Christ. Whether it is true or not depends upon whether it is a fact that Jesus of Nazareth was and is God's holy love for his world. Whether, in turn, we can know that to be true, is in large measure an eschatological question. But we have provisional aids by which we can test our statements: the Bible, the creeds and the worship and experience of the Christian Church (166).

Gunton also admits that model, metaphor and even a measure of demythologizing (though only for demarcating metaphorical from literal) are necessary in theology (150-53).[150] He understands theological statements as providing a map of reality—related, selective, true but not exact—and thus he appears nearer to the "critical realism" advocated above than to the severe realism of Torrance.[151]

We shall take leave from our discussion of "theology and the pressure of reality" at a point where key epistemological questions are begged. Torrance *et al.* claim that knowledge of God and Christ is at bottom *conceptual*, rather than intuitive or romantic (as, say, Paul Tillich would have it),[152] and that a Polanyian understanding of how science works provides a parallel.

Polanyi analyzed the 'tacit power' of the human mind to discern *Gestalten* or patterns in experience through a heuristic leap from parts to a whole in which patterns of coherence could be seen. The problem is a familiar one. What is it that enables us to move from a jumble of discrete, perhaps disorganized bits of experience, to a pattern which enables us to fuse these bits into an integrated whole?...It is an intuitive leap in which 'clues' are united in a single pattern.[153]

This is hardly the stuff of hard-edged realism, however. Some of the language used about such mechanics of cognition and discovery makes this "conceptual knowledge" into a most unfocused, intuitive thing indeed. According to Torrance,

> We are not concerned here with logical inferences or ab-
> stractive operations of thought but with *a movement of*
> *thought which cannot be described in explicit terms*, for
> while it does not entail explicit elements *it relies on im-*
> *plicit elements* which can only be learned in what Polanyi
> has so often called apprenticeship.... [It is]...*a proleptic*
> *grasp,* enabling us to engage in *an intuitive leap of un-*
> *derstanding*...in terms of which *other relevant clues be-*
> *come integrated into a comprehensive whole.*[154]

But surely Torrance has only *hinted* at what cognitive structures
might undergird these observed phenomena of comprehension and insight. He certainly does not probe them, and neither does Gunton.[155]

This sort of intuitive grasp has, however, been examined in
modern hermeneutics, and by theologians under its influence such as
Lonergan and Schillebeeckx (whom Torrance, for one, explicitly
criticizes). But there is another theological option, similar in certain
respects to those already labeled in this study as "conservative,"
which avoids any such liberal-style theological recourse. By attending to the Christian story alone this approach, informed by the new
insights of narrative theology,[156] considers Jesus Christ as he is portrayed in the gospels to be an immediately present, self-authenticating reality.[157]

Chapter Three

THEOLOGY AND THE
CHRISTUS PRAESENS

It is not so much *what* they say about the uniqueness and finality of Jesus that makes these "conservative" theologians different from those met above, but *why* they say it. Once again claims of revelation undergird their "conservative" position, but it is not a revelation rooted in the past (Torrance) nor one confidently expected in the future (Moltmann). Rather, their Christ is revealed as unique and final *in the present.*

Hans Frei is a post-liberal influenced by literary theory and narrative theology; he believes Jesus emerges as unique and final in the dynamic process of reading the synoptic gospels *in the present.* Dietrich Ritschl looks instead to the presence of Christ disclosed as unique and final (to those equipped to see it by *election*, I will suggest) in the church's liturgical worship.

HANS FREI

The late Hans Frei was a Yale theology professor and, eventually, a priest in the Episcopal Church. He exhibited many post-liberal currents characterizing the teaching of religion Yale-style. His program has much in common with that of George Lindbeck, to be discussed in Chapter 11, below. But if Lindbeck is a "radical" allowing Jesus no necessary uniqueness or finality, Frei, while every bit as disinterested in apologetic speculation as Lindbeck, nevertheless believes the uniqueness of Christ to be a crucial feature of Jesus' portrayal in the gospel narratives. Let us examine Frei's complex and subtle position by attending to his 1975 study *The Identity of Jesus Christ: The Hermeneutical Bases of Dogmatic Theology.*

We have here another sophisticated conservative rejoinder to idealist and liberal theology. Frei rejects all appeal to idealist generality in favor of the particular, event-character of the gospels. There he finds no pattern of universal human need and consistent divine response, according to which Jesus offers a particular version of a generally accessible remedy—this would reduce Christianity to a gnostic-style savior myth (57-60), albeit in modern existentialist garb (xi, 138). On the contrary Frei recognizes the particularity of Jesus' person as central to the gospel portrayal, arguing that "Unsubstitutable identity gained in unsubstitutable circumstances is simply not the stuff of mythological tales" (139). Nor is the historical Jesus important to Frei, of whom he believes little can be known with historical certainty (48, 51, 103). But, then, Frei does not think details of the historical Jesus' ministry would support a case for his distinctiveness anyway; such distinctiveness could only be discerned "at the end of the story," which means from the perspective of Jesus' resurrection (141-45). Frei sees the quest of the historical Jesus, delving behind the gospels and their stories as a search for what Gilbert Ryle called "the ghost in the machine" (14, 42). But he will not allow that the identity of a person can be properly grasped in this way—by any such abstraction—apart from an identity-revealing narrative. Nor does Frei believe one can trust any features one might excerpt from such a narrative because bias intrudes in the very choice of these features (90), and hence the tendency of questers old and new to produce historical Jesuses who are, in reality, clones of themselves.

Frei's point of departure, as identified in *The Eclipse of Biblical Narrative* (1974),[158] concerns the exile of enlightenment westerners from the biblical *Weltanschauung.* In response to this exile, liberals built bridges to the Cartesian, Kantian world which western theology had come subsequently to inhabit, in a sense mitigating the biblical vision to suit modern tastes. Thus a more reliable, empirical basis for belief was sought "behind the text" of scripture through historical investigation (truth as history, as fact, as reference), or else in eternal verities thought to be portrayed symbolically within the text, and here one thinks of trends from Kant to Kierkegaard to Jung positing an abiding human condition (centered upon a moral imperative, upon existential categories, upon a collective unconscious, etc.). Frei would far prefer that we stop fitting the bible to the prevailing post-biblical culture, however, and return to the biblical world as it is embodied in the narratives themselves.[159]

One aspect of this conviction is Frei's disdain for the apologetic task so characteristic of liberal theology. He is not convinced that one can be argued into faith by apologetics, nor indeed that any one path emerges as the royal road to religious conviction—except that actions speak louder than words (xii-iii, 7-8). Nor does he believe that apologetics actually work, arguing that apologetics mistakenly confuses the path to belief with the content of belief. Frei would no doubt prefer the way of Augustine, Anselm and Barth, the way of *fides quaerens intellectum*.

Frei's is a *Christus praesens* theology, which means that his Jesus is a living, present, self-authenticating reality rather than a unique human of the past (historical Jesus theology) or else a unique pattern of "timeless humanness" (idealist or existentialist theology). Both these standard modern approaches evade the actual dynamics of Christian experience by sundering Jesus' identity from his presence. If they *truly* knew who Jesus is, Frei argues, they would not have to debate how his presence today might be understood; properly, he thinks, these are given together: *"To have Christ present is to know who he is and to be persuaded that he lives"* (6). In all of this Frei wins the warm approval of Torrance, that relentless advocate of immediacy and critic of every idealist disjunction in theology. Torrance finds in *The Identity of Jesus Christ* "An outstanding exception to this kind of approach... [operating] ... with the unity of form and being, of identity and presence, in allowing Jesus Christ to interpret himself in his own uniqueness to our enquiry."[160]

To clarify Frei's position requires that we probe his understanding of the resurrection. The historical skepticism which warned Frei away from the historical Jesus remains when he considers the resurrection—a belief, he contends, that critical history cannot support (103). Nor does he believe the resurrection should be abstracted from the church's experience of Jesus as Lord as a separate event (in this Frei is totally opposed to the approach of Wolfhart Pannenberg, whose views will be discussed in Chapter 5, below). For Frei, it is the very experience of Jesus' Lordship itself which provides our evidence that he is risen, obviating any need for further support from historical events which critical history could never verify (xiii). "He *is* the resurrection and the life. How can he be conceived as not resurrected?" (146), Frei asks, maintaining that "Jesus the redeemer ...cannot *not* live, and to conceive of him as not living is to misunderstand who he is" (149). The resurrection is not the same as Jesus' presence, however: it provides "the necessary local basis" (16) for that presence, but experience of the presence is primary.

As to *why* Frei's Jesus is actually unique and final, we must look to the gospel story of which the resurrection provides both the completion and the hermeneutical key.

As mentioned earlier, Frei follows Gilbert Ryle in what we might call a "what you see is what you get" view of human identity (linguistic behaviorism). For Frei this means that Jesus' identity can be "read off" the gospel story itself. It does not abide in any part of the story's pre-history, nor is it grasped through comparison with other savior narratives (62) of which there are many, ancient and modern. It is not the best instance of something more generally accessible, then (as in liberal theology), but the *only* instance (65).

Frei recognizes that a story is encountered "on the surface," if you like—as a work of art is appreciated through the interplay of its parts, so a story works through narrative elements in its own structure rather than through references to "realities" beyond itself (51, 87, 101, 105). So Jesus' identity is given "in the action" (105), and Frei believes that this action has certain elements which render the Christian story unique.

The story Frei prefers is that of the synoptic gospels, in which he discerns a growth of Jesus into the fullness of his ultimate identity. Frei summarizes this development of Jesus, from the infancy narratives through the public ministry to the passion and resurrection narratives:

> In the first stage...he was described merely as a representative figure and not as an individual at all. In the second stage, he was much more nearly manifest as an individual in his own right, and yet he was more nearly identified in terms of the kingdom of God than in terms of him. In the third stage, he emerged fully as the one un-

substitutable Jesus of Nazareth—and this as much in the resurrection as in the passion (136).... At the end of the story, as at the beginning, there is full identity between Jesus and Israel. But whereas at the beginning it was the community that served to identify him, the reverse is now the case. He, Jesus, provides the community, as well as God's Kingdom and the stylized saviour figure, with his identity (137).

The end of the story is, of course, the resurrection. Here, according to Frei, Jesus' own control of events has reached its nadir in a death among the uncontrollable events of history. But it is precisely here that God is seen to be most active in raising Jesus from the dead, though in a way both hidden to objective history and veiled by the resurgence of Jesus to activity and centrality in the narrative (120-21). I would suggest that herein lies a theology of history, familiar from other "conservative" writers we have studied, in which the presence of God cannot be read off from history as the idealists would have it. But those who must live in the midst of history's apparently pointless flux can nevertheless take heart; it is people such as they who can best rejoice at this story of God's power at work in the absolute darkness and powerlessness of Jesus' descent among the dead (121). As a consequence of this vision every event, albeit meaningless and disconnected and unclassifiable under any grand historical schema, can nevertheless be discerned as the workplace of a hidden God. This is a *theologia crucis* of sorts, also reminiscent of secular theology's hidden God. There is a further element of hope redolent of Moltmann (and Pannenberg) to be discerned here, too, in Frei's statement that history will not reveal any meanings it might presently conceal except in the light of its end (161). This end is revealed proleptically in the story of Jesus, says Frei, but he is far more reticent even than Moltmann in his denial that *all* has been revealed in Jesus already.[161] Nor is he convinced that the New Testament demands such an affirmation: "The providential action of God over and in his creation is not that of a mechanical fate to be read off of one occasion" (163).

Frei compares the Christian savior story with other savior stories to highlight their differences. This is where the elements of Jesus' distinctiveness, as he identifies them, are revealed. Unlike the gnostic redeemer, Jesus does not share the alienation of every other spirit imprisoned in the gross matter of flesh. Rather, there is a congruence of Jesus' helplessness with his perfect obedience to God, so that his sharing in the need of all to be redeemed is a *vicarious* sharing and not the gnostic redeemer's *organic* sharing (58). But, then, Frei is also impressed by the non-substitutability of Jesus in the story—a simple thing, but for him the *real* difference between the Gospels and other savior stories. "The Gospel story is a demythologization of the saviour myth," he writes, "because the saviour figure in the Gospel story is fully identified with Jesus of Nazareth. The early Christians would substitute no other name" (59).

Other elements stand out, for Frei, when comparing the synoptic Christ with purported "Christ-figures" from modern literature. In particular he mentions the co-existence of Jesus' unsubstitutable individuality and his universal saving scope. Compared with Jesus, the hero of Herman Melville's naval novella *Billy Budd* is an insipid non-person; for all his oft-alleged power as a symbol of the human condition and designation as a Christ figure, he lacks individuality (66-68). Similarly, Frei is unconvinced by the tormented, existentialist Jesus of Nikos Kazantzakis' novel *The Last Temptation*. This figure is a Jesus for the robust rather than the weak, an exemplar in their struggle to defeat the self. But this Jesus has no "comfortable words" to offer "all who labor and are heavy-laden," and therein he lacks that universal saving scope typical of the gospel Christ: "himself he saved; others he could not save, is the theme here rather than its reverse in the Gospels" (72).[162]

While such narratives lack key aspects characterizing Jesus' portrayal in the gospels, nevertheless Frei does not deny them some "support role." "The central Christian story in its recited and performed reenactment is the bestower of meaning for other similar events," he allows, "and yet these other events have to evoke the original and breathe life into it" (170).[163]

By way of criticism, one wonders whether Frei's adherence is entirely to revelation alone, as is claimed. I suggest, on the contrary, that he *has* smuggled in some liberal-style dependence on human experience in asserting Jesus' uniqueness.

At the most basic level, I would point to the impossilility of avoiding bias in the way Frei claims. If seeking Jesus' identity in the liberal manner "behind the narrative" makes distorting bias unavoidable, as Frei rightly claims, can one avoid this simply by attending to the narrative itself? Will one's perspective not color interpretation at this level, too—indeed, at whatever level one chooses to look? It is, after all, a commonplace of contemporary literary theory that no reading of a text can be definitive, and that readers "construct" the meaning of texts according to their lights. The structuralists, whose influence on narrative theology is considerable, seek the meaning of a text in the literary dynamics of its internal structure, but surely these are not graven there indelibly. Post-structuralism would insist that each structural reading will find different aspects according to the reader's perspective. So Frei has not escaped the danger of importing *some* alien agenda, even a liberal theological one—his hermeneutic is not "virus free."

But there are more specific dependencies on human experience to be found. One thing Frei does appear to presuppose in his reading of the gospels is the loss of meaning in history currently sensed throughout western intellectual life and reflected in social conditions. It is precisely this which existentialists sought to remedy with their requirement that we ourselves become creators of meaning. Frei's Jesus saves us from this meaninglessness in revealing the locus of God's redemption right among the press of concrete events themselves. As we have seen, this illustrates for Frei how God's presence can still be discerned without needing to posit the sort of overarching historical vision reminiscent of Hegel and beloved of his descendants in idealist and liberal theology. Thus these existentialist concerns, and the much-discussed recent western experience of God's apparent absence, are important for Frei (we have seen how important is the latter factor in Moltmann's *theologia crucis*, too). Indeed, Frei's Jesus is alienated as others are alienated, albeit *vicariously* rather than *organically*, as we have heard it described. Existential perceptions are clearly at work, then, in Frei's understanding of Jesus and the atonement wrought through this vicarious identification. Is there a hint of some method of correlation here, recalling that of Tilllich, with Frei's Jesus providing by revelation the solution to an abiding human dilemma? The good post-liberal believes that this sort of alienation is quite culture-specific, however. By failing to take adequate note of this, Frei displays a greater proximity to liberal theology than he consciously allows.

Another place that experience creeps into Frei's picture of Jesus is at the more specific level of experience within the church, which he does recognize as preceding the gospel portrayal of Jesus. We have heard Frei refer to the church's experience of new life in Jesus as the basis of resurrection belief (recall his insistence that Christian claims to know Jesus as a living reality make it impossible to conceive of him as not having been raised). This also presupposes a link, a oneness, between earliest Christianity and its experience of the risen Christ with the experience of Christ's presence claimed by Christians today. So Frei *does* look behind the text—to the experience which gave rise to the text in the first place—just as he looks "in front of the text," too, for a corresponding Christian experience today. Herein is his real belief about the authority of scripture, I suggest; it does *not* lie in the text itself, but rather in the church's experience. And the approach which involves so grounding one's theological claims has a name—modernism.

If one looks this far behind the text, however, to the sort of experience it enshrines, then one suddenly finds oneself back in the mainstream of twentieth century biblical interpretation, from form criticism (which looked to the *Sitz im Leben* from which a text arose) to redaction criticism. Then the claims of Collingwood and existentialist historiography raise their head, as taken up in theologies open to the new quest of the historical Jesus by theologians such as Schillebeeckx (to be considered in Part III, below). This approach recognizes that experience must have a cause; it seeks to reconstruct the historical Jesus by examining the claims made on his behalf by the community which arose in his wake[164] (rather than in any actively sought isolation from those experiences, as in the original nineteenth century quest).[165]

It should be noted in this connection that narrative theology is bigger than the uses made of it by conservatives. Schillebeeckx and other liberals are now alive to the importance of story as a theological category, in part through influences from the hermeneutics of Paul Ricoeur. So a narrative approach attending closely to the gospel story need not be exclusivist, as in Frei's case. Frans Jozef van Beeck, whose major study *Christ Proclaimed: Christology as Rhetoric* (1979) is prominent among the alternatives to be mentioned in the Conclusion to this study, displays many of Frei's emphases *without* his insistence upon Jesus' qualitative uniqueness and his discontinuity with other experience.

All in all, it would seem that Frei has failed to mark out a justifiable claim of his own apart from liberal theology. A last observation to support this conclusion follows from his discussion of other savior figures. Frei nowhere establishes that Jesus is *totally* different from these others, but only that Jesus is more complete than they are—recall, for instance, his insistence that Jesus is *both* an individual *and* a savior of universal scope, while other savior figures were one or the other but not both. How does this differ from the standard liberal claim that Jesus most fully embodies a salvation which is found less fully embodied elsewhere? Has Frei's attempt (typical of the other "conservative" writers we have met) to present Jesus as *qualitatively* different really only managed to establish that he is *quantitatively* different, as liberal theology has tended to claim all along?

DIETRICH RITSCHL

Another with a *Christus praesens* emphasis is the German-American theologian Dietrich Ritschl (who is also a Reformed pastor with long parish experience, and a trained psychotherapist). His *Memory and Hope: An Inquiry Concerning the Presence of Christ* (1967), to be examined here, is yet another sustained attack on individualizing and interiorizing trends in western theology. A former graduate student of Torrance, Ritschl insists upon an objective Christological ground for Christianity. The manifestation of this "ground" is not episodic, however—it is not disclosed through divine epiphanies to individuals who are being "put right" by God after some pattern disclosed in Christ. Rather, he understands Christianity in terms of Christ's completed work—a work which lives in the church's *memory* and generates its *hope*.

These twin dimensions of Christ's presence, doxological and eschatological, are seen by Ritschl as tied essentially to the church's prayer and worship, rather than residing in its beliefs. Ritschl's views on the uniqueness of Jesus, which must be strained from his Christo-centric discussion of hermeneutics and theological method, are in-separable from this doxological framework. Any confession of Jesus' uniqueness is ultimately an intra-Christian confession, according to Ritschl, and meaningless apart from involvement in worship.[166]

For Ritschl, western theology came adrift with Augustine. Its meaning came to be seen as timeless (113-14), concerned to meet human need and focused on the *effect* upon recipients of grace rather than the *cause* of that effect (118).[167] Accordingly, the individual and "inner states" are deemed to be primary, and this is why Ritschl sees much of today's liberal emphasis in theology as really quite tradi-tional in its approach "from below"—that is, with the "human condi-tion" as its starting point (137). "This permits the somewhat exagger-ated statement," he suggests, "that there is ultimately little dogmati-cal difference between the theologies of Augustine, Billy Graham and Rudolf Bultmann. They all ask: How can I hear...that God's work in Jesus Christ calls *me* to a decision which will *mean freedom* and *salvation* for *me* in the future?" (34).

Ritschl finds no sense in all of this that Jesus Christ is of any decisive importance. Augustine's Christ, he believes, does no more than represent what God is doing anyway, as well as provide human-ity with an ethical example. He finds no hint of a completed event here, whereby salvation might be seen as having been secured and in which Christians might participate (121). Ritschl rejects all of this, however. He does not maintain a "traditional" theological focus on the human person by attending to the individual's accruing of spiritu-al gifts, say, nor does he look to the attainment of "authentic self-hood," or some other indicator, as anthropologically based liberal theology does. On the contrary, he directs attention to Jesus Christ. Ritschl believes that Jesus, alive in the church's memory, provides a surer path to insight concerning our human condition than can be had by attending to that condition directly (188).

For this and other reasons, Ritschl dislikes both idealist and ex-istentialist-liberal theologies, bringing him into direct conflict with approaches to be canvased in subsequent chapters. He opposes logos Christologies as inadequate to the two-nature paradoxicality of Jesus' person as conceived by Chalcedon—finding in Jesus an in-stance, albeit a special one, of the logos present everywhere leads to docetism on the one hand, with the logos deemed to move from God into the human form of Jesus, or else it leads to adoptionism, elevating a human Jesus into the form of Christ (205). According to Ritschl, however, too much "pre-Christological" knowledge of God is presumed by the former, and too much knowledge of the human condition by the latter.[168] Ritschl is also most critical of Bultmann's existential Christology. The focus there is on individual faith, and it is unclear to Ritschl why any Jesus so conceived should necessarily be unique (31).[169] There is no decisive initiating event in history, according to such views, but only a vague idea of God coupled with a complex view of the human condition (61). This involves a static God, manifest to individuals, as in Augustine—a God appealing to deists and enshrined in modern theology as Tillich's "ground of being" (45, 130-32). It also involves what Moltmann has called a *"theologia naturalis* of modern existence" (133) such as will be encountered throughout the subsequent two parts of this study.

The legacy of Bultmann in the period under consideration lies with his successors in the "new quest" who make much of existentialist historiography. Ritschl again rejects their individual focus, which he compares with that of eighteenth century pietism (40). The existentialist distinction between *Historie* and *Geschichte* locates the meaning of history in the relations of individuals to past events (37), so that "history is reduced to the historicity of the man who is concerned with history" (39). There is certainly something of Torrance in Ritschl's preference for objectivity, in which attention is directed to what God has done in Christ and away from what God might be doing for individuals whom he sees as being mired in their own subjectivity.[170]

But just as there is more to God in Christ, for Ritschl, than epiphanies to individuals (cf. Moltmann), more than can be found in the sacraments, more than the kerygma and its effect on the state of believers—just as there is an objective, event character at the heart of Christianity—nevertheless its reality is not reducible to events of the past alone (27-29). And hence Ritschl's embrace of the *Christus praesens*; while classical theology was not interested in the risen Christ as a present reality, according to Ritschl, he nonetheless is (29). Now, the church does not itself constitute this presence—it is no *Christus prolongatus* as has often been suggested (226). But

Ritschl believes the presence of Christ *is* known in the church's memory and hope, notwithstanding:

> Who then "is" the *Christus praesens? From the point of view of the Church*...he is that "power" or "interest" ...which makes the Church see that she is taken into possession, drawn into the history of promise and fulfilment, used in service, invited to hope; and this "power" is called Christ because the Church recognizes it in no one else than the one whom she remembers as the earthly priest Jesus of Nazareth and whom she expects in the future, though in no other terms than those of the promises of the past (218).

This is a new insight of twentieth century theology, thinks Ritschl, who follows Bonhoeffer in attending to it (20 n.4).

But at the point of stating just *how* this Christ is present, just what is the form and mode of his presence, Ritschl becomes opaque. This presence has its own mode, its own logic, he says (230); it is not addressable in terms of the kerygma, as we have seen, nor does it represent the self-consciousness of the church (the modernist reduction, one supposes).[171] But surely this is to follow Barth's retreat from the field of public accountability, as the post-liberals have also done in declaring defunct all generally accessible structures of public meaningfulness.[172]

How is it, then, that Ritschl's Jesus is unique? I suggest that, ultimately, it is a *fait accompli* of revelation, as for Barth. The basis of Ritschl's claim for Jesus' uniqueness is the resurrection. He does not believe that this can be given a status in incontrovertible history, however, as in Pannenberg's theology. Rather, it is all to do with experience within the church, with worship and participation in the collective story and practice of the faith community (207-08). There is none of Hans Frei's close attention to the dynamics of the gospel narrative here, however—Ritschl is by no means a narrative theologian. *But what he does share with Frei is a conviction that, apart from the faith community, there is nothing generally accessible about the uniqueness of Jesus.* "Theological thinking is a circle," he writes, "which has no distinct and definable beginning, such as the preexistent Christ, a definition of the invisible world, or the historical Jesus" (88), and so he sets his face against both traditional incarnationalism and more recent liberalism. It is simply the case for Ritschl that no-one but Jesus is so completely the agent of God and the agent of humanity—that in no one but Jesus can God and humanity be as fully seen and understood by Christians. He is quite right to state that this is an "assertion":

> *The assertion of the uniqueness of Jesus* regarding his "doing the works of the Father" and his "being the newness of men" *leads to prayer and flows from prayer.* In traditional language this means that the uniqueness of Jesus can only be preached in a worship service in which people pray. Preaching the uniqueness of Jesus on the street corners, i.e. without the beginning in prayer and the response to prayer, is "theoretically" absurd, and is possible "practically" only because the listeners on the street corner may still remember the prayer of worship services they once attended. This also applies to the first missionary activities of the apostles: they went to the places where the expectation of the Old Testament promises were still remembered (216).

Ritschl provides an instance of this. "Conversations with young people in the Soviet Union," he recounts, "indicate quite concretely that those who do not even abstractly "remember" worship cannot grasp statements about the uniqueness of Jesus even if they are willing to respect him as a man of high moral character and the like" (216 n.12).

As was the case in our consideration of Frei, however, one wonders whether all this is fatally circular. That is to say: believing that the resurrection establishes Jesus' uniqueness on the basis of his impact upon the church, while at the same time holding that the church can only confess the resurrection because of Jesus' impact upon it.[173]

And what of the heavy theological burden Ritschl lays upon the back of worship? [174] Surely he overstates the case in this matter. To employ an example ready to hand: many an Anglican priest knows that a lifetime of attendance at worship may elicit from the laity no more than a vague respect for Jesus' attainments which falls far short of orthodox Christology. Ritschl waxes far too lyrical about the impact and importance of worship on people, then, as liturgists and religious educators alike are often wont to do. This all-too-often misplaced enthusiasm is also found among theologically-minded therapists from traditions of depth psychology—those who make strong claims about the power of liturgical symbolism in the unconscious (remember that Ritschl himself practices as one of these therapists). And even among those strongly affected by worship, must we not admit that some are non-cognitivists in their use of religious language? Surely a good number among the rank and file occupy the range of non-realist approaches which Don Cupitt identifies in his book *Life Lines* (1986); I would be confident that Cupitt's category "aesthetic expressivism," for instance, is well represented among Anglo-Catholic laity and church musicians—not to mention clergy!

Perhaps it is not just attending worship which is required, therefore, but worship which incorporates a sufficiently strong emphasis on Christian uniqueness. However, this raises the question of whether the "worship component" is crucial in conveying the idea of Christ's uniqueness; would preaching be the key, perhaps, or would exposure to the idea in *any* context later recognized to have been formative suffice, and not merely that of worship?

What, then, *is* the deepest root of this idea for Ritschl? I suggest that it is Reformed theology's doctrine of *election* which undergirds the whole edifice. There can be little doubt about this. In *The Logic of Theology* (1984) Ritschl finds in "the election of Israel and the church ... the most important and most original theological notion of all" (292), though he interprets this election in inclusive rather than in exclusive terms (124), as we have also seen Moltmann do. Again, according to *The Logic of Theology*, "the doctrine of election, which is for believers what the proofs for the existence of God are for classical philosophers—stands out clearly in its key position for all theological theorizing" (122). In arguing thus, Ritschl is in step with his Reformed theological brothers Barth (for whom Jesus is the elect man), Moltmann and Torrance. But whereas Frei sought to explicate through narrative means the mechanism by which Jesus' uniqueness is established in the gospels, Ritschl requires no such measures; ultimately Jesus' uniqueness for him is a *fait accompli* of revelation. He claims that only exposure to worship will enable people to gain a sense of this uniqueness but, as should be obvious to anyone who makes as much of his pastoral credentials as Ritschl does, attending and even being moved by worship does *not* guarantee any such "true confession." Only election does this, and on this bulwark of his Reformed heritage hangs Ritschl's appeal to the religious disclosivity of worship.

To sum up: Dietrich Ritschl *asserts* the uniqueness of Jesus with no recourse to the human condition as conceived by the liberals. In this he is quite consistent. He does not find human solidarity in shared sin or guilt, nor in any anthropological consideration, as Augustine and Kierkegaard would have it. Only insofar as humanity is addressed by Jesus Christ is there human solidarity, says Ritschl (as does Barth). More recently, in *The Logic of Theology* (1984), Ritschl criticizes the Greek idea of a "normal person" (57). He also extends his earlier arguments to take account of anthropological insights into the incorrigible diversity of peoples, and post-modern thinking, all of which has risen to theological prominence since *Memory and Hope* (1967). Thus he argues that there is no *a priori* humanum (77, 197-201, 206-07). But this also frees up theology, Ritschl thinks, allowing it plainly to address people in all their concreteness and diversity and so allowing what he calls an "unmythological analysis of the natural" (234).

It is interesting to note, however, that Ritschl never reacts against another key feature of liberal Christology—the historical Jesus. At the time of *Memory and Hope*, the immediate theological past was not one in which the historical Jesus was important. Since Weiss and Schweitzer the historical Jesus' fortunes had been low, and major existentialist theologians of the period such as Bultmann and Tillich were certainly more interested in "the Christ of faith." And when *Memory and Hope* was written the new quest had not risen to theological prominence, as it has subsequently. So there was no need for Ritschl to reject the historical Jesus at this point. But neither does he in *The Logic of Theology*, and in light of the growth in importance of the historical Jesus since 1967 this omission is harder to understand. Moreover in *The Logic of Theology* Ritschl presumes a lot about the details of Jesus' life, referring to him as the "minimal man" since "he lived his life in complete vulnerability, with no possessions, unmarried and without protection, taking each individual as seriously as God" (174). But such untroubledly fulsome assertions are surely insensitive to the acknowledged complexity of distinguishing Jesus' actual person from his kerygmatic "personae" in the gospels.[175] So while in theory the historical Jesus is not important for Ritschl's Christology, in practice some uncritical use of the category is to be found, albeit a minor one.

In the final analysis, though, Ritschl has no need of "liberal props" like the historical Jesus or the human condition. He does not even need a narrative theology such as Frei's—another post-liberal attempt to probe Jesus' uniqueness. For Ritschl there is never any real question of justifying his belief. It is as if a divine breath of election and revelation has blown upon the dry bones of Wittgensteinian fideism and they have taken flesh! But this flesh is not vulnerable, as is Frei's hermeneutical flesh—indeed, as all flesh should be.

To find such flesh we must pass beyond the more or less invincible hermeneutical certainties encountered among these "conservative" approaches into the study of other liberal-tending theologies. There, doctrines such as election and revelation are explored rather than wielded! In justifying such a departure, however, we have more to prompt us than simply a desire for greater hermeneutical clarity; there is more beckoning us than merely a wish to see claims for Jesus' uniqueness cast in less unfalsifiable terms, as entailed by modern philosophy of science. The frequent emergence and apparent irrepressibility of liberal elements within the "conservative" theologies examined above, the veiled dependencies upon the historical Jesus and implicit claims concerning some human condition, compel the consideration of liberal theological counter-proposals. Thus we cannot avoid turning in a more liberal direction in view of the number of liberal weeds found growing tenaciously in the "conservative" garden!

PART II

IDEALIST

This "idealist" group stands in the middle of the "conservative" and "liberal" approaches—between those who tend to identify no clear meeting point between the subject and object of revelation, on the one hand, and those whose dependence upon unmediated revelation is virtually non-existent, on the other. As befits their position on the left of my typology, the "conservative" group make no real recourse to the historical Jesus nor to the human condition. The "idealist" group does, of course, though like the "conservative" writers their work is an explication of God's revelation through Christ in the process of history, and so it is essentially a theology "from above," rather than a theology "from below"—that is, one content to analyze and interpret the impact of Jesus, as the "liberal" writers in Part III below tend to do (even though they also rely upon the fact of Jesus' impact).

Three major figures are to be considered here. In Karl Rahner and Wolfhart Pannenberg we have two of the twentieth century's leading theological thinkers. Walter Kasper bridges their positions, repeating some aspects and improving upon others. He also points in the direction of Part III, sharing some affinities with those to be studied there.

Throughout this discussion various shortcomings in these approaches will become apparent—in particular, the way in which the *actual* role of the historical Jesus and the human condition is often overstated, with revelation or a heavily idealist philosophy of history adding far more weight to claims for Jesus' uniqueness and finality than those responsible will admit. Also, there is doubt in some cases as to *why* Jesus is accorded unique and final status, given the historical reservations which are voiced and the apparent inability of these writers to account for the genesis of such faith in the believer, or indeed to justify their belief in Christ's universal efficacy. In addition to these more general concerns, internal difficulties identified in the major approaches of Rahner and Pannenberg are found to render their elegant solutions rather less than totally convincing.

Chapter Four

TRANSCENDENTAL ANTHROPOLOGY

The theology to be considered here is "from above" in that it leans heavily on aspects of divine revelation, as well as natural theology in the tradition of Aquinas. Yet it has a strong element "from below," too, in its reliance upon the human condition and the history of Jesus to produce a unique and final "match." Here we find the most significant attempt from our period of interest to provide the meeting point between revelation and the human person identified as lacking among the "conservative" writers of Part I above.

KARL RAHNER, S.J.

Karl Rahner, certainly among the top few theologians of the twentieth century, was born in Freiburg and died at Innsbruck not long after his eightieth birthday in March 1984. His literary output was vast, and while it included books and the major collections he edited, Rahner is perhaps best known for his occasional writings which are gathered in English as the twenty-volume *Theological Investigations.*[1] He lived the disciplined life of a theologian within a religious order and for most of his career was a professor, at Innsbruck, Munich then Münster, before "retiring" in 1971 to the Jesuit writers' house at Innsbruck.[2]

Rahner was first and foremost a Jesuit and a priest. His Ignatian spirituality issued in a number of influential spiritual writings for priests and laity but, especially, it undergirded his whole theological vision of the world and human life as pervaded by divine grace.[3] Rahner also had an unfailing pastoral sense,[4] which supported his lifelong attempt to relate Christian belief in general (and Roman Catholic dogma in particular) to today's life-world. Rahner combined theological lecturing with pastoral work in Vienna and in rural Bavaria during the agony of World War II, further cementing his characteristic unwillingness to divorce theology from pastoral concerns.[5] Although Rahner's professional theological writings are notoriously difficult, the communication of the gospel to ordinary people was never far from his mind—this was, after all, a man whose spiritual guidance to young persons in Vienna was still sought after when he was nearly eighty![6]

And Rahner was a churchman. He was one of 190 or so *periti* (official theologians) at Vatican II and contributed much to its pronouncements on issues ranging from "anonymous Christianity" to the restored diaconate.[7] Rahner's pupil and sometime critic J.B. Metz pointed out that "In good Jesuit fashion, Rahner seems almost a natural churchman... he has the church in his guts, and feels its failures like indigestion."[8]

In a time of rapid change, doubt and soul searching throughout the Roman Catholic world, Karl Rahner undertook a sympathetic response to the church's critics and to the "cultured despisers of religion." He reinterpreted the church's faith in light of modernity, explicating even its most obscure elements (such as the Marian dogmas) as refractions of what he deemed to be most central—God's bringing-forth from the graced stuff of the world an absolute savior in the person of Jesus Christ.

Every Roman Catholic writer to be considered in this study owes a theological debt to Rahner. A "Rahnerian orthodoxy" has grown up on the strength of his synthesis, too; the Roman Catholic Church today is awash with his ideas, from popes to parish study groups. The center of Rahner's entire program was Christology, with Jesus Christ as God's final revelation to a world he believed was straining to find this revelation. So Karl Rahner is not only a singularly important recent theologian—he is also singularly important for his views over matters concerning us in this study.

Rahner wrote no systematic theology, but there are three main books. The two earliest, *Geist im Welt* (1939) (*Spirit in the World,* 1968) and *Hörer des Wortes* (1941) (*Hearers of the Word,* 1969), are the basis of Rahner's philosophical theology, while his *Grundkurs des Glaubens* (1976) (*Foundations of Christian Faith,* 1978) is a more systematic statement of the rational grounds for Christian belief and for particular doctrines (this last volume will receive closest attention in the discussion proper, to follow).[9]

In the previous chapter concerns were raised that "revelation" as "conservative" writers conceived it seemed to require a meeting point with the human world, though the existence of one was trenchantly denied. But this is no problem for Rahner. If revelation is the "key," then there is a divinely prepared "keyhole" in the human person ready to receive that key;[10] if there is a revealed Christology, then there is also a "searching Christology," undertaken by humanity, based on the need for an "absolute savior" (*heilsbedeutsam*). But this is not simply a natural theology to match a revealed theology—Rahner modifies his essential Thomism in this and other ways. Rather, it is a realization that humans are fundamentally constituted as "hearers of the word" within an overarching economy of divine outreach to the world which is at the same time divine presence in the world. "What is Rahner's theological vision?" asks Anne Carr:

> Perhaps it can best be described as an apprehension of the whole that maintains the distinction of its parts, unity in diversity: the sacred and the secular, essence and existence, the divine and the human, theology and philosophy, grace and nature, or in Rahner's characteristic language, transcendence and history. He advocates an approach to theology that takes account of both the a priori framework of interpretation, the 'transcendental', by which he means the conditions of possibility for Christian revelation and dogma, and the a posteriori, the 'categorical', the historical data. The unifying core of Christianity, for Rahner, is the message of the personal self-communication of God in the Incarnation and in grace ... to humankind and to the world, beyond the demands of nature, in such fashion that the world and humankind are both united to God in intimate relationship and set free in their own autonomy and distinction precisely by this relationship.[11]

And it is in Jesus Christ that the divine offer and the autonomous human response (albeit solely enabled by grace) achieve an unsurpassable, and hence unique and final, realization. For Rahner this triumph of human transcendence, this emergence at last of a fully human life, constitutes a turning point in the history of the whole cosmos, affecting *all persons* subsequently.

Because Rahner is so major and influential a figure we will do well to assay various influences upon him before proceeding to an examination of the work itself.

Rahner "successfully challenged the hegemony of a narrow and defensive neo-scholasticism in early twentieth century Roman Catholic theology."[12] The immediate context of Rahner's work was the mid-century ferment in Roman Catholic thought which had already led that church toward an embrace of ecumenism, biblical studies, patristics and liturgical renewal. The neo-scholastic orthodoxy which used Aquinas (while misrepresenting him at key points) in support of Rome's ultramontane, nineteenth century rear-guard action against modernity was being undercut by a spirit of *ressourcement*—impeccably traditional!—as well as the spirit of *aggiornamento* also associated with Vatican II.[13] "To understand Karl Rahner," then, as Vorgrimler explains, "one must...understand that he was already in the second generation of theological renewal."[14]

Karl Rahner had his place in the rise of so-called "transcendental Thomism," developing the ideas of a fellow Jesuit, Joseph Mårèchal. This involved a genuine attention to Aquinas coupled with that openness to modernity increasingly characteristic of Roman Catholic thought. Neo-scholasticism, following the polemical program of counter-reformation orthodoxy, preferred Augustine's disjunction between natural and supernatural orders to the rather softer line taken by Aquinas, for whom the world's concrete order was both an order of grace and one of salvation. Not so for Rahner, who opposed the "extrinsicism" of neo-Thomism, which saw the natural and supernatural as two parallel realities (following Augustine), in favor of their more complex interpenetration as perceived by Aquinas.[15] And hence Rahner's characteristic inability to see "nature" apart from "grace," nor any aspect of human knowing apart from knowledge of God.[16]

But between the metaphysics of Aquinas (with the possibility of analogical inference from human being in the world to the being of God) and our own times stands the metaphysical agnosticism of

Kant's "critical idealism."[17] "Transcendental Thomism" seeks to overcome this agnosticism by updating Thomistic metaphysics in the light of Kant's "Copernican Revolution," with its "turn to the subject," along with other aspects of modern enlightenment thought. This was the path Rahner followed, in the footsteps of Màrèchal.[18]

> In Rahner's philosophical theology, the Kantian cognitional a priori is transformed into a metaphysical a priori. ...According to this account, beyond the transcendental structures of reason which Kant argued make it possible for sense perception to become knowledge, there is the readiness to affirm being which serves as a kind of precondition for knowing anything at all.... A transcendental analysis of this readiness to affirm the being of beings and its inexhaustibility discloses that the human mind is structurally oriented to a horizon or backdrop of being (Rahner's notion of *Vorgriff auf esse*).... The horizon of being is disclosed as limitless, unrestricted or Absolute Being... which all call God—to paraphrase Aquinas....[19]

But it was in Heidegger's doctoral seminar at Freiburg in the mid-1930s that the young Fr. Rahner found his truest philosophical conversation partner. In his first attempt at a doctoral thesis, failed by the conservative Honecker but later published as *Spirit in the World*, Rahner studied Aquinas on the dynamism of the human mind in the light of Heidegger's fundamental question of being.

> Rahner's human subject, like Heidegger's *Dasein*, is a being in the world of sensible objects. For man can become aware of his own existence as a free knower only by setting the world over against himself in a judgemental affirmation.... Thus the human intellect, in order to come to know itself through the process of judgement, must have an implicit, pre-conceptual pre-grasp (*Vorgriff*) of Infinite Being. Heidegger... said that *Dasein* was the questioner whose fundamental question about Being 'runs through' the beings of the world in its pre-grasp of the world's horizon.[20]

But whereas Heidegger saw this openness leading nowhere, Rahner saw it leading to the infinite horizon which is God.[21]

We now explore Rahner's *Foundations of Christian Faith* (1978), albeit rather circuitously, taking account of other writings by Rahner where necessary.[22] The path to be followed here is dictated by the interests of this study, so we shall consider the human condition as Rahner sees it and the doctrine of revelation built upon it, and then the history of Jesus Christ as fulfilling that revelation, including Rahner's emphasis upon the resurrection as confirming that uniqueness and finality. Of central importance here are Rahner's views on the way Jesus' person and work extends to influence the whole cosmos—this, of course, is also central to our concerns.

For Rahner there are certain "inescapable" elements of the human condition—"the real and original experience of personhood and freedom, of subjectivity, of history and historicity, and of dependence" (43)—though he admits that today's plurality of philosophies conceive humanity in irreducibly divergent ways (7), and that people variously deploy the elements he believes to be constant (43).[23]

According to Rahner, to be human is to be fundamentally self-transcending and fundamentally linked to God, though also fundamentally different from God (119). Rahner is no materialist or behaviorist; he insists that we cannot be reduced to our components because we have a subjectivity conscious of these various components and so we transcend them (30-31). Rahner's human person is conscious of finiteness and senses, as an *a priori* of existence, an unthematic horizon defining this finiteness (19-20). Here we recall Plato's allegory of the cave and Kant's "leap of reason." So, unlike animals, to be human is not to deal with parts of experience only but "to live and act out of a formal anticipation of the whole" (191). For Rahner this horizon of looming mystery is encountered throughout all of human life, though it is the choice of each person whether to attend to it or not, thus making out of life either a path to salvation or else to its opposite (22, 39).

How then does God "get through" to persons, as Rahner conceives them? Most importantly, knowledge of God for Rahner is *a posteriori* knowledge—experience in the world provides the source, the carrying medium, and the language to articulate revelation as he conceives it (52). To be sure, the transcendental orientation of persons toward the mysterious horizon of their existence is the pre-condition for this revelation to be experienced and recognized.[24] But the *actual* revelation is more than merely a natural concomitant of human being; there is more than the "existential" of transcendentality involved here, but also a "supernatural existential." This comprises an elevation of natural human transcendentality by divine grace, an unveiling, which is always given by God (and so is "natural" only in the sense of being usual) but is not mere "nature"; while Rahner can reckon "the self-communication of God to man in grace as the transcendental constitution of man" (73), it is nevertheless a matter of a "supernatural elevation" of the natural. "If God were not to speak at all," says Anne Carr with reference to Rahner's thinking here, then "the message of human history would be God's silence, the silence of the infinite horizon of human spirit."[25]

More on the question of historicity as a part of human nature (*and* as a necessary component of revelation) shortly; for now it should be added that Rahner sees the revelation embodied in this "supernatural existential" as taking place everywhere (88-89), for everyone, as a hidden dimension of more general human transcendence (129). So there is no separate sacral realm, *nor are there any particular religious experiences* for Rahner (152), and here he wishes no doubt to distance himself from the philosophical theology of liberal Protestants such as Rudolf Otto and Ernst Troeltsch with their religious *a priori* separate from the rest of life.[26]

It should also be mentioned that Rahner sees revelation as a two-way street. This is most important for understanding both his view of the human person (and the high spiritual dignity of humans in the eyes of God),[27] on the one hand, and his Christology on the other (according to which Jesus is both divine offer and human response). Basically, Rahner believes there is no revelation if it is not *heard*. So he believes that "There is no revelation which could take place in any other way except in the faith of the person hearing the revelation" (142). Rahner is no Calvinist, then, with doctrines of total depravity, irresistible grace and election—of any invincibility on the part of God's Word in the face of human stubbornness; rather, he follows the teaching of Aquinas that the human will is a necessary component of revelation received aright.[28] Only when the divine self-offer is

matched by an adequate human response "is there an absolutely irrevocable self-communication on both sides, and only then is it present
in the world in a historical and communicable way" (195).

This historicity is important to Rahner—it is an existential of
the human person, and as such any salvation of the human person or
any lack thereof must be worked out in the public, historical arena
and not in any spiritualistic, private realm (41). Similarly, Rahner is
content "to call the history of the explicit self-interpretation of transcendental, supernatural experience in the life of the individual and
of mankind . . . the history of revelation" (154). This history of revelation and salvation which covers the whole of human history is not
specifically Christian though. While according to Rahner it is the
preserve of Christ, it is a Christ operating incognito.[29] In his view all
human life, all openness to "the other" in whatever form, even when
not explicitly religious (even at the simple level of following the
voice of conscience and living a moral life), can be an instance of
revelation received and acted upon, and hence of salvation (143-44,
152). The same revelation rejected, however, leads to the forfeiture
of salvation.

In what sort of divine economy are Rahner's "hearers of the
Word" located? Essentially it is an Irenaean rather than an Augustinian world which Rahner inhabits, a world predisposed toward the incarnation of the Word. The Word incarnate, understood simply as an
antidote for human sin (as Anselm classically expresses in his *Cur
Deus Homo*), is not the incarnation as Rahner understands it. Rahner
prefers to conceive the Word in a rather Johannine manner as making
its way in the world from the beginning "as an intrinsic moment and
a condition for the universal bestowal of grace to spiritual creatures"
(199)—though, of course, "the world knew him not." Rahner thus
sees the incarnation as part of the primordial process by which God
goes over into "the other" in order to come to expression, just as he
sees "creation as a partial moment in the process in which God becomes world" (197). This is quintessentially Hegelian, and it has
affinities with Teilhard.[30] But Rahner also sees that process by which
the stuff of the cosmos becomes conscious of itself in humanity as
necessarily requiring a final result (190), a high point, with higher
levels prepared for by lower ones (186).[31]

And just as the cosmos, through grace of course, is busy bringing forth its savior, Rahner believes the human race, for its part, is individually and collectively "on the lookout" for the advent of this savior. This he calls a "searching Christology," to match the searching out of humanity by God. This expectation is necessary if the actual "one who is to come" is to be recognized; according to Rahner, "We can find and retain something which encounters man in history only if there is present in the finding and retaining subjectivity of man an a priori principle of expectation, of searching, of hoping" (319). This search has been evident throughout the variegate religious history of humanity, he thinks: "Saviour figures in the history of religion can readily be regarded as an indication of the fact that mankind, moved always and everywhere by grace, anticipates and looks for that event in which its absolute hope becomes irreversible in history" (321). Thus hope is another constituent of the human condition; to be sure, this last extract sees hope as the fruit of the pressure of grace upon the individual, and so a "supernatural existential" rather than an "existential" pure and simple, but we can still call it a feature of the human condition remembering that Rahner's "supernatural existential," while not "natural," is nevertheless constant and universal.[32]

Thus in transcendentally oriented human persons, engaged in a "searching Christology," we have half of what Rahner gives us of a "Christology from below," or an "ascending Christology" (to match the "Christology from above" or "descending Christology" expressed in his recourse to dogma and in his talk of the primacy of grace). But there is another dimension of Rahner's "ascending Christology" apart from this detailed attention to the human condition, and that is the history of Jesus of Nazareth.

First, it must be said that the history of Jesus of Nazareth matters for Rahner because historicity as a whole matters, as we have seen. Rahner believes salvation is only accessible to fundamentally historical human beings as a *history of salvation* (41). So it is that Rahner attends to "what in its unique, irreducible and historical concreteness forms the basis of the existence and of the event of salvation" (177).

But it is not as if any "searching Christology" alone could identify Jesus of Nazareth unerringly as the long awaited one; such a "match" is not obvious at all, according to Rahner (211). It is only because the church has *already* made this connection as a matter of historical fact, and because individual Christians have found themselves assenting to this identification, that the identification is possible at all. Thus Rahner holds an Anselmian *Fides quaerens intellectum* perspective in that his "Transcendental Christology allows one to search for, and in his search to understand, what he has already found in Jesus of Nazareth" (212). Rahner admits that such faith-knowledge is circular (230).

As for the historical elements themselves Rahner admits that some uncertainty must intervene, this being the nature of historical knowledge (233). But he takes comfort from the realization that we can never be sufficiently certain of *any* historical facts to justify absolutely our various commitments in life, and so he decides that any set of historical reasons which might call belief in Jesus Christ into question is not as good as the set of historical reasons supporting that belief (234-35).[33] For instance, Rahner realizes the historical difficulties long-recognized with regard to Jesus' miracles. He has no doubt but that "Jesus was a miracle worker to some degree and extent" (255) while conceding that even if the New Testament miracles took place they need not have constituted interruptions to natural law (259). But he secures a special place for the resurrection in his argument for Jesus' uniqueness, noting that its distinctive character has been recognized since the earliest New Testament kerygmata, and that it "calls us in an essentially more radical way than the individual miracles in the life of Jesus" (264).

With respect to other historical elements in Jesus' life, Rahner has "no hesitation" about the following theses (247-49):

1. Jesus was a reformer within the religious milieu of his time.
2. Because of his radical sense of God's love for him, as for all people, Jesus was close to the religious outcasts. This accompanied his radical dethroning of the law: "He fought against legalism in order to move beyond a mere ethic of pious sentiments, and beyond a justification by works which was supposed to give man security against God" (248).
3. He came to expect that his mission would mean mortal conflict rather than the successful conversion of Israel.

4. He faced his consequent death as the will of God.
5. Jesus intended to gather disciples (clearly Rahner is arguing here for a dominical institution of the church, though Rahner does not comment on whether Jesus was seeking followers for his teaching only, or on the strength of his own person as an embodiment of that teaching).
6. Rahner admits a number of the standard historical questions concerning the pre-resurrection Jesus: whether he expected any future son of man, whether he saw any soteriological potential in his death (beyond Thesis 4, above), and whether he saw the church in his vision of the imminent advent of God's kingdom.

Rahner's main interest in the Jesus of history concerns his self-consciousness; after all, if revelation involves human response, as Rahner would have it, then Jesus must have understood and exhibited a uniquely extensive divine claim on his life in order to have been God's final and unique revelation. But with this contention comes the need to protect Jesus' humanity by maintaining a proper created distance between Jesus *qua* human being and God—Rahner wants there to be no hint of monophysitism, whereby Jesus would have no truly human consciousness but only a consciousness belonging to the divine *Logos* (249).[34] Rahner resolves this apparent paradox by distinguishing an "unreflexive consciousness" evident in Jesus' action, on the one hand, from "the objectifying and verbalizing self-consciousness of Jesus" on the other, which developed throughout his life (249). Thus Rahner can hold that while Jesus was implicitly conscious of his special relationship to God, he only grew into it *explicitly* as a result of his human experience with God throughout the course of a human life.[35]

In a major essay on this theme from the early 1960s Rahner rejects the view of Aquinas (and the neo-scholastics) that Jesus enjoyed an uninterrupted relationship with God for all of his human life—the beatific vision, in fact, which the blessed enjoy in heaven.[36] Rahner points to New Testament accounts of Jesus' agony in the garden of Gethsemane and his sense of dereliction by God on the cross as calling such ideas into question. In addition he refuses to countenance any "artificial layer Christology"[37] according to which Jesus' knowledge is divided between divine and human levels.[38] Instead,

Rahner sees Jesus' knowledge of God as developing; he is happy to "speak without qualms about a spiritual and indeed religious development in Jesus,"[39] and of Jesus' life in terms of a growing into what he already was, as Rahner believes all persons must do.[40]

> Rejecting the Greek reliance on knowledge as the simple measure of perfection, Rahner noted that freedom demands a *docta ignorantia* in order to preserve room for activity.... Here Rahner transformed the traditional Thomistic ascription of the beatific vision to Christ's humanity—in view of Christ's growth and sufferings—and termed it a *visio immediata*, as an interior and indispensable moment of the Hypostatic Union... for like every other spirit Jesus enjoyed an immediacy to God as the unthematic horizon of his consciousness. Then not only is there room for growth and development in Jesus' objective consciousness but also what was traditionally called 'infused knowledge' could then be interpreted as the gradual elaboration in reflex consciousness of what Jesus always knew unthematically as given in the *visio immediata*.[41]

Again, Rahner is aware that no unanimity of opinion is available among exegetes on this matter, as with other aspects of historical Jesus research. Nevertheless, he has no doubt that Jesus "understood himself as the eschatological event of salvation and the eschatological bringer of salvation," and certainly as greater than merely one more prophet "on a mission from God."[42]

Rahner is able to do this because he is not dependent on the history of Jesus alone for his claims, as are the bulk of writers in Part III, below, for whom the historical Jesus is much more important.[43] Rahner believes, as we have seen, that the whole dynamic of human experience with God requires a God-Man to bring its ultimate fulfillment and, moreover, that revelation involves human response. It seems, then, that Rahner is letting his theory determine the outcome of his historical questioning in advance—his exegetical engine, if you like, is running on dogmatic fuel! This is, after all, the way he sets up the argument in his central essay on this subject, making sure we understand the proper parameters for discussing Jesus' self-understanding before we begin any such discussion.[44] "Although Rahner constantly claims that his transcendental method takes the historical into account," comments Fiorenza, "he avoids such historical questions in his Christology."[45]

Rahner also supports the view of the new quest that there is no fatal disjunction between the Jesus of history and the Christ of faith (252, 265), as feared by liberals such as Harnack. What is more, Rahner believes that only the resurrection can account for the link between Jesus' historical life and the birth of faith in him as the Christ among the earliest Christians. But he modifies the more usual argument—that the resurrection alone can explain the birth of faith so soon after the death of Jesus—in a subtle and attractive way. If no claim to uniqueness and finality was either made by or associated with Jesus in his lifetime, if he was understood by himself and others to be no more than another in a long line of prophets, then why ascribe to this one prophet a victory in death when all the other prophets were thought simply to have died with their message? The resurrection alone can account for this, Rahner thinks (252).[46]

But before considering the resurrection, we must first note the elements of Rahner's belief in that uniqueness. There are three elements to Jesus' uniqueness and finality for Rahner, as Krieg identifies them.[47] These involve Jesus' self-understanding, his obedience to God, and the effect of this obedience on the rest of humanity and the cosmos.

We have seen Rahner's emphasis on Jesus' unique self-understanding as a major component (254). This is not the elevation of Jesus' "Abba relationship" with God (Jeremias) to the centrality it achieves for Schillebeeckx—indeed, Rahner declares as heretical (302) any Christology depending solely on Jesus' consciousness for its claims (one suspects Schleiermacher and his liberal Protestant descendants are targeted here, though, and not Rahner's contemporaries in Roman Catholic theology).[48]

Rahner also understands Jesus to have been uniquely given over to God, as the one in whom the human "Yes" to God was *qualitatively* (and not just *quantitatively*) superior to that of others because Jesus' "basic constitution," for all of his life, was one of radical and complete self-offering to God (303). We have seen some of

Rahner's arguments for this, and have heard his claim that the history of Jesus confirms it, but we have also been led to question whether this constitutes a circular argument, since the history of Jesus, for Rahner, appears to be the servant of his theological program and its needs.

Jesus' *finality*, for Rahner, lies in his status as the "final cause," the "cause or the moving power" (195), of salvation for the whole cosmos. Rahner does, for instance, seek to identify Jesus as the high point of the grace-empowered evolution of humanity into the fullness of its own life and of relationship with God. Part of his strategy here is to link the emergence of the God-Man with the maturation of humanity into consciousness.[49]

In sum, Rahner finds in Jesus not a denial of the divine presence dwelling elsewhere but, rather, its final and hence its unsurpassable breakthrough into history. As he puts it, concerning Jesus,

> We must bear in mind here that his word as God's final word can be understood to be definitive not because God now ceases arbitrarily to say anything further, although he could have said more, and not because he 'concludes' revelation, although he could have continued it had he just wanted to. It is the final word of God that is present in Jesus because there is nothing to say beyond it, because God has really and in a strict sense offered *himself* in Jesus (280).[50]

To further explicate Rahner's views on the matter we must now delve more deeply into his perspective on the resurrection,[51] and on the universal scope of the atonement wrought by Jesus as he sees it.

For Rahner the important thing about Jesus' resurrection is its event-character. It is not simply a metaphor for the birth of faith, as in Bultmann's understanding; Rahner is insistent that, since the New Testament understood the resurrection as an event and resurrection faith as arriving subsequent to it, so it must be understood today (237-41). But, then, no complete separation between Easter faith and Easter experience is deemed possible by Rahner either—they have been blended indissolubly since the earliest New Testament kerygmata.[52] Indeed, resurrection as he conceives it is co-terminous with belief in and experience of one's own salvation in nearness to God, and in a sense of the eternal validity of one's own life history.[53] Thus there is no mere, objective "salvifically neutral concept of resurrection" (267) for Rahner—"We dare to believe, in hope, in our own history," he says, "and this enables us to believe in the resurrection of Jesus."[54] *Belief in the resurrection, then, means conscious participation in God's new creation experienced and understood to be centered on Jesus.* So it is that Rahner makes no claims for its objective historical certainty; like all revelation, according to his schema, belief in the resurrection must include a participation in faith: "This is clear of course just from the fact that only the believers shared in the experience of the resurrection, while (Jesus') enemies did not" (244).

Of course in all of this Rahner is claiming more than the uniqueness and finality of Jesus Christ for Christian believers alone. He is convinced that Jesus is God's final word for the whole cosmos, despite the fact that only a tiny part of that cosmos knows it and acknowledges it. How can this be? Rahner's theory of the atonement is where an answer is to be found.

Rahner has no time for substitutionary theories of atonement, which imply that God's mind has in some way been changed by the sacrifice of Jesus. Rather, he sees the life and death of Jesus as the cause of God's salvific will insofar as God's will becomes irrevocable through that particular life and death. So, for Rahner, "the life and death of Jesus, or the death which recapitulates his life, possess a causality of quasi-sacramental and real-symbolic nature" (284).[55]

Furthermore, there is no limit to its extent. Rahner highlights the universal scope intended in the Old Testament, identifying in the New Testament too a saving efficacy of Christ and his Spirit which does not coincide with any conscious, explicit confession of it (148). Also, Rahner strongly affirms the truth and morality outside of Christianity (and outside of religion altogether); dialogue with those of other fundamental beliefs was most important for him.[56] He did not, however, assess the riches to be found outside Christianity as merely free-floating bits of religious wisdom—he was sufficiently sociologically-minded to declare essential the actual structures and practices of concrete religions as the necessary carriers and indispensable embodiments of any such wisdom. "According to Rahner," Knitter observes, "if Christian theology holds that Christians must work out their salvation in a religion, the same applies for Hindus and Buddhists."[57]

Furthermore, Rahner indicates how the universally extended work of Christ might be received outside of Christianity, claiming that "anyone who, though still far from any revelation explicitly formulated in words, accepts his existence in patient silence (or, better, in faith, hope and love), accepts it as the mystery which lies hidden in the mystery of eternal love and which bears life in the womb of death, is saying 'yes' to Christ even if he does not know it. *For anyone who lets go and jumps falls into the depths which are there, and not only to the extent that he himself has fathomed them*" (228, italics mine). This presence Rahner relates to the promise of Jesus, in Matthew 25:40, that he will be found "anonymously" among the brothers and sisters and those in need (311). Thus Jesus is also deemed to be present anonymously among persons of good will adhering to non-Christian religions, though through his *Spirit* (316).[58]

As for difficulties about tying this universal presence to the historical particularity of Jesus of Nazareth, Rahner is confident that "We get out of these and similar, unmentioned difficulties only by saying that the Incarnation and the cross are, in scholastic terminology, the 'final cause' of the universal self-communication of God to the world which we call the Holy Spirit..." (317). Now, for Rahner, "we are saved because this man who is one of us has been saved by God, and God has therefore made his salvific will present in the world historically, really and irrevocably" (284). How?—this is clearly the central question. Unfortunately, however, readers of Rahner's *Foundations* must be content at this crucial juncture with vague claims about "the essential unity of history and the solidarity of mankind" (284). Rahner does recognize just how foreign-sounding is this notion of "an assumption of the *whole* human race *in* the individual human reality of Jesus" (293) in a climate of western individualism, though it is the claim by which, I suggest, his views on Jesus' finality stand or fall. Rahner comes slightly closer to explaining this connectedness in an important earlier article:

The reality and experience of this intercommunicative existence which is so important for salvation is made concrete in the absolute quality and unfathomable depths of the love of one's neighbour, in the puzzling experience that in the fate of any individual we are confronted and put face to face with the fate of all human kind, and that this experience cannot be explained away rationalistically as abstraction, induction or the seeing of all 'cases' in a single 'case'. Everyone is aware of this in the experience of his being weighed down by a guilt which is not merely his own, in the experience of his own historicity. This historicity is on the one hand a co-determinant of the most ultimate aspects of one's own existence, and on the other hand it is itself partially the result of the historical decisions of other people. But one cannot draw a boundary between these two, between the passive and active effects of others.... This union of men in an intercommunicative existence ... exhibits the most varied elements— ... the physical unity of the cosmos, the space-time unity; biological unity; intercommunication in the unity of a single history of truth and love, untruth and hate; the unity of rootedness in God, etc.[59]

It is because of this connectedness, then, that Rahner believes Jesus Christ has become an influence on all persons. As Bruce Marshall observes,

In a genuinely evolutionary view of the world, temporal primacy is as good as ontological difference. In other words, in a world which continually surpasses itself by grace toward the life of God, the spiritual creature in whom this movement is first consummated inaugurates a new and final phase of the world's development, so that all who subsequently achieve the same fulfilment do so in dependence upon the one who first crossed the threshold.[60]

Necessary to support such a conception is the Platonic and Thomistic axiom that the highest in any genus is the cause of all others in the genus.[61] This is intolerably teleological to the modern, scientific mind, however, which believes in evolution toward states which are in no way real until they emerge, and which emerge under the impetus of purely random forces at that.[62]

Karl Rahner has attracted many critics. From the left, he has been criticized for too individualistic a conception of the human condition. So, for instance, J.B. Metz, his former pupil and long-time friend, challenged Rahner to conceive of humanity as more socially and politically conditioned than he normally allowed.[63] He was also criticized for being too traditional in his loyalty to Roman Catholic dogma;[64] but, then, Rahner's critics from the right thought him too radical—there were some rumblings from Rome,[65] and there was the birth of animosity between Rahner and Hans Urs von Balthasar. Once a friend, von Balthasar came to think Rahner too lenient toward those outside Christianity, and too affirming of "the natural man" before God: "for von Balthasar Rahner has been the great theological opponent who makes faith inadmissibly easy, who adapts to the needs of contemporaries, and trivializes the seriousness of God's history with humanity."[66] Also, he believed Rahner was too anthropocentric, denying the centrality of God,[67] which Moltmann sees as an inevitable failing of any theology colored by German idealism and its inescapable subjectivism.[68]

It can be said by way of mitigation that Rahner is not advocating any simple Thomistic natural theology against which a theology of the cross like that of Moltmann or, to a lesser extent, von Balthasar, might justifiably rail. Rahner's program is more subtle than this; without sacrificing a deep sense of the flawed nature of existence, which he shares with every theology of the cross, nevertheless his Irenaean spirit cleaves to the belief that God has been preparing the cosmos for its redemption by giving it a listening ear from the beginning, rather than by curing its deafness only when the message of redemption is at hand. In addition, such criticism simply fails to see how overwhelmingly God-centered is Rahner's whole theology; Rahner's is a whole world of grace, from first to last. His difference from the Augustinian mindset of von Balthasar and Moltmann is not a belief that humans can respond to this grace naturally—far from it.

Rather, he holds that divine initiative is so to the fore that it prepares the cosmos in advance for the advent of its savior. So one could argue that Rahner has a higher view of God and a fuller doctrine of grace than these critics, who have misread him as a less subtle, less complex follower of Aquinas than he in fact is. Rahner has learned the lessons of neo-orthodox critique, however, and he wields Tillich's "Protestant principle" mightily, so von Balthasar and Moltmann might find an ally rather than an opponent in Rahner. Indeed, it appears that Moltmann's recent awkward moves in the direction of a cosmic Christ[69] indicate some influence upon him from the movement in which Rahner centrally stands.

We have also to remember Rahner's emphasis on the subliminal influence of Jesus upon all reality as the final cause of salvation wherever salvation is to be found. So it could be argued that von Balthasar is the anthropocentric one for requiring salvation through Christ to be received in a self-conscious manner. Rahner's view of salvation includes participation by the subject, to be sure (he is too good a Roman Catholic to forget that), but nevertheless it need not be explicit or self-conscious participation; is von Balthasar's Jesus only present when confessed explicitly while Rahner's Jesus is universally and transtemporally omnipresent?

Moltmann has also criticized Rahner for a Christology celebrating "the survival of the fittest" (Rahner is obscured in Moltmann's thinking here, one suspects, by the real target, who is Teilhard de Chardin).[70] But, once again, this is not altogether fair. Moltmann believes that Rahner's Christ, understood as the leading edge of evolution, offers no good news to victims of that process who fall by the wayside. But Rahner's Jesus does not march ahead of the common horde ignoring the cries of failures stumbling in his wake; rather, like the Christ of the epistle to the Hebrews, his victory opens the way to a victory for all creation, which is taken up in his exultation. Rahner's Jesus does not triumph alone, then, like some Nietzschean "superman." On the contrary, he bears the whole creation in his (sacred) heart, and bears it in himself toward its own fullness in which all the suffering victims are redeemed just as Moltmann would have it. So this criticism involves too individualistic a reading of Rahner's Jesus, and too Teilhardian (i.e. too evolutionary and too much "from below") a reading of Rahner's "Christology within an Evolutionary View of the World" (1966), from which Moltmann takes his bearings.

Thus to the first of two major criticisms to be considered here. It is frequently pointed out that there is no necessary connection between Rahner's "absolute savior" and the actual person of Jesus—in short, that what is really unique is the role which only one human must play, and that Jesus just happens to fill that unique role.[71] Bruce Marshall sums up his assessment of this as follows:

> An analysis of Rahner's central christological argument shows that (at) the heart of . . . (it) . . . is a methodological decision or rule. Any attempt to answer the question, 'how can Jesus Christ be *heilsbedeutsam*?', so the reasoning goes, presupposes the answer to a logically distinct question. The independent and prior question asks about general criteria for, and thereby the most general features of, any reality which could possibly count as ultimately significant or 'significant for salvation'. In Rahner's case, the criteria are generated by a transcendental anthropology.[72]

Marshall prefers the approach of Karl Barth, for whom human beings cannot "know what's good for them" in advance of having it offered to them in Jesus Christ. Basically this shows the Calvinistic doctrine of "total depravity" at work, according to which we could not recognize an absolute savior without our warped perception first being set right.

Obviously, however, Rahner is no Calvinist; he believes that there are revealed pointers to help humanity find its absolute savior. But Marshall's primary inspiration lies not with Calvin or Barth but elsewhere, in the thought of his teacher Hans Frei[73] (in this study by Marshall, to paraphrase David Tracy's paraphrase of Genesis,[74] "the hands may be the hands of Calvin and Barth, but the voice is the voice of Hans Frei"). For Frei, as we have seen, the identity of Jesus Christ cannot be known in advance of Jesus' story in the gospels. So, for Marshall, it is Jesus' particular identity rather than an appeal to some set of general criteria which makes him the absolute savior, as it is for Rahner: "In a modern world which has grown tired of the Christian story, people will never take belief in Jesus Christ seriously, Rahner assumes, unless it can be made plausible to them that they are already "on the lookout" for what Christians claim Jesus brings —quite apart from whether they are convinced that he actually brings it."[75] And thus Marshall believes Rahner has betrayed his claim that Jesus is unique, because his idea of a savior is generally accessible apart from Jesus.

Herein we see the post-liberal mind at work, impressed as it is by the diversity of human experience rather than its similarities and, consequently, unimpressed with liberal belief in some universal human condition. Basically, Marshall does not believe that Christians are drawn to the figure of Jesus in the uniform way Rahner suggests:

> Just as Jesus Christ himself is inexhaustibly rich, the paths by which people come to appropriate that richness are irreducibly vague and unsystematically diverse. There is, one might argue, no single common pattern which includes them all.... On this view, it makes no essential difference to the logic of our existential access to 'that which is ultimately meaningful' whether we are 'on the lookout' for something like 'redemption'...(as, for example, Luther was), or whether we are not on the lookout for such a thing at all (as, it appears, Paul was not). (This) way allows for an irreducible cultural and historical diversity of patterns by which people appropriate Jesus as ultimately significant. This diversity is held together by its common bonding reference to Jesus Christ as a particular person rather than by any common denominator in the human subject.[76]

It remains, however, to see whether Marshall with his Yale-school approach offers a better alternative. A number of criticisms of Frei's approach were made in Chapter 3, above—Frei was thought to have overdetermined the meaning of gospel texts in advance of any reading, and to have presupposed some of the human questions to which existentialists cleave (Frei seemed to think the sort of thoughts to which Rahner might himself be prone, but decidedly not the sort of thoughts to which a thoroughgoing post-liberal ought to yield uncritical allegiance). It was also pointed out that the approach to Jesus' identity broadly favored by Frei can be carried through in a more liberal way, as by Frans Jozef van Beeck, for instance, in *Christ Proclaimed: Christology as Rhetoric* (1979). In the work of Schillebeeckx, too, we find some hermeneutical roots shared with Frei. But, most importantly, it was demonstrated that Frei failed to establish Jesus' *qualitative* uniqueness, but only his *quantitative* difference from other savior figures. Surely this inability must tell against Marshall's suggestion that a Frei-style approach exhibits a higher sense of Jesus' uniqueness and finality.

Has Rahner shown enough appreciation of post-modernity, so that his work is an obvious improvement in this respect upon the (individually focused) enlightenment thinking of the previous theological generation (now on the wane)?[77] Fergus Kerr calls Rahner "the deficient angel"[78] over this matter; "Rahner's most characteristic theological profundities," Kerr writes, "are embedded in an extremely mentalist-individualist epistemology of unmistakably Cartesian provenance."[79] Instead, his post-modern critics would have Rahner recognize the complexity of human being, its linguistic, sociological and cultural provenance, its newly-recognized malleability and general "soft-edgedness." This is part of the critique of all liberal Christology offered by the "historical skeptics" and "complete relativists" in Part IV below, where more will be said about it. To be sure, the later Rahner (he of the *Foundations*) is aware of this issue[80] but, nevertheless, via his transcendental anthropology he resists the relativist, post-modern trend in favor of an abiding kernel of human uniformity. As we have seen, there is a "supernaturally elevated" component to this, and so Rahner is not simply saying, as Thomistic "natural theology" and its various liberal inheritors contend, that there is a natural knowledge of God characterizing the generality of human beings. So his is not an anthropocentric "theology from below" at all. But, still, these new postmodern questions will bedevil every position which relies at all upon the human condition as theologically disclosive.

In sum, then, we have realized just how problematic all "liberal" talk of "the human condition" increasingly seems; we have queried the genuineness of Rahner's approach to the historical Jesus (seen to be more a servant than a master to Rahner's Christological vision) and, in addition, questions have been raised about the adequacy of Rahner's vague, universal connectedness of all things as sufficient for supporting his belief in Jesus' universal impact. All in all, then, there are grave doubts about all three foundations of that zone in Rahner's Christology declared to be "from below." But no one can deny Rahner's greatness in pursuing his broad objective— that of identifying a meeting point between the revelation of God in Christ and the world.

Chapter Five

PROLEPTIC ESCHATOLOGY

Here we encounter a major theological vision combining the metaphysical and phenomenological concerns of Rahner with the eschatological emphasis of Moltmann. Yet it avoids the blurring of theology "from above" with that "from below" identified in the former, along with some of the literalism and revelational positivism of the latter. Rather, this theology looks "behind" to the resurrection for its centerpoint, and "ahead" to the eschaton in which the reality of God and the meaning of all cosmic history will be fully revealed at last. It is a theology in which Jesus is absolutely unique and final as the incarnation of a God who is understood to be "the power of the future," yet whose fulfilling presence is known proleptically—in advance—in the resurrection. The historical Jesus and the human condition combine to support this highly distinctive and finely wrought claim. It is an "idealist" position in that revelation is understood to take place throughout the whole panorama of history, which will disclose at the last the face of God hidden within it all along (though disclosed in advance in the resurrection).

WOLFHART PANNENBERG

This Lutheran pastor, whose academic career led from Wuppertal to Mainz, and then, in 1968, to the chair of Theology in the University of Munich, has painstakingly built-up a vast dogmatic edifice—a rarity in a time of modest theological aspirations. His project is now beginning to bear mature fruit in the appearance of a systematic theology, following thirty years of ground-clearing and foundation-building in one major study after another.

"The intellectual task that Pannenberg has set for himself is a monumental one," writes Philip Hefner, "namely to construct a fundamental system of thought in which the primary ontological principle is futurity."[81] This futurity is that of Christian eschatology. It is understood according to Pannenberg's reading of Jewish apocalyptic, and its end is revealed proleptically in the resurrection of Jesus Christ. This centrality of the resurrection is evident in all Pannenberg's theology; his understanding of historiography is amenable to it, his metaphysics depends on it and his Christology takes shape around it. The resurrection is the center of Pannenberg's world, which is why there is no doubt about the uniqueness and finality of Jesus Christ in his theology.

Pannenberg was born in Stettin (now a part of Poland) in 1928. As a boy his interests were musical and rather intellectual, and he did not receive a Christian upbringing. He participated in the dislocation of wartime, facing death by bombing and starvation. As a teenage conscript in the last days of war, Pannenberg survived the Russian advance only because an illness cut his military service mercifully short.

Pannenberg's conversion to Christianity followed upon what appears to have been an intense mystical experience on the Feast of the Epiphany in 1945, involving a timeless sense of absorption into the setting sun while on a long country walk. Pannenberg's recollection of the meaning of this event is instructive for understanding the future development of his thought, with its Christological focus and its overarching ontological claim:

> I did not know at the time ... that in that moment Jesus Christ had claimed my life as a witness to the transfiguration of this world in the illuminating power and judgement of his glory. But there began a period of craving to understand the meaning of life, and since philosophy did not seem to offer the ultimate answers to such a quest, I finally decided to probe the Christian tradition more seriously than I had considered worthwhile before.[82]

So it was that, having studied Marxism in detail in Berlin (thus accruing a body of knowledge which would later stand him in good stead), Pannenberg settled on a theological career and studied at Göttingen, Basel and Heidelberg. He had already conceived a love for scholastic theology,[83] but was also much influenced by his patristic studies and by the theology of Karl Barth, though he thought the latter to lack philosophical rigor.

Pannenberg has never succumbed to anything like a positivism of revelation, nor to any retreat into private experience in the manner of Schleiermacher's "religion of feeling." Instead, he came to find revelation through history alone and, in this sense only, his theology is "from below." "I came to realize," he recounts, "that history presents that aspect of the world of our experience which, according to Jewish and Christian faith, reveals God's presence in his creation. In this discovery, I owed much to Karl Löwith's lectures on the theological rootage of modern philosophies of history as well as to Gerhard von Rad's interpretation of the Old Testament."[84] This recognition was decisive for Pannenberg, bringing him to realize how philosophical reflection on the question of God (which he loved) and biblical exegesis (which hitherto had failed to interest him) together provided a privileged medium to discuss the reality of God. Pannenberg reasoned "that there is no direct conceptual approach to God, nor from God to human reality, by analogical reasoning, but God's presence is hidden in the particulars of history."[85]

Very important influences on Pannenberg's understanding of history were the philosophies of Hegel, Dilthey and Heidegger. For Hegel history was the means by which the "ideal" of "being" was actualized; an Hegelian theology is one which sees God programatically revealed through the events of all history.[86] But, as Carl Braaten recognized, Pannenberg saw that a Christocentric theology of universal scope "must take care lest it repeat Hegel's failure to take seriously the finitude of human experience, the real openness to a still incalculable future, and the uniqueness of the individual, which Søren Kierkegaard underscored in his attack upon "'the system,' meaning Hegel's philosophy."[87] Here Pannenberg turns to Dilthey, who moved not "from the whole to the particular," if you like, as did Hegel the generalist, but "from the particular to the whole." Thus Pannenberg came to believe that the ontology of things, including God, would only be known at the end of history, "when all the facts are in."[88] Clayton believes that this idealist or "totalist" insight lies at the very heart of Pannenberg's theological methodology.[89]

A central theme in all of this for Pannenberg was human reason; its importance to him is pointed out by Richard Neuhaus.

> He came inquiring of theology because he was a thoughtful young man with the kinds of questions about which theology presumed to speak: life, death, destiny, the purposiveness of the universe. He was not persuaded by theologians who asked him to compromise or abandon reason. Critical reflection was as reliable a friend as he had, and, having brought him to this point, he was not about to forsake it now. He suspected, however, that the Christian viewpoint might be more reasonable than its experts allowed. Perhaps through some failure of intellectual nerve they found it necessary to seek sanctuary in the fortress of specialized language and subjective experience surrounded by the moat of revealed knowledge.[90]

Thus we see how the foundations for Pannenberg's impressive synthesis were laid: he combined the insights of biblical theology with modern philosophy of science and an empiricist turn of mind not always found in German theologians, while maintaining the holistic vision of meaning characteristic of German idealism. Also, he conceived those elements of his theology which are "from below" with reference to history and a phenomenology of hope (influenced by Bloch through his readings in Marxism) rather than a more usual reliance on the human condition statically conceived. But while finding such "signals of transcendence" in human experience, he does not sacrifice the hidden God of his Lutheran heritage to any doctrine of analogy; his God needs to be revealed *à la* Luther and Barth. This revelation was not in any safe preserve of "the Word," however, apart from the public domain as understood in modern philosophy of science and historiography, but precisely *in* that public world. So Pannenberg combines the publicness offered by doctrines of analogy with a denial of any "purely natural" revelation.

My analysis of Pannenberg's work begins with his earliest major contribution, his "Dogmatic Theses on the Doctrine of Revelation," which formed part of a noteworthy collaborative effort, begun in the early 1950s, entitled *Offenbarung als Geschichte* (1961). The collection appeared in English under the title *Revelation as History* (1968).[91]

Central issues were the nature of revelation, the way in which biblical tradition witnessing to that revelation dovetails with wider human experience, and the link from revelation (deemed to be primary) to the Word of God (deemed to be secondary).

In his essay Pannenberg rejected natural theology while maintaining human reason as indispensable for the recognition of revelation. Revelation is declared to be woven into ordinary history, rather than occurring through distinct theophanic events (Thesis 1), and it is universally accessible to "natural knowledge" without any secret gnosis required to grasp it (Thesis 3). But such revelation is only *complete* at the end of history, though occuring throughout history (Thesis 2).

This revelation is tied particularly to the history of Israel, according to Pannenberg (Thesis 5), but it is only in the fate of Jesus Christ that *full* revelation is anticipated (Thesis 4). In all of this, Pannenberg relies upon the apocalyptic view of history found in the Old Testament, as he understands it (145). He is convinced that history is the primary reality, rather than the static regularities of the world as it is: "Experience of the reality of history," he writes, "is superior to that connected with contemplation of the cosmos" (141).[92] So it is that Pannenberg declares the Christ event to be ultimate—its eschatological character declares it to be final in that nothing more can follow, by definition. The end of our world will thus be a cosmic recapitulation of what has already happened in Jesus (142).

Pannenberg believes that history after the Christ event bears the mark of Christ, with God effectively constrained to work toward the future thus prefigured (143-44). This universality of Christ is also thought to have had its impact within the generality of cultures, apart from the Old Testament milieu of Jewish apocalyptic.

As for the fairly obvious problem that notions of a resurrection from the dead might not speak to those from a non-biblical culture, Pannenberg employs what is effectively a pragmatist solution. Insofar as spreading Christianity drew the world of classical thought into the church's orbit, Pannenberg believes that the finality of Christ thereby found a cognitive location outside the world of its inception. In effect, the historical developments through which Christianity became universal were at the same time the ongoing historical revelation of Christ's ultimacy.[93] This emphasis was to recur in his work.

The expression of these initially apocalyptic ideas in new environments led the church to employ Greek ideas about the immortality of the soul and, in our own century, anthropological perceptions about the constitutive openness of human persons to their environment. Both of these point to *a common end for all humanity* (148), which is the parallel Pannenberg finds with apocalyptic thought in these subsequent elaborations. This move allows Pannenberg to bring back theophanic and incarnational ideas of revelation which he earlier deemed to be unacceptable, using this newly-opened back door—because of what amounts to a structural similarity with apocalyptic ideas, and because the ongoing march of (revelatory) history has brought these objectively unacceptable themes within a Christian orbit, Pannenberg now recognizes in such non-Jewish ideas of revelation that "the universality of the eschatological self-vindication of God in the face of Jesus comes to actual expression" (149) (Thesis 6). So, for instance, Pannenberg admits that "gnostic thought about revelation . . . was the means by which the eschatological significance of the Christ event could be expressed" (149) and that "the incarnation is a final resumé of the God of Israel's history of revelation" (151).

Pannenberg completes this most significant essay with a discussion of "the Word" as related to revelation in terms of "foretelling, forthtelling and report" (Thesis 7). This involves another subtle maneuver. Pannenberg understands revelation as historically located and written in the language of facts—a language which will be fully translated and understood only in the eschaton. He has declared that revelation is not in the "reception" of historical testimony by the believer—it does not lie between the events and the interpreter but is woven into the history itself. In this way Pannenberg resists the reduction of revelation to the kerygma, which Bultmann entertained in an atmosphere of historical skepticism. Thus the spirit, according to Pannenberg, speaks the language of history, not hermeneutics.

But Pannenberg manages to have his cake and eat it over this matter, too, just as he did when, having denied gnosis and incarnationalism, he retrieved and provisionally blessed them as alternative pointers to the insights most deeply captured in the apocalyptic vision. Thus, in a necessary adaptation, *Pannenberg broadens his conception of history to include interpretation*, in the manner of Collingwood. So when he maintains that "The events in which God demonstrates his deity are self-evident as they stand within the framework of their own history" (155), he means that the necessary interpretative framework is also a part of that history, with the interpretation arising within history as an event in its own right. So there is a place for the kerygma, according to Pannenberg, but only as reporting on the revelation which proceeds it and undergirds it: "The word of the kerygma is not its own revelatory event in any isolated fashion, but is an aspect of the event of revelation in that it reports the eschatological event. It is this eschatological event that is the adequate self-vindication of God and that activates a universal proclamation through which it is also made explicit" (155).

So, despite a strong dependence on biblical theology (which we have met in Moltmann), Pannenberg also finds a place in his system for hermeneutics and for the contribution of anthropological considerations to understanding the universality of Christ; here he is closer to Rahner. Indeed, Rahner is favorably received throughout Pannenberg's *Jesus—God and Man* (1968). But it is to Pannenberg's early anthropological study *What Is Man?* (1962, ET 1970) that we must first turn for a closer examination of his theological dependence upon the human person.

According to Pannenberg the uniqueness and finality of Jesus is tightly woven together with his understanding of the human condition. But there is none of the more fulsome reliance upon transcultural, universal constants of human nature found in other writers on the right half of my typology, such as Kasper and Küng; Pannenberg is thoroughly post-modern in *What Is Man?* in his recognition of fundamental cultural diversity. Both conscience and sexual roles, for instance, are declared to be mutable and culturally variant where natural law theorists have long deemed them to be essential fixtures (87, 91-92, 110-11). In arguing thus Pannenberg draws upon the insights of anthropology and anticipates the work of Foucault. He recognizes the biological and anthropological *leitmotif* of human immersion in and total dependence upon the natural environment (51, 110). Also, he appears to be on the way to something like linguistic naturalism, denying any selfsame center to each human person apart from the public fact of linguisticality; "Without language," he writes, "there would be no silent thinking in conceptual pictures and no inner world of consciousness" (21; cf. 48). So Pannenberg is far more willing to embrace post-modern insights than is Rahner, and indeed many far more thoroughgoing liberals. In this he treads a similar path to Moltmann, whose "conservative" status in this study belies a radical awareness of relativizing and destabilizing trends in recent thought. Indeed Don Cupitt, an example of thoroughgoing theological radicalism, has only embraced linguistic naturalism since the late 1980s,[94] albeit in a more complete form than that of Pannenberg (who does not efface *all* signs of underlying constants in his vision of the human).[95]

One might briefly summarize the position of *What Is Man?* as follows: that the essence of the human is *openness*, but the environment to which humans are open is best understood in historical rather than ontological terms and that this history, in turn, is only properly understood in the light of Jesus' life, death and resurrection.

This openness is an openness to God and to the resurrection life, says Pannenberg, whether or not the religious nature of this longing, this missing term in all human dealings, is properly understood by those who experience it (53). Of "man" Pannenberg writes: "in his infinite dependence he presupposes with every breath he takes a corresponding, infinite, never ending, otherworldly being before whom he stands, even if he does not know what to call it" (10). In addition to this overarching horizon (and one so Rahnerian), Pannenberg finds other constants of human nature in the universal need for community and the equally universal quest for understanding. "Men seek community," he writes. "This shows that the destiny of all men is the same" (83). He claims, also, that "The process of understanding between individuals presupposes in every area that only one truth can be valid for all men" (84). So despite his post-modern rejection of natural patterns of existence, Pannenberg nevertheless discerns trends as broad as these, to which he adds the further conviction that it is human nature to change the world—a belief in

Homo faber (perhaps this is Pannenberg the serious student of Marxism speaking). None of these allegedly constant features of the human are static, however; they are broad pointers to a human nature which is only unchanging in the fact and manner of its immersion within a broader reality which is historical and ever-changing.

Pannenberg shares with Moltmann a phenomenology of hope. He holds that it is impossible to live for the day only, that "the suppressed question about the future" (41) is ever present. And, like Moltmann, he believes that "Only the person who is certain of his future can calmly turn to the present day" (44). But Pannenberg is also drawn to existentialist insights, especially the conviction that human essences are not given in advance of actual existence, and that such existence is threatened and unsure, so that outcomes cannot be known in advance. Therefore, with Dilthey, Pannenberg will only talk of meanings in the context of the whole, and of the meaning of human lives in the light of their end. This is why he believes that "history" is the category most closely approximating the actual lived state of human life, yielding up less abstract pictures of the human than do biology or anthropology or sociology (137-38).

It is also worth noting that he does not simply present the resurrection as a *fait accompli* of biblical truth in this connection; rather, he links its appeal very firmly to features of the human condition he has discerned. So he sees resurrection belief as more conformable to modern insights into the human person as a psychosomatic unity, rather than a disembodied soul, a "ghost in the machine" or any other conception of it, according to any other form of dualism (51-52).[96]

But, again like Moltmann, Pannenberg believes that the historical vision which so powerfully commends itself to him has a biblical root. Rather than a static Greek cosmos, the bible celebrates a history of involvement apart from which God cannot be known aright. The unity of this history only comes into focus in Jesus Christ, he claims. Similarly, the sense of one world, and a comprehensive unity of world history beyond the rise and fall of nations, "has emanated from the West and... has its ultimate root in Christianity's universal historical consciousness" (148). Thus in Jesus Christ, for Pannenberg, the world is given a unifying center by God—it has no natural center.

In all of this there is evidenced a complex relationship between the human condition on the one hand and the biblical testimony on the other, both of which are seen as vehicles for divine disclosure in history. The Old Testament arose from a people whose dealings with God taught them to think historically, believes Pannenberg. This historical consciousness spread with the biblical faith, and its presence unlocked the latent creative capabilities of humanity, especially by allowing us to conceive the world and its history as a whole, and to have hope (143, 145-46). So God reveals a universal horizon to humanity, as well as allowing a hopeful openness toward the future.[97]

One cannot help wondering, consequently, whether human nature *really* contributes to the basis of Pannenberg's theology, or if it is all really a matter of a biblical literalism after all, though far better concealed than we find it in Barth, or in Moltmann for that matter. A discussion of Pannenberg's major Christological work, with occasional reference to other sources as needs be, will demonstrate that this issue continues unresolved, as does the matter of how belief in Jesus' uniqueness and finality is arrived at by those who believe in it.

The main source of Pannenberg's Christology, *Jesus—God and Man* (1968), is in three parts. Part 1 is basically a refutation of alternative modern Christologies (the kerygmatic approach of Bultmann, as well as logos Christology) on the basis of Pannenberg's resurrection emphasis. Part 2 examines human nature in the light of Christ, considering the perfecting of humanity in Jesus, and the atonement. Part 3 looks at the incarnation, along with the uniqueness, sinlessness and lordship of Jesus, again in light of the resurrection. Thus Pannenberg works out an interpretation of all the central Christological issues on the basis of his resurrection focus.

We have seen Pannenberg reject the notion that revelation lies in the human construal of what is primarily an historical revelation. So in *Jesus—God and Man* he refuses to follow Hermann and Schleiermacher in placing the experience of the redeemed at the center and merely inferring Jesus' authorship of that experience—without the historical reference, he argues, the kerygma would be a myth (25-27). So although he knows that confession of faith in Jesus cannot be separated from soteriological concerns, nevertheless he will not allow this confession to be reduced to them (38); Pannenberg insists that Jesus' significance is a matter of his person and not just his work, and here he explicitly parts company with Kant, Schleiermacher, Bultmann and Tillich (48).

Part 1 of the study introduces Pannenberg's resurrection emphasis. Not only is it insufficient to base Christology on what Jesus means for us; it is also insufficient to depend on Jesus' "abba relationship" with God—apart from some confirmation by God, any such claims by Jesus about an especial closeness to God would remain empty assertions (66) (Schillebeeckx, who makes much of the "abba relationship," would agree).

Although revelation is not found in the interpretation, nevertheless we have seen Pannenberg's willingness to understand historical events as *including* their own interpretation. This is certainly the case here—the eschatology of post-exilic Judaism, as Pannenberg perceives it, precedes, underlies and explicates the early Christian proclamation of Jesus' resurrection as the single, long-expected fruit of Israel's hope (74). And, as faith degenerates into myth without an historical base, so too will faith degenerate into myth without an eschatological hope to support it (83).

But there is more than apocalyptic expectation at work in the background of resurrection belief; Pannenberg also makes some appeal to the human condition as providing certain elements of pre-understanding necessary for conceiving and appropriating such belief. Hope is one element: "One may presumably characterize it as a generally demonstrable anthropological finding," Pannenberg claims, "that the definition of the essence of man does not come to ultimate fulfilment in the finitude of his earthly life" (83). So Pannenberg follows Bloch's phenomenology of hope (84). He recognizes a human yearning for life beyond death, an openness beyond every situation (85), and the fact that absence of hope can speed us toward death (in instances involving voodoo, as among the aged, and suicides) (85 n.78). Indeed, Pannenberg holds to the indispensability of hope in the fostering of full humanity (86).

But this falls short of the reliance upon human nature we find in Rahner. Pannenberg does not simply appeal to the presence of a universal human structure like hope as a pointer to the actuality of resurrection, but views the fact of resurrection as establishing the unity of humankind in a way that appeal to any such natural structures cannot: "The unity of mankind," Pannenberg writes, "expresses itself in the concept of the resurrection of the dead in that this event is expected as universal fate that will involve all men" (88). Thus Pannenberg takes the "divinely revealed human unity" introduced in *What Is Man?* one step further. Regarding hope as a human attribute, then, he falls somewhere between Moltmann and Rahner.[98]

The resurrection is important for Pannenberg—without it there can be no ongoing viability for Jesus' claims, which would thus be seen to have "miscarried on the cross" (112). But, in keeping with his eschatological focus, Pannenberg will not declare the invincibility, finality and generality of the resurrection to be a *fait accompli*; it remains incomplete (107, 112) and is only glimpsed proleptically in the resurrection of Jesus.

What was the resurrection of Jesus, according to Pannenberg? Certainly, he recognizes that the gospel traditions are highly legendary and historically unreliable (89). In this he is in keeping with a large body of recent critical opinion. Pannenberg does not know what sort of experiences the appearances of Jesus were (92) and, although they were visionary in the sense that not all are reported to have seen them (93), they were obviously distinguishable by the early Christians from other sorts of ecstatic visions (94). Pannenberg realizes the inevitability and necessity of the Jerusalem community positing an empty tomb as a presupposition for the resurrection kerygma (100, 103), but he cites the independent origin of empty tomb and appearance traditions as making good evidence nevertheless.

The resurrection is an historical, public reality according to Pannenberg because it provides the best explanation of the facts. As long as there is no narrow scientism asserting that "the dead do not rise," then he believes there is no better theory to account for the evidence of early Christian experiences that Jesus had risen and that the tomb was empty (109). There is a pragmatist element, too, in Pannenberg's recourse to the power of the Christian theological system as a whole in illuminating and guiding the lives of Christians (107):

> Thus the resurrection of Jesus would be designated as a historical event in this sense: If the emergence of primitive Christianity, which, apart from other traditions, is also traced back by Paul to appearances of the resurrect-

ed Jesus, can be understood in spite of all critical examination of the tradition only if one examines it in the light
of the eschatological hope for a resurrection from the
dead, then that which is so designated is a historical
event, even if we do not know anything more particular
about it. Then an event that is expressible only in the language of the eschatological expectation is to be asserted
as a historical occurrence (98).

Once again, this illustrates a conception of the historical which welcomes preunderstanding and interpretation in addition to facts into
the fabric of history.

Pannenberg is strongly dismissive of allegedly scientific skepticism about the resurrection. Such criticism hinges on a poor philosophy of science, he argues:

First, only a part of the laws of nature are ever known.
Further, in a world that as a whole represents a singular, irreversible process, an individual event is never completely
determined by natural laws.... Therefore, natural science
expresses the general validity of the laws of nature but
must at the same time declare its own inability to make definitive judgements about the possibility or impossibility
of an individual event, regardless of how certainly it is
able, at least in principle, to measure the probability of an
event's occurrence. The judgement about whether an
event, however unfamiliar, has happened or not is in the
final analysis a matter for the historian and cannot be prejudiced by the knowledge of natural science (98).

Thus Pannenberg further clears the way for an interpretation of the
resurrection as history.

It is on the basis of Jesus' resurrection that all the other dogmas
of Christology hinge, according to Pannenberg; "If Jesus as a person
is 'the Son of God,'" he writes, "as becomes clear retroactively from
the resurrection, then he always has been the Son of God" (141). The
virgin birth is deemed to be a secondary doctrine explicating the significance of Jesus, shown in his resurrection, with reference to his ori-

gin (143-50). The pre-existence of Jesus, thought by Pannenberg to be incompatible with the virgin birth in accounting for his origin, is also seen to be a derivative doctrine (143).[99] Not for Pannenberg (nor for Moltmann, as we have seen) the prevalent prioritizing of the incarnation in Christology;[100] an incarnational focus misrepresents the true nature of revelation, mistaking the theophanic for the historical (158).[101]

Part 2 of *Jesus—God and Man* begins with discussion of human nature. Like everything else with Pannenberg this nature is not something given in advance of its end—in this case, of its eschatological fulfillment. Insofar as this fulfillment is given in advance in Jesus, then it is in him that the fullness of human nature is to be found:

> The destiny of man is not present all along the internal
> structure of individuals as what is common to them, but,
> so to speak, it comes upon them from outside as their fu-
> ture. Therefore, it can constitute Jesus' uniqueness that in
> him that which is man's destiny as man has appeared for
> the first time in an individual and thus has become acces-
> sible to all others only through this individual (189-90).

So it is the humanity of Jesus which illuminates the human nature of everyone else, which for Pannenberg "cannot be derived from the average empirical content of human existence or from its universal structure" (190). The test, however, is in Jesus' unquestioned soterio-logical significance and in "the universal significance of his particular humanity" (190)—a pragmatic test based on the successfulness of Christianity in the world, as we have seen elsewhere in Pannenberg's thought.

Pannenberg lists the ways Jesus has been seen as humanity's representative before God (198), but denies that this simply reflects the changing ideal self-image of humanity, as Schweitzer argued was the case in the nineteenth century quest of the historical Jesus (200). Instead, Pannenberg understands that human ideality so conceived "involves elements of Jesus' own particular individuality which have been recognized in their universal significance" (204), apart from which the ideal would be derived from general anthropological insights rather than from Jesus himself. Pannenberg realizes, too, that it is only such universal significance which allows people to identify and have community with this Jesus.

Wherein lies the universality, then? Pannenberg finds it in the universal human hope for a true home, for liberation, for just rule—the hope found in Israel and in the resurrection (206).[102] Not in any universalizable message or teaching, then (207-09), nor in any supernatural link to earth throughout Jesus' lifetime, as in divine man Christologies which fail to take seriously his humanity and his suffering (223-24), but in the resurrection of Jesus only is humanity shown its true end and driven toward an ultimate decision by God (244). There is also a sense in which Jesus' death is a universal death, according to Pannenberg: Jesus dies as a blasphemer instead of the true blasphemers, all of whose claims to ultimate authority, political or religious, are undermined by his sacrifice (261). In addition the nerve of the law, linking deeds to their proper consequences, is cut; the Jews had borne this burden, on behalf of all humanity, but in the death of Jesus a new freedom is born in which all humanity can vicariously participate (263).[103] In addition, the separation from God evident in Jesus' despairing cry from the cross and highlighted in the doctrine of his descent into hell (272) further assures Pannenberg of Jesus' universal salvific efficacy, albeit anonymous, for those who share the separation from God to which these actions point.

Part 3 of Pannenberg's study begins with a critique of Chalcedonian incarnational orthodoxy. Jesus is not the unity of two substances, Pannenberg says, but is *himself* God, in the whole of his human life (283). Both the Alexandrian conception of a human nature assumed by the logos and the Antiochene alternative in which the whole man is assumed both strike Pannenberg as devaluing Jesus' concrete humanity (291), as does talk of a *communicatio idiomatum* (301). Comments such as these are common in recent critiques of incarnational doctrine, but Pannenberg's conclusions are by no means typical. He is not simply intent on asserting the historicity of Jesus as an alternative to the metaphysics of incarnation, as are many other recent critics of incarnational orthodoxy. He is, rather, operating from his conviction that human essence and identity cannot be given in advance of the living out of a whole human life (304). In the case of Jesus he makes this insight of Dilthey, and of existentialism in general, refer to the resurrection in which Jesus' true nature is revealed. Thus it is not the incarnation which establishes God's unity with Jesus, for Pannenberg, but the resurrection; the incarnation, albeit an indispensable doctrine, is at best a way of talking about the life which was not known to be definitively of God on any basis other than God's posthumous vindication of that life. According to Pannenberg, then, "the concept of the incarnation can be paraphrased in terms such as these: out of his eternity, God has through the resurrection of Jesus, which was always present in his eternity, entered into a unity with this one man which was at first hidden" (322).

How, then, does this unity with God evident in Jesus' resurrection express itself throughout a life seen in retrospect to have been an incarnate life? It is here that historical Jesus issues make their appearance. Pannenberg looks to Jesus' activity to find out about his person; he makes no recourse to Jesus' self-consciousness, as if this would establish his status, but only to that self-consciousness as made evident in Jesus' deeds throughout his life (328, 361n.82). Jesus' personal community with God, his "sonship," abided in his obedience, in his human dedication (335);[104] for Pannenberg this represents a more fulsome assertion than does the Chalcedonian notion with its synthesis of two natures, *and* it preserves the humanity of Jesus. "Precisely *in* his particular humanity," Pannenberg writes, "Jesus is the Son of God" (342). Rahner is echoed, too, in Pannenberg's assertion that only through Jesus is true humanity revealed, alongside whom "all other human personality appears as an imperfect experiment" (346).

It is in his obedience to God that Jesus brings true human nature to light, which finds its fulfillment in human freedom lived in accordance with the will of God rather than in individual assertion against God's claims. Herein is the basis of Jesus' sinlessness, according to Pannenberg (344-45). Pannenberg doubts, however, that there is enough historical evidence from the gospels to assert Jesus' unflinching, single-minded dedication to God with confidence. Thus he raises the sort of questions those theologians labeled as "historical skeptics" will be seen to find unanswerable in Part IV, below. He even states that a history-based claim for Jesus' sinlessness must cope with the extra difficulty of showing that he never once lapsed, and this is an obstacle that does not normally arise in such discussions. And besides, Pannenberg adds, the reduction of sin to moral infringements constitutes a trivializing of it (360-61).

Thus Pannenberg shows a very interesting response over the matter of Jesus' sinlessness. "Historical skeptics" such as Dennis Nineham will be seen to reject Jesus' sinlessness for want of adequate historical evidence, so the invention of historical arguments is not going to constitute a compelling defense. Pannenberg does not respond in this way, however. Instead, he cuts his losses and responds on other fronts: first, he sidesteps any moral interpretation of sinlessness (as relied upon by Nineham and others) in favor of an emphasis on Jesus' dedication to God; second, he hammers the radical consequences of incarnational belief, insisting that a sharing in our human lot by Jesus must mean a sharing in human sinfulness, apart from which the radicality of sin is not taken seriously enough (362); third, he asserts another historical basis for Jesus' uniqueness apart from that of his sinlessness—the resurrection. Thus Pannenberg thinks he has nothing to fear from historical skepticism:

> That Jesus overcame sin under the conditions of existence of the general bondage to sin, that he lived in openness to God, can only be asserted in the light of the resurrection. It cannot be derived from the dedication to God that Jesus' pre-Easter existence expresses when taken by itself. Jesus' earthly conduct appeared thoroughly ambiguous (362).

It is not that there was no superlative dedication during Jesus' life, according to Pannenberg; his point is that such dedication could not be confidently asserted apart from God's vindication of Jesus.[105]

The book ends with a final discussion of Jesus' lordship. Pannenberg follows Barth in claiming the election of Jesus as the basis of all other election (383) and Rahner in identifying Jesus as the leading edge of human evolution (387). Combined with a recognition that the world is unified only through the presence and ordering power of the human, Pannenberg's message here seems to be, "humanity makes the world, and Jesus makes humanity":

As one eschatological summation, as the reconciliation of
humanity across all dividing chasms, the Christ event establishes not only the unity of human history, but thereby
also establishes the unity of the universe. This assertion
presupposes that the totality of the material world does
not possess its unity in itself apart from man, but that this
unity is only structured through man.... The lordship of
man over nature is essentially—like the form of all lordship—activity that establishes unity.... In this sense, the
history of Jesus, on the basis of which humanity is embraced into the unity of a single history, is at the same
time the consummation of the unity of the world. As humanity in its history, so too the material universe is only
brought together to the unity of a world through its relation to Jesus (390).

Thus Pannenberg reiterates his rejection of any logos Christology—
his Jesus "is not the law, but the reconciler of the cosmos" (395) because "only through Jesus is the creation of the world fulfilled"
(397).[106]

An issue which should be canvased before more fully assessing
the approach of Pannenberg is his attitude to Jesus' uniqueness and
finality in the light of the world religions. We will briefly consider
two contributions, written nearly thirty years apart.

In a 1962 lecture, later published as "Toward a Theology of the
History of Religions" (ET 1971), Pannenberg dismisses a number of
then popular assessments of the religions and asserts a Christocentric
reading of their history. Pannenberg's discussion is quite post-modern, making much of the diversity and context-dependence of the religions at a time when the prevailing orthodoxy in religious studies
asserted their common rootedness in universal human experience. He
denies the phenomenological generalizations of Mircea Eliade as
failing to take this contextuality seriously,[107] and he rejects the religious *a priorism* of Troeltsch and neo-Kantianism.[108] The alternative
focus Pannenberg chooses, apart from the religious interiority of
human persons, is that of "reality" itself as the true referent of the religions, and especially the reality of the mystery of being to which

the various religions point.[109] Pannenberg adds to this the perspective
on history he shares with Moltmann, that in Israel's emerging eschatological thought an historical understanding of the world grew up.
This was inherited by Christianity, subsequently coloring the rise of
our modern secular world view with its acknowledgement of a common "history of religions."[110] Thus Pannenberg asserts the centrality
of Jesus in the history of religion, deemed by him to be the fulfillment of Israel's historical yearnings: "From this standpoint," he
claims, "the history of religions even beyond the time of the public
ministry of Jesus presents itself as a history of the appearance of the
God who revealed himself through Jesus."[111]

So the early Pannenberg asserts, with no wider justification,
that Jesus is the unifying center of the religions because he is the unifying center of history on the basis of his resurrection; he believes
the religions would have no commonality apart from the historical
impetus revealed to Israel and bearing fruit in Jesus. Thus the view
we encountered at the end of *Jesus—God and Man* is echoed here:
the unique and final one is the one in whom unity appears, who is
thus the creator and center of all.

Pannenberg offers essentially the same argument in "Religious
Pluralism and Conflicting Truth Claims" (1990)—an essay in a volume opposing the "religious pluralists" such as John Hick. Pannenberg
again emphasizes plurality among the religions and within religious
experience (far more than Hick does, in fact, whose views are considered in Chapter 10 below). And, once more, though not denying "some
dim and provisional knowledge of God in all humankind,"[112] Pannenberg insists that the very ability to think in terms of *one* God is a result
of the revelation of that one God in Jesus Christ.

Pannenberg rejects John Hick's understanding of salvation in
terms of any present "reality centeredness" of human life because of
Jesus' eschatological claims, which also serve as early proof that
Christianity understood itself in unique terms insofar as Jesus believed his mission represented a final phase in revelation, as did his
followers (this clarifies the meaning of "reality" in his earlier religions paper). Accordingly, Pannenberg rejects Hick's belief that inclusive understandings of salvation for all persons through Christ are
nothing but "epicycles" added to the hardline exclusivism of Christianity's "Ptolemaic" tradition. Pannenberg argues, on the contrary,

that inclusivism was an *early* Christian position, appearing in the belief that Christ descended into hell and so made salvation available to
those who had died apart from an actual earthly encounter with him,
and also in the second century logos theology of Justin Martyr.[113] So
Pannenberg offers a straight inclusivist position, as found in Rahner:
"Even in the case of those who will participate in the kingdom of God
without having encountered Jesus in their earthly life, Jesus will be
their saviour no matter what form of religion they were following."[114]

In setting a test for truth among the religions, Pannenberg asks:
"how compatible is the transformation of life they promise with the
vision of the eschatological transformation wrought in Jesus Christ?"
Pannenberg tempers this strong stand, however, with an eschatological proviso: he concedes that Christianity itself is by no means perfect and complete in advance of the eschaton,[115] allowing as a consequence that interreligious dialogue is important for Christianity's
own formation.[116] And he reiterates the pragmatist argument, touched
briefly in the earlier religions paper,[117] that the truth of a religion
should be assessed according to "Whether a particular tradition
proves superior in illuminating the people's experience of their life
and world."[118] But revealed truth remains the bottom line; its importance in this context highlights its centrality (albeit more carefully
concealed elsewhere) in the whole of Pannenberg's argument for
Jesus' uniqueness and finality.

A considerable critical literature has grown up around Pannenberg's work; his project has struck many as controversial, winning
both admiration and opposition from the start.[119] Much of this debate
is not relevant to the matter at hand, but there are a number of related
issues bearing upon the question of Jesus' uniqueness and finality
which deserve mention.

There is certainly an historical basis for Pannenberg's faith in
the uniqueness and finality of Jesus, and that is the resurrection understood as an historically meaningful and factual event. But what of
the two elements in my typology separating those on the right side
from those on the left—the dependence upon the human condition
and upon the historical Jesus? While Pannenberg makes frequent recourse to the historical Jesus and is notable in recent theology for his
extensive grasp of the critical debate in biblical studies, nevertheless

the historical Jesus teaches Pannenberg nothing apart from its confirmation in the resurrection. And while he finds in Jesus both the savior and the crown of humanity, occasionally recalling Rahner's theological anthropology, nevertheless there is no natural theology of the human person, nor even any correlation-type understanding of God's revelation to the human person, as in Rahner. Albeit more subtly than Moltmann, Pannenberg has recourse to revelation as constituting the human person in the first place. So Pannenberg's attempt at a "theology from below" is underpinned by a "theology from above."[120]

With regard to the historical Jesus, we have seen Pannenberg reject the recourse to Jesus' "abba relationship" of those claiming to establish Jesus' uniqueness on the basis of his inner life.[121] Like Gilbert Ryle, Pannenberg prefers to look at external behavior rather than speculate about inner states. Well and good, but how much does he *really* depend on Jesus' acts, and does his evaluation of them pass muster?[122] O'Collins rightly accuses Pannenberg of leaving out the ministry of Jesus, as does Moltmann in *Theology of Hope* (1964).[123] But while Moltmann at least attempts to correct this inattention in *The Way of Jesus Christ* (1990), Pannenberg's Christological writings still do not recognize in the life of Jesus any confirmation of his uniqueness apart from the resurrection, and the light that event casts back over his life.[124]

Questions are also begged about the foundation of Pannenberg's system. Does the revealed "pre-understanding" of the resurrection, found in his reading of Jewish apocalyptic, really stand up? Does he really offer as much historical evidence for the resurrection as his claims demand? And is the resurrection as he sees it more a matter of the interpretation of history in faith rather than history itself, which very thing he deplores? Ultimately Pannenberg is found to be too rationalistic, failing to account for the actual mechanics through which faith in the uniqueness and finality of Christ—his ultimacy for the church and for the believer—is arrived at.

Regarding the human condition, doubts have been raised by some critics that Pannenberg's version of it is not as general as he claims. Could Pannenberg's human person be more the product of his theological agenda and less the reflection of any real person? Cobb wonders, for instance, "whether the *anthropos* so brilliantly discussed is not the male of the species and whether it is not North Atlantic 'man' who is in view... ?"[125] In a similar vein, Burhenn points out that Pannenberg reflects a particular existentialist, Marxist-colored stance in anthropology, representing only one option among many in current thinking on the human person.[126] But while aware of cultural diversity, linguistic naturalism etc., all of which are central to post-modern thinking on the human person, Pannenberg maintains the sort of recourse to a universal anthropology which is condemned in the theology of Rahner by his post-modern critics.[127] All of this illustrates a belief on the part of Pannenberg that there is an optimum interpretative strategy for understanding the human; one could well ask, therefore, whether this perspective calls for the very identification of revelation with interpretation he elsewhere eschews.[128]

Having considered the human condition and the historical Jesus as bases of Pannenberg's theology, and having found this reliance to be compromised by other veiled dependencies, we now consider the main basis for this theology, the resurrection of Jesus. Questions can be asked about the adequacy of Pannenberg's understanding of Jewish apocalyptic, on which his resurrection belief depends. One might also ask whether this event, deemed so confidently to be historical by Pannenberg, is not more a matter of the *interpretation* of history, the primary category being faith rather than fact?

First, with regard to apocalyptic, what are we to make of its importance in the thought of Pannenberg? He asks us to see apocalyptic "not merely as the historical setting of the teaching of Jesus but as a presupposition of our own believing too,"[129] and of course this is problematic. Burhenn questions the appropriateness of Pannenberg's requirement that we step out of the shared life-world of late twentieth century thought back to the first century.[130] He points out that this is not the sort of perspective from which historians operate, just as they do not operate with that openness to the transcendent which Pannenberg claims to be characteristically human.[131] Nor do they operate with a strong determinist view of history, as Pannenberg appears to do.[132] So it is simply not the case that late Jewish apocalyptic can be one of the current historian's tools of trade; just because Pannenberg attempts to show its relevance to modern philosophical anthropology does not mean that he has earned for this ancient world-view any rightful historiographic currency. As Burhenn rightly observes, to attempt this constitutes a *revision* of actual historical method rather than its proper use as claimed.[133]

One can also ask if Pannenberg properly understands this late Jewish apocalyptic—over this he has been much criticized. "Basically," explains Grenz, "these criticisms maintain that the apocalypticists were not concerned with history as the sphere of God's revelatory activity, but with the eschaton, when the present evil world would be done away with.... Likewise there were no universal hopes in apocalypticism, as is definitely the case in Pannenberg's understanding."[134] And, of course, there is a question as to whether belief in a general resurrection was as well established in Jewish thought and culture as Pannenberg would have it.[135] McGrath points out that Pannenberg's understanding of late Jewish apocalyptic, emphasizing the delay of full revelation until the end, along with a general resurrection and the final recognition of God's universality, is based on the work of Dietrich Rössler which he labels "controversial."[136]

And what of the resurrection itself in Pannenberg's thought—is it fact or interpretation? Peter Carnley offers a number of insightful observations about the *real* loyalties underlying Pannenberg's resurrection belief, pointing to a far greater role for faith interpretation than a purportedly historical theory ought to allow. On the resurrection appearances, Carnley accuses Pannenberg of confusion and circularity. Regarding the confusion, he suggests that something as publicly accessible as Pannenberg believes the appearances to have been would not have come to some as private "visions" and not to others, as we see in the gospels. There must be an element of publicness if an event is to be deemed historical. Regarding the circularity, Carnley finds Pannenberg understanding the appearances in the light of their consequences (not in terms of Christian experience but of doctrinal elaboration, such as the discussions of Jesus' oneness with God) while justifying these very consequences in light of the appearances.[137] Nor does Carnley think Pannenberg *really* believes the resurrection to be historically accessible. He singles out an occasion of indecision about the power of the evidence in which Pannenberg's claim that history establishes the resurrection is immediately followed by a warning that this is only to the extent that evidence allows.[138] We recall, too, Pannenberg's professed agnosticism about the actual *details* of Jesus' resurrection, and his recognition of many legendary accretions in the gospel accounts.[139] Given his inability to find a decisive foundational role for the historical Jesus in his theology, Pannenberg's sole dependence on an event he can only vaguely describe is a case of "putting all his eggs in one basket," according to Carnley.

> For if the resurrection experience ratifies and confirms what was only ambiguously and uncertainly revealed in the events of Jesus' historical life, then it must be an event of quite decisive clarity and force. But how can it confer clarity and force, when it is itself so unclear? How can it provide the historical basis for dogmatic construction when its own historicity is so questionable?[140]

The whole issue of interpretation versus the facts themselves is thus raised. For one who believes that revelation lies in the facts and not in the interpretation, Pannenberg seems to give us a resurrection which is at best an interpretation of facts which are nowhere as clear as he thinks. Though he adds pragmatist arguments to his attempts at confirming the resurrection, claiming that resurrection belief best accounts for the rise of Christian faith, best fits his reading of the human condition, best illuminates life in the world,[141] etc., nevertheless Pannenberg cannot escape the interpretative character of even this further recourse. There is nothing wrong with such a solution— many modern theologians hold that the resurrection is an interpretation, just as Pannenberg holds that other Christological doctrines are themselves interpretations (though based on the resurrection itself). But this is not what Pannenberg claims to offer.

Ultimately, it seems that the very uniqueness and finality of Jesus as Pannenberg understands it is a matter of theology and interpretation rather than of history and fact. Various commentators have found Pannenberg's assertion of the proleptic fulfillment of history in Jesus to be a theological rather than an historical one, charging him "with imposing faith on reason, while not seeing clearly that faith is in actuality an aid to the assimilation of history."[142] From the first New Testament writings, Christians have interpreted Jesus in the light of their faith in him; the gospels spring from this faith, they construct the history of Jesus according to this faith and they aim at the production of this faith in those who receive them. This is the insight of redactional and structural analysis in current critical study—but it is far from the recourse to history which Pannenberg claims.

For one thing, it is not the usual way with matters declared indisputably factual that there remains considerable difference of opinion over them. But this is just what Paul Althaus shows to be the case in Pannenberg's proposal—if the resurrection is an unquestionable fact of history, then why does everyone not recognize it? Why is it so hidden in history that, presumably, "divine assistance" is needed to believe in it? (which very thing Pannenberg refuses to accept).[143] Besides, if all the facts have to be known before any such assessments can be made, according to the historiographical insights Pannenberg carries over from Dilthey, then how can an event be seen to prefigure the fulfillment of the whole in advance of the end, when "all the facts are in"? Avery Dulles concludes that there must be other revelatory events in creation or salvation history to allow their fulfillment in the Christ event to be recognized,[144] albeit provisionally. This apparent dependence of the resurrection upon other revelation to confirm it, coupled with Pannenberg's refusal to allow other revelation apart from its confirmation in the resurrection, shows that he is unable to ground his resurrection belief as he claims to do.

It is also important to consider how faith is born and how it is sustained. In this regard, Pannenberg is widely criticized for failing to recognize the present experience of Christ as central to what Christians say about their belief. By locating the origin of Christian believing in the past, in claims for the (allegedly self-interpreting) event of Jesus' resurrection, Pannenberg is separating the object of faith from the believing subject; and although his motive is to get away from the liberal subjectivism of Kant's legacy in theology, he creates his own subject-object divide nonetheless.[145]

Frans Jozef van Beeck heightens this critique, accusing Pannenberg of imposing a complete discontinuity between the faith of eye-witnesses to the resurrection and those who came to believe in later periods—a discontinuity foreign to the New Testament. "The eschatological congratulations addressed to those who have believed without seeing make the point forcibly," argues van Beeck.[146] Rather than the resurrection, then, seen as a past event, van Beeck believes the Christological *a priori* to be the experience of Christ present in the Spirit. He proceeds to question what epistemological dependencies are involved in a claim of Pannenberg that "Certainly, the believer knows very well that Jesus not only lived then, but that he is also the One presently alive as the risen and exalted one."[147] Certainly there is no ecclesial dimension here; van Beeck observes that nowhere in *Jesus—God and Man* "is there a hint that present worship and witness—and the knowledge involved in them—are the ways in which the Christian experiences the actual presence of the living Lord."[148]

In sum, van Beeck denies that the witnesses to Christ should effectively become epistemological substitutes for him, and that the historicity of Jesus' resurrection ought to be allowed to supplant the historicity of Christian experience:

> To call the Resurrection itself an historical event is an unnecessary historical postulate predicated on Jesus' death and burial and on his appearances, which *are* historical events. What is directly *historical* about the Resurrection as the beginning of *the actual presence, in the Spirit, of the living Lord to his Church* is: *the lives of the witnesses expressed in their confident testimony.* . . . They do not merely believe the witnesses' *kerygma that* Jesus lives, they also believe in Jesus alive. The particularity of the (earliest) witnesses' faith in the living Christ who has appeared to them is carried on in the particularity of all those Christians through the centuries who realize that their faith *now* is a very particular *calling*. This calling has made them new people, "in Christ"—people for whom the shape of the things to come has already become a living reality.[149]

This is not to fall into the subjectivism which Pannenberg despises, however. The recourse taken by van Beeck is *collective* in its orientation, as is that of Ritschl in *Memory and Hope* (1967), who affirms Christ as a present reality for the church and its worship while trenchantly denying the subjectivism which he traces from Augustine to Bultmann.[150]

Perhaps Pannenberg could salvage something from this sort of critique by further expanding his understanding of the resurrection. He could overcome the criticism that present ecclesial experience is overlooked in his approach by allowing the resurrection to include its reception in the life of the faith community. This is what John Macquarrie does in discussing the "Christ event,"[151] seeing it as larger than the life of Jesus—as expanding to include the impact of that life. By such recourse, Pannenberg could keep his focus on the resurrection as the center of the Christ event, allowing it still to illuminate the life of Jesus, while offering Christians' felt experiences of Jesus' presence the place in critical theology they clearly demand. This would not compromise Pannenberg's view of history, in that the inconclusive nature of historical assessments in advance of history's end can remain; indeed, Pannenberg would thus be allowing the future to illuminate and interpret the past—in this case, later interpretations of Jesus further filling out our assessment of his person—without sacrificing the pivotal role of the resurrection. And if interpretation is part of history rather than hermeneutics, as Pannenberg insists, then this recourse would ensure an historical link between the resurrection event and its present reception. If Pannenberg does not allow something like this, then there is no obvious connection between alleged facts in the past and experience in the present. Rahner was criticized above for failing to explain the links which he perceived between the Christ event and subsequent happenings throughout the universe— links he described in rather "new age" terms. But at least he made that attempt. This attempt is also made in the theology of Walter Kasper, who offers a "Spirit Christology" linking the resurrection to present experience (but more of that in the subsequent chapter).

In concluding this discussion of Wolfhart Pannenberg, it is important to remember just how significant is his ongoing contribution to twentieth century theology. According to Elizabeth Johnson, Pannenberg's eschatologically based Christology has "effected the first arguable (sic) successful marriage between the results of historical critical exegesis and the concerns of classical dogmatic Christology."[152] Pannenberg's focus on the resurrection in a consistently eschatological Christology earns from van Beeck the accolade that his work is "an important event in the history of Christology."[153] His thought meets the contemporary atheistic critique head-on, it builds on critical dialogue with the scriptures and the Christian tradition, and it proceeds from an interdisciplinary conversation with both human and natural sciences.[154] The universal scope of his program and the unashamed invocation of reason marks Pannenberg out among his contemporaries, ensuring him a grateful following in the present theological climate; "one senses that thoughtful people are weary of derivative and auxiliary theologies," writes Neuhaus, in praise of Pannenberg—"of theologies that are drawn from and ancillary to definitions of reality unrelated to the Christian proposition. There may be a new climate of Christian readiness, and cultural readiness, for the audacity of truth."[155] But, in the light of our discussions, we are obliged to temper our appreciation with the suspicion that Pannenberg's truth is too audacious, or perhaps not audacious enough.

He is suitable for classification as an "idealist" because of his high dependence on revelation as coming through history, and for his metaphysical vision—vast, overarching, based on futurity. His place on the right side of my typology comes with his professed reliance upon the historical Jesus and the human condition. But we have seen cracks appear in the edifice.

The historical Jesus and the human condition as they appear in Pannenberg are very much the dependent variables, with the independent variables in his equation for Jesus' uniqueness and finality being provided by the revelation and the metaphysics. This is quite normal among those discussed in Part II, but it is important to mention it as it largely distinguishes the "idealist" writers from those designated "liberal" in Part III below, who depend far less on these factors. We have seen in Pannenberg's Christology a predominance of the resurrection and of the man revealed in it—the ministry of that man (historical Jesus) and the life of other "men" (human condition) are viewed solely in the light of that event, with no genuine confirmatory role of their own.

The power of the resurrection to illuminate the past deeds of Jesus and to ensure the church's faith in him is only possible through Pannenberg's specially constructed view of history, which Clayton calls "retroactive causation."[156] This is one of many stratagems we have identified by which this theologian changes the rules of the public bodies of knowledge and methodological frameworks with which he claims to be in dialogue (mainly history and natural science) to the point that the whole body of his conclusions appears to be the stuff of privileged information. So it is that despite Pannenberg's constant assertion that revelation lies in public facts, I am led to suspect that Pannenberg's Christology really depends on private interpretation, drawn from sectional perspectives, and hinging on the very "gnosis" he decries.

As with Moltmann we find in Pannenberg a heavy dependence on revelation, and his claims that anything in advance of the eschaton is purely provisional cause Pannenberg to surrender none of his apparent certainty (neither did they with Moltmann). We also find the effective denial of any fundamental religious disclosivity in the human condition, though there are hints of a *de facto* anthropology underlying Pannenberg's synthesis, as was also identified in our discussion of Frei in Part I, above. As with Rahner, there is a whole ontological philosophy in Pannenberg which requires justification before its probative force can be admitted, *and* there is the question of how the Christ event was "extended" to affect people subsequently—Rahner's answer to this was found wanting in our discussion, above, and so has Pannenberg's.

This raises the related issue of wherein actually lies the uniqueness and finality of Jesus for Christians—in past fact or present experience? Pannenberg is certainly aware of the unavoidability of interpretation, de-emphasizing it while at the same time attempting to draw it under the rubric of history and his idea that revelation emerges through the events of history. But this is an unclear area in Pannenberg's thought; he never quite convinces us that he has subsumed hermeneutics under history as he claims. Pannenberg has never given us the real reason *why* it is that Christians believe in the uniqueness and finality of Jesus.

Chapter Six

A BRIDGING FIGURE — WALTER KASPER

Walter Kasper represents a "phased descent" from the metaphysical heights inhabited by Rahner and Pannenberg. He is more dependent on the historical Jesus than are these two "idealist" writers, though less so than the "liberal" group in Part III below. His perspectives on the human condition (correlated strongly with the historical Jesus in the manner typical of those on the right side of my typology) are similar to those of Rahner and Pannenberg. His emphasis on the Logos, present everywhere but incarnate in Jesus, links him to the "Logos Christology" of Schoonenberg and Robinson, to be considered in the next chapter. Kasper is a "bridging figure" between Rahner and Pannenberg, as between their metaphysically elevated "idealist" theologies and the "liberal" styles of Part III.

Walter Kasper is a Roman Catholic theologian strongly associated with the University of Tübingen, as a sometime professor of theology and a current representative of the venerable school of theological thought which flourished there in the nineteenth century. Born in 1933 this Swabian priest, once described as middle-of-the-road (between conservatives of the right and radicals of the left in post-conciliar Roman Catholicism),[157] is now the bishop of Rottenburg/Stüttgart.

The Tübingen school in Roman Catholic theology offers an Anglican-sounding triad of dependencies—reason, tradition and scripture. An approach typical of the school would be to combine respect for the institutional church and its traditions of belief and worship (as mediators rather than inhibitors of Christ in the present) with a recourse to scripture informed by historical critical method, and all this in an atmosphere of active engagement with the currents of modern thought.[158] Another feature of the Tübingen school is its ecumenical openness; it arose partly in response to the challenges of Kant and other Protestant thinkers in the European enlightenment, and Kasper himself is much influenced by Luther's theology of the cross. The "reason" looked to by this school was largely German idealism; they dialogued with Hegel, Strauss and the subsequent tradition of Protestant thinkers. For Kasper, however, his main influence comes from the later thought of Schelling,[159] in whom he finds an idealism issuing in greater openness to the complexity and vicissitudes of history than either Rahner or Pannenberg has inherited from idealist thought. Yet like them Kasper makes much of the resurrection as the center of Christian faith in the uniqueness and finality of Jesus. Also, he is committed to the theological importance of both the historical Jesus and the church's contemporary experience in the Spirit (as mediators of a reality uniquely present for the first time in Jesus). This commitment, characteristically respectful of scripture and tradition in the Tübingen manner, when coupled with an attention to the human condition informed by the insights of contemporary existentialism and Marxism, makes Kasper's Christology an interesting mix of features also found in the Christologies of Rahner and Pannenberg.

Kasper shows more real dependence on the historical Jesus than do either Rahner or Pannenberg, though his dependence on the human condition falls between the relatively high level of Rahner's thoroughgoing transcendentalism and the rather lower reliance of Pannenberg (who exhibits the sort of "revelational positivism" also found in Moltmann, though to a lesser extent). Kasper is distinguished in this company by his attempt to avoid problems identified above in the approaches of these two major figures—Rahner's difficulty in identifying Jesus as the absolute savior, and Pannenberg's failure to count anything from current Christian experience as evidence for Jesus' uniqueness and finality.

Kasper's study *Jesus the Christ* (1974, ET 1976), emerging alongside other major works about Jesus by Küng and Schillebeeckx in what Loewe has aptly termed "the continental Christological eruption of 1974," is the major source for his Christology.[160] It is an obvious product of the Tübingen school, combining historical critical insight, the tradition of the church and current speculation—for this reason, Clarke has described *Jesus the Christ* as the best introduction to Christology in English.[161]

The features Kasper seeks to include in his Christology are a fidelity to the historical Jesus, a plural approach to philosophy involving a refusal to confine theology to any one world-view,[162] and a holding fast to the actual *person* of Jesus through maintaining the ancient link between Christology and soteriology (20-22). Furthermore, Kasper believes the starting point of Christology is the decidedly non-abstract reality of Christian faith lived out in the community of Christian people—"The only trace which Jesus has left behind," he writes, "is the faith of his disciples. He takes effect in history only by virtue of that faith" (28).

Kasper by no means restricts himself to the historical Jesus as sole ground of faith, then, but nor is he willing to sever the link with Jesus and replace it with a "kerygmatic" faith that is ultimately only faith in the church as bearer of the kerygma (34). Kasper wishes the church's experience of Jesus' impact and the critically recovered witness of Jesus' own history to challenge and interpret one another. In this he is helped by finding revelation not just in Jesus' life, and not just in the church's life in the Spirit, but also in the resurrection, which is distinct from both (35). Here we find an obvious parallel with the thought of Pannenberg. All of this leads Brian McDermott to recognize that

> Kasper's formulation of the Christological criterion is a complex one. The primary criterion is the earthly and exalted Jesus Christ.... The secondary norm is the living faith of the Church, both in its foundations testified to in the NT and its ongoing life of worship and witness through the ages. The subordination of the Church and its faith to the primary criterion, the reality of Christ, is evident in Kasper's formulation.[163]

Having declared the historical Jesus central to the Christological enterprise, Kasper offers a major discussion of Jesus' life and ministry as he sees it emerging from critical New Testament study. While clearly recognizing the nature of the gospels as faith reflection and proclamation rather than history pure and simple, nevertheless he is able to offer a list of assured outcomes, concluding that "The Jesus we have as a result is a figure of unparalleled originality. Attempts to maintain the opposite can safely be left to amateur theologians" (65). Kasper believes Jesus to have been a mysterious, highly original, largely unclassifiable figure consumed by a vision of God's kingdom—apart from this recognition Kasper does not believe that Jesus can be appreciated aright.[164]

The strong historical certainties claimed by Kasper concerning Jesus' life are suddenly deepened when we come to the crucifixion, in which he claims Jesus "experienced the darkness and distress of death more fully than any other man or woman" (118). This sort of statement simply cannot be verified, of course, even if it can be understood as meaningful. The "historical skeptics" to be considered in Chapter 9 below, find such allegedly historical claims for a unique level of human experience in Jesus to be totally unsustainable and unconvincing. But Kasper *also* emphasises the separate fact of Jesus' resurrection as highly evidential for his uniqueness and finality. Thus "the Resurrection is part of the foundation of faith, as it has the functions of legitimating the historical Jesus . . . and of providing the new content Kasper deems essential for the achievement of a non-reductionist Christology."[165] As Rosato puts it, "according to Kasper, the absolute uniqueness of Jesus' ontic human life can only be understood in terms of the unquestionable universality of his resurrected and glorified existence."[166]

The "proof" for Jesus' resurrection, according to Kasper, lies in its impact among Christians *to this day*. He sees the empty tomb tradition as secondary, offering complementary evidence at best (129), and the appearances as colored by faith also—as "believing seeing" experiences (139).[167] Instead Kasper looks to the whole apostolic tradition and to present experience, finding in the resurrection of Jesus their necessary structure (140).

In this light, Kasper understands the resurrection/glorification of Jesus as the birth of a new world of gracious possibilities for human freedom which can be tested and confirmed through experience. Kasper is fulsome in his declarations that something final has thus happened, in a manner redolent of Karl Rahner's approach, but there is also some implied criticism of Rahner's inability clearly to describe or account for Jesus' redemptive influence upon the rest of creation:

The new existence in Jesus Christ is not however some mysterious potion which quasi-magically transforms man and mankind. The eschatological reality granted in Jesus changes the objective situation of all men, and makes it possible for all men to enter that new reality by faith and baptism. Insofar as Jesus Christ belongs objectively and ontologically to the situation of every man, the Resurrection is a power or an 'existential' which precedes our decision and qualifies it and requires it. Whenever a man gives himself through faith and baptism to that reality, he is a new creation in Jesus Christ... (156).

Kasper sees the resurrection as freedom from fear because it is victory over death; as well, it is the basis of Jesus' presence in the eucharist—"In that sense," Kasper writes, "we may say not only that Jesus was 'raised into the kerygma,' but that he 'rose again in the liturgy'" (158). Thus, in a manner recalling Ritschl and van Beeck, Kasper finds a basis for ecclesiology (and, in his case, Roman indefectibility too) in the resurrection.[168]

In the final third of the book, Kasper offers a discussion of the mystery of Jesus Christ in which he interprets traditional credal formulations in the context of their history. It is also where he offers the heart of his Christological vision, showing how the historical Jesus and the human condition combine to support his conception of Jesus' uniqueness and finality.[169]

Kasper reiterates his conviction that the human situation is now different from what it would otherwise have been apart from Jesus, but here he spells out more thoroughly the nature of the change. He sees the incarnation as changing the innermost being of people by creating new possibilities, removing the encumbrances of humanity's former situation. What is that situation? For Kasper the human person is an incomplete and yearning being: "Of himself he is a torso, a fragment. In his freedom he is hunger and thirst for the unconditional, definitive and absolute" (213). But no solution to this condition is available from within our own orbit, and in our own powers; Kasper believes that the human condition is poisoned by selfishness—a denial of our essential outward-directedness. In Jesus, however, this selfishness is overcome in a life of signal dedication. Rather than exhibiting the self-subsistence prized by the Greeks, Jesus was the man for others (217). And rather than "solidarity in disaster" (223) remaining our lot, solidarity together and with God has now been opened to us through Jesus.[170] In Jesus' obedience to death, according to Kasper, all anti-human forces are overwhelmed:

> Jesus takes on himself our guilt-entangled history, but, through his voluntary obedience and his vicarious service, gives it a new quality and establishes a new beginning. The history of disobedience, of hatred and lying is brought to a halt in his obedience and service. Even more: in his suffering and dying on the cross, where his obedience and service reach their supreme perfection, these powers of injustice wear themselves out on him and rush to their death; since he does not respond to them, he swallows them up—so to speak—in his death. His death is the death of death.... Jesus Christ then is not only a member of mankind, but the beginning of a new humanity.... Thus he recapitulates the whole previous development and at the same time opens up a new history (218).

According to Kasper, Jesus' mediation of this salvation is through his human obedience, as we have seen, but it is *at the same time* the action of God—Kasper will not surrender his strong emphasis on divine initiative as required to effect every bit of this.[171] He emphasizes the incarnation as the Spirit's work, and even insists upon the virginal conception of Jesus as a doctrine necessary to safeguard such pneumatological involvement—"In an abstract theology of hypothetical possibilities," Kasper declares, "combined with a 'soulless' theological positivism, one can indeed say that God could have acted otherwise" (251) (but not apart from that, one supposes).

Kasper's discussion concludes with an attempt to link the resurrection as locus of revelation (above and beyond anything revealed in the life of Jesus) to the world in which that revelation is to be received. Brian McDermott observes that "The most significant way in which Kasper uncovers the 'more' in the Resurrection is by developing the outline of a 'Spirit Christology.' The life, light, and creative

power released in the world by the Resurrection, Ascension, and out-
pouring of the Spirit are the surplus of being and life of the Risen
One shared with the universe which groans for redemption."[172] We
note, however, that Kasper's Christology remains one of "incarnation" rather than "inspiration," unlike the "Spirit Christology" of Geoffrey Lampe, for instance.[173] Kasper remains fairly close to Rahner
here, though the talk is more of Spirit than of Logos. He recognizes
the presence of the Spirit throughout human experience in the world
(267), while its presence in Jesus is deemed to be not only quantitatively greater than it is in others but also *qualitatively*; Jesus "is not
simply moved by the spirit but conceived and formed by the spirit"
(256). Kasper ends by reiterating the Christian conviction that in
Jesus the Spirit has brought the Logos to unique, definitive expression (267-68).[174]

Rosato notes that both Kasper and Pannenberg find singular
proof of Jesus' unity with God in the resurrection.

> But whereas Pannenberg feels that the Resurrection
> wholly precludes the necessity of any kind of Spirit
> Christology which might falsely imply adoptionist cate-
> gories, Kasper is of the opinion that a Spirit Christology
> which takes its lead from an analysis of the role of the
> Spirit at the Resurrection can avoid adoptionist overtones
> and actually enhance the essential unity of Jesus with
> Yahweh from the beginning of his human existence and
> even before it. It therefore seems that, contrary to Pan-
> nenberg's own refusal to adhere to any form of Spirit
> Christology, he in fact bases the permanent unity of Jesus
> with the Father on the retroactive clarity of the Resurrec-
> tion event, which in turn is explicitly attributed in the
> New Testament to the Spirit, as Kasper points out by his
> references to Rom 8:11 and 1 Pet 3:18.[175]

So it is that Kasper fills a gap which Pannenberg claims to leave va-
cant—the inclusion of contemporary experience among the evidences for Jesus' resurrection; as the above-mentioned references to

Romans and 1 Peter make clear, the Spirit is far more important in building faith than the rationalistically-minded Pannenberg will allow, with his deep distrust of theological subjectivism.[176]

We have found in Kasper a resurrection-centered Christology recalling that of Pannenberg, and also an echo of Moltmann's skepticism about the disclosive power of unaided philosophy. Kasper invokes an idealist philosophy, albeit one like that of the later Schelling who sought the cohesion of all things in divine revelation rather than in any obvious underlying structure (unlike Hegel, Teilhard and, to a lesser extent, Rahner). Thus in Kasper and his Tübingen school approach we find an alternative in Roman Catholic theology to the transcendental Thomism of Lonergan and Rahner.[177]

Kuschel observes that "Kasper is more obviously and consistently concerned with a concrete historical understanding of the person and cause of Jesus than Pannenberg, Jüngel and Moltmann; more so also than...Karl Rahner."[178] In addition, we have seen the importance of theological anthropology for Kasper, whose linking of the historical Jesus and the human condition is typical of those on the right side of my typology. Krieg notes that "By uniting historical data about Jesus' last days with the theme of freedom Kasper has used an argument to identify Jesus as a figure of unusual freedom...."[179] Combined with claims for Jesus' unique impact in history, and in the present, in the Spirit of his resurrection (upon which event Kasper bases his main evidential claims) we find in this theology a combination of key insights from Rahner and Pannenberg.

Yet there is no overconfident idealist philosophy, as Kasper finds in Rahner, nor any of the rationalism he criticizes in Pannenberg. Instead, the Tübingen synthesis which Kasper effects propels him in the direction of Schoonenberg and others to follow in Part III. Unlike "liberal" thinkers, of course, he has a high dependence on revelation, in the form of a reliance on Jesus' resurrection which is stronger than theirs, and a high ontology, albeit in the moderated form of Schelling's late idealist synthesis. So Kasper's Christology is no *mere* blend of Jesus' history with a particular reading of the human dilemma yielding an "optimum fit," as would be typical of a "liberal" like Hans Küng, for instance.

The "idealist" writers have sought to understand revelation as linked to the human world and history, and as involving human response, in ways which mark them out clearly from the "conservative" group of Part I. Yet they retain a focus on Jesus as the unique and final center of revelation and divine action. Problems were seen to arise in three main areas for Rahner and Pannenberg, however.

With respect to the historical Jesus, it was suggested that both these major figures had inserted Jesus into their philosophical worldviews, without giving sufficient attention to historical Jesus issues, as they claimed to do—even Kasper makes fulsome claims for Jesus' specialness which ought really to be tested in light of the critical discussion. The human condition as it emerges here was also thought to pay insufficient attention to the deconstructive insights of postmodernity (with Rahner thought to be the chief offender). Questions were raised about the way faith in Jesus was thought to arise, too, with an unclear chain of cosmic influence in Rahner matching a too-swift refusal to consider Christian experience in Pannenberg.

While Kasper mitigates these challenges somewhat, an approach is called for which adheres more closely to human life in the world and to the history of Jesus than the "idealist" group appear able to offer, despite their strong claims to do so. Thus we proceed to the "liberal" writers, away from theologies which are conceived "from above."

PART III

LIBERAL

"Liberal," for our purposes, means that these writers are interested in the historical Jesus and the human condition as correlated elements of any claim for Jesus' uniqueness and finality.

The particularity of Jesus and the details of his life are important here. This represents an emphasis upon Jesus' concrete person which is not always found among the "idealist" writers, above. We find an interest in Jesus' psychology and self-understanding, too, and comparisons with other leading figures of history. There is an appreciation of post-modern difficulties in defining the human to be found here, also, with a common core sought out and defended; some features of humanity as it is conceived here are familiar from Rahner's transcendental anthropology while other aspects are new, such as Schillebeeckx's prioritizing of human suffering.

But all is not entirely based on the human Jesus and the human condition, whether the emphasis is on revelation (the "Logos theology" writers) or salvation (Christologies "from below"). The resurrection and the present impact of Jesus are very prominent, as we have found them to be in the preceding chapters. Metaphysical speculation is not absent here, either—it has an important supporting role for the writers of "Logos Christology," though those offering Christologies "from below" have little interest in it. For both groups, however, the balance is shifted toward the correlation between Jesus' life and our own—away from resurrection, metaphysics, eschatology and other pivotal elements of Christologies dealt with on the upper half of my typology.

Certain questions raised concerning the "idealist" group remain unresolved among these "liberal" writers, however. Even among

147

those emphasizing the historical Jesus there are doubts about the true extent and historical credibility of their recourse. And there is some uncertainty as to just why Jesus as he is conceived here is the unique minister to the human condition.

Chapter Seven

LOGOS CHRISTOLOGY

The notion of Christ as a cosmic force is as old as St. Paul and his Deutero-Pauline disciples writing in the New Testament, while Christ as the incarnate Logos is as old as the Johannine Prologue. This approach characterized the Alexandrian school of Christian antiquity in contra-distinction to the school of Antioch, which was less metaphysically speculative in its commitment to safeguarding Jesus' humanity. The understanding of the logos used in liberal theology today is not primarily that of Plato, according to which the logos was a middle being between God and the world. Rather, it is that of Heraclitus, according to whom the logos was conceived panentheistically as grounding the world's unity, although the identification of Jesus as the one appearance of the whole logos in the flesh represents aspects of both understandings—this identification, attributable to Tatian, remains a mainstay of logos Christology.[1]

Those considered here are unlike Teilhard, and even Rahner, however, in that their central interest is not the metaphysics of the logos and accounting for its incarnation but, rather, the dynamic of God's revelation to humanity in Jesus—to this the metaphysical issues concerning the logos are entirely subordinate. In this regard they are far more committed to the fact and details of Jesus' life and the nature of his impact, as we find to be the case in the full-blown theologies "from below" to follow.

Schoonenberg and Robinson primarily address the history of Jesus and the historical experience of human persons in the world—it is on this basis that they seek to justify their fundamental beliefs about Jesus' uniqueness and finality. So although there is ontological underpinning for their Christology, recalling that of writers located on the upper side of my typology, nevertheless they are more readily aligned with a theology "from below." These versions of "Logos theology" approach the thoroughgoing "liberal" positions to be addressed in the subsequent chapter where no ontological dependence whatever is sought; but they do not achieve the genuine theology "from below" that we will find there.

PIET SCHOONENBERG, S.J.

In 1966 the Dutch Jesuit Piet Schoonenberg published an article on Christology, as did his fellow theologians Schillebeeckx and Hulsbosch. Thus began the so called "Dutch Christology" or "New Christology" with its distinctive focus on Jesus' humanity.[2] These beginnings opened a controversial chapter in recent theology, which led to the censure of Schillebeeckx by the Sacred Congregation for the Doctrine of the Faith under Cardinal Ratzinger following an earlier, indirect condemnation of Schoonenberg's work by the same body under Cardinal Seper, of which more later.

The centerpiece of Schoonenberg's Christology is a 1969 study, first translated into English in 1972, entitled *The Christ* (1974). There we find similarities with Rahner and Kasper, but also with Pannenberg—especially the latter's conviction that Jesus is *in person* the Son of God, along with something of his eschatological perspective. There are aspects of process thought to be found, too—a sympathy shared with Robinson.

Schoonenberg begins *The Christ* with a ground-clearing exercise concerning the nature of God's action in the world. He denies any notion of divine intervention from outside the natural process in favor of God working within the closed weave of cause and effect entirely through natural processes—a denial of extrinsicism which we have also met in Kasper and will meet again in Robinson. Like Rahner he understands God's action in terms of final rather than efficient causality, with the efficient causes being all natural (39-40).[3]

Jesus' entry into the picture comes via preliminary comments on the human condition. Schoonenberg finds a correlate for "grace perfecting nature" in the need for fundamentally open and unfinished human persons to be formed through their interaction with others.[4] And insofar as human society and language are necessary for forming persons, so the grace of God is required for their completion:

"Thus it appears to lie wholly in the line of evolution that man is a being open to unmerited, bestowed help and fulfilment, from his fellow men and ultimately from God himself" (38). "In a totally unique way this is true for Jesus Christ" (44), writes Schoonenberg; in Jesus the fullness of humanity is mediated, albeit teleologically and "eschatologically," as he prefers to put it—"The 'through him' must be explained by the 'for him' or 'to him'" (39).[5]

Schoonenberg then takes up his main theme in *The Christ*. Having sought to understand divine action as always taking place "in, with and under" natural actions in the world, he seeks to understand Jesus' person in the same way. This he does in conversation with the Formula of Chalcedon, and its doctrine of Jesus as both divine and human. Schoonenberg certainly does not wish to deny Jesus' divinity, dissatisfied as he is with recent Christologies content with a high view of Jesus' status based on historical reconstruction of his person alone, along with evolutionary Christologies like that of Teilhard. Nevertheless, he doubts that Chalcedonian notions of nature and person can communicate a credible "high Christology" today (65).[6] Schoonenberg prefers to begin his assessment from what he *is* sure of—with the oneness of Jesus' person. Rather than any internal interaction between natures, as would tend to divide Jesus' person, the gospels only ever speak of Jesus' dialogue with his heavenly Father, who is *outside* his person (68-69). So where Rahner had difficulty in going beyond the generic humanity of Jesus to affirm that he was *a* man, a human individual, this recognition is foundational for Schoonenberg.

Schoonenberg then asks how this one person, this human person, can be understood to be a divine person. He is convinced that the transcendence of Jesus is to be seen in his humanity, and that this was the New Testament position (90). Thus Schoonenberg denies any commencement "from above" such as that of Leontius of Byzantium, according to whom Jesus' human person was enhypostatic in the person of the Logos (apart from which he had no hypostasis, or ground to his own personhood, of his own) while affirming the notion of God's word coming to unique expression in Jesus nonetheless. Thus he preserves both the divine initiative in Jesus and the genuineness of his human life, avoiding biased perspectives arising from both the Antiochene and Alexandrian schools of Christian antiquity. Thus, in seeking a high Christology which affirms both full humanity and total divine initiative in the person of Jesus—an "integral Christological humanism" whereby Jesus *himself* is the Son of God—Schoonenberg arrives at the inversion of Leontius' formula for which he is famous: rather than the person of Jesus being enhypostatic in the person of the Logos, Schoonenberg declares that the Logos is enhypostatic in Jesus' human person. "Our concept could now be called the theory of the enhypostasia of the Word," writes Schoonenberg, "or in other words: of the presence of God's Word, or of God through his Word, in Jesus Christ, and indeed in such a way that this Word enters him wholly, that it becomes in him a historical person, that it becomes flesh" (89).[7] It is important to note that Schoonenberg avoids any adoptionism here; it is an incarnational Christology he presents, asserting of Jesus that "if God fulfills this man in all his dimensions then he does so from his origin" (93).

Schoonenberg devotes the second half of *The Christ* to exploring Jesus' human transcendence. He mentions the "abba relationship," along with Jesus' self-pronouncements, prayer, and the Lord's prayer, as instancing a relationship with God of great "clarity and immediacy" (100). Likewise, Schoonenberg is convinced that Jesus made a "totally unique impression" (53) on his followers. Like Rahner, he rejects the Thomistic notion that Jesus enjoyed the *visio beatifica* in his lifetime and that his knowledge was supernaturally extraordinary—with Rahner he denies the Hellenistic and scholastic notion of knowledge as a perfection. But he *does* hold that Jesus knew of his special relationship with God and that, through perfectly natural astuteness, he knew that his own death was likely (124-129). Schoonenberg sees Jesus as a man of faith, though one taken possession of more and more by God throughout his life. Yet there was a unique characteristic of Jesus' faith: "His faith was not faith in the proclamation of another Christ," writes Schoonenberg, taking up the theme of Jesus' immediacy with God once again, "but an...unmediated surrender to God himself" (150). This unique, though human, closeness involves sinlessness in spite of Jesus' real capacity to sin and be tempted; says Schoonenberg, "he is sinless, not through an incapacity for sin which merely makes Christ's temptations external and their results decided in advance, but through the strengthening, the hearing of God which makes Jesus conquer the real possibility present in him to sin" (145).

In all of this, however, Schoonenberg is by no means overconfident of his historical sources. While he obviously believes there is much that can be known of Jesus through critically reading the gospels, nevertheless he is clear that they are documents of post-Easter faith and provide no clear history of Jesus in the modern sense (110-13). So, for instance, in an admission which would delight "historical skeptics" like Dennis Nineham, Schoonenberg says we cannot objectively establish that Jesus suffered more than others—even his sinlessness is a matter of faith for those grasped in faith by Jesus' person (95). In this Schoonenberg is more skeptical than Kasper. But the issue of history is not ultimately the crucial one, according to Schoonenberg; "Even if we, in our historical knowledge of Jesus, were to equal the knowledge of his contemporaries," he declares, "our faith in Jesus' person and mission would be no easier... for us than for them" (113). Thus the question arises of where faith in the uniqueness and finality of Jesus finds its support in the theology of Schoonenberg, if only partly in the historical Jesus.

The resurrection was a central piece of evidence for Rahner, Pannenberg and Kasper, but this is not the case here.[8] For Schoonenberg, unlike Pannenberg, "the resurrection of Jesus is not an historical fact, it is one of the possible and therefore free ways to interpret what comes over us if we are seized by him after Jesus' death" (158). So where does the proof of Jesus' uniqueness lie? Clearly it is in the eye of the beholder,[9] though this is not how Schoonenberg expresses it. In a manner redolent of Kasper, who also links revelation to interpretation, he speaks of God's Spirit as interpreter and mediator of Christ. Schoonenberg closes *The Christ* with a further affirmation that God and Christ are now present to the church in the Spirit (187) and that this Spirit leads to true discernment—presumably, too, in the matter of Jesus' uniqueness and finality.[10]

The conservative critique of Schoonenberg begins at the Vatican and extends from there. The Sacred Congregation for the Doctrine of the Faith under Franjo Cardinal Seper, in seeking to defend the doctrines of Trinity and incarnation against "some recent errors," appeared to have Schoonenberg in mind—especially with regard to the non-eternity of the Logos as a person within the Godhead, and the non-eternity of the Trinity. "Those who think in this way," states the report, with reference to those seeking Jesus' transcendence in his human life, as does Schoonenberg, "are far removed from the true belief in Christ, even when they maintain that the special presence of God in Jesus results in his being the supreme and final expression of divine Revelation."[11] Other, more strident criticism is to be found; Schoonenberg is, as Pujdak points out, "more often caricatured than represented." Milet misunderstands Schoonenberg entirely, labeling him a death of God theologian;[12] Bernard Lonergan thinks him an Ebionite with a purely human Jesus,[13] while Kasper dismisses Schoonenberg on the basis of his Trinitarian ideas (despite some agreement on methodology).[14] On the other hand (and rightly, I believe) fellow Jesuit Michael Cook defends Schoonenberg against the Vatican's charge of adoptionism, highlighting Schoonenberg's insistence on identifying the divine initiative throughout Jesus' life.[15]

Clearly, Schoonenberg has received the usual treatment reserved for those labeled "radical"—he has been misunderstood and denounced by conservative forces in his church and its hierarchy.[16] His intent, however, was to keep as high a Christology as possible in an intellectual climate favoring ideas of evolutionary development and human freedom. His aim was "both to avoid all dualism and to recognize the autonomy of created reality, without reducing the weight of the divine initiative."[17]

But does Schoonenberg's confidence in Jesus' uniqueness and finality, unsupported by the relative certainties exhibited by those discussed in Chapter 2, above, amount to an insufficiently grounded perspectivism? One wonders what saves Schoonenberg's claim from sliding toward the relativism we will encounter in Part IV below.[18]

JOHN A.T. ROBINSON

Bishop John Robinson, who died of cancer in 1983,[19] was one of the Anglican Church's leading recent theologians. His *Honest to God*[20] introduced a popular audience to the thought of Bultmann, Bonhoeffer and Tillich, and the idea that belief in a "panentheistic" God, "the beyond in the midst," could redeem theism in a secular environment. This greatest theological bestseller of all time (over a million copies) was one of many books in which Robinson combined New Testament scholarship, theological exploration, ethical concerns and, occasionally, visionary suggestions for liturgical reform. Robinson's roots were firmly in the church establishment; he was no radical in the abrasive, deconstructive sense. Nevertheless his liberal views were censured by the hierarchy and he never received a diocese of his own.[21] Robinson's Christology is most thoroughly expressed in *The Human Face of God* (1973), which we will consider in detail. Other sources will be mentioned in passing, but they contribute little beyond this major work.

In *The Human Face of God* Robinson seeks a Christology which will speak to a world which has outgrown the natural-supernatural distinction. Like Schoonenberg, in *The Christ*, Robinson understands divine action as taking place *within* natural processes rather than impinging upon them from outside.[22] Thus he sees Christology as making sense of human life in the world, rather than attempting to commend some remote supernatural person or equally remote salvific transaction (2, 4). Concerning present conditions, Robinson shows an awareness of the post-modern decline in our former certainties.[23] He mentions four key elements of the current intellectual climate in the west: 1) a dethroning of the mythical world-view whereby myth is now a subset of meaning, no longer constituting the overarching web of meaning as formerly (20); 2) the decline of metaphysics, in the sense that our world is now explained on its own terms rather than in terms of another, higher world (21-23); 3) the dissolution of absolute monism in favor of plural truth—Robinson declares that "The model for our age is not so much the Gothic arch as the mobile" (24); and 4) the rise of historical thinking, issuing in skepticism over the veracity of Jesus material in the New Testament (27-32).

All this does not lead to deconstruction and complete relativism, however. Robinson still believes in a fixed center to human experience despite all this, as we shall see; "there are sticking-points where one must not sell out," he writes, maintaining "that fidelity to the quality of relationship is the deepest test, that *persons matter* more than any precepts or sabbaths" (25).[24] Like the sociologist Peter

Berger, in *A Rumour of Angels* (1971), Robinson believes that there remain reliable signals of the transcendent in the plural world of today. Staying with his image of the Gothic arch as a symbol of a (now defunct) cosmos rendered meaningful by the great chain of being, Robinson holds that while nowadays "One cannot hope to complete the arch, yet these multiple broken columns are shafts of transcendence thrusting beyond themselves, meeting points of secular mysticism, where the unconditional is made flesh, and afterwards one may say, like Jacob, 'The Lord is in this place, and I did not know it'" (26). He knows that any Christology done in this environment will inevitably seem reductionist before the more confident Christology of yore—"compared with that done in the more "full-blooded" (but actually rather bloodless) categories of classical ontology" (34). But he insists upon such new emphases if the humanity of Jesus is to be preserved, and hence the importance of Christianity for people no longer willing to conceive the sacred as remote from the world and its people.

I would like to highlight two dimensions of Robinson's program in *The Human Face of God*. First, there are his discussions of Jesus' humanity and the possible interpretation of traditional Christological dogma—these deserve to be taken together, as together they represent the correlation Robinson seeks between Christological dogma and contemporary questions. But there remain the *reasons* why Robinson accepts Jesus' uniqueness and finality in the first place. There are a combination of factors, which need to be gathered together, from which Robinson's own firm belief in Jesus' uniqueness emerges by way of a cumulative case. To be considered first, however, is his reinterpretation of Christological dogma with its emphasis on Jesus' humanity.

Robinson's Christology turns upon his commitment to the *full* humanity of Jesus; in this he is typical of recent English theology with an empiricist bent, though he is no dogmatic reductionist as we shall see. The *fact* of Jesus' human life for Robinson is as important as any historical details of that life, too. He deplores the ready denial of Jesus' humanity throughout the church's history, from docetism through notions of an "impersonal humanity" (38-41) to neo-scholastic emphasis upon what amounts to Jesus' "superhuman" attainments (71). For fear of losing the sense of God's involvement and salvific initiative in Jesus' life, Robinson thinks, the church has compromised Jesus' share in our humanity long reckoned to be equally important for salvation.

Jesus' full humanity, according to Robinson, requires his full immersion in the natural process through which humanity evolved and all individuals are brought to birth (43, 54). Central to Robinson's case at this point is his disavowal of the virginal conception, on the grounds that it would remove Jesus' true solidarity with every part of human existence which St. Paul and the writer to the Hebrews demand (52-53).[25] The thought that God miraculously created human genetic material to provide Jesus with all the appearances of human paternity (including, Robinson supposes, the physical characteristics of non-existent paternal ancestors) seems as absurd to him as are claims that God created fossils and placed them in the rocks (51).

Robinson follows mainline exegesis and theology in recognizing the virgin birth story as theological rather than historical and gynecological (119), insisting that the initiative of God in Jesus' life does not require a miracle of this sort: "Human intercourse is no more ruled out than it was in her [Mary's] cousin's miraculous pregnancy—equally the result of the Word of God, for whom nothing is impossible" (50). "We shall never know humanly speaking who was Jesus' father," concludes Robinson, who discerns hints about Jesus' illegitimacy in Matthew's introduction of four morally dubious women to precede Mary in the genealogy; yet Robinson is confident that "we can be free to be as indifferent as we are ignorant—on the ground, as Matthew boldly asserts, that [Jesus'] divine significance is entirely unaffected" (63).[26]

In his overall interpretation of Christological dogma, Robinson prefers to think of Jesus as God's true man—unique in the divine plan to be sure, but a true man rather than an enfleshed deity. This certainly does not mean that Jesus had every human quality (69-71); rather, Robinson's Jesus is an icon of human normalcy. He is an individual who takes the unique step of simply being himself, thus allowing the truest and most inclusive expression of humanity to emerge: "What attracts and judges us is not the man who has everything—that merely oppresses us—but the man in whom we can glimpse a vision of the essential" (73). This obviously implies a common, deep well of humanity intuitively accessible to all of us:

"To call Jesus the Christ is to acknowledge that somehow he has that which has made men say, in their thousand different ways, 'This is *it*'" (75).[27] This is the Christ which Blake liked, an accessible figure displaying a universal humanity (74-75). So rather than a divine man stripping off his attributes to become human, in a metaphysical kenosis, Robinson sees a human being uniquely sacrificing his ego in self-giving to God in an obediential, this-worldly kenosis (166).

Rather than two stor*eys*, then, with a higher-order being coming to earth, Robinson sees the incarnation in terms of two stor*ies*—two ways of speaking about the one Jesus, as both a man *and* the unique manifestation of God. This represents the prioritizing of the functional over the ontological so characteristic of Robinson's theology—he compares Jesus with the king of Sweden, who is a commoner raised to royal office and in no way indelibly, "ontologically" royal in the British sense (184-85). Of course this is adoptionist, and Robinson offers no defense. He simply declares such thinking to be closer to the Jewish prophetic mode, deploring its condemnation in the tradition. This is a degree Christology, with Jesus *quantitatively* rather than *qualitatively* different from the rest of us. As we have seen, however, this is *not* a matter of Jesus excelling in unmatchable human perfections;[28] rather, it focuses on his openness to God. "The uniqueness of Jesus," concludes Robinson, "was the absolute uniqueness of what God did in him" (211).

This functional approach to Christological dogma is lent some metaphysical weight, however, via an invocation of the Logos. Robinson rejects the anhypostasia view, according to which the Logos provides Jesus with a basis for his human personhood. Rather, with Schoonenberg, he sees the Logos as enhypostatic in Jesus' fully human person (105). Robinson's is essentially an inspiration Christology, then, in which Jesus is empowered by the Logos, as are all persons open to God—there is no miraculous power making Robinson's Jesus essentially different, such that a second nature is called for to account for it (112-13).[29]

Robinson is strongly opposed to any exclusive reading of God's presence in Jesus, who is *totus deus* rather than *totum dei*—wholly God rather than the whole of God (10, 229). And certainly, for Robinson, "The finality or universality of Christ is not to be identified with the finality or universality of the Christian religion" (229).

Robinson's version of incarnational faith, then, is reminiscent of Rahner's. "What happened at the Incarnation," writes Robinson, "if we can so put it, is that God, the power of nature and history, the Logos or principle of the evolutionary process, began to be represented in a new way. The appearance of Jesus marked the emergence of a world 'come of age.' ... For he dared to accept the role of sonship, of standing in God's stead" (217-18).[30]

Related to these "dogmatic reflections," and supporting them, are Robinson's actual *reasons* for belief in Jesus' uniqueness and finality. He trusts the gospel portrayal of Jesus as historically accurate in everything that matters, further insisting that no significant gap could have existed between the man and his portrayal.[31] He also accepts the fact of Jesus' resurrection as a setting apart by God, though he remains skeptical about the *physical* resurrection, as we shall see. Robinson adds to these central convictions an interesting case for Jesus' sinlessness, positing also a unique level of psychological integration to accompany his claims for Jesus' unique openness to God. He lends additional support to his case by comparing Jesus with other religious founders and their religions.

The only detailed argument Robinson offers here is largely negative, however, based on the assertion that Christian claims for Jesus could not have been sustained had the credibility gap been too wide (125, 130)—"the correspondence must have been *sufficient* to have provoked the response, 'To whom else should we go?' (John vi.68)," argues Robinson, in the belief that no uniqueness claims would have been made "if Jesus really had thought of himself as a poached egg or been profligate or even just another Zealot...."[32] So although Robinson admits the possibility of historical disproof for Christian claims, nevertheless he thinks the "burden of disproof" lies with the skeptics,[33] whose case he believes is neither obvious nor sustainable.

The resurrection has an important evidentiary function for Robinson, as was not the case for Schoonenberg. He sees it as a necessary occasion for the birth of a new faith, though he does not seek any miracle involving Jesus' body to establish it.[34] "What precisely happened to the old body will never be cleared up," he writes. "The mystery ... is subsequently interpreted ... not as the disaster it first appeared, but as a confirmatory sign of the action of God. But unless there had been the new transforming reality of life in the Spirit, combined with the psychic phenomena, the physical evidence would not have been construed (let alone constructed)" (137).[35]

Resurrection belief seems to have a present experiential component for Robinson as well. He goes so far as to speak of a "scandal of imparticularity," claiming that Christians must know atonement and resurrection in their own experience if they are to accept Jesus' unique role, denying that the sole grounds for their belief must be found in any "particular" past events. Thus atonement and resurrection are wider and more inclusive than simply *the* atonement and *the* resurrection (230-31). Contemporary experiences of reconciliation undergird belief in the atonement, according to Robinson, and other experiences "from below" support belief in everything else given a "capital letter" in the tradition: Creation, Resurrection and Ascension (234). So while he has no desire to sever links with history, nevertheless for Robinson "Christology has to start with the flesh of God now, with his *prosopon* in the present tense. For that is the Christ incarnate today. The clue to this is indeed the Christ who has been and the Christ who will be" (241).[36]

In accord with his claims that Jesus could not have been too different from his portrayal in the New Testament, Robinson argues for Jesus' sinlessness. But again the case is negative. He insists that Jesus must have undergone the normal course of human development, learning obedience and becoming perfected through suffering (80-83) as Hebrews states. Jesus must have undergone genuine temptation, according to Robinson, from his encounters with fallen women to the rigors of Gethsemane, and he must have been genuinely free to sin, to the extent of even wishing to do so. But this does not compromise his sinlessness, concludes Robinson, for whom Jesus "was fallible—yet when the crunch came, he did not fail" (93). This claim he supports by two arguments. First, Jesus in the gospels offers no self-deprecating remarks about his own sinfulness, which is "so universal a mark of saintliness, from Paul onwards..." (97). Robinson assumes this is because Jesus quite clearly was never weighed down by any sense of sin whatever, unlike Paul and the saints. Second, Robinson notes that while the gospels defend Jesus against allegations of transgressing sabbath laws and the like, never is there any attempt to tone down other potentially damaging accounts. How easy it would have been, Robinson suggests, for Jesus' opponents to have twisted the Zacchaeus episode into a story of collaboration, or to render into very damaging form the accounts of Jesus' encounter with the dubious woman who fawned over his person—behavior on Jesus' part that could well ruin a priest's reputation nowadays, as Robinson the bishop wryly observes (97-98). But no such allegations about any sort of impropriety were ever forthcoming, despite Jesus' own sardonic description of his reputation as "a glutton and winebibber, the friend of tax collectors and sinners." All this strikes Robinson as genuine evidence that the claim of sinlessness captures Jesus' true nature—"The astounding claim of the church," he concludes, "is therefore considerable testimony to the character of Jesus..." (98).

Robinson proceeds from such considerations to speculate about the psychology of Jesus.[37] That Jesus developed and had to integrate negative elements into his psyche, as all mature people must, seems obvious to him. He finds plenty of evidence in the gospels that Jesus dealt with various human drives—libido, temper and intolerance, anxiety and fear of death. In addition, his Jesus would have had to incorporate "the Shadow," as Jung terms it, apart from which he would remain a half personality, a cardboard cutout rather than a human being, as he is often imagined and portrayed (80, 86-87). "The Shadow" contains the things people frequently wish to disown, as individuals but also as a society—Robinson mentions suffering, the absurd, the impersonal and the feminine as things with which Jesus was able to cope, while many cannot or will not.[38] Robinson finds proof of this incorporation in Jesus' ability to tolerate the flaws of those he encounters in the gospels: "To accept the unacceptable in others," Robinson explains, "depends upon not finding it a threat to oneself. What seems to have impressed his contemporaries was precisely his self-possession, his poise, his authority, his peace" (88). Thus, for Robinson, Jesus actualized the "archetype of the self" which Jung sees as slumbering in the human unconscious awaiting the appearance of someone in history to activate it (204).[39] As we know, Robinson finds this psychological power unlocked by many other images and individuals sacred and secular, but nowhere more so than in Jesus' case:

Thus in its central and distinctive mystery of the cross and resurrection Christianity integrates and transfigures the light and the dark sides, I believe, more profoundly than in the coexistence, for instance, within Hinduism of Krishna and Kali, the figures of dalliance and destruction; it deals with the problems of suffering and above all of sin, more radically and dynamically than the impassive serenity of the Buddha, however moving; and ... it incorporates the feminine more fully than the patriarchal religions of either Judaism or (especially) Islam.[40]

Robinson concedes to post-modernity that the different religions refer to different aspects of human experience, but insists that one must choose which vision addresses reality best—a personal one or a non-personal one (229). His final choice, as a committed "personalist" in philosophy, is a Christian one, according to which the personal "finds its prism and its promise in Jesus as the Christ" (229).[41] According to Robinson,

The Christian who asserts that for him Jesus Christ is the all-embracing principle of interpretation is asserting that there is nothing in his experience that requires any *other* explanation; for everything 'coheres' in him. He makes this judgement—and calls himself a Christian—because he does not find this is true of Buddha and Mohammed, not because he does not find any truth in them. For him Christ represents the definitive revelation of God—and this is a less misleading word than final—because it is inconceivable to him that there should be any higher revelation of God *in human terms* than 'pure unbounded love.' And he judges that empirically it is true that no one comes—or has to come—to the *Father*, that is, to God conceived in the intimacy of '*abba*,' but by Jesus Christ. Jeremias is justified in calling this one of the distinctive marks of Christianity. Certainly it is not true of Moses or Mohammed, Buddha or Vishna (sic), Confucius or Lao Tzu (221).

Thus the high premium on love and intimacy with a personal God in Christianity underscores Robinson's belief in the uniqueness of Jesus by comparison with other religious founders; and as the only "founder" who seeks to mediate that sort of God, Robinson's Jesus is in fact the one who most thoroughly does so.[42]

In concluding this discussion of Robinson's Christology, it is important to mention that he is the only major figure in the period of interest who has so emphasized the psychology of Jesus, in tandem with his understanding of the human condition. He is a "Jungian," as are many more "popular" writers in the Anglican and Roman Catholic world today, in his apparent identification of the deep structures of the world process, the divine Wisdom, Logos or Spirit, with the deep structures of the human, here pretty clearly matched with the "archetypes of the collective unconscious" identified by C.G. Jung.[43]

The human condition as Robinson thus conceives it is nowadays making heavy weather in a post-modern environment. It provides one of the few ways to resist the siren song of cultural relativism currently heard throughout the humanities (with which we will engage in Part IV below), but it has many detractors. At its heart is the idea that an "archetype of the self" dwells within each and every human psyche, and responds to things and persons who "resonate" with it. Jesus provides the optimum instance of this resonance, for Robinson—and all of this despite his recognizing considerable cultural diversity (in particular, that there are both personal and non-personal poles in all the world religions giving rise to fairly fundamental differences in perspective). Clearly they are not fundamental for Robinson, however, who sees the personal as the deepest and most inclusive category, so that the archetype of the self will resonate most fully with something that is fully personal.

There are problems when we move from the human condition to the other element of Robinson's correlative undertaking—the historical Jesus. Certainly, his ideas about the priority of John (that the fourth gospel was written first) and the early dating of Hebrews are controversial to say the least. This unconventional dating serves his program by establishing an early pedigree for the kind of high-though-functional Christology he wishes to offer, but it casts doubt on the extent to which he *really* relies upon the historical Jesus. But in addition to this Robinson also affirms a strong level of historical recollection in what the synoptic gospels have to say about Jesus. So a conservative approach to the historical Jesus in the New Testament supports a decidedly non-conservative theology.[44] The problem here, though, is that he does not give enough evidence of engagement with the exegetical labors of those who *can* decide what is and what is not historically authentic.[45] Thus the historical Jesus and the Christ of faith are largely blurred together in *The Human Face of God*. It is not the dogmatically elaborated Christ of faith to which I refer of course—Robinson has demythologized that figure—but rather his own Jesus, the astonishingly attractive and well adjusted embodiment of God's universal wisdom which he finds in the New Testament. But this figure is not the Galilean rabbi, undeniably foreign to us in many respects, who emerges from the consensus in current historical Jesus research, and who is to be found in the pages of theologians who *genuinely* attend to this research, such as Schillebeeckx.

The type of correlation Robinson effects between Jesus and the human condition is different from that we will find in Schillebeeckx and Küng, below. With them it is a matter of Jesus uniquely meeting the human need for salvation. With Robinson the emphasis is on revelation and the person of Christ, rather than salvation and the work of Christ; Robinson's Jesus reveals the depths of God in the heights of the human, and this is as close to talk of salvation as he gets. In this he is like Schoonenberg.[46]

Robinson is also different from Schillebeeckx and Küng in his continued reliance upon the Logos as a metaphysical element in his argument, superadded despite strong claims that his is a theology "from below."[47] Really, as Robinson admits, his is a method of correlation—what his theology from below amounts to is working-out today's right questions "from below" in order to enable access to static, eternal answers "from above." So Robinson shares with the writers discussed in Part II above, something of a "head start" in his Christology, identifying a metaphysical niche into which the historical Jesus will fit—in Robinson's case, Jesus is the icon of what is at once divine love, cosmic wisdom and human interiority. This is not theology "from below" as it is more fully represented in the next section, however, in which the human condition is delineated without any such recourse to metaphysics.

At the end of the day, Robinson has offered a phenomenological method for establishing Jesus' uniqueness and finality. His link between Jesus and the human dilemma is intuitive, for no arguments are offered other than intuitive ones for the superiority of the Christian vision to a more "eastern," non-personalist one. He also seems to have let his Christ image, of a uniquely well-adjusted man who proves to be the acme of divine revelation, color his portrayal of the historical Jesus (an almost universal flaw since the birth of historical Jesus research to be sure, but one which must continually be brought to light). Nor has Robinson offered reasons for the uniqueness and finality of Jesus strong enough to survive accusations of subjectivism and relativism in his favorable comparisons with other religious leaders.[48] As this challenge of relativism also stands against his understanding of the human condition—that it is too western, psychologistic, middle-class, etc.—and as doubts have been raised about how genuinely he depends upon the historical Jesus, it would appear that Robinson's case hinges on whether we accept those aspects of his theology which remain tenaciously "from above."

In the next section all theology really is "from below," in that attempts to explicate the incarnation of a metaphysical reality such as the Logos do not feature prominently. Instead, the dependence upon the historical Jesus and the human condition is foundational, if not always convincingly argued. Whereas Rahner, Pannenberg and Kasper achieve a head start in their reliance upon various forms of revelation and ontology to support their claims for Jesus' uniqueness and finality, with Schoonenberg and Robinson not totally free of this either, the thoroughgoing "liberal" writers receive far less assistance in their quest. Theirs is the only approach to Jesus' uniqueness and finality met thus far which is genuinely "from below."

Chapter Eight

CHRISTOLOGY "FROM BELOW"

Here we consider two major writers of wide influence and some notoriety. Meier notes that "with the exception of a few scholars like Raymond Brown, Catholic exegetes are not terribly well known to the Catholic public at large. Küng and Schillebeeckx, to the contrary, tried to absorb Scripture studies on the historical Jesus into a larger theological whole and make the results available to the Catholic in the street. In the process, they got into trouble."[49] They make much of the human condition, and in this they recall Rahner and Kasper, but they interpret it in conversation with a wider range of contemporary dialogue partners than Rahner, arriving at results which evince far more awareness of historical relativism and the contributions made by ideology.

Both Schillebeeckx and Küng find in Jesus a unique instance of God acting to save humanity, though their understandings of this are significantly different. Both offer what they see to be a reinterpretation of traditional Catholic Christological orthodoxy fit to reach and challenge a post-Christian society. For their trouble, both have been investigated by the Vatican authorities, with Küng officially deprived of the title "Catholic theologian" (though in effect he continues to operate as one with enhanced popularity).

There are various non-negotiable pinning-points in the arguments of both men, as we shall see, which show their inability to mount a case without recourse to some of the certainties claimed by the "idealist" writers discussed in Part II above. Nevertheless, the types of theology to be considered here represent the premier attempts in the period of interest to understand Jesus as unique and final in the light of historical study and the contours of human existence alone.

EDWARD SCHILLEBEECKX, O.P.

Born in Antwerp in 1914 Schillebeeckx is now an old man, though his theological output continues—a book on a major theme of his thought, hermeneutics, is still forthcoming. His entire life's work exemplifies a distinctively Dominican spirituality combining communal life, academic engagement and pastoral involvement, as is evident in his vision of theory and praxis mutually interacting within community. This spirit of the order he loves is what he seeks to have realized in the church as a whole.[50]

Having entered the Order of Preachers at Ghent in 1934 he was sent to the Dominican House of Studies in Louvain for his initial philosophical and theological training. There he was influenced by a brilliant young friar, Dominicus De Petter—a Thomist working out a theory of knowledge in conversation with sociology, phenomenology and hermeneutical theory, "emphasizing the role of intuition as the key to bringing together empirical reality and the human mind."[51] Schillebeeckx has never ceased to pursue his work in this spirit, welcoming dialogue with these and other major currents of twentieth century thought. His central concerns ever since have been hermeneutical, evincing a desire to understand the nature of revelation, salvation and the church's relation to the wider world.[52]

From teaching theology at his former seminary as a young priest during World War II, Schillebeeckx then went to Paris. There he imbibed both existentialism, in the ascendant at the Sorbonne and elsewhere, and the *nouvelle théologie* which held sway among the Dominicans at Le Saulchoir, and the Jesuits at Lyon-Fourviére —the former delving into medieval sources and the latter into patristic ones.[53] While working in Paris with the great Dominican exponents of *nouvelle théologie*, Yves Congar, and M-D Chenu,[54] Schillebeeckx also met, studied and conversed with Camus and Merleau-Ponty.

There followed a decade of teaching Dominican students in Louvain, after which Schillebeeckx went to be the Professor of Theology and the History of Theology at the Catholic University of Nijmegen in the Netherlands in 1957; he remains Emeritus Professor in Nijmegen, having retired in 1983, and continues to live at the Albertinum—the Dominican house of studies there. He has been very involved in the Dutch church, contributing behind the scenes at Vatican II as a theological adviser to the Dutch bishops. His long stay in the Netherlands explains why this cosmopolitan thinker,[55] Flemish by birth, is often referred to as a Dutch theologian.

In 1960 Schillebeeckx presented a new understanding of the sacraments in his very influential study *Christ the Sacrament of Encounter with God* (ET 1963). There he anchored the theology of the church's sacraments in the prior sacramentality of Christ, seen as the great sacrament of the encounter of God with humanity—an encounter extended to the present through the participating sacramentality of the church.[56] Thus he moved beyond the Aristotelianism of neo-Thomistic sacramental theology toward an "encounter model" of revelation. This shift was based on what he had learned about the human person in the post-war philosophical schools of Paris, and from his historical studies with the Jesuits in the area of patristics, from whom he learned a less mechanistic notion of sacrament as *mysterion*. Sacraments are not things, he taught, but actual *encounters* with the living Christ through the church in existentially significant moments of life.

In all of this we find as early as 1960 both the historical method and the concept of "encounter" which are absolutely central to Schillebeeckx's mature Christological works. In addition, there is already in this 1960 study much evidence of an already sophisticated appreciation of historical critical literature on the New Testament, the mastery of which has so distinguished his more recent Christological forays.

Schillebeeckx has contributed other major theological studies in the area of sacraments, especially those of eucharist, holy matrimony and holy orders, along with his Christology; all these studies are characterized by the serious historical engagement characteristic of *nouvelle théologie* along with the personalist emphasis evident in his work on the sacraments. Needless to say, all of this also represents a commitment to venture into controversial realms in the study of difficult, topical subjects.

After the council, Schillebeeckx moved away from sacramental theology to consider God's interaction with the world on a wider front. As Philip Kennedy observes,

his early writings discuss the family Rosary and Roman
Catholic Sacraments, whereas his latest articles debate
biological engineering and ecological despoilation.... In
his initial publications he talks about God and Christ in
the context of Church and sacrament. His latter-day publications speak of God and Jesus in categories of politics
and suffering.[57]

Schillebeeckx schooled himself in modern hermeneutics, critical theory and historical critical studies of the bible, growing in sympathy
for the praxis-oriented approach of liberation theology. From the critical theory of Max Horkheimer, Jürgen Habermas, Herbert Marcuse
and Theodor Adorno, of the neo-Marxist "Frankfurt school," Schillebeeckx learned to view humanity in more social and historical terms,
leaving behind some of his earlier personalist emphasis.[58] He also
drew from them a characteristic theme of his later work—his rather
gloomy assessment of the human condition as one characterized by
only occasionally relieved suffering.

In keeping with the highly skeptical assessment of modernity
typifying the Frankfurt school,[59] and their consequent repudiation of
historical progress as proclaimed by the enlightenment, Schillebeeckx made his own the eschatological emphases we have encountered elsewhere in 1960s theology (in the work of Moltmann and
Pannenberg). He saw the eschatological proviso as a sign of hope in
the face of the manifest contradictions evident in humanity's tragic
history of suffering.[60] He also developed a praxis-oriented approach
from his encounter with critical theory, coming to see the gospel as
something to be *done* and deepening his characteristic refusal to see
it in purely conceptual terms.

According to Philip Kennedy this new emphasis on hope and
praxis represents a major shift in Schillebeeckx's epistemology, "a
turn from a theoretical participation in, to a practical anticipation of,
absolute meaning."[61] It was in keeping, too, with a confidence abroad
throughout European theology in a time of cultural ferment that theology might have something to say of use to the wider culture.[62]
Schillebeeckx has never lost the political edge to his theology first
developed at that time.[63]

Another major aspect of Schillebeeckx's activities in the 1960s, following the council, concerned his place in the so-called "Dutch Christology." We have already considered the contribution of Schoonenberg at this time who, along with Schillebeeckx and the Dutch Augustinian Ansfried Hulsbosch, did much for the renewal of Roman Catholic Christology. All of them emphasized the humanity of Jesus, which is why historical studies of Jesus' person came to be so important for Schillebeeckx—he needed to know the details of Jesus' life if that life was uniquely disclosive of God.[64] Obviously, he benefited in this endeavor from the new openness to critical biblical studies allowed by the Vatican since the mid-1940s and reaffirmed at the council, and from the "new quest" which had returned the historical Jesus to Protestant theology after a long absence.[65]

The crowning achievement of Schillebeeckx's life is the massive three-volume trilogy which forms the basis of our discussion to follow. In this developing work, strictly a prolegomenon to Christology rather than a Christology outright, "this Dominican scholar has provided perhaps the most detailed study of the person of Jesus Christ to have appeared in the twentieth century."[66] Not all were appreciative of these massive labors, however. Schillebeeckx underwent and survived an investigation by the Sacred Congregation for the Doctrine of the Faith in 1979 over his orthodoxy in the light of his major works on Christology—works deemed by his accusers to be fairly minimal in traditional terms. Challenged once before, in the late 1960s, over his work on revelation, Schillebeeckx was again challenged in the early 1980s over his book *Ministry: A Case for Change*,[67] issuing *The Church with a Human Face: A New and Expanded Theology of Ministry* in response.[68] Schillebeeckx's weariness and wariness after this prolonged experience of attack and defense is evident in the tone and content of the last of his aforementioned trilogy *Church: The Human Story of God* (1990).[69]

But if Schillebeeckx has his detractors in Rome, his widespread and ecumenical support and worldwide popularity must offer some solace. His enormous exegetical exertions, combined with his deep appreciation of contemporary human experience (as illuminated, chiefly, by critical theory), have produced a singular and powerful attempt to reclaim Chalcedonian orthodoxy in our day. Jesus emerges from the seemingly endless pages of Schillebeeckx's great trilogy less encumbered by philosophical and dogmatic determinants than we have seen hitherto in this study.

Despite hints of a more plural perspective emerging in the last volume, for he has grown in his appreciation of cultural and linguistic contexts through the 1980s,[70] Schillebeeckx's consistent project is to find in Jesus a unique and final instance of humanity before God.

> His governing Christological aim or interest is to explain in what sense Jesus is the manifestation of a universal salvation stemming from God. In his early Christology he explained Jesus' uniqueness and mediation of universality by relying on the definition of Chalcedon: Jesus saves because he is a God-man. In the later Christology, however, the universality of divine salvation is mediated through Jesus' praxis aimed at emancipating the poor, and in the praxis of those who seek to emulate Jesus.[71]

The "liberal" style of this project is thought by Schillebeeckx to provide the only viable way a Chalcedonian vision can be conveyed in our day.

In his massive study *Jesus: An Experiment in Christology* (1974, ET 1979) there is much that is open-ended and even confusing. Jesus' uniqueness and finality emerge, for instance, through a combination of disparate criteria, including not only the historical Jesus and his unique addressing of the human condition, but also the resurrection, and the impact of Jesus on (and "in") the church then and now. All of this is worked through in an awareness of post-modern concerns about history and the human person, though without succumbing to them as have the "complete relativists" in Chapter 4, below. Schillebeeckx's somewhat untidy book, however, stands as an important contribution to contemporary Christology: as Fergus Kerr observes, comparing Schillebeeckx with other major contributors,

> There is little sign in their writings that the preceding generation (Karl Rahner, Hans Urs von Balthasar, and so on) ever opened a modern biblical commentary. Schillebeeckx's book on Jesus... is the first by a Catholic the-

ologian to build a doctrinal approach to Christ on the
basis of the gospels rather than on the teachings of the
Council of Chalcedon.[72]

Of course, Schillebeeckx argues that he *is* offering a reinterpretation
of the Chalcedonian formula, as we shall see.

The uniqueness and finality of Jesus is not reduced by Schillebeeckx to either unique events or to the church's interpretation in
faith of certain events as unique. So it is not a matter of fact alone or
of value alone. Rather, Schillebeeckx locates Jesus' uniqueness in a
combination of both event and interpretation. Thus he avoids the distinction which appears in form criticism and subsequently in theology between the Jesus of history and the Christ of faith. Schillebeeckx
recognizes that "All early Christian traditions are both 'kerygmatic'
and recollection of Jesus of Nazareth" (85), believing that the Christ
of faith is a largely justifiable interpretation of the Jesus of history,
while at the same time holding that Jesus of Nazareth is the norm
and criterion for any true interpretation. So neither nineteenth century liberals like Harnack are right, for whom interpretations of Jesus
in the New Testament were corruptions, nor twentieth century liberals like Bultmann, for whom there can be no meaningful access to
the Jesus of history. Rather, Schillebeeckx follows the new quest in
attempting to reconstruct "the historical Jesus" so as to allow access
to "the Jesus of history" (recognized as not totally irreconcilable figures); after all, thinks Schillebeeckx, it was the latter who inspired
the church to interpret him as the Christ of faith. In this dialogue,
widened to include the human condition as he understands it,
Schillebeeckx sees Jesus' uniqueness emerging.

The first point to be made is that Schillebeeckx is ideologically
committed to the importance of Jesus' historical particularity:

> ...whereas Rahner develops his Christology from the
> basic datum that Jesus was a human being and therefore
> had the spiritual potentiality of a human being as de-
> scribed in Rahner's anthropology, Schillebeeckx tries to
> be much more specific in speaking of Jesus as an individ-
> ual with ascertainable characteristics—the concrete his-
> torical Jesus.[73]

So not for Schillebeeckx the reduction of Jesus to the status of an idea, as we see it in Strauss and Bultmann, for such ideas can vanish—"In that way Christianity loses its universal purport and forfeits the right to continue speaking of a final saving activity of God in history" (76). Such a reduction of Jesus to the status of an idea emerged in the enlightenment, in which there arose a trend to regard him as a repository of universalizable human values and nothing more. The corollary is that Christianity becomes merely one more expression of a uniform underlying human religiosity. But according to Schillebeeckx this denies the heart of Christian kerygma: "the fundamental connection between Jesus' person and his message of God's approaching rule" (588). Such so-called "first-order" statements are the stuff of New Testament assessments of Jesus, Schillebeeckx argues, and it is *this* faith which Chalcedon seeks to express in its "second-order" philosophical language (559-67).

Now, what of the details? Schillebeeckx is confident that we know *a lot* about the historical Jesus, though less than the nineteenth century quest claimed to recover (66). He denies that there is any knockdown historical proof for Jesus' uniqueness, realizing that his life can be interpreted in terms *other* than those of God's definitive salvation (74). Still, Schillebeeckx is convinced that the records we have, while falling short of "a historically exact record of events," nevertheless "do give us a full-length picture of him" (83). "In spite of not inconsiderable distinctions," he writes, "Jesus 'comes across' everywhere in the early Christian traditions in the selfsame way. The unity turns out to be more universal and profound than the pluralism" (515).[74] So convinced is Schillebeeckx of this that he lays the burden of proof upon those who would argue that New Testament pictures of Jesus are chiefly interpolative.[75]

There are many aspects of Jesus as portrayed in the gospels which Schillebeeckx believes are historically authentic, from his baptism by John (137) to the institution of a memorial meal at the last supper (307)—this latter is not always acknowledged by scholars, being thought by some to reflect no more than early church practice. Summarizing his assessment of Jesus' praxis, Schillebeeckx declares that "one of the most reliable facts about the life of Jesus is that he broached the subject of God in and through his message of the coming rule of God; and that what this implied was made plain first and foremost through his authentic parables and the issues they raised: namely, *metanoia* and the praxis of God's kingdom" (266). According to Schillebeeckx, this message

> was given substantive content by Jesus' actions and way of life; his miracles, his dealings with tax-gatherers and sinners, his offer of salvation from God in fellowship at table with his friends and in his attitude to the Law, sabbath and Temple, and finally in his consorting in fellowship with a more intimate group of disciples. The heart and centre of it all appeared to be the God bent upon humanity. Of this God's rule the whole of Jesus' life was a 'celebration' and also 'orthopraxis'.... The bond between the two—God's rule and orthopraxis—is so intrinsic that in this praxis itself Jesus recognizes the signs of the coming of God's rule. The living God is the focus of this life. Against the background of the... movements which isolated themselves into 'remnant' communities, Jesus' message and praxis of salvation for all Israel without exception... are difficult to place in a historico-religious context. For that reason we are bound to enquire whether Jesus' message and praxis do not become intelligible only when we presuppose his special, original religious apprehension of God. For the question is: whence does Jesus obtain the unconditional assurance of salvation to which his message of God's coming rule as final wellbeing for men so positively testifies? (266-67).[76]

The answer to this key question for Schillebeeckx is, of course, Jesus' unique "abba relationship."

Schillebeeckx's Jesus "knew nothing of the convulsive quest of people for self-identity; he was an utterly free person, his living rooted in the sovereignly free God whom he called his *Abba*" (402). Herein Schillebeeckx finds the deepest clue to Jesus' uniqueness: "Of Jesus' standing out in a historico-religious context, purely on the grounds of his addressing God as *Abba*, there can be no question, *per se*. Jesus' uniqueness in his relationship to God undoubtedly lies in its unaffected simplicity; and the marks of that in late Judaism, though not absent, were really rare" (259). This rarity of usage on Jesus' part convinces Schillebeeckx of its historical authenticity. The project of unearthing Jesus' private self-understanding is not something Schillebeeckx values, admitting that we are "powerless to reach into Jesus' own psychology" (137-38). But he does believe (following Ryle) that the message and mode of life of a person are enough to shed light on their self-understanding. This allows him to deduce "an extraordinarily pronounced consciousness of a prophetic role" (257) on the part of Jesus—a conclusion evidenced by the "abba relationship."

Yet there is more to Schillebeeckx's ascription of uniqueness and finality to Jesus than this. He also makes much of Jesus' impact upon his disciples then and now. This impact includes the resurrection, as well as the phenomenon of faith. Schillebeeckx is aware that the Easter kerygma does not stand alone in the New Testament; he points out that the first three of the trajectories he identifies in the New Testament (*maranatha, theos anér,* and "wisdom" Christologies) proclaim Jesus' exaltation apart from any resurrection (538). And the very fact of the gospel form convinces him that the earliest Christians had seen the resurrection as intimately connected with the rest of Jesus' life (73, 111). So whereas Pannenberg is almost totally reliant upon the resurrection in his argument for Jesus' uniqueness and finality, Schillebeeckx remains far less so. Nevertheless he claims that there is no good news without the resurrection, just as there is no good news without a contact point between Jesus' life and the present (111-14) (recall van Beeck's critique of Pannenberg on this score in Chapter 5 above).

The resurrection "event," whatever that was, is inseparable from its interpretation within the early church according to Schillebeeckx, who does not believe that any pre-linguistic resurrection event can be entirely "strained out" of the interpretation mediating it to us (392). What is more, he understands the "reality" testified to by the resurrection as independent of traditions which grew up around the Jerusalem tomb and the resurrection appearances; these he sees as already presupposing the Easter faith (397).[77]

Schillebeeckx discerns three elements in this variegate experience of resurrection: an initiative from Jesus himself, an element of acknowledgement and an element of witness or commitment to mission (353)—for Schillebeeckx, "Jesus is presented as the risen one within a collective-ecclesial-experience. The source of this talk of Jesus as risen...is the experience of a new being or existence" (352). These are experiences of "Christological seeing," according to Schillebeeckx, with a high point reached in the recognition by Thomas in Chapter 24 of St. John's gospel (360).

Schillebeeckx accounts for the rise of resurrection belief by conjecturing a protophany to Peter, around whose newborn faith that of the other apostles coalesced.[78] Thus, according to Schillebeeckx,

> They all of a sudden 'saw' it. This seeing may have been the outcome of a lengthier process of maturation, one primary and important element of which was enough to make Peter take action and bring the disciples together again. About this initial element there was obviously a collective exchange of ideas—'they doubted'—until a consensus emerged. Even the oldest pre-Pauline credal formulae are the result of an already protracted theological reflection and not the instant articulation of the original experience (391-92).

We have seen Pannenberg discuss the resurrection as an historical event, just as we have seen Schoonenberg deny that anything need have happened to Jesus' physical body. What is Schillebeeckx's position on these important matters? Regarding the involvement of Jesus' body, he argues that "A 'vanished corpse' is not in itself a resurrection, and an actual bodily resurrection does not require as its outcome a vanished corpse" (331). But this is not to suggest that resurrection is a kerygmatic reality for believers only, while Jesus "himself still lingers 'in the realm of the dead'" (647).[79] It appears that a real transition of Jesus to the life of God is what Schillebeeckx intends, while remaining essentially non-committal over the fate of Jesus' earthly remains, just as he equivocates over the question of Jesus' virginal conception (554-56).

According to Schillebeeckx the resurrection "event" itself "no longer forms part of our mundane, human history; it is, *qua* reality, meta-empirical and meta-historical: 'eschatological'" (380). This insistence is quite different from Pannenberg's that the resurrection is accessible to us in ordinary human history. But, then, Pannenberg's argument was based largely on the *impact* of Jesus' resurrection, which was found to undergird his claims for its historicity. This Schillebeeckx will allow, sharing with Pannenberg the new quest insight (based on existentialist historiography) that past events are known through their subsequent impact. But Schillebeeckx will not reify the founding event of resurrection faith, excerpting it from the complex nexus of New Testament kerygmata among which it is only one component. So the "proof" of Jesus' resurrection is not an historical matter, in the way it is for Pannenberg. At this point Schillebeeckx is closer to another in the school of hope, Jürgen Moltmann, in his insistence that the truth of Jesus' resurrection will only be definitively established at the end of history: "The real legitimation, evident to all, remains thus totally eschatological" (643).

Before proceeding it is worth noting grounds upon which Schillebeeckx does *not* base claims for Jesus' uniqueness and finality. First, miracles are not considered to be evidential. Schillebeeckx accepts the growing exegetical opinion that Jesus *did* perform cures and exorcisms, apart from which the New Testament could admit of no "glad tidings" (189). But he recognizes the "epic concentration" through which the miracle tradition was expanded by invention to highlight Jesus' significance for the first Christians (80, 182, 188). So Schillebeeckx rules out any supra-historical interpretations of Jesus from the start, preferring to seek the special activity of God solely as immanent within the natural order (633) in a manner similar to that of Schoonenberg. Schillebeeckx prefers to ask about the *meaning* of the miracle accounts, rather than posing the modern question, "did they really happen?" (79). The miracle accounts testify to him that the earliest Christians found in Jesus a decisive overcoming of the power of Satan: "As for whether natural laws are being broken or respected, nobody has a thought about that..." (184). He also plays down the virginal conception of Jesus as a minor New Testament tradition, speaking more of the ascendancy of the Spirit of God in Jesus' life, rather than the question of his paternity (554-56). All in all, it seems that Schillebeeckx denies any supernatural understanding of the miracles whatsoever, and does not speculate on the events which he believes must have stood behind the miracle accounts. He prefers to look at what the accounts were saying about Jesus.

One wonders of course just what *did* happen to spur such interpretations, and suspects that Schillebeeckx might have sacrificed his
usual insistence upon "event" in favor of "interpretation" at this
point. Surely one who seeks out the historical Jesus at such length to
see if his kerygmatic interpreters are right should be more rather than
less intense in his probings at a point where, by his own admission,
the gap between event and interpretation is great. Not to attempt an
account of Jesus' miracles, however, now that scholars are ready to
admit more of an historical basis to the accounts than old-fashioned
rationalistic liberal exegesis was prepared to countenance, appears to
be a weakness, although Schillebeeckx is certainly not alone among
current theologians in this failing.

The other area in which Schillebeeckx is loath to base his
uniqueness claims is that of Jesus' death. His theology, drawing upon
the emphases of critical theory at this point, will not admit any
salvific role for suffering—it is an evil to be overcome, rather than a
virtue to be courted. So while he is quite certain that Jesus must have
foreseen the likelihood of his death (299), and thinks it likely that
Jesus may have sought to integrate that possibility into his life (302),
nevertheless he refuses to allow that death the soteriological centrality it has achieved in the western church. Rather, he sees the death as
continuous with and expressive of the whole shape and content of
Jesus' life, rather than an event of a different order (282). It is the *life*
of Jesus which is salvific, according to Schillebeeckx, for whom elements of the passion tradition describing Jesus' death as salvific are
neither original nor important (291).

In the absence of proof, Schillebeeckx admits the necessity of
faith for those who wish to claim the uniqueness and finality of
Jesus. We have seen his insistence upon interpretation, his denial of
any access to pure facts, and noted the important role of "intuition"
in his hermeneutics (which reaches back at least to the early influence of Fr. De Petter). Nevertheless Schillebeeckx is confident of
much about the historical Jesus, as we have seen, and of his unique
impact. However, Schillebeeckx admits that this impact is not evident to those who are not caught up in it. So for Schillebeeckx the
"revelation" of Jesus Christ comes not in pure uninterpreted events;
rather, it includes the response of faith to those events. As he puts it,
"Revelation then issues in the response of faith: yes, indeed! This is

how a truly human existence has to be lived. The eschatological presence of God in Jesus and man's ultimate comprehension of reality are correlative" (635).

This further step in Schillebeeckx's argument raises questions about his correlation of the human experience of reality and the experience of Christ. And this brings us to the central feature of all those Christologies discussed in this third chapter—the nature of the "fit" between what can be known of the historical Jesus, on the one hand, and what is involved in our human condition on the other. At one point Schillebeeckx makes this requirement explicit beyond contention. "The only way," he states, "in which the affirmation of Christian belief can be shown to have credibility is twofold: (a) on the one hand by the historical study of Jesus'...life and death...and (b) on the other hand by showing how the Christian claim to universality is substantiated in the true humanness of 'being human," as that confronts us in Jesus of Nazareth" (605). To be sure the resurrection has a complementary role for Schillebeeckx in establishing Jesus' uniqueness and finality as part of the process of revelation beginning with historical events in Jesus' life and ending with the reality of faith. But no faith would arise, no revelation would take place, unless Jesus uniquely ministered to the human condition. How does Schillebeeckx understand that condition?

Certainly there is no naive, ahistorical conception of humanity of the sort for which Dennis Nineham castigates liberal theology, as we shall see in the next chapter. On the contrary, Schillebeeckx shares the post-modern awareness of historical diversity. But he does not emphasize discontinuities between past and present expressions of Christianity at the expense of continuities, as thoroughgoing "historical skeptics" such as Nineham insist upon doing:[80]

> The anti-historical posture of enlightened and enlightening Reason is at the moment coming under more and more general attack....On that basis the Enlightenment went on to talk about an ideal universal humanity, the *humanum*, without any historical, particular and real mediation....Since the Enlightenment, after many sorts of untoward experiences, our age has come to see that mankind does not have at its beck and call this *humanum*;

what is truly worthy of man is not something we all
know and have within our power. It is 'outstanding'; a
sought essence of humanity. We have rightly come to
speak of *homo absconditus* (E. Bloch). A general concept
of humanity is always in itself ambiguous; it needs a critical point of reference, a criterion; and this is in fact
given by the record of human suffering ... (591).

Thus we see two key elements in Schillebeeckx's understanding of
the human condition. The first is its openness to the future, its unfinished quality (there is a similarity with the work of Moltmann at this
point). But this is part of a more constitutive openness, to the world
and to others; like Rahner, Schillebeeckx understands human beings
in terms of their possibility for communication (614). This openness
is particularly evident when faced with the suffering and ambiguity
which he believes are "a permanently thriving parasitical 'epiphe-
nomenon' of our history" (620). This is the other pole of the human
condition as Schillebeeckx sees it. He rejects the idealist press to impose a too-simple closure upon history, as in Hegel's system; he admits the complexity, the mingling of sense and non-sense, of the absolute and the absolutely plural, which are characteristic of real
human history (615).[81]

It is primarily this fact of suffering, however, which delineates
the human condition—by showing us what is missing from our lives
as they are, if you like. So, for instance, Schillebeeckx recognizes
"an implicit craving for happiness" which he finds very suggestive:
"*qua* contrast experience it implies indirectly an awareness of a positive call of and to the *humanum*" (622).

This universal meaning yet to come is rendered definitively in
Jesus, according to Schillebeeckx. Certainly, Jesus meets Schillebeeckx's basic definition of what being truly human means: "'Being
human for the other' is a task as it were sketched into the structure of
our 'human constitution.' ... That is why Jesus' being human for the
other is an important presupposition and a precondition for making
sense of any more exact qualification of his Christological uniqueness" (606-07).[82] This "more exact qualification" Schillebeeckx
seeks in Jesus' response to the fact of human suffering—and not just

in his historical life, either, but in the ongoing efficacy of his struggle against suffering which will only deserve to be called unique if it is operative at both personal and societal levels, and thus able to address the sum total of things.[83] For Schillebeeckx, then, it is only through Jesus that we can believe that the facts of evil and suffering can be reconciled with our constitutive hope for a final good (625). Why is this?

Schillebeeckx's difficulty is how to present an event within history as a definitive act of God, let alone a unique human act, while denying the notion of special divine intervention (preferring to understand divine action as a kind of depth dimension to natural and human action, which comes to conscious expression as "revelation" in the experience of faith). But at the point where he might have been expected to answer the question, "why Jesus?" Schillebeeckx seems content with saying "let us proclaim the mystery of faith." That is, he simply declares "that in the human life of Jesus the ultimate point of man's existence has been expressed in word and action—and that in a normative and exemplary sense" (635), though only as it appears to those who have faith. While mentioning the "abba relationship" and the fiasco of the cross as a major encounter with the fact of human suffering, Schillebeeckx seems unable to say just why Jesus is definitive, and not someone else: "there could be some hard and long discussion about that," he admits, "but the question ignores a very concrete datum already to hand: namely, that Jesus has appeared in our concrete history, can no longer be spirited out of it, so that the recollection of the thing will always be an irremovable historical challenge" (639).[84]

Thus the cocktail is finally mixed: Schillebeeckx at last manages to link unique closeness with God and unique closeness to humanity in Jesus, claiming in addition that this definitive encounter has evoked a uniquely powerful response from those who interpret Jesus and live from him. Thus we have a unique event alive in interpretation and praxis in a uniquely powerful way.[85] So it is that the facts of Jesus' life (as history can access them), and the lived experience of the vindication of that life by God in the church, against the backdrop of a human dilemma nowhere more thoroughly and effectively experienced and addressed, constitute the cumulative grounds for Schillebeeckx to assert the uniqueness and finality of Jesus in this major volume. His later books have things to add to our discussion, however, which will receive brief attention before we move on.

Schillebeeckx's next major volume was *Christ: The Christian Experience in the Modern World* (1977, ET 1980). This study, longer than its predecessor, is mostly an investigation of Jesus' impact, based on New Testament material apart from the synoptics. Without extending to this book anything near the attention accorded its predecessor, nevertheless we will note here Schillebeeckx's attempt to explain and deepen claims made in *Jesus* about the human condition, the nature of suffering, and just why it is that Jesus can be described as unique and final.

Schillebeeckx's awareness of how post-modernity has relativized all thinking about the human person has increased in this second major volume. He sees, in the midst of today's cultural pluralism, a call upon humanity to do what it has never had to do before, and that is to conceive universally valid ethical norms and implement them in the face of a looming global catastrophe (654-61).[86] And he reiterates his claim that humanity is unfinished in advance of the eschaton, adding that "no reflection on oneself can arrive at a crystallization of a kind of general substratum of rationality among all men, independently of time and space" (731).[87]

New to this volume, however, is a list of *anthropological constants* which essentially constitute the human condition as Schillebeeckx sees it. They incorporate post-modern uncertainties as dimensions of the human, rather than finding in them a denial that any human condition exists. In this he avoids the criticisms which Rahner has attracted for failing to recognize this aspect of the late twentieth century's philosophical and cultural environment. Schillebeeckx's list offers no abiding essence of the human as in Aristotle, Aquinas or Spinoza; on the contrary "in very general terms these anthropological constants point to *permanent* human impulses and orientations, values and spheres of value, but at the same time do not provide us with *directly* specific norms or ethical imperatives" (733). Nevertheless, Schillebeeckx does believe they must be taken into account if human life is to be rendered livable.

The *first* of these constants is our relationship to human corporeality, nature and the physical environment: here we have a relationship with boundaries that must be negotiated by individuals and societies—boundaries which cannot be pushed too far. Salvation for humans, then, rather than angels, must touch this dimension of our existence (734-36). According to Schillebeeckx's *second* constant, being human involves other humans. Here he recognizes that individuality is limited, and that hominization requires right dependence on others and on society (737). *Third* there is the connection with social and institutional structures which Schillebeeckx (no doubt in the light of sociology) recognizes as having a life of their own. Given the unavoidability of structures and institutions in human life, then, the ethical and salvific task must include the challenging and reforming of structures (737-38).[88] *Fourth*, Schillebeeckx acknowledges the conditioning of people by time and space—the post-modern challenge of pluralism in a nutshell. So our historical and geographical situation determines who we are, our strengths and weaknesses, and what we can achieve (so do our religious traditions which can provide norms for action when critically remembered) (738-39). *Fifth* there is the criterion of praxis—that theory and practice are in mutual relationship and that humanization in our world requires this realization (740). The *sixth* criterion is that humans have a religious or para-religious consciousness. Schillebeeckx means by this that there seems to be an unavoidable utopian element in human consciousness: "faith and hope—whatever their content—are part of the health and integrity, the worthwhileness and 'wholeness' of our humanity" (741). Without this dimension Schillebeeckx sees us falling into various neuroses, or else embracing horoscopes or some such. Schillebeeckx's *seventh* and final criterion emphasises that these constants form an irreducible synthesis, in the sense that failure to take any one into account leads to our forfeiting possibilities for any truly holistic liberation (741-42).

What Schillebeeckx is able to show on the basis of all this is that genuine salvation cannot be a wholly mystical affair, nor purely economic and political. It must touch the whole person as constituted with these many dependencies. This Schillebeeckx believes Jesus does *par excellence*. We are now in a better position to appreciate the expanded solution he goes on to offer for the problem of Jesus' uniqueness and finality. Jesus is unique for Schillebeeckx because he uniquely ministers to the experience of human suffering, as it is disclosed against the anthropological constants he delineates. "In general religious terms and in individual religions God may have many names," he admits, "but he shows his *true countenance* to Christians in the unselfish involvement of Jesus as the good shepherd in search of his wandering and lost sheep" (639).

The spelling out of this by Schillebeeckx remains rather vague, but four elements emerge clearly enough (802-03). The first concerns Jesus' success in providing the impetus for a movement which survives to this day—the fact that *he did it*, as was also pointed out in *Jesus*, discussed above. As Schillebeeckx understands the interpretation of any life to be included within the effect of that life, and hence as part of that person's identity, he thinks it likely that Jesus justified such fulsome interpretations of his own person. Secondly Schillebeeckx offers historical evidence for Jesus' special relationship to God, and his special self-understanding as an eschatological prophet, concluding that "the historical influence of the message and life-style of Jesus was also intended by Jesus himself" (802). Schillebeeckx adds a third point, in effect his standard caveat, that faith and participation in the Christian community are necessary for this uniqueness to be acknowledged: "Jesus' light burns in this world only with the oil of our lives" (846). Then, fourth, he invokes the "mad, bad or God argument" (cf. 832)—one which I must say I would more usually associate with popular evangelical apologetics. According to this argument the uniqueness of Jesus' apparently inflated claims would tell badly against him unless there is corroborating evidence based upon the positive impact of the claimant throughout history, in the light of which Jesus is given the benefit of the doubt. Schillebeeckx goes on to assert that this is a salvation made available to all through Christ, and universal in that sense, as well as being universal in addressing all the elements of human being identified among his anthropological constants.

The last book to be considered here is *Church: The Human Story of God* (1989, ET 1990). It presents a wide-ranging discussion which coheres around Schillebeeckx's already familiar ideas that human experience is the realm of revelation, that Jesus is central for God's dealing with human suffering (despite God's universal redeeming presence throughout history) and that a properly constituted and functioning church is essential for the conveying and substantiating of any such claims. The treatment of Jesus' uniqueness and finality in the book is deeply woven into the understanding of divine action and the human dilemma found there. Yet it is not as clear as it might be— in addition to elements carried over from the previous books, Schillebeeckx's latest book adds a far from complete discussion of Christian claims in the face of religious pluralism. To follow is an attempt to encompass the key elements of this most recent discussion.

The question of relativism is certainly to the fore for Schillebeeckx here, for whom, now, "we have to be able to explain why Jesus, confessed as the Christ, is the only way of life *for us*, though God leaves other ways open for others" (43). Schillebeeckx aims for "the expression of the uniqueness of Jesus Christ on the one hand without discrimination against other religions on the other hand without falling into 'religious indifferentism,' suggesting that all religions are equal" (102). This last point recalls his critique of enlightenment rationality from earlier in the corpus, and the concomitant notion that every religion taps into one experiential substratum common to all humanity (163).[89]

How does Schillebeeckx argue for Jesus' uniqueness and finality here? There is a new argument to the effect that the universal claim of Jesus is rooted in the universal claim of the Old Testament, testifying as it does to God as universal creator (143). "It becomes clear here," concludes Schillebeeckx, "that... the God of Jesus is a symbol of openness not of closedness" (167).[90] This appears to represent an argument of the following form: religions claim different things, and universality is not necessarily appropriate to all of them, but as the claims of Jewish salvation history are universal, and as Jesus comes out of that tradition, then the possibility of his universality must be countenanced in this case where elsewhere it need not be. This is fleshed out, of course, with reference to Jesus' powerful effect in mediating salvation to human beings within history, as we have seen in the earlier works. Schillebeeckx here describes this effect in terms of freedom from sin, guilt and despair, freedom from fear of disapproval by God, freedom from fear of death and freedom for goodness and disinterested commitment toward others, all of which is seen as a foretaste of the coming total redemption and as justifying our faith in the uniqueness of Jesus. The fragmentary realizations of these eschatological outcomes enable the confession "of what Christians now already...albeit with some hesitation, and in fact quite daringly, call the uniqueness of Jesus Christ" (134).

So once again we have a variety of dependencies. Jesus is unique because of his relationship with God, and because of his success at focusing salvation from God, which is now explicitly seen to be larger than church, Christ and religion. This salvation is understood in terms of human wholeness broadly conceived, which is glimpsed in Jesus' praxis and supported by its presence in the life of his disciples.[91] Yet this is not an exclusive thing, denying other religions their "place in the sun," nor is it provable apart from faith and in advance of the eschaton.

Schillebeeckx has won wide support as well as some telling criticism for his work. Unlike Hans Küng, however, he has escaped serious Vatican censure, arguing to the end that his work is carried out in the spirit of orthodox church belief and teaching. Nowhere is he more insistent about this than in the realm of Christology, maintaining that he is, simply, an interpreter of Chalcedon for modern times. "Chalcedon for me is the norm of all my theological research," he writes, in response to conservative critics: "I want to initiate Christians into this dogma, surfeited as they are with books which declare that 'God is dead' or that Jesus was no more than a man or a great prophet. If Chalcedon were a dead letter for me, I would hardly have had the desire or the courage to write two books totaling more than 1400 pages."[92]

Of course, the incorporation of historical Jesus research into mainstream Roman Catholic theology has been Schillebeeckx's great contribution to the field. But how does this theologian rate in the complex, subtle and shifting world of professional exegesis? John P. Meier, a leading Roman Catholic scholar in the field of historical Jesus research, is very complimentary about Schillebeeckx's achievement. He sees in Schillebeeckx's program a greater methodological sophistication than he finds in Hans Küng, particularly concerning his distinctive and resolute refusal to separate the historical Jesus from the Christ of faith (recall that Schillebeeckx saw the various Jesus portrayals *in the gospels* as interpretative portraits, in the same way that later Christologies were interpretative).[93] According to Meier, "we have in Schillebeeckx's *Jesus* a genuine integration of the quest for the historical Jesus into a systematic Christology. Whatever its failures, this is the book's claim to lasting fame. In the future, no Catholic Christology can turn the clock back to the pre-Schillebeeckx era and still hope to be taken seriously."[94]

As to exegetical difficulties, the main ones mentioned by Schillebeeckx's critics concern his reliance upon the Q hypothesis, the "abba experience" and aspects of his views about the resurrection.[95] For his part, Meier thinks that Schillebeeckx is uncritically reliant upon the wrong exegetes at crucial moments. In particular, he thinks him insufficiently sensitive to the first century Jewish environment.[96] This is an important criticism: it points to recent trends in historical Jesus research which have sought to investigate and situate Jesus more fully against his first century Jewish environment,[97] which very thing Schillebeeckx prides himself on doing.

Schillebeeckx has certainly welcomed criticism from professional exegetes, and has changed emphases between his books *Jesus* and *Christ*. Nevertheless, he does not think that specific exegetical difficulties threaten to undermine his work while they remain minor. He does not feel that substantive problems have been brought to light.[98]

It is also possible to discern some features of the nineteenth century quest in Schillebeeckx's work. It is clear, for instance, that the self-understanding of Jesus is *very* important, despite his claims not to depend on Jesus' psychology. Gerald O'Collins points to the importance of psychological speculation in the first Jesus book, in which Jesus was described as "no fanatic" (301), "rational and purposeful" (299) and as having a particular attitude toward his death, seen as a service to God and humanity (311).[99] This psychological undercurrent in the work of Schillebeeckx, and especially in his placing a distinctive "abba relationship" at the center of his claims for Jesus' uniqueness, recalls the emphasis of Schleiermacher, for whom Jesus' uniqueness lay in the depth and extent of his God consciousness. Another feature of the nineteenth century quest, which Schillebeeckx's "new quest" approach has not been able to remove to the satisfaction of all critics, is the projecting of contemporary traits and preoccupations onto the figure of Jesus. Has the "liberal Protestant face" of Jesus from the nineteenth century quest (in reality, a projection onto Jesus of the quester's own face) become a twentieth century face in

Schillebeeckx's portrayal of Jesus? While admitting that something like this is probably inevitable, nevertheless Rosemary Radford Ruether accuses Schillebeeckx of creating an eirenic, apolitical Jesus in his own image—one who does not stand out in his environment (a foil to the punchy, unclassifiable figure "discovered" by that apparently more combatitive personality, Hans Küng).[100] That Louis Dupré could make substantially the same criticism, while finding a more political, radical Jesus in the work of Schillebeeckx, is explained by the fact that he had read *Christ* (where Ruether at the time of her criticism had not) in which Schillebeeckx was offering something far closer to liberation theology (as well as a critical edge with respect to the Roman hierarchy), compared with what went before.[101]

"From an historical standpoint," writes Richard, concerning Jesus as he appears in Schillebeeckx's work, "it is impossible to determine whether a human being bound by time and history has a universal definitive and distinctive significance for all human beings."[102] Richard knows that Schillebeeckx is aware of this and that he does not attempt such an historical proof, nor will Schillebeeckx argue for the uniqueness of Christianity based on comparison with other religions, as Küng attempts in *On Being a Christian* (1974). But Philip Kennedy, in his comprehensive and most sympathetic study, is concerned that Schillebeeckx *still* claims too much about Jesus on the basis of his self-understanding and his subsequent impact. Regarding the importance for Schillebeeckx of Jesus' alleged unique closeness to God, Kennedy replies that a "rationalist in the line of Lessing ... could claim that Jesus was a self-deluded megalomaniac"; concerning Jesus' unique impact on his followers, Kennedy replies to Schillebeeckx that "a rationalist skeptic could point out that many figures in history have had legions of followers. Yet their lives and conduct need not be of perduring significance for all people at all times."[103] This seems to me a fair criticism, and it would be terminal for Schillebeeckx's efforts were he not equally committed to other grounds for Jesus' uniqueness and finality. To an evaluation of these other bases we now turn.[104]

The human condition is the other major feature of Schillebeeckx's argument, with Jesus uniquely ministering to the fact of human suffering. I have two questions here. First, *has* Schillebeeckx shown just *why* it is that Jesus is the unique answer to this universal human predicament? His invocation of a range of anthropological constants, and an elaboration of his ideas about suffering, are evident in the book *Christ*, but their juxtaposition leaves the human dilemma as he sees it rather unclear from one who so confidently asserts the appearance of a unique solution to that dilemma in the person of Jesus. The other question concerns the adequacy of "suffering" as a universal human norm. Surely there is more to suffering than its physical component; suffering is a function of our whole person, a spiritual reality, and so I suggest there are *more fundamental* human needs and structures which underlie it. In this regard, critics have suggested that Schillebeeckx has underrated human guilt, which they see as an equally likely contender for this human norm, insofar as he has underrated the death of Jesus in his theology.[105] Perhaps Schillebeeckx might answer that the root causes of suffering *are* many, and too culturally diverse for any one of them to constitute a universal fact of human experience, yet at the once removed level of suffering there *is* some universality of experience.

In downplaying Jesus' death and resurrection, Schillebeeckx's work is, of course, distinctive. "In many traditional Christologies either the death of Jesus or his resurrection was taken to be the point of disjunction or discontinuity," writes Joseph Ramisch, "and it is precisely that position that Schillebeeckx has worked to reverse through his historical approach to Jesus."[106] Nevertheless the death of Jesus is very central in the New Testament, so that declaring Jesus' life to be salvific *despite* his death does not address the singular emphasis on that death found throughout the various strands of New Testament tradition.[107] Others go beyond this avoidance of obvious exegetical facts to ask about the downplaying of atonement in Schillebeeckx's theology. Should he not make more of the saving impact of Jesus' death as the New Testament and the tradition clearly see it, and as the human dilemma might well demand?

In concluding this discussion of Jesus' uniqueness and finality in the thought of Edward Schillebeeckx, it is worth noting what an improvement his program constitutes in the face of much that has come before us in this study.

Schillebeeckx has all the realism represented by theology of hope, as we found it in Moltmann, though he grounds this hope in human experience rather than in a positivism of revelation, for which Moltmann was criticized in Chapter 1, above. Schillebeeckx also recognizes the demand for a savior as integral to the human condition, along with Rahner, though he avoids Rahner's failure to account for more recent post-modern uncertainties concerning that human condition. Schillebeeckx knows, as does Pannenberg, that no account of Jesus' uniqueness and finality can disregard the resurrection, and like Pannenberg he knows that access to the resurrection is through the faith of earliest Christianity. But unlike Pannenberg he does not argue for the unquestioned historicity of Jesus' resurrection on this basis; rather, he admits that it is a complex and metahistorical reality. Schillebeeckx also acknowledges the role of *contemporary* church experience in accounting for resurrection belief, and for faith in Jesus as a whole; this is not what we find in Pannenberg, however, whose recalcitrance in this regard, as pointed out by van Beeck, was discussed in Chapter 5 above.

It bears mention that Schillebeeckx has taken more trouble over matters of exegesis than *anyone else* discussed in this study— Kasper and Schoonenberg, not to mention Rahner, do not match him in this regard; he is certainly more exegetically effective than Moltmann tried to be in *The Way of Jesus Christ*; and his historical-critical program is vastly more thorough and problem-free than that of Pannenberg in *Jesus—God and Man*, whose whole approach was seen to falter if questioned too closely over the understanding of apocalyptic it presupposed (and this despite questions raised about Schillebeeckx having underrated the importance of Jesus' death in the New Testament).

Nevertheless there remains a major weakness, albeit a simple one: Schillebeeckx does not say just *why* it is that Jesus is the unique minister to universal human suffering, even if he has begun to build a case for the fundamental and universal nature of that suffering. Schillebeeckx has addressed the problem of fragile humanity before God, offering Jesus as the unique solution to it, without *really* saying just *why* it is that *Jesus* is unique and final, and not another.

So to Hans Küng we now turn. He is not of Schillebeeckx's obvious exegetical caliber, but his *On Being a Christian* (1974) at least *tries* to answer this question of "why?" by *comparing* Jesus' person and praxis with various alternatives, both religious and secular.[108]

HANS KÜNG

Hans Küng is a quintessential occupant of my Position 3, as defined in this study. The historical Jesus and the world of human experience are critically correlated in his theological method. What is more, the comparison between Jesus' life and what is offered by other religious leaders and secular world-views—a comparison studiously avoided by everyone else encountered in this study apart from Robinson—forms the centerpiece of his most popular and influential book, *On Being a Christian* (1974). Indeed, as Richard observes, "The whole thrust of Küng's *On Being a Christian* is to prove that it is better to be a Christian than anything else."[109]

Küng's career as a Roman Catholic theologian has been brilliant and particularly controversial.[110] He was born at Sursee, near Lucerne, in 1928, commencing at Rome in 1948 a rigorous seven years of priestly formation at the Collegium Germanicum and the Pontifical Gregorian University. This intense neo-scholastic education, conducted in Latin and involving much rote learning, coincided with the zenith of papal authority in the person of Pius XII, toward whom the youthful Küng was initially a loyal enthusiast. His disillusionment grew in time, however, as he witnessed the neo-scholastic triumph of *Humani Generis* (1951), the suppression of the French worker priests (1953), and the infallible declaration of Mary's assumption into heaven (1954), all of which began to strike him as reactionary, fearful, anti-modern and anti-ecumenical.

The radical, vivifying spirit of *nouvelle théologie* was in the air, however, and Küng breathed it in as did Rahner and Schillebeeckx before him; Küng knew Yves Congar during his student years in Rome, where this great theologian had chosen to live out his silencing and exile from France. While in Rome the promising student tutored in Marxist thought and sociology, commencing also the study of Barth which bore fruit in his famous doctoral thesis on justification which Küng completed during a year and a half at the Sorbonne and the Institut Catholique in Paris, where he was sent after his ordination in Rome. This attempt at reconciliation between Barth and Trent on justification, soon to be published,[111] both established Küng's ecumenical commitment and led to the commencement of his dossier at the Sacred Congregation for the Doctrine of the Faith.

In the lead-up to the council Küng began writing on the church, in the light of the historical emphasis he had learned from *nouvelle théologie*, while fitting in a curacy in Switzerland and a year assisting Hermann Volk at the University of Münster, followed by a move to the chair of Roman Catholic theology in Tübingen at the age of 32.

His works on the church and authority multiplied through the 1960s, during which time he was both an official theologian (*peritus*) in Rome for Vatican II and a controversial figure in the United States, where a notorious lecture tour featured various bans and lockouts from Roman Catholic universities. Despite popular support and help from a number of prelates, Küng was censured by the Sacred Congregation in 1968 over his book *The Church* and more severely in 1971 over his assault on the hierarchy in *Infallible*.[112] It was *On Being a Christian* (1974) which sealed his fate, however, despite attempted clarifications of his Christological position in *Does God Exist?* (1976) and an appeal.[113] The price Küng paid for his forthrightness was the removal of his *missio canonica* in 1979, and hence his right to teach in the Roman Catholic Theology Faculty at Tübingen, though this carefully orchestrated maneuver was partially thwarted when a post as Professor of Dogmatic and Ecumenical Theology in an independent institute was made available to him, along with certain visiting professorships in the United States.

Küng's troubles with Rome have been put down to the popularity of his books—*On Being a Christian* sold hundreds of thousands of copies worldwide—and hence the dangers he poses to those outside a traditional theological readership.[114] Others have found Küng to be an ecclesiastical provocateur. Nevertheless, outside the world of Roman Catholic theology as it is circumscribed by the fathers of the Sacred Congregation, Küng continues as perhaps the world's most popular and influential theologian today, both inside and outside the Roman Catholic world.

Since 1979 Küng has further developed his systematic treatment of central doctrinal matters with a more recent shift of attention to methodological issues, to the paradigmatic nature of theological truth and doctrinal development, to a search for criteria of truth and ethics in a post-modern world and to new departures in a more pluralist direction regarding world religions (of which more later).[115]

In an essay first appearing in 1985, Küng enlightens us much about his approach, his priorities and his underlying assumptions. He rejects, for instance, the sort of grand system-building we have met already with the likes of Pannenberg, preferring flexibility and the capacity to incorporate new insights (182). He names Karl Rahner as a great inspiration, for whom dogmas could be completely rebuilt while maintaining their literal form. To witness this remarkable dialectical juggling act is one of the great joys of reading Rahner, and depending on one's theological tastes it can be either delightful or infuriating. For Küng it came to be inadequate, because he came to doubt whether the plain meaning of official texts could be bent in the way Rahner bent them (as we saw him do, for instance, when he sought to broaden traditional exclusive language into the inclusivistic, eirenic doctrine of "anonymous Christianity").[116] Of course, Küng has his own form of dialectic—a more straightforwardly Hegelian one,[117] seeking always a synthesis beyond thesis and antithesis. As with Roman Catholic and Protestant doctrines on justification, then, so with Christianity and any other conversation partner in the world of religions, Küng does not see positions as fixed and mutually exclusive, but as stations on the way to a synthesis preserving the best features of both.[118]

Küng eventually moved away from Rahner, for, in the light of Rahner's maintaining the natural/supernatural distinction (and falling in with the Curia over the matter of papal infallibility), Küng was able "to recognize him for what he was, the last great (and stimulating) Neo-Scholastic" (188). He goes on to indicate his indebtedness to Barth who, it appears, helped Küng cut the nerve of his neo-scholastic schooling. From Barth, in turn, Küng was returned to a proper Catholic affirmation of a point of contact between humanity and God by Bonhoeffer, who rejected Barth's "positivism of revelation."[119]

Though he had as a student attended lectures by the outstanding exegete Stanislas Lyonnet (later silenced), Küng was little schooled in historical critical biblical studies before arriving to teach in Germany. There he studied Bultmann, whose commitment to existentialist readings of the human condition, the centrality of the kerygma as the point of Christianity and evangelical commitment to demythologizing Küng appears to have largely absorbed, though he preferred the position of Käsemann when it came to the historical Jesus.[120] Nevertheless, Küng does not embrace the new quest's strong link between the historical Jesus and the Christ of faith—a link particularly evident in Schillebeeckx; instead, he maintains something of a distinction between the two figures in the nineteenth century liberal manner, as we shall see.

The resulting method is one of attending both to the horizon of human experience and the historical Jesus, who *in person* is identified as the Christian message and program. This is a method of correlation similar to that of Schillebeeckx and Tracy, though distinguished from that of Tillich, who severed the "new being" from the historical Jesus. As we shall see, Küng is no naive exponent of enlightenment rationalism in his addressing of the human condition, having learned post-modern lessons. Nevertheless a definite profile of the human condition does emerge in his works, to which the historical Jesus uniquely ministers.

In *On Being a Christian* (1974) Hans Küng seeks to discover the deep needs of the human, and the way these are met by the God disclosed in the life of Jesus, as it emerges from a critical reading of the New Testament.

He composes his picture of the human condition against the backdrop of allegedly liberating options in the contemporary world such as capitalism and technological progress, socialism, and the major world faiths like Buddhism and Islam, all with an eye to the history of suffering and the widespread experience of alienation characteristic of this century in the west. What he seeks to offer is a humanism superior to any other on offer.

Like Schillebeeckx he makes much of human suffering, and this no doubt emerges from the same source—the critical theory of the Frankfurt school. But unlike Schillebeeckx he adds guilt, alienation and despair to the fact of suffering (298, 579), seeing them as equally fundamental.[121] Thus, inspired by existentialism, he speaks of the human dilemma known to all religions, of "man's alienation, enslavement, need of redemption," of "man's loneliness, addiction, abandonment, lack of freedom, his abysmal fear, anxiety, his selfish ways and his masks" and this in addition to "the unutterable suffering, the misery of this unredeemed world and the sense and nonsense of death" (92).

Küng is at pains to deny that this is any "simple concept of an immutable, universal human nature," however, preferring to start from the dynamic, changeable, complex and at least partly self-directing world in which we actually live, and from the human and social sciences which have arisen to describe it—"These sciences offer an increasing abundance of assured anthropological conclusions and information relevant for action" (516). Thus, while insisting on human autonomy and responsibility in the wake of the enlightenment, Küng still manages to find a constant and explicable human essence by pragmatic means, and one no less uniform because he sees it as a matter of probability (539) rather than one fixed and eternal.[122]

The need for meaning and basic certainty is very central to Küng's definition of the human (75). At the center of his apologetic is a belief that humans operate with a "basic trust in reality." "Any assumption of meaning, truth and rationality," he writes, "of values and ideals, priorities and...norms presupposes a *basic trust in reality*: in which man rejects nihilism, accepts reality in principle" (534). And it is this human *factum* of basic trust which most clearly raises the question of God for Küng, for whom "whenever, even in a purely immanent humanism [such as he seeks in fidelity to the enlightenment], something like unconditionality is postulated in the light of man's freedom...his openness to the future, there is in fact a reference to that ultimate dimension of unconditionality as the condition of possibility, even though it is not named" (535). Thus, like Kant (535), he comes at the question of God via practical rather than pure reason, for there are no proofs of God in Küng's schema.

For Küng the fundamental human longings which Horkheimer (436) and existentialism identify can only be met by God; he lays the typical neuroses of our society at the feet of the decline of religion, apart from which Küng does not believe that humans will thrive (59). Küng hinges his view of the human on the insight that "if man wants to realize himself at all, if as a person he wants to gain freedom, identity, meaning, happiness, he can do so only in absolute trust in him who is able to give him all this. Man's basic trust seems in the best sense to be "sublimated" in trust in God..." (588). This experience of wholeness "is based, as the psychology of religion makes clear, on an empirical unity of knowing, willing and feeling, which is understood not as our own achievement but as a response to an encounter with God" (80-81). Thus Küng sees the human condition as fundamentally incomplete, apart from its vivification and "salvation" by God: "The Christian element," he writes, "is neither a superstructure nor a substructure of the human. It is an elevation or—better—a transfiguration of the human, at once preserving, cancelling, surpassing the human" (602). So it is that Jesus is the savior of humanity for Küng, because he brings about the emergence of a new humanity, "a different, a new man: a radically changed awareness, a fundamentally different attitude, completely new orientation in thought and action" (249). Yet this is not to say that Jesus brings a different human condition from the existing one; *rather, he brings the present one to perfection in himself and as gift and task among his followers.* This is why Küng believes Christianity is the best humanism, for it best solves the human dilemma as he sees it—releasing people for a true humanity rather than creating for them something new and altogether different. In this light Küng's memorable concluding comments are to be understood:

> So we have asked: why should one be a Christian? The answer will certainly be understood now if we reduce it to a brief recapitulatory formula:
>
> > *By following Jesus Christ*
> > *man in the world of today*
> > *can truly humanly live, act, suffer and die:*
> > *in happiness and unhappiness, life and death,*
> > *sustained by God and helpful to men* (602).

The question for us, now that we have analyzed Küng's understanding of the human condition, is: Why is it that the historical Jesus uniquely ministers to that condition, bringing it to fullness?

Before even discussing the details of the historical Jesus as Küng understands him, the simple *fact* of Jesus' life in its particularity is central for Küng's understanding of Jesus' uniqueness and finality. He makes much of Christianity's perennial attention to Jesus' *irreplaceable person*—that it is not simply a world-view or an idealism (120, 123). This is one reason why Küng refuses Rahner's theory of "anonymous Christianity": "Christianity cannot be reduced or 'raised' to a nameless—that is, anonymous—Christianity" (126). So with a similar anti-idealist emphasis to that of Hans Frei (see Chapter 1, above), Küng states that "Jesus himself in person is the *program* of Christianity" (174). For Küng this individual, historical focus constitutes a great strength of Christianity today, in the face of other claims more universal and abstract (411): "As a concrete, historical person, Jesus possesses an *impressiveness* which is missing in an eternal idea, an abstract principle, a universal norm, a conceptual system... Jesus possesses an *audibility* which makes ideas, principles, norms and systems appear to be mute" (546, 547).

Küng constructs his historical Jesus without attempting to offer a psychological profile (318), as was ostensibly the case with Schillebeeckx. Regarding the "abba relationship," which was most important for Schillebeeckx, Küng admits of its authenticity and distinctiveness but does not grant it special emphasis alongside many other aspects of Jesus which he finds rare and noteworthy (314). Nevertheless Küng *does* point to Jesus' special relationship to God in which "his basic attitude is rooted, an attitude which can be described in one word: his *freedom*, which is infectious and opens up for the individual and for society in their one-dimensionality a *really different dimension*, a real alternative with different norms, values and ideals" (317).[123]

Küng's portrayal of Jesus is woven together with his description of the Christian ethical and political task (which he conceives on the basis that Jesus *in person* is the Christian program).[124] His Jesus is neither priest nor theologian (178), but rather a public storyteller (179). His Jesus had no sympathy with the conservative law, aristocracy or government nor, on the other hand, with Hellenistic open-mindedness (180). No sweet romantic or stolid ecclesiastic, he was close to being a revolutionary (186), though for Küng the story of Jesus' temptations points to his rejection of political messianism (188). His revolution was a non-violent one, changing human nature (191). Küng's Jesus bears no taint of "gloomy social-revolutionary abstemiousness" (190).

All in all, writes Küng, "even though the Gospels provide no insight into [Jesus'] psyche... they do show that his outward behaviour cannot exactly be described as "normal" in the light of behaviour patterns of the time" (193).[125] As Küng sees him, Jesus

had not played any of the expected roles: for those who
supported law and order he turned out to be a provocateur, dangerous to the system. He disappointed the activist revolutionaries by his non-violent love of peace. On
the other hand he offended the passive world forsaking
ascetics by his uninhibited worldliness. And for the devout who adapted themselves to the world he was too un-
compromising. For the silent majority he was too noisy
and for the noisy minority he was too quiet, too gentle for
the strict and too strict for the gentle. He was an obvious
outsider in a critically dangerous social conflict: in opposition both to the prevailing conditions and to those who
opposed them (278).

Regarding Jesus' death Küng is certain, as was Schillebeeckx,
that Jesus expected it and worked it into his program, the last supper accounts being understood as pointing to this (321-24). But
where Schillebeeckx saw nothing positive in suffering, and hence
made little of Jesus' death, Küng is far more fulsome. He is willing
to acknowledge the possibility of growth through suffering. But in
arguing this it is largely by comparison with what can be known of
the deaths of other religious leaders and great men. And here, in
this program of comparison with alternative beliefs and persons,
we move toward the heart of Küng's case for Jesus' uniqueness and
finality.[126]
The message and praxis of Jesus is universally accessible, according to Küng; it is not for superior people, as he sees Confucian-
ism to be, nor chiefly for a monastic community as in Buddhism, nor
is it a matter of caste, as in Hinduism (267). It is not exclusive in the
sense that Jesus merely pointed a way that others might follow, as
did the Buddha—for Küng, it is possible that Jesus *himself* sent out
disciples. He also points to Jesus' insistence upon love of enemies
(258-59), just as he points to the absence of any prophetic call in
Jesus' life, as we find with Moses, Muhammad and the prophets
(286)—these, too, are unique features.
In making much of Jesus' manner of death, in comparison with
that of other religious leaders, Küng employs a once popular apologetic, now fallen on hard (post-modern) times:

Anyone who thinks that all religions and their "founders" are alike will see the *differences* which appear if he compares the deaths of such men. Moses, Buddha, Confucius, all died at a ripe old age, successful despite many disappointments, in the midst of their disciples and supporters, their "span of life completed" like the patriarchs of Israel. According to the tradition, Moses died in sight of the promised land, in the midst of his people, at the age of 120 years, his eyes undimmed, his vigour unfaded. Buddha died at the age of eighty, peacefully, his disciples around him.... Confucius... spent his last years in training a group of mainly noble disciples, to preserve and continue his work.... Muhammad, after he had thoroughly enjoyed the last years of his life as political ruler of Arabia, died in the midst of his harem in the arms of his favourite wife.

Here on the other hand we have a young man of thirty, after three years at most of activity, perhaps only a few months. Expelled from society, betrayed and denied by his disciples and supporters, mocked and ridiculed by his opponents, forsaken by men and even by God, he goes through a ritual of death that is one of the most atrocious and enigmatic ever invented by man's ingenious cruelty (334-35).

Further, Küng claims that Jesus enjoys a different bond with his followers than that enjoyed by those with other allegiances.

Why did there arise that bond to the master which is so very different from the bonds of other movements to the personalities of their founders, as for instance of Marxists to Marx or enthusiastic Freudians to Freud? Why is Jesus not merely venerated, studied and followed as the founder and teacher who lived years ago, but—especially in the worshipping congregation—proclaimed as alive and known as the one who is active in the present time? How did the extraordinary idea arise that he himself leads his followers, his community, through his Spirit? (345).

The answer to this question is to be found in Küng's analysis of Jesus' resurrection, which is closely related to what he has to say about Jesus' ongoing impact on his followers.[127]

The resurrection is a real event, and crucial,[128] so that for Küng "Christian faith stands or falls with the evidence of Jesus' resurrection, without which there is no content to Christian preaching or even faith" (346). He sees the appearance traditions as the nub of it all, and with Schillebeeckx views them as vocational, like the call of the Old Testament prophets (376)—"Reality and significance are therefore one in the resurrection" (378-79). Yet the status of Jesus' body in the resurrection is unclear for Küng. He goes as far as we have seen Moltmann and Schoonenberg go in denying that the resurrection requires any corporeal element, pointing out that the New Testament word *soma* means more than the physical body only, but the whole self with its history. So Küng can allow "that the *crucified lives forever with God, as obligation and hope for us*" (356) and that "In death and from death he *died into* and was *taken up* by that *incomprehensible and comprehensive ultimate reality* which we designate by the name of God" (358) while requiring "no continuity of the body: questions of natural science, like that of the persistence of the molecules, do not arise."[129]

So the resurrection is of first importance in establishing Küng's claims for Jesus but, as with Schillebeeckx, this is a matter of affirming Jesus' completed life, rather than providing additional revelation beyond that found within Jesus' life. For both theologians it is a matter of asserting that Jesus' life and praxis are unique and final. For Küng, "Jesus' assumption into the life of God therefore does not bring the revelation of additional truths, but the revelation of Jesus himself: he now acquires final credibility" (383). Obviously, without the resurrection Jesus would have no finality for Küng, who is in this sense typical of all those treated in this study who retain Jesus' uniqueness and finality.

We have seen Küng's comparison of Jesus' life and death with those of other leaders religious and secular. This he continues in similar terms discussing Jesus' unique impact: "this one man has so changed the course of history that with good reason people began to date the years of the world from his birth," writes Küng, pointing out by contrast the limited scope of Jesus' ministry in space and time and life experience. "And yet how great his influence has been," he writes; "every fourth human being, about a thousand million human beings, are called Christians. Numerically, Christianity is well ahead of all world religions" (149). Küng asks how it was that the condemned heretic became messiah in the minds of his followers, becoming in person, and so quickly, the center of proclamation—"not only the Gospel of Jesus, but Jesus himself as the Gospel" (344). He asks how the movement survived the crushing failure and ignominy of Jesus' death, allowing the church "to explain the shameful gallows as a sign of salvation and to turn the obvious bankruptcy of the movement into its phenomenal new emergence?" (344). In particular, Küng points to the power of the gospel to transform suffering, robbing it of its absolute status and even turning it into an opportunity for hope and freedom (579). All of this he sees as adequate proof for the uniqueness and finality of Jesus as God's instrument for revelation and salvation, seen at the same time as the perfecting of humanity.

In Küng's own words, in which he interprets the credal orthodoxy of Jesus as both God and man:

> All statements about divine sonship, pre-existence, creation mediatorship and incarnation—often clothed in the mythological or semi-mythological forms of the time— are meant in the last resort to do no more and no less than substitute the uniqueness, underivability and unsurpassability of the call, offer and claim made known in and with Jesus, ultimately not of human but of divine origin and therefore absolutely reliable, requiring man's unconditional involvement.... As true man, by his proclamation, behaviour and fate, he was a model of what it is to be human, enabling each and everyone who commits himself to him to discover and to realize the meaning of being man and of his freedom to exist for his fellow men. As confirmed by God, he therefore represents the permanently reliable ultimate standard of human existence (449-50).

One might summarize Küng's position on Jesus' uniqueness and finality in *On Being a Christian* as follows: *the historically verifiable (and hence "real") person of Jesus, in himself constituting the Christian vision and program, uniquely solves the human dilemma compared with other leaders and their programs, showing himself uniquely close to God and humanity, which he entered into so deeply that he disclosed through the ongoing impact of his life, death and resurrection hitherto unrealized and subsequently unsurpassed possibilities and freedoms.*

There are some related exegetical and theological problems with Küng's program in *On Being a Christian*. These concern the thoroughness and the rightness of his portrayal of the historical Jesus, along with the possibility and the necessity of asserting Jesus' uniqueness in the way he has.[130]

We recall the criticism of Rosemary Radford Ruether that the Jesus of *On Being a Christian* reflects Küng's own personality and anti-hierarchical ecclesial concerns, as the figure portrayed in Schillebeeckx's *Jesus* portrays Schillebeeckx's concerns.[131] Meier agrees that Küng's Jesus is personally colored, but this in the context of a far graver concern; he makes the obvious, though nonetheless telling, criticism that Küng takes insufficient care and invokes not nearly enough detailed argument in his reconstruction of Jesus' historical person.[132] Nowhere in *On Being a Christian* are Küng's criteria of historicity set out in full, and hardly anywhere are they explicitly employed. The book reads like a piece of popular liberation theology in this sense, with insufficient justification for the choices of this or that phrase or incident as historical. Küng appears to read the historical Jesus "off the surface" of the gospel, rather than delving into the text in the manner of Schillebeeckx, for whom the criteria of historicity are clear and everywhere employed.[133]

As for what Küng does with the historical Jesus whom he recovers, there are problems with his use of comparison. Paul Knitter challenges Küng over his assessment of Jesus alongside other religious leaders, asking whether these others might be seen as unique and final in their own cultural orbit; he wonders whether today's absence of those pressures which made Christianity sectarian and defensive in its early centuries might not allow a more pluralist Christianity to emerge in our day, as it might have done from the beginning had Christianity grown up in the more syncretistic culture of India, say.[134] Of course, Küng's whole argument in *On Being a Christian* is that humanity today is so compromised that *only* the Christian vision, embodied in Jesus, will suffice to deliver it, and not any tolerant pluralism akin to that offered by Knitter.

But can such a comparison work? It is now generally accepted that cultures form more or less self-contained units or *Gestalten* which cannot be compared willy-nilly; success in one culture may be regarded as weakness in another, for instance, as is often witnessed. Knitter and those prone to cultural relativism simply deny that there are underlying human norms which can be appealed to in this regard, as we shall see in Chapter 10 below. Even a Roman Catholic theologian like David Tracy, whose method is similar to that of Küng (who has also collaborated with him, and defended him against the Vatican), is nevertheless unconvinced by anything but purely existential arguments (here read "subjective") for Christian "decisiveness":

> For the fundamental theologian, to show that decisiveness—or, in the more classical terms, that "finality"—more historically would demand, I believe, a dialectical analysis of Christianity in relationship to the other world religions: a task which would demand a full-fledged use of history of religions...and would, in the final analysis, prove a theological task whose successful completion would require a complete Christian dogmatics....[135]

Of course, Küng would want to suggest that this is just what he has attempted to do in *On Being a Christian*. But his assessment of the human condition, upon which so much depends, would strike many as no more than an existentially inspired and, hence, quite relative cultural product of the modern west.

Even so, it is still a matter of contention whether and to what extent Küng has been able to establish Jesus' uniqueness and finality *even within the purview of his own system*. In their surveys of the whole field of recent Christology and theology of religions, both Gerald O'Collins and Lucien Richard raise this concern. For O'Collins, Küng is unable to assert anything more than a difference in degree be-

tween Jesus and others—certainly not a difference in kind.[136] Richard
agrees, for whom Küng's "historical and inductive methods cannot
establish the normativity of Jesus Christ; they cannot establish why it
is Jesus who becomes God's representative rather than another."[137] In
fairness to Küng it is important to point out what many critics fail to
see: that it is *not* just Jesus' history which establishes his uniqueness
and finality for Küng, but only when that history is combined with his
assessment of the human condition, further supported by claims for
the unique impact of Jesus upon his followers and the world, which in
turn are largely a function of his resurrection.

Yet even if this is conceded, it is not by any means certain that
Küng has established Jesus' finality or unique impact. It is dangerous to argue, for instance, that Christianity is superior because its
adherents numerically exceed those of other religions (149). The
current increase of militant Islam throughout the middle east, In-
donesia and in the southern Republics of the former Soviet Union
raises the prospect that, one day, Christianity might not be numerically superior—in such a world, Muhammad might be declared
unique and final if this were the only criterion (this shows one danger in any comparative approach, according to which Jesus' uniqueness and finality is a quantitative matter only, and not a qualitative
one). Consider, too, that the other religions have evolved much, and
might further evolve to the extent that one day Küng's unfavorable
comparisons would lose their force. Thus one takes a risk in linking
the uniqueness and finality of Jesus to the fortunes of the religion
which bears his name. One might add that any case emphasizing
Jesus' impact on his followers ought not to be content with comparing Jesus in the full panoply of his effects, on the one hand, to other
religious founders in their particularity alone, deprived of the testimony of their followers. Surely the comparison should take into account their impact as well.

Whatever he has failed to achieve in making a watertight case
for Jesus' uniqueness and finality, Küng has certainly offered an un-
forgettable portrait of Jesus in *On Being a Christian*. Obviously this
figure recalls the Jesus found in Bornkamm and Käsemann, as Meier
points out,[138] and yet even critics testify to the power and vividness
of this figure.

The concrete Jesus who appears in these pages is more real than the persons we meet each day, more ideal than the best characters of fiction. It is true that at times Küng engages in exaggeration, in one-sidedness, and in broadsides against hierarchs. Without doubt, this displeases some who are seeking a calm, dispassionate and scientific account of the master. However, once one accepts the fact that Küng is writing in order to bring a person alive for modern man, one can begin to see in his rhetoric a device for conveying with feeling and emotion the passionate and vibrant vitality of the man who was Jesus Christ.[139]

In this chapter we have moved away from the idealist metaphysics encountered in Part II above, toward approaches adhering more closely to Jesus' person and his impact upon others. To be sure, the "Logos" theology of Schoonenberg and Robinson was more metaphysical in its interests than the work of Schillebeeckx and Küng was found to be, though all in all their attention to the life and ministry of Jesus and to the human condition as he illuminated it makes Schoonenberg and Robinson sit far more comfortably in the company of Schillebeeckx and Küng than they would with Kasper, Pannenberg and Rahner.[140]

A variety of emphases concerning the historical Jesus were unearthed throughout Part III, and different readings of what was deemed to be most central in human experience. Post-modern insights into cultural diversity were also found in abundance, though a definable human experience uniquely plumbed by Jesus remained prominent in varying degrees. In Robinson and Küng, too, we have rare attempts in the period of interest to offer a comparison between Jesus and other founders and leaders, sacred and secular, based on their human qualities.

The arguments for Jesus' uniqueness and finality considered throughout this chapter have been in the nature of cumulative cases, which have been found to involve some diffuseness of argument. As we have seen, a failure to be really explicit in this area has weakened both Schillebeeckx and Küng in the cases they have argued. The nature of that weakness is laid bare and much exploited by the "radical" theologians to be discussed in the next three chapters.

PART IV

RADICAL

Now I come to those here designated "radical"—the small, diverse though expanding cluster of theologians who reject belief in Jesus' uniqueness and finality. They are grouped according to three broad categories.

"Historical skeptics" are basically modernists seeking Christ's reality in the Christian present and wary of ascribing special importance to the historical Jesus or the period of Christian origins. Their awareness of cultural relativism is accompanied by a spirit of historical skepticism about the life of Jesus, along with an appreciation of "myth" as a respectable alternative to historical accounts in the mediation of religious meaning.

"Complete relativists" take these issues to what they see as their logical conclusion. The thinkers considered here deny any accessibility to the meaning of things in themselves apart from their interpretation. Condemned, therefore, to almost complete relativism they countenance no absolute uniqueness claim for Jesus or for the Christian religion.

"Religious pluralists" remain essentially liberal theologians at heart. Some of them still claim access to the historical Jesus and some to discern a human condition—the two poles of "liberal" approaches which I have identified. But they differ from most liberals in their primary attention to the issue of how Christianity should respond in the face of challenges to its belief from the other world religions. They are also united in rejecting exclusivist and inclusivist theories and thus Jesus' uniqueness and finality as well. The concerns of both "complete relativists" and "historical skeptics" are represented among them, but usually "religious pluralists" shy away from the relativism of the one and the agnostic spirit of the other.

Throughout these chapters, however, serious doubts will be raised about just how much of a threat these challenges might actually pose to a hermeneutically sophisticated "liberal" case for Jesus' uniqueness and finality.

Chapter Nine

HISTORICAL SKEPTICS

No one to be considered here denies that Jesus was wonderful, that his impact was and is astounding, and that his story is absolutely foundational for Christians. Uniqueness and finality claims are not countenanced, however—those to be considered here see such claims as derived from the faith of early Christianity rather than establishing it, as unsustainable in the face of cultural pluralism, and even as unnecessary if divine action in history is understood as all-pervading, rather than focused at one particular high point (as Wiles would have it). The most they will say is that Jesus is unique for Christians, but this is an intra-ecclesial confession only, rather than an objective reality. Hints of liberal theology remain, however, as in the rather uniform trans-cultural idea of God we find here, conceived along enlightenment lines. This chink, admitting liberal-type arguments, is found throughout Part IV; it will be pried open in the Conclusion, to follow.

DENNIS NINEHAM AND JOHN BOWDEN

Dennis Nineham, a former Warden of Keble College and professor at London, Cambridge and Bristol Universities, continues to write theology in his retirement. His portrait, prominent in Hall at Keble, captures strikingly his rare position in England as both senior churchman and theological radical: the standard conservative foreground has Nineham kneeling at a prayer desk in scarf and hood while, in the background, an expressionist painting dominates. Nineham's radicalism is particularly sharp over issues considered in this study.

With his "Epilogue" to Hick's symposium *The Myth of God Incarnate* (1977) Nineham first led me to ask whether, in maintaining their belief in the uniqueness and finality of Jesus' historical person and work, despite their revising of Christological dogma, many of today's theologians have failed to deal adequately with modern historical consciousness and its concomitant cultural relativism. Ronald Preston observes that for his trouble, both in this "Epilogue" and in *The Use and Abuse of the Bible* (1976), Nineham has come to be seen as a bogey man, more abused than heard.[1] Yet as Nineham has quite rightly maintained from the beginning, though his approach may seem startling he is only conveying what has long been recognized in New Testament studies.[2]

For Robert Morgan the publication of Nineham's commentary *Saint Mark* in 1963 constituted a watershed in English religious thought, insofar as the German historical critical tradition had never been brought home so forcibly to theology[3] (contrary to Morgan, Nineham himself thinks it was John A.T. Robinson's *Honest to God*, from the same year, which performed this service).[4] The contribution of this "boat rocker" in English New Testament studies is assayed appreciatively by Don Cupitt for a commemorative number of the journal *Theology*.[5] There we read of Nineham's emphasis on the historicity of Christianity beyond any talk of timeless essences *à la* Hegel, any "religion of love" as conceived by Schweitzer, or any Bultmannian "doctrine of man." For Cupitt, Nineham has consistently attacked the typically English fondness for reading back any such developed orthodoxy into the New Testament. The implications of this approach for the issue of establishing Jesus' uniqueness and finality will be addressed in what follows.

First, let it be said that Nineham has no doubt that Jesus' life was of sufficient impact to produce the results it did in the life and writings of earliest Christianity. His point, however, is that we cannot know how. The New Testament speaks of the matter in first century terms, most of which Nineham finds utterly foreign. At the same time his modern historical skepticism allows him very little from the gospels to build an alternative account.[6] In particular he is suspicious that the projection of modern ideals rather than valid historical reconstruction is behind granting Jesus titles like "'the man for others,' 'the one who was completely open to God and the future' (Bultmann), 'a man who dares to act in God's stead' (Fuchs) or 'the one in whom existence was completely transparent to essence' (Tillich)."[7] Similar titles are used throughout *The Myth of God Incarnate* as alleged improvements upon "orthodox" incarnational language, and they are conveniently listed by John Rodwell: "the 'as-if-God' (p.39), 'the unique focus of (man's) perception of and response to God' (p.42), '*the* man of universal destiny' (p.57), the exemplar of a faith based on 'homopraxis' (p.62), the proclaimer of the 'principles of Spirit' (p.209), 'God-acting-towards-mankind' and 'God-in-relation-to-man' (p.181)."[8] Nineham's concern in his "Epilogue" to that work is that his co-authors and others still claim a factual, historical basis for such assertions. He is too skeptical even for this liberal "act of faith."

Nineham cannot accept Hick's belief in the overwhelming God-consciousness of Jesus,[9] a belief no doubt redolent of Schleiermacher, nor that of John Robinson in Jesus as a vessel totally emptied of self and filled with God, nor Arthur Peacocke's (Teilhardian) assessment of Jesus as a new species of human (186-87). These English views, which would once have followed naturally from belief in the revealed truth of Jesus' literal divinity, now stand alone without dogmatic underpinning. But although it is no longer a revealed "given," incarnational belief is allowed to survive in such a perspective as a deduction from the alleged historically ascertainable facts about Jesus (188)—once incarnational belief gave rise to talk of Jesus' human perfections; now, belief in his human perfections gives rise to talk of his incarnation.

Yet Nineham cannot see how such "perfect humanity" could ever be historically discerned. He is convinced that despite the strong savor of consistency attending the character of Jesus in the gospels, full records and even constant observation throughout Jesus' life could never definitively establish his sinless perfection (188). Nor, following H.J. Cadbury and C.G. Montefiore, does Nineham see enough unambiguous evidence that Jesus himself followed the teachings ascribed to him (189-90). Instead, Nineham is concerned that Jesus' moral perfection went unquestioned by gospel writers because of its necessary place in vindicating their supernatural claims about Jesus. He questions, too, whether moral originality is not a modern category to which first century persons would not have been sensitive (193-94). And, regarding claims for the moral greatness of Jesus, Nineham recalls Schweitzer's warning that the wide cultural gap separating us from the first century might lead to our being struck, were we to meet Jesus today, by his strangeness rather than his greatness (195).

A solution is sought by focusing not upon "historical" (*historisch*) nor on "historic" (*geschichtlich*) knowledge, but on what Norman Perrin calls "faith knowledge." This grows not from history but from proclamation, developing from and itself developing the kerygma. Indeed myth and saga can ground such faith knowledge just as well as history can. And justifying it is simply a matter of pragmatic considerations: in terms of the ultimate reality it mediates, the faith, experience and praxis it enables etc. (198-99). Nineham thus shows himself rather Bultmannian in his recognition of the preached Christ as the primary reality for the many who are drawn to the figure of Christ and empowered thereby (200). Nevertheless he expressly rejects Bultmannian recourse to an unchangeable fundamental structure of human nature with which the kerygmatic Christ might resonate (200). Thus primary elements of the liberal Christologies examined above—those of a confidently reconstructed historical Jesus and a firmly established human nature—are both rejected by Nineham. He concludes the "Epilogue" with his view that it has only been an ever-changing Christ-image that has enabled new generations to find this faith knowledge (200). It is enough to say that through the historical Jesus, God has kindled much of humanity into a richly salvific relationship with himself (202-03). Nineham can even share Maurice Wiles' confidence that the link between historical Jesus and preached Christ will never be deformed to breaking point (200-01).[10] Yet this relationship cannot be probed. For Nineham, "God's secret" lies in the whole Christ event—a compound of fact and interpretation which will not yield up its indissolubility to historical method (203).

Nineham's views on cultural relativism also bear on the issue in question. In an historical age we have become increasingly aware that our understanding of things, including our science, morals, politics, rituals and religious beliefs, are conditioned by a dominant set of ideas undergirding our culture.[11] Languages have deep structures by which we are socialized into our culture's presuppositions about the way reality is to be divided and categorized.[12]

Throughout *The Use and Abuse of the Bible*, Nineham rejects any notion of universal human nature apart from such cultural conditioning. Although we have certain basic drives and urges, he sees these as relatively unspecialized and poorly programmed, so that a lot depends on the way we are led to understand and indeed to develop them.[13] Nineham finds these cultural determinants in all the things we are not disposed to question about our world-view—in R.G. Collingwood's "absolute presuppositions" and T.E. Hulme's "doctrines felt as facts."[14] Such totalities will not be readily explicable one to another, and to highlight this Nineham has his favorite quotes and illustrations. From the American literary critic Lionel Trilling he learns that "to suppose ... we can think like men of another time is as much an illusion as to suppose that we can think in a wholly different way,"[15] and from Charles Galton Darwin that "London in 1750 was far more like Rome in AD 100 than like either London or Rome in 1950."[16]

The differences between perceptions of things in various historical periods is illustrated in Nineham's comparison of various treatments for a collapse from what we would now call diabetic coma. In the first century an exorcist would be summoned, in the sixteenth a chirurgeon who would use a cupping glass for blood-letting and so restore the humors to balance, in the twentieth an injection would be given, and in the twenty fifth ... who knows?[17] He is, therefore, confident to say that what impressed people about Jesus in the first century may well fail to impress us today, and vice versa. Nineham emphasizes how distinct were first century cultures from our own (the "machine universe" of modernity, for instance, being conceivable only since large machines were available to provide the analogy, etc.).[18] So it is, therefore, that miracles and such-like are less believable now that we know more of what would be involved in them than our ancient forebears could have known. Clearly, then, there is a wide gap in how properly to interpret Jesus between ourselves and those whose cognitive spectacles were provided by credal orthodoxy—those Christians of the patristic era and since whose motives were those of *fides quaerens intellectum,* saving the literal truth of scripture and building a coherent system.[19] And before such relatively later doctrinal projections were made upon Jesus there were certainly lineaments of first century Jewish culture along which the figure of Jesus in the gospels was constructed.[20] Viewing him as they did, there was much the early church would not have questioned, including his sinlessness and the literal truth of all he said.[21] For Nineham, too, it is hard to know whether Jesus claimed to be the Son of God, or if such words were only put on his lips once the belief had arisen.[22] Neither can the history of Jesus and the story of God sending his Son to fulfill the Jewish expectations be separated in the gospels, for this was not an age of objective, modern historiography.[23] Nineham decides that even the notion of a unique divine intervention may reflect nothing more than Jewish apocalyptic expectations which modern westerners cannot be expected to share. Wiles and Young agree on this point.[24]

But if we cannot justify literal readings in the gospel accounts of Jesus, neither will Nineham allow us to modernize the figure met there—we must not assume that someone from a past cultural totality will appeal to our own, and especially if the God behind it all is thought to be faithful to the historical character of his creation,[25] and hence a respecter of the closed nature of various historical totalities. So Nineham, while sympathetic to Bultmann's historical skepticism about Jesus, rejects as highly procrustean his boiling down of the various expressions of a first century Christian world-view drawn from the New Testament into different ways of expressing one selfsame truth,[26] and a truth according to modern existentialism at that. And though he thinks the post-Bultmannian "new quest" has much to commend it, Nineham cannot countenance its attribution of modern attitudes and disclaimers to Jesus, preferring Jesus the stranger who passes us by in the pages of Schweitzer.[27] He suggests therefore that New Testament interpreters have feared confronting the "pastness" of Jesus in case he does not speak to them.[28]

Concerning the historical Jesus, Nineham does not doubt there is much to learn from the gospels and that some reconstructions of the life and activity of Jesus are more plausible than others. Indeed, Nineham has his own definite ideas on this matter which he is prepared to defend. Yet the crucial factor for Nineham is that there are considerable gaps in our knowledge which preclude definite conclusions.[29] With most other scholars he has no serious doubts that Jesus lived and moved around Palestine exorcising, counseling, teaching and preaching (often in parables), that he fell foul of the Jewish authorities, was crucified by the Romans, and that the gospels contain faithful reports of Jesus' various activities. But scholarly disagreement arises when we ask precisely *which* activities are historically certain.[30] So while C.H. Dodd preferred to accept the truth of New Testament accounts and not deny their historicity unless compelled, Nineham prefers the historical spirit of R.G. Collingwood—an initial skepticism which comes to conviction only through sifting and "torturing" the primary evidence.[31] As Nineham put it recently, "Being impressed by the figure of Jesus portrayed in the Gospels gives no one the right to pass judgment on its historical authenticity."[32]

Nineham has no doubt that God was powerfully active in the life of Jesus to establish the community through which Christians find salvation. For him this is as certain as any historical fact. The evidence for this lies in the vigor of early Christian responses to Jesus and the ongoing capacity of that community to mediate the salvific reality of God.[33] So Nineham is a modernist basing his faith on the experience of life and salvation known through the concrete reality of modern Christian existence, rather than in any postulated historical origin of that life. His God is to be experienced and believed in what happens *now*, rather than in any formative past about which there can be no ultimate historical certainty. He goes so far as to make a virtue of faith from the necessity of his historical skepticism and cultural relativism, believing God has providentially brought the church to this uncertain pass. It should "relax," therefore, knowing that absolute "bedrock" is to be found not in historical reconstructions but in our understanding of the Christ event as collective and as ongoing. The really important historical fact for Nineham, therefore, is also the plainest—that a new community with God arose, that it continues in our day, and that Christians share in it.[34]

His advice, then, is that we must not look for more certainty about Jesus than God in his providence has vouchsafed to us in this historical age.[35] Following John S. Dunne, and with a strong flavor of post-liberal concerns, he would have the church stand far more loosely by biblical literality than it has. When it does appeal to the bible however, it should adopt the approach of suspending disbelief and "passing over" into the story of Jesus, yet without denying its foreignness. Thus it will respect the pastness of its scriptural past and value its dialogue with that past, to be sure, though without naively or faithlessly fleeing to it in the face of modern doubt.[36]

Thus Nineham sees in Jesus the powerful activity of God, and finds his to be the paradigmatic story in dialogue with which the church is brought into dialogue with a God still active in its midst. But to talk about the uniqueness of Jesus is to overstate the case, just as it is to mistake the intentions of a God whose providence is compatible with both historical skepticism and cultural relativism.

Before proceeding I express some reservations about Nineham's case. First, Nineham is as committed as anyone in Part III above, to the powerful impact of Jesus, but this impact is not really probed; *why* did Jesus achieve so extraordinary a degree of influence? I suspect Nineham would identify the genetic fallacy in a question such as this, however, claiming that Jesus' place in Christianity cannot be reduced to his own personal input, but that the developing tradition about Jesus drew from many quarters—essentially, that all the water in a river does not come from its source only. Be that as it may, however, Nineham might still be expected to deal with the case of Jesus' impact on the earliest Christians (apart from the cultural background of the day and its influence on what has been said about Jesus subsequently). We have, after all, seen such an inquiry carried out with considerable methodological sophistication by Schillebeeckx—himself unafraid of skeptical conclusions.

Second, Nineham and the other "historical skeptics" in this section admit a unity in the experience of God and in God's essential attributes which appears to belie any thoroughgoing relativism.

A third argument to consider, in which the whole force of Nineham's cultural relativism is challenged, is that offered by John Barton in his essay "Reflections on Cultural Relativism" I & II (1979). Like Nineham, Barton is no advocate of a historically, transculturally fixed human nature.[37] But where Barton differs strongly from Nineham is in rejecting the latter's notion of cultural totalities. Such appeal to closed paradigms or epistemes cannot even be maintained within the biblical world itself, argues Barton: if angels and

demons are supposed to be part of a cultural *gestalt* which could not
have been questioned in New Testament times, he asks (193-95),
then how could the Sadducees' party deny the existence of angel and
spirit and resurrection, as we read in Mk 12:18? Such notions of cultural isolation strike Barton as a little old-fashioned nowadays, as if
the possibility of translation and the fact of cultural overlap were not
well established (196-97).[38] He makes much of our capacity to communicate in the gray area of partial understanding, despite culture-
specific perspectives, arguing that while all human speech is in some
sense broken, it is never incomplete (197-98).

David Edwards echoes these concerns about Nineham, pointing out that while evidence for the dissimilarity of cultures can be
piled up, so can evidence for their kinship and mutual understanding;
as in linguistics there are found to be common structures between
languages, so too is this the case regarding societies and mytholo-
gies.[39] As G.M. Newlands put it in his discussion of Nineham, with a
generous splash of *reductio ad absurdum*, "Despite their differences
I do not see, *mutatis mutandis*, why the Warden of Keble should not
have been able to embrace Helen of Troy."[40]

Returning to the theological issue at hand, Barton insists that

> Relativism is the beginning of theological method, not its
> end: it tells us that we can expect to find only hints of ul-
> timacy, not Euclidean chains of proof.... Once we thus
> broaden the discussion, and examine the relativity of all
> human expressions of meaning, cultural relativism is
> shown up as essentially a trivializing of the mystery of
> communication. Communication *does* occur; what is true
> for me can be true for you, even though its context in the
> totality of your thoughts and experiences must be so dif-
> ferent from its context in mine as to make, theoretically, a
> mockery of the suggestion (198-99).

Given the possibility that shared meanings, communication between
people across history, and even anthropological constants might not
be susceptible to the relativizing critique, the possibility of some liberal-style case for Jesus' uniqueness and finality survives. But more
of this in the Conclusion of this study, to follow.

John Bowden is a long-term and successful publisher of liberal and radical theology at London's SCM Press, and an author in his own right. In his avowedly unoriginal book *Jesus: The Unanswered Questions* (1988)[41] he nevertheless provides an important compendium of recent challenges to the doctrines of Jesus' uniqueness and finality. He worries at Nineham's bone of contention from several angles, as well as raising other issues which will be discussed more fully in the subsequent treatment of "religious pluralists" and "complete relativists." Though a priest like Nineham, and possessed of a lively Christian faith, Bowden is nevertheless what we might term an "omni-skeptic."

For Bowden the rise of science and modern culture is the decisive watershed for theology and hence Christology—any clinging nowadays to pre-critical views is no longer faith but ideology (Ch. 1). The former divine certainties of dogma have thus been taken from us—he cites recent English controversies over the incarnation as an illustration of how a once authoritative given has come now to be seen as merely an historical artifact in theology, time-bound and by no means inviolate (72-89). Thus Nineham-style historical skepticism is a major feature of Bowden's case. He likes Nineham's aforementioned "Epilogue" to *The Myth of God Incarnate*, appreciating what a radical threat it poses for those wishing to maintain Jesus' uniqueness and finality without traditional dogmatic support. So, he argues,

> having rejected the arguments for the metaphysical uniqueness of Jesus, i.e. that by virtue of the doctrine of the Incarnation Jesus may be believed in as both God and man, theologians cannot fall back on arguments, say, for the moral uniqueness of Jesus, the man for others, the best man who ever lived. There is no rational way in which such arguments can be defended. So we cannot escape from the problems of the church's formidable and archaic doctrines into the simplicity of a Jesus who was demonstrably the paragon of all virtues and a supreme example of human nature. Even if we had far, far more evidence—which we do not—that would be impossible to demonstrate (90).[42]

This last point is supported in his Ch. 3 where Bowden criticizes the new quest of the historical Jesus for attempting too much historical reconstruction with too little plain and incontestable historical evidence—evidence mostly limited to the synoptics and colored by their various theological agendas. Where others might find much agreement among the Jesus portraits "recovered" by this movement, he finds their diversity pointing more realistically to a fundamental inconsistency and incompatibility (e.g. 45-46).

Nineham's concerns about cultural relativism are effectively reiterated here, too. Bowden also mentions Bultmann among those who have shown him how remote from us is the world of earliest Christianity, along with E.P. Sanders and his Schweitzer-like emphasis upon the impossibility of understanding Jesus apart from the apocalyptic matrix of first century Judaism.[43] Like Nineham, Bowden is convinced that Jesus will be trivialized and his impact lost if this strangeness is overlooked in a modernizing rush to make him "relevant" (Ch. 9); as was the case with Nineham, then, the influence of Ernst Troeltsch is prominent in Bowden's conviction that Jesus cannot be unraveled from the seamless garment of history (Ch. 10).

Yet precisely because of this pastness and remoteness certain recent assessments of Jesus, in their unfavorable conclusions, have highlighted the problem of ascribing uniqueness or perfection to the figure met in the gospels. Bowden mentions that English writers from Bertrand Russell to Philip Toynbee have found Jesus unattractive, while the Jewish scholar C.G. Montefiore saw in him a figure "not good enough to be God." So, too, Richard Robinson, in *An Atheist's Values*,[44] is mentioned for condemning Jesus as bereft of an ideal of truth and knowledge, as effectively lacking humanism and without an adequate social or political consciousness (Ch. 7). And if Jesus is made to fit our time, as Pelikan and others[45] show is attempted in every age and place, then Bowden foresees difficulties squaring the various modern figures thus produced with oddities of the New Testament Jesus. Thus a modern Jesus such as "the man for others" appears odd in his dismissal of the Syrophoenician woman (Mk 7:24-30) while "the Liberator" is unaccountably heard to say "the poor you have with you always" (Mk 14:17 // Mt 26:11) (Ch. 4).

To these concerns of Nineham, Bowden adds an ideology critique of the way Jesus has been construed as an oppressive figure by many and hence a poor candidate for the appelation of uniqueness. He reminds us of what has been learned from black and feminist theology—that a white male savior can actually be a figure of oppression for women and blacks (Ch. 6). Indeed, history has been full of attempts to sacralize political hierarchies and sanctify unworthy projects by associating them with Jesus—from the Roman imperial Christ to the Aryan Christ of Nazi-influenced Christianity in wartime Germany to current opposition on the part of conservatives toward the ordination of women because of Jesus' maleness (Ch. 8). For Bowden this "dark side of the tradition" (182) can only be broken down when a unique and uniquely authoritative Jesus (under whoever's control) is deposed. Like Nineham he would prefer we were more open to the creative present than shackled to an authoritarian past.

Bowden also canvases the various recent responses of Christianity to other religions over the matter of Jesus' finality (Ch. 11). Beyond "exclusivism" (Barth, Kraemer) and "inclusivism" (Rahner *et al.*) his sympathies are with the pluralist stance of John Hick, Wilfred Cantwell Smith and *The Myth of Christian Uniqueness* (1987), of which more subsequently.

Bowden's many questions are not answered, but he does offer a strategy for dealing with them. Following H. Richard Niebuhr, Jean Milet and others he favors a halt to what we might call the "creeping Christocentrism" of modern theology with the focus shifted back from a unique and final Christ to God (Ch. 13). The criteria upon which such a "God focus" is deemed possible, however, are experiential—essentially the liberal Protestant recourse of Rudolf Otto or Friedrich Schleiermacher to types of deep, common human feelings deemed religiously disclosive (Ch. 12). Bowden turns to Gerd Thiessen's *On Having a Critical Faith* and Philip Toynbee's *Towards the Holy Spirit* for his insights here.[46]

Thus an emphasis on one of the two major poles I have identified in liberal Christology today, the human condition, remains present for Bowden in some form, although a confidently reconstructed historical Jesus is vigorously denied. This is surely odd, however, from one who so emphasizes cultural relativism in his arguments. For if taken to its extreme, as it is by the "complete relativists" discussed below, any possibility of a universal human experience or type of feeling is denied. Like John Hick, then, Bowden ultimately employs the argument from religious experience, however broadly conceived, to ground his belief in God. There are Christological consequences, though, for anyone who maintains such an essentially liberal commitment. If our images of God—surely no less historically varying, culturally dependent and open to misuse than those we have of Christ— are somehow purified, established and even vindicated by their resonance with some deep human experience, then a similar argument might prove workable for Christ. Such an approach is, of course, the "liberal" position, which will be brought more fully into dialogue with this "radical" one in the impending Conclusion to this work.

MAURICE WILES AND FRANCES YOUNG

In this discussion of "historical skeptics" I now move from two whose expertise is in New Testament studies to Wiles and Young, who have distinguished themselves in the field of patristics. There is a shift, too, to a more fulsome theological agenda, and although the contribution of Young is relatively small, in Wiles we meet a major English theologian whose radical program is nowhere better focused than over the issues concerning us in this study.

Maurice Wiles preceded Keith Ward as Regius Professor of Divinity at Oxford. He shares with Nineham and Bowden the same liberal Anglican heritage and generally the same sense of historical skepticism and cultural relativism.[47] But Wiles the theologian is not content with questions raised in the tradition of Troeltsch; he proceeds to give (appropriately qualified) answers in the liberal tradition of Hegel and Schleiermacher.

Wiles champions a "non-incarnational Christology," but unlike other such Christologies met among English liberals like Robinson, Lampe, Goulder and the early Cupitt the uniqueness and/or the finality of Jesus is also surrendered. This is not always recognized, and rightly so, for Wiles' position over this issue is by no means uniformly clear. David Brown thinks Wiles actually maintains the uniqueness and finality of Jesus while viewing the incarnation as a myth[48]— a favorite compromise of English idealism, which he also associates with Robinson and D.M. Baillie. Prusak, however, recognizes that

Wiles' position is somewhat less definite: "Whether it is simply a contingent historical fact that the truth about humanity's relation to God came alive in our particular tradition through the figure of Jesus, or whether his life and all that stemmed from it are essential to the full and effective realization of the union of divine and human in a person's life, remain open questions for Wiles."[49] I fear, however, that both are incorrect and that although Wiles may occasionally and notably hint at a belief in Jesus' uniqueness and finality here and there, he has effectively abandoned it. To establish this, however, will involve searching high and low through the Wiles corpus, and dealing with some evidence plainly to the contrary.

It is helpful to begin with a summary statement of theological likes and dislikes provided by Wiles at the end of the 1960s.[50] He flatly claims that the days of neo-orthodoxy and an existentialist theology without ontology are gone.[51] Rahner's attempted juggling of the Roman Catholic tradition with the modern world is labeled as intolerable, while Pannenberg is only praised for the openness of his theology to historical biblical criticism. And though Wiles likes Küng, he finds him lacking in "Protestant astringency" and sophistication. Here, therefore, proponents of the first three positions considered in this study pass in review and are found wanting. The only modern movement receiving Wiles' unqualified approval is process theology which he sees as resolving *the* theological problem of the age—the reconciling of an immutable God with a world now known to be one of constant flux. Note, however, that process theology need not in principle require a unique and final Jesus to complete the process or provide it with a high point, although this alleged requirement is often asserted.

It comes as no surprise, then, that something like a process view is central to Wiles' approach, with divine action understood to take place only within and never apart from the natural course of events in the world, including human responses to a divine love intuited in history and experience. This is a major reason why Wiles refuses to see the incarnation and the life of Jesus in terms of divine irruptions or interventions—they are a part of the whole, smoothly continuous with all divine activity.

To begin at the beginning, let us consider a very flat denial of Jesus' uniqueness and finality for reasons that such talk is hopelessly out of date. In his inaugural lecture as Professor of Christian Doctrine at the University of London, entitled "Looking into the Sun" (1976), Wiles associates belief in Jesus' radical distinctiveness with an apocalyptic view of God's dealings with the world predominant in parts of New Testament Christianity (156). He thinks it is this predominant expectation, rather than the early church's convictions about Jesus' importance for it, which led to so uncompromisingly high an assertion: "It was within this eschatological context—the context alike of Jesus' own mission and of his first followers' proclamation of him immediately after his death and resurrection—that a sense of the radical ultimacy of Christ's work first took place" (156).

Wiles follows Pannenberg here (as, perhaps, did Nineham), agreeing that Jesus' resurrection was seen as an anticipation of the general resurrection and the consummation of history, and that this accounted for the ascription of revelational status and uniqueness to his life. But while Pannenberg takes all of this literally, Wiles does not (160). He sees such ideas as the product of an ancient world-view no longer tenable. He rejects, too, the Platonic variant of such views, as found in the two-nature doctrine of Christology's post-semitic, Greek-influenced development. Sounding here like a logical positivist, Wiles appears to label such views as strictly meaningless, unable either to be affirmed or denied (161). But then he adds something that will frequently reappear: the conviction that such talk is not nonsense—that it demands restatement and reappropriation.

Some equivocation over this matter appears, however, in "Does Christology Rest on a Mistake?" (1972). There, Wiles seeks to link the fortunes of the incarnation and the redemption to those of two other doctrines with which they are inextricably bound: creation, which in the Irenaean vision the incarnation completes, and "the fall" which in the Augustinian vision is reversed by the redemption (4). In recent times both these doctrines have come to be dissociated from single events—creation is now commonly seen as co-terminous with the evolutionary process, while "the fall" is appreciated for providing a psychological window into the experience of "everyman" rather than recounting "some datable aboriginal calamity" (5, 6). So too, thinks Wiles, can the incarnation of God and the redemption wrought through Christ best be understood as woven into the whole cloth of history rather than cut from it as single events. As was the painful task with doctrines of creation and "fall" for past theology, then, so Wiles would have today's theologians separate the key theological assertions involved in talk of incarnation and redemption from particular historical occurrences once thought necessary for their instantiation. Thus "two stories" must be told: a scientific/historical story and a frankly mythological one[52]—"In the first place a human story of the partial overcoming in human lives of that repudiation of the fellowship with God of which the doctrine of the fall speaks. And also a mythological story of God's total self-giving, God's compassionate acceptance of pain and evil whereby that overcoming is made possible and effective" (9).

The specter of Jesus' uniqueness looms large here, and Wiles seems quick to disavow any strong and particular link between historical and mythological stories in the case of Jesus. In so doing he echoes Nineham and Bowden in their unwillingness to allow a retreat from talk of incarnation to talk of the historical Jesus' moral perfection, his great impact in the emergence of the church and so on, though for a different reason. While their main reason was that it *could* not be done, Wiles feels it *should* not be done, for traditionally the Christian focus has been more upon the divine action in redemption rather than Jesus' human response—though both features must still be highlighted if Jesus' own contribution is not to be understated (10). Yet elsewhere in the paper he appears to hedge over the possibility that Jesus' life might still have been unique, even though ontological support to establish this is no longer deemed necessary; "Nevertheless it *could* still be *reasonable* to give to the life of Jesus a special place in illuminating, as no other life, the significance of the whole story, as bringing home *to us* effectively the transcendent divine truth which the mythological story in its own way is designed to proclaim" (9) (italics mine), and "There are many things to be said which give grounds for seeing the life and death of Jesus as a part of the human story which is of unique significance in relation to seeing the human story as a true story of divine redemption at work" (11). Yet all of this is found in an essay where Wiles, like Nineham and Bowden, entertains grave doubts about the historical facticity of Jesus' story, as well as courting cultural relativism (10) and the challenge of religious pluralism (11).

Thus Wiles rejects the incarnation while equivocating about the uniqueness of Jesus' life and the amount of divine agency involved in it. But ultimately he seems to realize that establishing the uniqueness is impossible. Despite whatever other things he says, Wiles does say this (in a good impression of the post-liberal position): "there comes a point at which we reach a limit question, where we have to say 'I can give no further reasons for seeing the thing as I do; this is my vision; do you not feel drawn to share it too?'" (11).

The potential confusion for Wiles here described appears closer to resolution in another article from the same period in which the aforementioned interweaving of divine and natural action is more fully discussed. In "Religious Authority and Divine Action" (1976) he seeks to understand authoritative moments of religious disclosure in terms of a faith community's response to them rather than through any heightened divine presence or activity in the events themselves:

> I do not think that we can properly speak of God being more creative in one place than in another.... Nevertheless I think we may speak of certain aspects of the created order as particularly potent vehicles for human awareness of divine creativity.... For the Christian the life of Christ, and certain other events also within what is commonly referred to as 'salvation history', have an outstanding potency of this kind and are seen as special divine actions (138-39).

Thus the emphasis is more fully on the significance of the events for those who appreciate them rather than on any universal importance such events might have. This is quite in keeping with the basis of this "radical" position in allowing the uniqueness and finality of Jesus to function as a way of expressing devotion for Christians "intra-ecclesially," though not "extra-ecclesially" in relation to the whole of history or the diversity of other faiths.

Wiles extends the argument in his Hulsean Lectures of 1973.[53] In discussing the person of Christ he mentions how the poor prospects of historically reconstructing Jesus' life and the impossibility of ever providing historical "proof" for the major Christological assertions (45-49) herald a much-needed shift in Christology "from concentration upon the individual figure of Jesus to the whole Christ event" (50f).[54] This strategy, encountered in earlier parts of this study, looks to the collective experience of twenty Christian centuries for the "Christ event," recognizing the difficulty of pinning all of this to the man Jesus and a single decisive divine intervention.

In a subsequent chapter on the work of Christ, Wiles seeks to show that an adequate atonement theory can also be had without any special focus of divine activity. Basically, he cannot see how a once-for-all action could overcome evil and human sin if "the fall" is understood as a description of all life rather than a single event (67-68) and if evil is seen to be woven into the stuff of personal and social existence and no longer personified as "the devil" (64-65). Wiles cannot accept that notions of propitiation (65-66) and sacrifice (66-67) can point to any non-metaphorical reality as once-for-all events at this historical distance. Nor is the sympathetic involvement of God in human suffering or his victory over death thought to depend on any once-for-all incarnation or resurrection. After all, both elements were already present in the Old Testament (69-73). Just as the incarnation can be understood as a dimension of the ongoing Christian experience, then, so traditional aspects of the work of Christ can be seen in the same way.

Because of this, and because the story of Jesus' passion still undeniably releases great power for changing lives, Wiles concludes that a subjective theory can adequately preserve the divine objectivity of atonement in Christ, its "eternal representation and historical effectiveness" (81). Its "objectivity" rests on the plain fact that people are still drawn into it, that *it works*. Thus the "Christ event" is a sacrament of the sympathetically suffering presence of God and God's atoning activity within and throughout the ongoing process of evolving creation and human history; it is not a "final" divine act inextricably linked to a unique, historical person.

Wiles' opinions achieved notoriety in *The Myth of God Incarnate* (1977). In the first of two contributions, "Christianity Without Incarnation?" Wiles identifies the incarnation as only an interpretation of Jesus; it was suitable, perhaps, for the patristic era but is so no longer. As the church found it could still appreciate the eucharist without the doctrine of transubstantiation (2) and, more recently, that it could affirm incarnation without belief in Jesus' virginal conception (3), so Wiles is convinced that Christianity will not collapse if the incarnation comes to be viewed as a myth. He does, for instance, recognize that a weaker sense of the doctrine can be maintained in that Christianity is anti-dualistic, and as such remains an "incarnational religion" (7).

But if Wiles' historical skepticism and awareness of cultural relativism preclude any ascription of human perfection to Jesus, nevertheless he maintains a strong sense of Jesus' significance for Christians: "On no showing can the records of his life have absolute significance for us; on any showing to which the name of Christian could conceivably be given his life would remain of substantial importance for us" (8).

Yet Wiles is immediately up to his old tricks of equivocating over this issue. The following quote, taken out of context, would indicate *prima facie* an "idealist" or "liberal" stance:

> So, it may be claimed, it is supremely through Jesus that the self-giving love of God is most fully expressed and men can be caught up into the fullest response to him. For Jesus was not merely a teacher about God; the power of God was set at work in the world in a new way through his life, ministry, death and resurrection. On such a basis it is reasonable to suggest that the stories about Jesus and the figure of Jesus himself could remain a personal focus of the transforming power of God in the world (8-9).

Yet immediately thereafter Wiles approvingly cites John Hick's pluralistic approach in an apparent contradiction: "It does not involve the judgment that all religions are of equal truth and worth. It does rule out the judgment of the superiority of one religion over another in advance of an informed knowledge of both faiths. Such a change can only be regarded as a gain" (9).

Perhaps the presence of such apparent anomalies finds its implicit explanation in a conjecture, from Nineham's "Epilogue" to *The Myth of God Incarnate*, that theologians are simply not adequately appreciative of how newly problematic are the uniqueness and finality of Jesus, once incarnational dogma has been surrendered.

In his second essay, "Myth in Theology" (1977), Wiles discusses theological uses of the term "myth" since the nineteenth century. He mentions how doctrines of creation, fall and resurrection can now function as myths, there being a deeper "ontological truth" to which they bear evocative witness. The parallel reality with regard to incarnational doctrine is identified by Wiles in the personal relationship with God of which believers speak: "if this union of divine and human at the heart of the human personality is a reality, however hard to identify or to describe, may that not be the ontological truth corresponding to and justifying a mythological understanding of the incarnation?" (161). For Prusak, what Wiles advocates here appears to be the straight incarnational vision of Hegel as appropriated by D.F. Strauss, "a mythological account of a potential union of the divine and the human in the life of every human."[55] But this is not quite right. Wiles does, after all, emphasize that this is a church-specific rather than a general phenomenon; it is an expression of Christian experience through history rather than an item of idealist generality. He later comes to call the incarnation an "historical myth" to indicate this specificity (163-64).

Some care must be taken over what historical claims about Jesus are deemed necessary to undergird this incarnational myth. According to Wiles,

We would want, I suggest, to be able to affirm two things. First that his own life in its relation to God embodied that openness to God, that unity of human and divine to which the doctrine points. And secondly that his life depicted not only a profound human response to God, but that in his attitudes towards other men his life was a parable of the loving outreach of God to the world. Now both those things are firm features of the traditions about Jesus. And while we cannot be sure how much of the detail of the accounts we have is later interpretation, it is most unlikely that the kind of historical knowledge about Jesus available to us or that may become available to us in the future could ever deform that picture to such a degree as to rule out the appropriateness of linking the incarnation myth in this special way with the person of Jesus (162-63).

Crucially, however, the historical link Wiles requires does not depend on the man Jesus only, but on the relationship between Jesus and the experience of grace among contemporary believers.

> This can be affirmed in a weaker or a stronger form. The weaker form would simply state as a matter of contingent historical fact that this truth about man's relation to God came alive in our particular tradition through the figure of Jesus. The stronger form would give to Jesus a more indispensable role. While refraining from giving any distinctive metaphysical account of Jesus' person, it might still claim that his life and all that has stemmed from it are essential in practice to the full and effective realization of this union of divine and human in the life of man. The grounds for such a claim would have to be historical and psychological reflection on the way in which man's spiritual life has been and is formed within Christian faith. Its validity could only be tested by the course of future history (163).

Clearly this "stronger form" is what I have called the "liberal" position. Though a firm preference is not declared, Wiles seems to locate the burden of proof with advocates of this "stronger form," hinting loudly that the "weaker form," a good example of the "radical" position here under discussion, is the more believable. Thus what might have been another spasm of uncertainty over the uniqueness and finality of Jesus in the first of these two essays from *The Myth of God Incarnate* appears again to have been brought closer to resolution.

In his subsequent summing up of issues in what has come to be called "the myth debate," Wiles briefly mentions "the finality, uniqueness, universality or centrality of Jesus."[56] His sympathies are clearly with non-exclusive Christologies; he wishes to maintain "the categorical character of the religious demand" yet without an absolute or metaphysically favored Jesus. This is all he believes to be justifiable from the Christian's standpoint "within one particular stream of religious and cultural development." We are then referred to another article, written at the time of *The Myth of God Incarnate* but appearing later, in which Wiles' position on this matter is spelled

out more fully. In "Christian Theology in an Age of Religious Studies" (1979), driven to greater explicitness perhaps by its pertinence
to the issue under discussion, he certainly seems to have yielded the
doctrine of Jesus' uniqueness in yielding that of Christianity itself
among the religions:

> For we would not be able to speak of it as the truth for all
> peoples and for all times. But I do not believe it would
> diminish one iota of its real spiritual message. For we
> would still be able to speak of the Christian gospel as the
> primary form in which the truth of God has come to us *in
> our culture*; we would still be able to speak of it as one of
> such profound spiritual worth that it ought to be shared
> with other people throughout the globe. And some at
> least of those who hear it so presented may be freer to re-
> spond, because *they will no longer be offended (justifi-
> ably offended) by the feeling that what may be a truth ap-
> prehended by the preacher is being presented to them as
> the truth without qualification.* And this will be achieved
> without that gospel being robbed of its particularity, its
> history, its images—all those things that give it vitality—
> and being turned into some all-embracing and all-dead-
> ening generality [57] (italics mine).

There are some points worth noting in Wiles' discussion of
Jesus in *Faith and the Mystery of God* (1982). First, while he offers a
fuller "new quest-style" discussion of Jesus' life than ever before, a
not fully critically self-conscious story based on Jesus in the gospels
is all we actually get, though the status of what we are reading is
made slightly clearer than it is by, say, the liberation theologians.
Thus Wiles can declare how "First and foremost I see him (Jesus) as
one for whom God is an all-encompassing reality" (56-57) and find
in the death of Jesus "the supreme example of parabolic speech
about God" (70), that "It is through the cross that he (God) is most
clearly seen as the God for whom nothing is expendable except himself" (72). But Wiles does not see such statements implying the
uniqueness and finality of Jesus for anyone but those who respond to
the story in this way. This is clear when he reiterates the role of his

own Christian perception along with past Christian interpretation in producing the figure of Jesus which he sees: "When I stand back from my reading and seek to respond to it as a whole, then history and interpretation combine to give rise to a vision of God in relation to the world, for which the figure of Jesus and the movement that stems from him are central" (60).

So, despite appearances, including the occasional adjective a "liberal" might use, Wiles seems content to see the life and death of Jesus as an enacted parable of God's love and presence *as they appear to Christians*. The "power," moreover, lies in the story and its ongoing life in the church—a story understood to draw on the ever present current of God's creative and redemptive activity in history.

This denial of specific divine intervention in favor of a quasi-process view occupies Wiles in his 1986 Bampton lectures *God's Action in the World*, with which I conclude this examination of his work. In a discussion of God's action in Jesus, Wiles speaks of "my faith in God as supremely revealed in Christ" (93). He can also speak (on the same page) of no single event being made special by God, but only by those who either do or do not appreciate it. Incarnation and resurrection emerge, as I have shown before to be the case with Wiles, as parables for "those with ears to hear," if you like, of God's love victorious over death. This conviction owes as much to contemporary Christian experience as it does to the thick mix of event and interpretation we meet in the various New Testament portrayals of Jesus.

I think a case can be made, then, despite contrary evidence, that Maurice Wiles is a "radical" rather than a "liberal" over the matter of Jesus' uniqueness and finality. In the spirit of Schleiermacher his God-talk is also "world-talk"[58] envisioning an unbroken natural process as the arena of God's working, and so denying any specificity to divine action. There is also a debt to Troeltsch here, whose method of correlation in historiography refused to split events into special (miraculous) and ordinary dimensions.[59] The Hegelian flavor in all of this has been noted, too, as has the influence upon Wiles of Hegelian souls from the realm of process theology. It seems reasonably certain that Wiles' Jesus lives in the church's experience of a loving God, providing a unique parable of that experience for Christians; but there is no need or way to assert his uniqueness and finality more generally.

Before considering Frances Young's interesting variations on these themes I express two concerns. First, Wiles denies that God's smooth action in the world process requires a high point. But writers such as Rahner, Schoonenberg and Robinson insist upon such a high point, while conceiving of the world process in substantially the same way (as did Teilhard, too, for that matter). To insist on continuities and deny particularities as Wiles does risks overlooking an essential feature of the evolutionary process, however—that it proceeds by discontinuities and mutations, involving the sudden emergence of new levels of complexity. So Wiles' reading of this situation is by no means compelling.[60]

Second, as with Bowden and Nineham so too with Wiles—their God seems to be clearly in focus despite the alleged fog of cultural relativism which obscures both the human condition and the historical Jesus, and hence prevents any Christological benchmark from being arrived at. Why is Christ obscured but not God, however? The next writer to be considered is very certain about God (exhibiting more of Schleiermacher's influence), too, though she supports her essentially pietistic stance with a stronger sense of the human condition than does Wiles.

Frances Young is Edward Cadbury Professor of Theology at the University of Birmingham and a contributor to *The Myth of God Incarnate*. Like Wiles, she finds in the incarnation, uniqueness and finality of Jesus a cluster of ideas now outmoded through dependence on a remote Christian past and invalidated through incompatibility with a pluralistic Christian present. But if Wiles is driven to this conclusion by his desire to give a credible, modern account of God's action in the world, Young's abiding concerns are far less "speculative." As a Methodist minister, her background is not "once-born," Anglican and focused upon *incarnation* but, rather, "twice-born" and focused upon *redemption*. Young is also modernist and pragmatist in her theological sympathies, but it is the experience of salvation which matters most. This experience is accessible in the church (modernism) through its story of a suffering God defeating evil via the cross of Jesus Christ—a story which works, and thus is sufficient (pragmatism). An incarnate Christ, or even just a unique and final one, would add nothing of importance for Young to this pivotal experience of atonement, whose Christological motto might well be: "take care of the soteriology and the Christology will look after itself."

There are, nevertheless, one or two lapses back into "liberal" language. But whereas Wiles' occasional indiscretions of this sort tended to one of the elements I identify as "liberal" (basing unique-ness-talk on historical claims about Jesus) Young's minor capitula-tions tend toward the other element (postulating a clearly delineated human nature with which the figure of Jesus is in unique accord).

The substance of Young's argument is found in two contribu-tions to "the myth debate." In the first of these, "A Cloud of Witness-es," Young's major contribution to *The Myth of God Incarnate* (1977), theological reflection is appended to a detailed search for the concept of incarnation in the New Testament, along with a study of its use among the fathers. Details of this scholarly investigation mat-ter less, for our purposes here, than the conclusions: the diverse Christological witness of the New Testament, despite including high views of Jesus as God's representative, is found by Young to fall short of affirming the incarnation. Similarly she comes to view incar-national orthodoxy of the patristic era as timebound dogma far re-moved from the biblical vision of a God involved with the world, and thus as tending to docetism (14-30).

In her subsequent reflection Young declares her preference for focusing Christology upon soteriology. Not only has she found this to be a feature of which she approves in New Testament and patristic discussions, but she thinks It necessary for any adequate response to the problems of evil, suffering and sin (30): "For me, experience of suffering, sin, decay and 'abnormality' as a constituent part of the world, would make belief in God impossible without a Calvary-cen-tred religious myth... without the cross it would be impossible to be-lieve in God" (34-35).

As with Wiles there is no desire to sunder the unbroken web of events in search of direct divine causation. Recourse is also made to talk of two stories, one "scientific" and the other "mythical" (31ff).[61] With Jesus, there is one story of an archetypal believer suffering for his God-centered life choices, and another story of God involved in the reality of a dying, compromised human life (37). Young grounds this second, mythical story (recall Wiles' apologia for myth in terms

of its corresponding "ontological truth") in the recognition that suffering love is "Godlike"—that it is creative and redemptive and a
part of the way things are (presumably, part of a divine order thought
to be discernible in the manner of all natural theology) (36). For
Young the holding together of these two stories is a deeply felt imperative of Christian experience (37) and Jesus is naturally, therefore, the supreme disclosure and unique focus of this Christian
salvific vision. But she has no desire to see such claims universal-
ized, just as she has shown herself happy to abandon the ontological
claims for incarnation upon which they would once have rested:

> Truth about the world is found nowadays not in unique
> particular exceptions, but in statistical averages: many
> witnesses are more convincing than one. In a world con-
> text, the witness of differing prophets and differing faiths
> to the 'beyond' is more important to all religions than the
> exclusive claims of any one. Of course, for the New Tes-
> tament writers, for the church, for all believers, Jesus
> Christ undoubtedly holds a unique position; no one else
> has the same role for faith. But in the case of outsiders,
> has it not become increasingly difficult to maintain that
> faith in Christ is indispensable for salvation? The idea of
> Christ's finality is surely linked with the eschatological
> presuppositions of the early church, presuppositions
> which were central and fundamental to them but which
> we can only make our own in some kind of 'demytholo-
> gized' form. Within one cultural stream, namely the Ju-
> daeo-Christian European tradition, some case can be
> made for seeing Christ as a kind of 'coping-stone' to reli-
> gious developments in the ancient world, the spiritual cli-
> max, as it were, of Hellenistic philosophy, which deter-
> mined the subsequent religious culture of Europe; but to
> claim that Jesus as the cosmic Christ has the same ulti-
> mate significance for all mankind irrespective of time,
> place or culture is surely unrealistic (40-41).

This position is very familiar from Young's fellow "historical skeptics."[62] She adds that Jesus has only been seen as an image embodying

salvation among widely varying peoples and cultures because they have projected their various ideals upon him (42). It is in this way that she understands Jesus' capacity for being "all things to all men."

Second, and even more briefly, I consider Young's essay "The Finality of Christ" (1979). There, in dialogue with the New Testament and patristics, she determines that "a general acceptance among Christians that Christ was the final revelation pre-dated the recognition of his full divinity" (183). She is thereby able to preserve the underlying convictions about Jesus' uniqueness and finality called for by Christian self-understanding while allowing the later overlay of incarnational doctrine to be peeled off. Thus Young's conclusion in this paper is the same as that of her earlier essay for *The Myth of God Incarnate*:

> No human individual, institution or movement can claim absolute or universal validity for its beliefs. Yet each human individual and group has a right to its own identity and dignity. So Christianity too may claim a right to its particular identity, and may foster the preservation of its tradition and its peculiar religious insights, even though claims to overriding absoluteness have to be abandoned. In abandoning exclusive claims to a unique and final divine revelation in Jesus, and recognizing that all mankind has not and cannot be expected to see God in him, we should not be tempted to reduce the centrality of Jesus for Christian belief. Jesus Christ as the one through whom God has confronted us must surely continue to play a central role in Christian theology, for it is an essential element in Christian consciousness. We have to stick with the problem of christology, not abandon it or reduce it (186).

As was the case with Maurice Wiles, however, Frances Young has not preserved herself from some slight equivocation over this matter. Elsewhere in the Goulder symposium she comments that "the cross is regarded as the 'classic case' of God's presence in the midst of human sin, suffering and death."[63] And in a fine, earlier study of the ancient notion of sacrifice and its potential applicability in modern theology she concludes by committing herself to an assessment of the work of Christ as psychologically powerful to a unique extent: "In some strange way the human response to Christ's sacrificial death is instinctive.... In some mysterious way, the Man upon the Cross retains his place in the human imagination as the timeless symbol of reconciliation through sacrifice.... In art, music and literature, he is unlikely to lose it completely" and "to those who respond to the symbol, to those who sense its truth, the cross is the power of God and the wisdom of God. Age-old religious instincts enable us to make that response, whether we can explain it or not."[64] What is the basis of any such deep psychological appeal, but for the "best fit" proclaimed by "liberal" theologians such as John Robinson between the Christ and the human condition?

There is no suggestion here, however, that Young is genuinely in doubt about her conclusions as Wiles might appear to be—there is an inconsistency within this last quotation itself which undermines any "liberal" reading: while "In some strange way" all are initially said to be drawn instinctively to the crucified, Young concludes her statement by limiting the appeal of the cross "to those who respond to the symbol, to those who sense its truth." If the appeal were truly psychologically universal, however, surely *all* would be convinced and won over by it, and not merely the Christians who respond.

That "liberal"-style survivals of the doctrines in question, however dim, are not extirpated totally by even the most hard-headed of these "historical skeptics," however, confirms that the uniqueness and finality of Jesus does indeed constitute a blindspot and a potential pitfall for theology late in the twentieth century.[65] "Liberal" elements are very much in evidence in the next group of "radical" writers to be considered, too.

Chapter Ten

RELIGIOUS PLURALISTS

The contribution of these thinkers to this study is based on their writings about the Christian theology of religions. Hick and Cantwell Smith are the major exponents of "pluralistic" or "Christ-together-with-the-religions" views, according to which Christ and Christianity lose that primacy in the world of religious persons and movements traditionally accorded them in Christian thought. The Christian religion thus becomes but one among many reifications of a more fundamental religious vision. So, accordingly, the uniqueness and finality of Jesus Christ is surrendered as all but a "mythological" part of intra-Christian discourse.

They remain liberal Protestants, however. Each in his own way maintains the fundamental oneness of human experience, while Hick occasionally oversteps his position and waxes lyrical over Jesus' superlative qualities as a divine agent. Other elements of liberal theology are to be found, too, as shall be shown. But any such recourse to the historical Jesus and the human condition does not commit them to the implications about Jesus' uniqueness and finality drawn by the "liberal" group of Part III.

Paul F. Knitter has provided a critical survey of recent Christian theologies of religion. He, too, belongs with the "religious pluralists," though with more genuine awareness of relativism than we find in Hick and Cantwell Smith. He leads the discussion in the direction of the more thoroughgoing relativists, to follow in the next section.

237

JOHN HICK

John Hick is a prolific English theologian, a Presbyterian minister, and now retired from his chair in the Philosophy of Religion at the University of California, Claremont Graduate School. He was much influenced in his pluralistic thinking through an earlier tenure as University theology professor in the multi-racial religious melting-pot of 1970s' Birmingham. Hick's published views are everywhere reprinted, updated, summarized and much discussed. Something of a mature "final position" can, however, be seen to have appeared in his Gifford Lectures of 1986/87, expanded and published as *An Interpretation of Religion: Human Responses to the Transcendent* (1989) (subsequently, a mature assessment of the man and his critics has begun to emerge in the journal literature).[66] It is fitting, therefore, that Hick's overall program be introduced via this major study in which all his past and present theological and philosophical preoccupations are drawn together in what amounts to "nothing less than a short history of religion."[67]

Hick's "Copernican Theology" replaces an old "Ptolemaic theology"; no longer is Christ at the center in the universe of faiths for Hick, nor nowadays even "God" as understood in theistic traditions. Rather, "ultimate reality" is at the center; Hick conceives it broadly enough to embrace both theistic and non-theistic interpretations. As one of Hick's former students and present critics, Gavin D'Costa, put it, "over the years he has moved from *Christocentrism* to *theocentrism* to a *Reality-centrism*."[68]

In *An Interpretation of Religion* Hick clearly exhibits his Kantian vision of a transcendent, ultimately real (or "divine") *noumenon* knowable only as it is refracted through various histories and cultural totalities into the differing *phenomena* of the great world faiths. He begins with Wittgenstein's concept of "family resemblance" to justify the grouping together of *the religions* under the category *religion*.[69] He then turns to a comparativist, phenomenological account of religion as it has emerged since the epoch Karl Jaspers called "the axial period." This crucial era between 800 and 200 BCE witnessed a flowering of religious genius throughout the ancient world (the Buddha, Confucius, the major Hebrew prophets, etc.) and, according to Hick, the rise of autonomous, individual consciousness. The character of "post-axial religion" is thought by Hick to be *soteriological*, primarily concerned with the deliverance of humanity from the (allegedly) newly recognized "travail of existence" rather than with metaphysical speculation (although, crucially, all subsequent religions are seen to be cosmically optimistic). Herein there is an "improvement" on the apparently existentially untroubled life-world enjoyed in pre-axial "primal religion."

There follow two parts recalling Hick's long engagement in the 1950s and 1960s with the philosophy of religion. With regard to the traditional philosophical agenda of western Christian theism, especially the "proofs of God's existence" ancient and modern, he admits that the equal tenability of naturalistic explanations for phenomena formerly thought to be of divine origin makes "God" and the truth of religious belief unprovable. For Hick, however, it is nonetheless reasonable to trust religious experience; the potential fruits of religious living provide sufficient warrant for religious belief. He also maintains that the ultimate meaningfulness of religion is guaranteed by the prospect of "eschatological verification."

"The real" thus disclosed cannot be known *an sich* but only through its various *personae* (Jahweh, Krishna etc.) and *impersonae* (Brahman, Nirvana, Sunyata, etc.). Hick's criteria for grading the religions are soteriological and ethical: that the religions facilitate the shift from self-centeredness to reality-centeredness (salvation), and that they all advocate something like the "golden rule" (understood as a Kantian "categorical imperative"), justifies them alongside Christianity as equally valid paths. As to the future, Hick expects that the pluralistic view will one day become as standard for Christians as its "inclusive" predecessor has become.

This overall understanding of religion is perceptively analyzed by Twiss (in terms recalling the typology of theological approaches offered by Lindbeck).

> Hick's theory of religious pluralism is a sustained attempt
> to account for the diversity of religions by combining elements from two views of and approaches to religious
> belief and practice: a Wittgensteinian-grammatical view,
> on the one hand, and a more traditional propositional-
> realist view, on the other. In this hybrid account, the

diverse religions are conceptualized as cultural-linguistic grammars or idioms for engaging in soteriologically oriented forms of religious life that ultimately refer to one radically transcendent reality.[70]

According to Twiss, Hick establishes his theory via "a two-tiered epistemology of religious belief: a this-life pragmatic justification oriented to the authenticity of religious forms of life combined with an eschatological confirmability-in-principle of their implicit central truth-claims about the nature of reality."[71]

Certainly there are implications for the question of Jesus' uniqueness and finality in this "Copernican revolution," and Hick's contributions to significant recent symposia will serve to explicate them: *The Myth of God Incarnate* (1977), *The Myth of Christian Uniqueness* (1987), a Claremont colloquium entitled *Encountering Jesus: A Debate on Christology* (1988) and, in passing, the seminar convened by Michael Goulder in *Incarnation and Myth: The Debate Continued* (1979).

First, however, it should be noted how the once Christologically conservative Hick (who thought even D.M. Baillie's "paradox of grace" Christology insufficiently orthodox[72]) has since moved entirely to abandon not only belief in the incarnation but in Jesus' uniqueness and finality as well. In tracing the changing of his mind I closely follow Chester Gillis' most useful chronological summary.[73]

With regard to Baillie's view, in *God Was in Christ*,[74] that Jesus' incarnation consists in the *extent* of his human dependence upon God, Hick asserts that incarnation is traditionally seen not as a matter of *degree* but rather of *kind*; otherwise any sufficiently Godly soul is a potential candidate for such divine honors. Thus Baillie is accused of understating the deity of Christ in the attempt to preserve his humanity. Hick affirms, at the time, that "It is in the historical figure of Jesus the Christ that, according to the Christian claim, God has in a unique and final way disclosed himself to man";[75] so while in his first book *Faith and Knowledge* (1966)[76] Hick was prepared to allow some creativity and latitude in Christological formulation, this was not to be had at the expense of Nicene and Chalcedonian orthodoxy.

By the time of his *Christianity at the Centre* (1968),[77] however, Hick was willing to sacrifice much of that penumbra of secondary dogmas surrounding the divinity of Christ—a divinity which he had come to see in terms of "God's Love Incarnate." But in the article "Christ and Incarnation" (1966),[78] deferring to the challenge of other world religions, he abandons Chalcedonian talk of a hypostatic union altogether. Instead he offers a Jesus with a human nature and will, though motivated by God's agape. His earlier disapproval of D.M. Baillie has certainly vanished.

Hick's "Copernican Revolution" appears in "The Christian View of Other Faiths" (1972),[79] wherein a shift from Christocentrism to theocentrism is called for and the incarnation is relegated to the realm of mythology. In "Whatever Path Men Choose Is Mine" (1974)[80] he declares that his newly pluralistic solution has been formulated to avoid any exclusivity in Christian salvation claims. And in "Christ's Uniqueness" (1974)[81] he rejects Jesus' theological pre-eminence and sole salvific role, now believing that such notions contravene the limitless love of God. Finally Hick "comes to the now famous formula: the myth of God incarnate, a transposition, he says, from metaphysical to metaphorical language."[82]

I propose to continue Hick's story where Gillis leaves off, with a contribution to *The Myth of God Incarnate* (1977) entitled "Jesus and the World Religions." Here the uniqueness of Jesus is explicitly rejected. What we know of the historical Jesus, says Hick, comes from communal memories in the synoptic gospels. And though Hick discerns an impressive figure through these accounts he finds no evidence therein for any incarnation or uniqueness, but only that the earliest church wished to exalt Jesus because of the soteriological experience they associated with him. In addition Hick compares this process with the progressive exaltation of the Buddha in the rise of Mahayana. He fails to see any meaningful content, beyond paradox, in the orthodox two-natures formula (178), nor does he see any substance remaining in inclusivist theories of extra-ecclesial salvation through Christ (180):

> If, selecting from our Christian language, we call God-acting-towards-mankind the Logos, then we must say that *all* salvation, within all religions, is the work of the Logos and that under their various images and symbols men in different cultures and faiths may encounter the

Logos and find salvation. But what we cannot say is that
all who are saved are saved by Jesus of Nazareth. The
life of Jesus was one point at which the Logos...has
acted; and it is the only point that savingly concerns the
Christian; but we are not called upon nor are we entitled
to make the negative assertion that the Logos has not
acted and is not acting anywhere else in human life
(181).

Thus while Hick believes Jesus to be the Christian gift to the world,
this is no longer to be interpreted in the old, western imperialistic
categories; Jesus is "bigger" than the church's teachings about him
(though by no means in the inclusive sense demanded by Rahner).
So, for Hick, the incarnation is nothing more than a statement of the
Christian sense that "God was in Christ" (284).

For all that, however, Hick joins Maurice Wiles' notorious descent into ambiguity over the historical Jesus' accomplishments by
occasionally asserting Jesus' human superlativity, if not uniqueness.
Thus having begun with reference to the "largely unknown man of
Nazareth" (168), Hick begins to wax lyrical in a now familiar way:
"I see the Nazarene, then, as intensely and overwhelmingly conscious of the reality of God...his life a continuous response to the
divine love...so powerfully God-conscious that his life vibrated, as
it were, to the divine life" and, at the same time, "a wholly unpreten-
tious working-class young man" (172). Here there is very little sense
of historical skepticism and cultural relativism, as Nineham critically
observes of Hick and others in his "Epilogue" to *The Myth of God
Incarnate* (187).

In one of his short pieces for Goulder's collection *Incarnation
and Myth* (1979), entitled "Evil and Incarnation," Hick further defines his newly metaphorical conception of the incarnation. If incarnating means strongly expressing or "embodying," so that Churchill
can be said to have "incarnated" British defiance, for instance, then
for Hick "It is in this sense that we can very properly say that the divine love, the divine attitude to mankind, was incarnated in the life
of Jesus—that the Logos was made flesh" (83-84). With what could
well be reluctance, Hick then indicates that he has learned the lesson
of those labeled "historical skeptics," above:

It would, as Dennis Nineham reminds us in his contribution to *The Myth of God Incarnate*, be a leap beyond the historical evidence to assert that God's love was *perfectly* or *absolutely* embodied in every moment of Jesus' life. But it is entirely possible that the divine *agape* has been more fully incarnated in this life than in any other. At any rate we know that God's gracious and demanding love was embodied in Jesus' love in so powerful a way that we ourselves are grasped by it today, some nineteen centuries later (84).

So by the late 1980s Hick seems to have got the message, as is his usual way in learning from others' critiques of his program. In 1989 he makes reference to Jesus' considerable continuity with other Jewish teachers of his day (as shown by biblical scholarship in the last decade), not to mention Jesus' similarities with aspects of the Bhakti tradition in Hinduism, with Sufism, Amida Buddhism, with the compassionate vision of Mahayana, the rabbinic tradition, as well as the founder of Sikhism, Guru Nanak.[83] And in "The Non-Absoluteness of Christianity" (1987) Hick expresses doubt about asserting a fuller incarnation of the "divine purpose" in Jesus than in others:

> Whether it happened more fully in the case of Jesus than in that of any other human being, or even perhaps absolutely in Jesus, cannot properly be settled a priori (though that seems to be how Baillie and Lampe settled it) but only on the basis of historical information. This means in practice that it cannot be definitively settled, for we lack the kind of evidence, touching every moment and aspect of Jesus' inner and outer life, that could entitle one to make such a judgment (32).

In this essay, as more fully in his contribution to a Claremont symposium (with John Cobb and others) entitled "An Inspiration Christology for a Religiously Plural World" (1988), Hick not only continues his call for a Christology without Jesus' uniqueness and finality, but begins to suggest the form it might take. In fact he brings his earlier emphasis on the Logos to a new pitch, embracing the thrust of Geoffrey Lampe's "inspiration Christology" and D.M. Baillie's "paradox of grace." Crucially, though, while for Baillie the paradox of grace in Jesus was "complete and absolute" and for Lampe the spirit in Jesus provided "a perfected form of inspiration," for Hick these are unnecessary extras.[84] Having come explicitly to share Nineham's skepticism about establishing the historical Jesus' uniqueness (21), Hick, in the "Inspiration Christology" essay, simply wishes to see Jesus as an inspired man among other inspired men, with the "extent" of his inspiration deemed indeterminable. Writes Hick, "A return today, in our pluralistic age, to this simplest, least theoretical or speculative, and most directly experiential understanding of Jesus seems to me to offer great gains, both for the Christian community and for the wider human family" (24).

Among the influences on Hick's pluralistic theology of religions and his perception of Jesus are Kant, Troeltsch and Schleiermacher. For a start Hick's own development clearly follows that of Troeltsch, whose views in *The Absoluteness of Christianity and the History of Religions*,[85] with its talk of Christianity as "absolute," "unique," "final," "normal" and "ultimate," had given way, by 1923, before a deepening pluralism and Hick-like talk of "relative absoluteness."[86] And Schleiermacher's ghost walks wherever the divinity of Jesus is conceived as a matter of degree, in the intensity of his (purely human) God-consciousness.

We have seen the influence of Kant's *Critique of Pure Reason* (1781) in Hick's non-speculative agnosticism—his careful distinction between the *noumenon* of "the real" and the *phenomena* of the religions. It is likely, too, that Kant's *Critique of Practical Reason* (1788) stands somewhere in the background when shared human moral experience, the categorical imperative, is invoked as evidence for the "reality" of the *noumenal*. And perhaps Kant's *Critique of Judgment* (1790), with its notion of "common sense," contributes to Hick's confidence in the uniform contours of human religious and aesthetic sensibility as crucial justifiers of religious belief.

The extent of Kantian influence suggests just how uniform is human nature in Hick's mature vision. So while recognizing the variety of phenomenal reifications, through different linguistic and cultural totalities (a diversity which, admittedly, Troeltsch and the "historical skeptics" make more of than does Hick), nevertheless deep structures of human nature and experience remain as a crucial feature in Hick's understanding of religion. These deep structures enable the one deep unity to be grasped beneath the obscuring blanket of multi-fold religious diversity. So, for instance, Hick in "Jesus and the World Religions" (1977) can appeal to "a tendency of the religious mind" (170), "the one world of our common humanity" and "the global consciousness which is emerging" (182), while in *An Interpretation of Religion* (1989) recourse is made to "structures of our mind, which in turn reflect cultural variations *within the basic human form*"(202) (italics mine).

Thus not only has Hick's preference for the historical Jesus over the developed, dogmatic Christ been noted, but his recourse to human nature as well. And these are, of course, two epistemological pillars of the "idealist and "liberal" positions outlined above.

Clearly, therefore, Hick's case constitutes an anomaly. It is through this anomaly, however, that Hick's separateness from the "liberal" writers is shown up, though he remains a liberal Protestant and refers to himself as such. The difference is that the "liberal" group match the historical Jesus and the human condition to their claims for Jesus' uniqueness. Hick, on the other hand, refuses to do this. Why? First, he claims far less dependence on the historical Jesus than nearly all the "liberal" writers. Second, he is unlike nearly every "liberal" considered above in reversing the trend in modern theology by turning from Christocentrism to theocentrism.[87] Thus he eliminates Christology as a distinctive source for knowledge of God. And third, the human condition serves Hick differently than it serves the "liberal" writers. For them it provides a Bultmann-style pre-understanding defining, if you like, an "itch" which only the historical Jesus can "scratch." But for Hick this human condition works as part of a Kantian epistemology by disclosing the gracious reality beyond all religious phenomena and certainly beyond Jesus. So while he *is* a liberal theologian his position, relative to that of the "liberal" group discussed in Part III above, is not Christocentric; he demands less from the historical Jesus, and finds the human condition pointing not to Christ but to "the real" which lies beyond Christ—indeed beyond all human religion.[88]

All of this, however, still involves a confident recourse to the one behind the many, the *noumenon* behind the multivariate *phenomena*, and this is precisely what post-modern relativism questions. Despite his occasional application of a Wittgensteinian "grammatical" view of religious truth *à la* Peter Winch (see n. 68), nevertheless this is not carried through to its most radical conclusion, as it is by a Don Cupitt (or a Michael Goulder).[89] Shifting from God-centeredness to reality-centeredness certainly indicates Hick's appreciation of non-theistic approaches to ultimate reality, but only insofar as he has acknowledged the multiplication of *phenomena*—his sense of the single *noumenon* is unchanged, though he has renamed it "reality" rather than "God." So he has not really escaped this criticism which applies also to the "historical skeptics": that they are not consistently radical in their commitment to cultural diversity. The same will also be evident with the next writer considered.

WILFRED CANTWELL SMITH

Wilfred Cantwell Smith is now Professor Emeritus in the Comparative History of Religion at Harvard University having formerly taught at Dalhousie and McGill Universities in Canada, where he was ordained a Presbyterian minister. Through his many writings, as in his innovative leadership within the academy, Cantwell Smith has been a most influential historian of religion. He began as an Islamicist and Oriental linguist, and the comparative study of religions has always been his concern, rather than systematic theology. Yet he does explore the theological implications emerging from his primary historical work moving, in the last decade, toward outlining a "world theology" which is thoroughly pluralist.

The texts to which I now turn illustrate this theological aspect of Cantwell Smith's work, in which he most definitely surrenders the uniqueness and finality of Christ. His approach differs significantly from that of Hick, with one of several distinctions being his lack of methodological interest in the historical Jesus. But he does share with Hick strong recourse to the human condition as the basis of all he does and so, like Hick, there is some resemblance to the "liberal" writers discussed above.

Cantwell Smith's view of theology as the legitimate heir of historical study, asserted in the face of the bastard usurper secularist reductionism, is propounded in "Theology and the World's Religious History" (1987). On the subject of truth he believes that our western culture has backed the wrong enlightenment horse in its preference for science rather than history (69). Science has subsequently led to a somewhat truncated assessment of "the natural" at the expense of a more fulsome "humane understanding," banishing much of great human value to a new realm of "religious belief"— whereupon it is counted a poor cousin to "scientific knowledge." History, on the other hand, shows that religion is far less the optional addendum to human life that a scientizing secularism would deem it (68)—Cantwell Smith argues that life is everywhere underscored and bracketed, rather than merely punctuated here and there, by religion. He believes an accurate and deep exploration of history actually leads to the brink of theology: "It is, frankly, preposterous to imagine that anyone insensitive to the presence of God can understand or interpret human history in any but drastically inadequate ways, given the extent to which human lives have been lived in that presence" (55). This is how Cantwell Smith works his magic. He begins with human religious experience and by employing realist epistemology he infers God's existence, setting his face against all naturalistic explanations.

Cantwell Smith's mature position is most fully expressed in the Cadbury Lectures he was prevailed upon to give at the University of Birmingham in 1980, appearing as *Towards a World Theology: Faith and the Comparative History of Religion* (1981). Not only are his perennial concerns revisited there but also his fullest engagement with the theological task is given, in what was for Langdon Gilkey his "most important and adventurous proposal."[90]

Cantwell Smith begins by arguing that world religious history is unified, full of interconnections and mutual influences among the religions; by no means is it merely a loose collection of wholly disparate traditions. He reiterates the view, which made him famous in *The Meaning and End of Religion* (1962), that each of these "*cumulative traditions*" variously represents the light of divine revelation as refracted through the prism of a more fundamental reality, that of human "*faith.*" To fixate upon and then to dismiss the tradition's "beliefs," blind to the deeper reality of "faith," constitutes the unpardonable sin of enlightenment rationalism for Cantwell Smith. Beyond the resultant highly artificial reduction of religion to "natural" and "supernatural" (hence "true" and "false") he champions a "humane knowledge" far more open to the universality of religious feelings and phenomena. The corporate, critical self-consciousness he advocates is broader than any narrow and parochial bias masquerading as "objectivity"; it keeps channels open to religious participants as well as to scholars.

Having thus established a view of religious studies which is open to theological conclusions, Cantwell Smith discusses versions of ultimate reality accessible through the several religious traditions. In this broad context he undertakes the more specific consideration of comparative religion from the perspective of Christian theology. Then, in his crucial eighth chapter, he makes two significant Christological points. First, he rejects a so-called "big-bang theory" of religious origins—the essence and identity of religious traditions is to be found in their present life (of course, in conversation with their past) rather than by reconstructing their origins. It is in the present we are "saved" (a this-worldly reality for Cantwell Smith, as for Hick). As Alan Race observes, "By "saved" here Cantwell Smith means that which has enabled a truly moral life, that which has released the drive towards living with more than a mundane reference colouring one's goals and aspirations, that which has kept the forces of despair and meaninglessness at bay. All of this, he believes, can be demonstrated historically, as a matter of fact, through one's friendships with people of other faiths."[91] Yet while this is observably obvious for Cantwell Smith he also finds it to be part and parcel of viewing Christian convictions about God and Christ aright. Thus his second major Christological insight—the cause, too, of much confusion among his interpreters—is that Christians need not doubt the presence of salvation within the non-Christian religions if God is the sort of God they meet in Jesus Christ. And he is quick to point out how God's salvation comes *through* (not in spite of) all religious traditions, contra any inclusivism. The Christian vision, according to Cantwell Smith, rules out any salvific exclusivism (170-71). It is because of Christ, as Cantwell Smith sees him, that Christians need have no doubt about this.

So revelation is a present reality, says Cantwell Smith, and accessible across the spectrum of religions. This is because he understands revelation to impinge upon actual persons in their concrete place and time. It is no abstraction nor, in any meaningful sense, is it "past."

Before discussing these issues, and encountering some of the confusion about them among Cantwell Smith's interpreters, let us immerse ourselves a little more in his Christological views via some more direct writings. Most commentators lament the paucity of explicit Christology in the Cantwell Smith corpus. Indeed, he admits this paucity himself.[92] Rose Tadsen, whose doctoral thesis on Cantwell Smith's Christology can but prove useful in a discussion such as this, suggests that "Perhaps it should at least be considered that Smith may himself not yet be clear on the place or meaning of Christ."[93]

Briefly, then, let us take note of two essays, one early and one recent, which are more directly concerned with Christology.

A Montreal lecture of 1961, "The Christian in a Religiously Plural World," broaches the issue of pluralism's challenge to Christian theology. The missionaries' failure to convert the world religions is noted—as Canon Max Warren (then head of the Church Missionary Society) put it, "We have marched around alien Jerichos the requisite number of times. We have sounded the trumpet. And the walls have not collapsed" (cited on 110). For Cantwell Smith the theological implication is that this is the way God wants it, therein presaging his later "faith vs. belief and cumulative tradition" stance.

Cantwell Smith rejects the traditional Christian logic which damns outsiders despite their obvious spiritual and humane attainments (123) along with the traditional Christian spirit which approves of such damnation. For Cantwell Smith this flies in the face of that mercy of God which Christians should recognize in Christ (118ff, 126-27) along with Protestant belief in free grace rather than "works" (127). Observing the realities of salvation in these other religions and standing alongside them in the task of building a better world[94] are both Christian imperatives for Cantwell Smith. But, crucially, the world religions can no longer be left out of account in formulating Christian theology, as he classically states:

The time will soon be with us when a theologian who attempts to work out his position unaware that he does so as
a member of a world society in which other theologians
equally intelligent, equally devout, equally moral, are
Hindus, Buddhists, Muslims, and unaware that his readers
are likely to be Buddhists or to have Muslim husbands or
Hindu colleagues—such a theologian is as out of date as
is one who attempts to construct an intellectual position
unaware that Aristotle has thought about the world or that
existentialists have raised new orientations or unaware
that the earth is a minor planet in a galaxy that is vast only
by terrestrial standards. Philosophy and science have im-
pinged so far on theological thought more effectively than
has comparative religion, but this will not last (112-13).

That theologians are nowadays realizing not only this but more
is evident with the appearance of a book such as Hick and Knitter's
symposium *The Myth of Christian Uniqueness* (1987). Cantwell
Smith's contribution therein, "Idolatry in Comparative Perspective,"
is an important source for his latest Christological emphases. Idols
are revalued by Cantwell Smith who argues that all such visual as
well as *doctrinal* images provide, for good or ill, necessary albeit
limited mediations of God. He goes on to condemn the western
Christian arrogance about others' "idolatry" which fails to perceive
how idolatrous its own dogmas can be. As he puts it,

my thesis is that all of us on earth are prone to an error,
one that Western theology, unfortunately, has tended at
times to bless: the error of identifying with the divine,
with the truth, with the final, with transcendence, the particular form in or through which we have been introduced to it, by way of which It or He or She has come
into our particular lives—rather than relating that form to
It/Him/Her, subordinating it, relativizing it in relation to
the Absolute that it serves (58-59).

Thus seeing religious truth the way we do, whichever cumulative tradition we might inhabit, is a matter of perception limited to our own

community process and its internal self-understanding. Christian exclusivism is thus undermined by Cantwell Smith in a new way:

> For Christians to see Christ as divine is a perception
> ...that their own personal experience, and two thousand
> years of Church history, elicit and confirm. It is, however,
> impossible to *perceive* him as the sole such mediator; although one can hold this as a theological proposition, inferred by logic from what one does see. One cannot perceive the non-divinity of Krishna, or of the Qur'an. (That
> these are not forms of God for oneself one may know.
> Whether they are or are not for other people one has to ascertain by investigation). To believe that other groups'
> forms are *not* divine is a purely doctrinal construct. To
> hold that Buddhist, or post-Biblical Jewish, life is not the
> locus of God's salvific activity, fully comparable to God's
> activity in Christian life, is a sheer man-made hypothesis.
> The position has—inescapably—no direct grounding in
> reality. The doctrine of the divinity of Christ is a conceptual form of Christians' knowledge of God. The doctrine
> of other religious patterns' non-divinity is an intellectual
> formulation of ignorance: an ignorance of the life of those
> for whom those patterns are rich (60-61).

For Cantwell Smith, however, there can be no doubt that Christ is the touchstone of God's dealings with Christians: "I myself certainly see the figure of Christ in the piety of hundreds of millions of Christians over the centuries as a form in which transcendence, God, has participated in our lives (and/or vice versa: a form in which we have participated in its life). In fact, it would seem to me obtuse for anyone to fail to see this, and silly to deny it (for any perceptive Muslim, for example, or atheist). I speak as an historian" (63). But no uniqueness is implied thereby. Likewise, a similar state of affairs is seen to pertain throughout the religions:

> No doubt, some Christians have understood Christ Himself, or various Christian authorities, as saying that God
> has acted effectively only in this one case, or surpassing-

ly so. It is equally sure that some Muslims have understood the Qur'an or various Islamic authorities as saying
much the same thing in their case. A claim to uniqueness
is not unique. Its incidence is simply one of the significant facts of which the modern mind takes note before
theorizing about religious or spiritual matters. It is, of
course, true that Christ is unique. It is also true that the
Qur'an is unique, or K'ung Fu-tse (64).

Cantwell Smith appreciates how Christians could once take comfort
in their exclusivism, but advises them they can do so no longer (68
n.12).

Consequently Cantwell Smith is drawn to join the growing
chorus of theologians who have come to understand the incarnation
as a myth. But he sees this as a matter of gain rather than loss for
Christians; not only can "truth" be communicated better by myth
than proposition (so says Cantwell Smith from his broad experience
of comparative religion) but the surrender of aggressive dogmatism
thus enabled would be a major contribution to world peace (so says
Cantwell Smith the statesman of religious studies) (65-66).

By way of assessment I will first consider Cantwell Smith's
idea of God, with his attendant notions of epistemology and truth.
Thus enabled, issues germane to this study will then be brought into
focus—the presence of quite foundational notions about the human
condition, and the apparent absence of interest in the historical Jesus.
This latter will involve some mention of points made by Rose Tadsen
about Cantwell Smith's Christology.

As Philip Almond rightly observes, personal truth presupposes
the existence of a transcendent focus of faith for Cantwell Smith, for
whom "the objective existence of God is not so much a conclusion to
the decision religiously to believe, but a basic presupposition of living religiously."[95] Cantwell Smith's version of God is normatively
theistic, but he does recognize how the transcendence he identifies
has non-theistic reifications also (e.g. in Buddhism).[96] But he makes
less of this than Hick, who is far more circumspect in his use of
words such as "God," "theology," "faith" and "salvation."

On the matter of Cantwell Smith's epistemology, Langdon Gilkey observes that "Smith openly moves onto the battleground of philosophy of religion, but the arsenal he brings with him is that of the historian of religion; and that is what is novel about it."[97] Cantwell Smith has a realist epistemology and, as has been observed, he is very critical of reductionism and current preoccupations with our construction of reality rather than reality in itself. Also, he conceives the business of *knowing* more broadly than do the empiricists, finding in it moral and aesthetic dimensions as well. So it is that the good, the true and the beautiful are conjoined in Cantwell Smith's Platonic heart.

Cantwell Smith also employs an argument from religious experience (faith) which echoes the liberalism of Schleiermacher. This experience he finds more ontologically disclosive than would Rudolf Otto, however, not to mention either William James or Carl Jung. Indeed, Cantwell Smith is so sure in his assertion that faith is the medium of divine disclosure that he combines the emphasis of Schleiermacher with what amounts to a Barthian-style positivism of revelation. In addition, note that Cantwell Smith is also a moral realist—values for him are objective, real and knowable.[98] As Edward Hughes observes in his study of Cantwell Smith's theology, "It is perhaps unusual to find such an active neo-Platonic imagination in the twentieth century; but the neo-Platonic model legitimizes those insights into reality that a sceptical and reductionist philosophy fails to perceive."[99]

While recognizing human diversity, nevertheless Cantwell Smith is firmly of the opinion that human nature is fundamentally uniform as well as religiously disclosive. This is the typical liberal understanding met also in Hick; these two "radical" theologians, in many ways, remain liberals at heart. So, for Cantwell Smith, "human beings are that kind of reality... that any given two of them—no matter how close together, no matter how far apart, in space, time, culture, temperament—any two of them can arrive at an understanding that is neither 100 per cent nor zero. There is no person on earth that I can fully understand. There is and has been no person on earth that I cannot understand at all."[100] It should be noted, though, that in his eagerness to postulate underlying structures Cantwell Smith is less readily dismissive of human diversity than Hick. The primary unity of

human experience to which he holds only presents itself to his view
after much scholarly laboring over the secondary diversities:

> One of the most determinative characteristics of any
> human being is whom he or she means in saying 'we'.
> Neither the academic intellectual, nor the person of faith,
> can any longer be content to mean less than 'we human
> beings', across the globe, across the centuries: we per-
> sons on earth, in all our vast diversity of historical devel-
> opment, cultural particularism, and in our case religious
> commitment. It requires erudition, critical acumen, imag-
> inative sympathy and penetrating understanding; it takes
> time, effort and dedication; but it is now possible, and
> therefore now requisite, to learn to say, and to mean, that
> we human beings on earth are diverse but not incongru-
> ous. Our solidarity precedes our particularity, and is part
> of our self-transcendence. The truth of all of us is a part
> of the truth of each of us. It is self-consciously we who
> differ. Therefore, we differ, yet we are not disparate. In-
> deed, yet we ultimately converge. True knowledge of
> man is self-knowledge, but now on a global scale, and on
> an historical.[101]

Cantwell Smith could not be clearer on the matter of a religiously
disclosive "human condition" than this.

But where Cantwell Smith differs from Hick most decisively,
for my purposes, is over the historical Jesus. As Rose Tadsen points
out, "Smith thinks that the 'Christ figure' of continuing faith has been
more significant, operative, consequential, and historically real than
the vague figure of Nazareth. . . . For Smith this ever contemporaneous
figure is the true historical figure."[102] She adds that he rarely speaks of
Christ except in terms of personal responses to him. There is no unconditional talk of Jesus as God's revelation pure and simple;
Cantwell Smith believes that revelation is always revelation to some-
body.[103] He gives a personal example of this, stating how Christ has
revealed God to him more fully than was the case twenty years ago,
and how he hopes that this will become even more the case. But he
also recalls that, as a questioning undergraduate during the depression

years, he found God speaking to him more through the Old Testament social critic Amos than through Christ.[104] Thus Cantwell Smith shows there is no objective givenness about revelation through Christ, or indeed anyone else. It appears that for him Christ is basically a dimension of the Christian's cumulative tradition—the "cumulative" aspect being especially important, as the latest "installments" in this tradition are as much or more important than the first.

Now, however, some confusion arises. Two possible instances of veiled Christocentrism in the work of Cantwell Smith will be discussed.

Tadsen identifies hints of the first possible type of Christocentrism when Cantwell Smith looks to Christ as the revelation *to all* that God is loving, universal savior—"he does not ever mention the Qur'an or the Buddha or any other central religious form or figure in this respect."[105] Tadsen adds that she has heard Cantwell Smith say privately that Christ provides the best access to this gracious, salvific reality (212). Elsewhere, however, Cantwell Smith states that it is for Christians alone that the good news emerges in this way—that the salvific capacity of the other religions is not *proved* by Christ in advance of the evidence, but is simply established *de facto* by observing the reality of salvation which the religions foster (in providing the matrix wherein God-centered lives are created and established). Hick, as we have seen, does this far more explicitly, without a hint of Cantwell Smith's recourse to any "methodological Christocentrism."[106]

But while we might accept that Cantwell Smith has rejected Christocentric thinking of this sort, as Hick also claimed to do, a different kind of case can be made in which Hick and Cantwell Smith *are* exposed as far less pluralistic than they claim to be. Gilkey points out that Cantwell Smith's God is active, merciful, moral and revealed to us through history, and this sounds to Gilkey like the Christian God.[107] Indeed, we have heard Cantwell Smith base his assurances about the mercy of God toward adherents of the non-Christian religions on the fact that the God he meets in Jesus is a merciful God—not that Jesus is the savior of all these people, but that God will save them because he is the sort of God whom we meet in Jesus. Thus the tolerant, universal deity of the "religious pluralists" is found to be conceivable only because of Jesus Christ?[108] Surely, however, such a God would not emerge from the riot of options and the strong dualism characteristic of the Hindu pantheon, nor from the troubled religious melting pot of Judaism and Islam in today's middle east.[109] It seems, therefore, that Cantwell Smith's tolerant theocentrism involves a deeper, more subtle Christocentrism, insofar as his tolerant, inclusive God is unthinkable for him apart from what Christians believe Jesus has shown them of God. Hence this view of God might be seen as but one more "epicycle" to the inclusivist position—itself an epicycle in the "Ptolemaic" Christian cosmos Hick and Cantwell Smith claim to have overturned.

One can go on to argue, as does Mark Heim, that these "pluralist" thinkers are anything but pluralistic in their undercutting of genuine religious diversity. Rather than respecting what the different religions say about ultimate reality, there is a western liberal imperialism in these approaches every bit as dismissive of the non-Christian religions as traditional Christian exclusivism was thought to be.[110] The roots of such imperialism are found in the separation of religious and secular realms in the rise of science and the English enlightenment,[111] with the resultant banishing of religious truth to the realm of personal perception and preference—ultimately, to that of *phenomena* rather than *noumena*.

All this can now rightly be seen as just the sort of western cultural imperialism which "religious pluralists" have deplored in the worst exclusivist excesses of our missionary past. As effectively as our expansionist colonial forebears in the west co-opted missionaries in their task of subjugating foreign cultures, therefore, so today's expansionist western culture finds unwitting allies among the theologians here considered—we discern in these "religious pluralists," with their universal God beneath the superficial flux of religions, the hegemony of western enlightenment thought. And this, in turn, is inseparable from specifically Christian ideas about God and the world.

Before proceeding to discuss the "complete relativists," who alone in this chapter escape these charges of closet foundationalism, there is a variant on the pluralist position which deserves our attention—one far more open to the fact of inter-religious diversity. And that is the "complimentary uniqueness" case of Paul Knitter.

PAUL F. KNITTER

Paul F. Knitter is a Roman Catholic theologian of religions. Formerly a religious in a missionary order he is now a married layman and Professor of Theology at Xavier University in Cincinnati. Knitter's book *No Other Name?* *A Critical Survey of Christian Attitudes Toward the World Religions* (1985), as well as being the most extensive of its sort to date, presents a world theology of its own. I also consider an essay "Toward a Liberation Theology of Religions" appearing in *The Myth of Christian Uniqueness* (1987), a volume jointly edited with Hick, in which Knitter begins to take account of the anti-foundationalist challenge and its implications for world theologies.

In *No Other Name?* Knitter seeks to disabuse Christianity of its dogmatic self-assertiveness in the face of world religions. Instead of a single divinely sanctioned religion with a unique Christ, he offers a world theology accessible through inter-religious dialogue.

This dialogue is for all who are committed to their own religions but who remain imaginatively open-minded and search for the deep unity which Knitter believes can be found beyond religious diversity. But the dialogue proposed will not lead the participants *past* their individual commitments to a transcendent beyond, as Hick would have it, nor *beneath* each religious tradition to the one reality of faith undergirding and energizing them all, as Cantwell Smith would have it. For Knitter the religions are not so much interchangeable pointers to "the whole" *but, rather, distinct, necessary components of its complete representation.*

The world theologies met thus far have been more or less relativistic, as if the religions were various paths up a mountain, providing views of the terrain from various perspectives on the way up but disclosing the same overall view once the summit has been attained. Hick uses the ancient Indian proverb of blind men with an elephant to illustrate this point: one has hold of the trunk believing it to be a snake, another finds a leg and thinks it a great living pillar, a third takes the elephant's tusk for a ploughshare, and so on.[112] The blind men are severally limited to their own perceptions of the whole, while the noumenal elephant stands unrecognized beyond each individual's phenomenal grasp. So it is with religions and the true nature of "the real," thinks Hick, at least until the eschaton—the point when, at last, blind eyes will be opened or else the summit attained.

How might Knitter's perspective resolve this parabolic dilemma posed by Hick? I suggest Knitter would have the blind men talk among themselves about what they thought they had found, thus making correct identification of the elephant far more likely. Such a version of Hick's parable would involve dialogue between the blind men in touch with trunk, leg, tusk, etc. to the end that an adequate picture might be compiled of the whole beast. Hick's strict Kantian separation of noumenal and phenomenal would thus be circumvented.

This, I believe, is Knitter's own special contribution on this issue. Following David Tracy he holds the view that all individual truths have universal relevance. That is to say, all truth if it is true "for us" is in some sense true "for all" (36).[113] For Knitter each religion will correct oversights and compensate for blind-spots in others so an overall picture can be built up (221). In this process *every* contribution is unique—without Jesus, for instance, Knitter cannot see a full and adequate picture of God emerging: "All peoples, of all religions, must know of him," he writes, "in order to grasp the full content of God's presence in history."[114] To illustrate this I return to my metaphor; without knowing about the trunk, for instance, the blind men may never fully realize what they have hold of, though from the trunk alone the elephant cannot be identified. So it is that Jesus is important for Knitter, though he will not allow bald assertion by Christians that Jesus is in any sense *uniquely* disclosive of God.

There are some now familiar reasons which Knitter gives to support this prohibition: the presence of low Christologies in the New Testament which should give pause to today's advocates of a high Christology, the limitations of either-or thinking inherent in what he calls the "classicist mindset" of westerners, and the suggested origin of the apocalyptic/eschatological context in which early Christian talk of Jesus' uniqueness is a form of "survival language" (181-85). For Knitter, Christians must realize that such confessional language preceded the earliest assertions of Jesus' uniqueness and finality and it must again suffice today.

But for Knitter there is another reason, less familiar. His dialogue model will not allow any religion to claim unique insight apart from the dialogue itself. Knitter admits that Jesus may indeed prove

to be unique, but this will only be evident through the process of dialogue.[115] Similarly, if Christianity were to surrender its traditional
claims to Jesus' uniqueness, the ability to do so would also come
only through inter-religious dialogue:

> The spiritual adventure of dialogue, an adventure that
> will take time and that Christians are only now really be-
> ginning, will provide the praxis that can verify *or* qualify
> the traditional Christian claim that in Jesus of Nazareth
> God has 'surprised' us and offered the fullest expression
> of divine truth, the symbol that will confirm, complete,
> and correct all other religious symbols and thus unify hu-
> mankind. Without dialogue, such a truth might be sus-
> pected and suggested, but it cannot be known (207).

I now turn to Knitter's 1987 essay "Towards a Liberation Theology of Religions." Here even more centrally than in *No Other
Name?* the role of religious dialogue in the world peace process is
emphasized (178-79). But there is also a new recognition of the
struggles for liberating praxis among the oppressed as a "privileged
hermeneutical ground" (185) for religious insight. This is because
since *No Other Name?* Knitter has had to face the challenge of anti-
foundationalism. He now wishes to look elsewhere for the basis of a
world theology. Not that he is any friendlier than before to "the pap
of relativism" (181), but clearly the "common ground" between religions which he was happy to take for granted in *No Other Name?*
has now vanished. Having read Richard Rorty and others, therefore,
Knitter confirms that "We are urged by the philosophers to resist the
siren lure of objectivism and bravely to give up our search for foundations or a "common ground" above or outside the plurality of
views" (183).

But although Knitter has abandoned Hick-the-liberal-theolo-
gian's philosophical realism he appears to have retained a Hick-
style moral realism, for a compelling moral reality remains to fill
the gap left in the foundations of his former world theology. It is the
liberation theologian's "preferential option for the poor and the non-
person" (185).[116] Knitter urges that this is no new foundationalism,
however, but only "an approach, a context, a starting point that must

itself be clarified as it clarifies and creates new common ground of understanding" (186).

It is in this new context of liberation that Knitter's commitment to the disclosivity of dialogue re-emerges. Only in dialogue between those committed to struggling for justice among the oppressed will a true world theology come. But this is because the focus will have shifted from theology or Christology to *soteriology*, so that inter-religious dialogue can proceed where Knitter (echoing Aloysius Pieris) believes the religions have more in common (188).[117]

But once dialogue has been re-established on a new footing (not, we are told, a new "foundation") Knitter returns to familiar territory. Again he tells us it may be the case that Christ and Christianity are proved unique through such dialogue. But, he asks, "has such praxis taken place? Have Christians actively learned from and worked with other religions to such a degree that they have experienced the uniqueness and normativity of Jesus over all others? Has their praxis of dialogue with other believers been extensive enough to make the universal claim that Jesus surpasses and is therefore normative for these other faiths? I think not" (192). Were this atmosphere of greater understanding to be established, thinks Knitter, a *consensus fidelium* might arise in which Christians were prepared to surrender their claims for Jesus' uniqueness and finality (194). Alternatively, only through such a praxis-based dialogue could an adequate comparison and hence a grading of religions take place. Only thus could traditional Christian convictions about Jesus be either disproved or established.

Apart from such an undertaking, according to Knitter, there is no place or need for Christian exclusivism concerning Jesus. In addition he believes, with Cantwell Smith, that what Christians learn about God through Jesus not only gives them confidence that salvation is available *extra ecclesiam* but constrains them to engage in non-absolutist exploration with others (196). Also, as in *No Other Name?* he offers the essentially post-liberal sentiment that simple confession of personal faith will serve the evangelistic cause, if such is one's aim, far better than dogmatic assertions (193, 196). Adding this to his conviction that only in dialogue, if at all, will the truth come out about Jesus, Knitter's proposed relaxation therapy for exclusivist-minded Christians is complete—he offers them the carrot of possibly establishing their exclusivist case on a firmer footing than heretofore, that in so doing he might coax even the most narrow-minded Christian into religious dialogue. By no means does he fore-close entirely on Jesus' uniqueness—a concession to critics perhaps. But nor by any means does Knitter assert it outright.

It bears mention that Knitter's is a far more Catholic program than that of the Protestants Hick and Cantwell Smith. Inspired by Schleiermacher, and by currents of Protestant thought before and since emphasizing personal faith and religious experience, Hick and Cantwell Smith see religious individuals as directly in touch with ultimate reality, though aided to some extent by religious traditions. In all, the collective dimension of religion is secondary—perhaps even bypassable. But for Knitter contact with "God" is achieved only through participation in a religious tradition. Personal faith or religious experience is not abstracted from this holistic, collective reality in a more typically Protestant manner. So it was that Knitter could find no path through to "the whole" but that allowed by dia-logue between different religious traditions, for no deeper or more direct insights were deemed possible. Thus dialogue is even more essential for Knitter than for Hick and Cantwell Smith, for whom "mystics" of all religious stamps might apprehend "the eternal one" apart from the sharing of insights with others. But not so for Knitter. The blind men cannot suddenly find their sight and so pass on to full and direct disclosures beyond their former gropings. Only in di-alogue will the elephant be known aright, even if through a drench-ing in Knitter's newfound anti-foundationalism the elephant might have changed its spots![118]

We have noted that Hick and Cantwell Smith think like liberals about a religious absolute disclosed through experience. But unlike the "liberal" group considered in Part III above, they choose to focus on religious diversity and not to exclusively identify Jesus with that absolute. Serious doubts were raised, however, about the extent to which they *really* escaped the Christocentrism which they so earnest-ly denied. The veiled Christocentrism of their God-idea calls into question the success of their pluralist program.

This problem did not arise for Paul Knitter, who showed him-self far more aware of actual diversity. Nevertheless, his "cumulative uniqueness" perspective treats the diverse religions as really quite compatible, such that Christ, the Buddha and other figures can fit together alongside each other, as it were, as pieces of the same puzzle.

The "complete relativists" we next consider share none of the interest shown by "religious pluralists" in accounting for the diversity of religions, since for them diversity is all; they take *plurality* for granted where liberals are committed to the notion of *unity*. They are imbued with the spirit of cultural relativism met already among the "historical skeptics," considered above, and they do not look for new foundations in the face of anti-foundationalism, as we have seen Knitter do. Indeed they lack confidence in any religious absolute of the liberal variety whatsoever. Thus the question of equating Jesus with any such absolute will not even arise—neither as a temptation for them nor even as a possibility.

Chapter Eleven

COMPLETE RELATIVISTS

The theologians now to be encountered take up and indeed move beyond the radical challenges posed by "historical skeptics" and "religious pluralists." The post-modern, post-structuralist challenge to modernity was discussed in the Introduction above. It envisages a world no longer able to tolerate talk of absolutes—neither as divinely revealed, nor as humanly discerned through examining either the fortunes of history or the contours of human life. Its deconstructive, Nietzschean spirit searches out and exposes all talk of given meanings, especially those entailed in Descartes' "turn to the subject" and the subsequent confident individualism of modernity. Language and culture assume far greater primacy in a world where meaning is humanly, often passively made. Thus conservative and liberal Christianity are both faced with authority crises. Two key emphases of liberal Christologies—the accessibility and automatic appeal of an historical Jesus along with a definite human condition with which this Jesus "fits"—are both denied. Nor can any idealist vision of history as the veiled march of divine spirit survive, unless it be reclassified as poetry.

Two writers will receive primary attention here. Don Cupitt now shows himself a confident Christian atheist who has drunk the cup of post-modernity to its dregs. He has of late abandoned a distinctive though nonetheless minimal earlier conception of Jesus' finality. The new American school of post-liberal theology will be mentioned via its major spokesman, George Lindbeck. His work on doctrine advocates an abandonment of dogma and absolutism—doctrines *express* the story of Christ, and are to be taken seriously by

Christians, but this story offers but one possible construal of history and experience. Thus the story of Jesus can support none of Christianity's former absolute ambitions for it, and Lindbeck will not insist upon Jesus' uniqueness. It is by no means certain, however, that Lindbeck has succeeded in dismissing the "liberal" type of case, as will be argued.

DON CUPITT

Don Cupitt, an Anglican priest, Fellow of Emmanuel College and a divinity lecturer at Cambridge University, has delivered an increasingly radical stance in English theology since the late 1960s. And as he has become an outspoken "Christian atheist" since the early 1980s, so too has he moved away from his early beliefs about Jesus' finality. They were, nevertheless, distinctive—we consider them briefly before examining the more radical, later views.

In "The Finality of Christ" (1975) Cupitt identifies Jesus' irony and religious iconoclasm as the basis for his finality—there is no superseding the themes to which he bore witness. In "The Leap of Reason" (1975) Cupitt asserts that Christianity embodies in its central myths the philosophy of spirit toward which Jesus was working far better than any other religion. Jesus' finality lies not as much in the content of his message as in its accessibility to everyone (rather than to some spiritual elite), and on that no more need be said. *Who Was Jesus?* (1977) is even more effusive, displaying a marked devotional tone; of Jesus, Cupitt writes: "The message is final: nothing more can be said in language. And because Jesus grasped and lived it, he is rightly called saviour, mediator, redeemer, not because of what he is in himself, but because he was so possessed by that to which he bore witness. In that sense he is rightly called the absolute in time, the one who shows the way to the perfect world" (92). This is quite a high Christology, though it is functional. It is echoed in Cupitt's short piece "Professor Stanton on Incarnational Language in the New Testament" (1979): "But if I have found salvation through Jesus' voice and person, I can quite intelligibly speak of him as the human ultimate and the crown of creation; the man who, by mirroring God, shows what the world was meant to be" (169). In *Jesus and the Gospel of God* (1979) Cupitt also exalts "Jesus as high as possible without compromising monotheism" (18). He suggests that other religions capture the same realities as those to which Jesus pointed, mentioning Amida (Pure Land) Buddhism and some forms of Hinduism. But with critical reservations the full panoply of traditional Christological titles is still allowable:

> Jesus can be called the final cause of creation in the sense that in him the highest goal is attained and the world comes to fruition, and he can be called the first-born of all creation in the sense that in him the creature at last enters into its perfect relation to the Creator and the Creator's work is complete. ... He anticipated—seized in advance—the end of all things. In that strictly eschatological sense he may be called divine (73).[119]

Insofar as Jesus made an existing message universally accessible, the early Cupitt was willing to ascribe finality to his person—as a kind of reward for services rendered, if you like. This does not represent the traditional Christological focus on Jesus' person, but rather the enlightenment focus on Jesus as teacher of reasonable religion, though colored by a little of the apocalyptic spirit Cupitt inherited from Schweitzer and Nietzsche. To be sure, Jesus' person *is* featured in the discussion and a finality ascribed to it. But the focus is chiefly upon Jesus' teaching; it is the message which matters, with any finality ascribed to Jesus' person being largely fortuitous. To offer an illustration, it is as if Jesus were one of many sperm attempting to fertilize an ovum—only one will succeed, though any one might have done so. So it is with Cupitt's Jesus in this early period—he is but one among many bringers of what is essentially the same message, the one who just happened to succeed in making that message universal.[120]

But even this minimal claim has been abandoned by Cupitt in his more recent work. Cupitt has, since *Taking Leave of God* (1980), passed beyond any literal theism into what I have elsewhere called his "later period."[121] For the later Cupitt not only is God dead but the self as well; no longer either a conservative or a liberal in theology, he has eschewed the modern project of enlightenment individualism. For him all is now language and culture, but with some prospect re-

maining for human desire ("life energy") to assert itself and so hold
off any collapse into complete passivity in the face of social and cultural pressures to conformity.[122]

There is an easy, anarchic attitude to truth in all of this. Meaning is seen as a totally human creation or, better still, it has become a
culturally, linguistically and temporally diverse human creation supported by no human condition, no ground of being, no logos, and no
liberal-idealist optimism that history is still "going somewhere."

Cupitt occasionally hints that all of this finds optimal expression in the myth of the incarnation—read as a story of the scattering
and dispersal of absolute meaning. Just as in his "early period" he
saw in the historical Jesus a picture (at that time, a "final" picture) of
what his spiritual vision entailed, so in his "later period" Cupitt finds
this vision evoked by the incarnational myth. But this is only a story
he likes. He has no confidence in our ability to reconstruct the historical Jesus any longer, no human condition or essence to match him
with, nor any overall view of history in which to locate a high point.
Thus there can be no uniqueness or finality of Jesus; all one sees is
Cupitt occasionally referring to what for him is a favorite story. Let
us trace this development in Cupitt's thought through the 1980s and
into the 1990s.

In *The World To Come* (1982) Cupitt sought a vision of spiritual life in the face of the "post-Nietzschean" void which he saw as
presaged by the historical Jesus and symbolized by the exalted Jesus
Christ. Thus he saw in Jesus Christ a Christian symbol for the new
world which we humans alone can make. In *The Sea of Faith* (1984)
Cupitt points beyond "the Babylonian captivity of realism" to a religion free of authoritative absolutes, content to limit its disputes with
other religions to the question of which can best explicate and address the human condition (32). Christianity, for Cupitt at this time,
fulfills the best both in Nietzschean humanism and in Buddhism,
combining the radical humanist challenge of the one with the lofty
spiritual attainments of the other (33). There is a touch of "liberalism" here: religious truth is a function of its capacity for answering
the human question with Christianity as the best answer. This echoes
Cupitt's early view of Jesus' *message* as ultimate and final. But in
Only Human (1985) Cupitt begins to fall firmly into the clutches of
post-modernity via the claims of linguistic naturalism. He leaves be-

hind liberal attempts at finding a fixed definition of the human. But a favored place for the Christian symbols remains in *Life Lines* (1986). There, Cupitt sees God and Christ incarnate as symbols of our human situation in the face of the void—perhaps they are still the "best" symbols. The New Testament provides a story of the decentering and scattering of God, of Christ and his people (214). It is a vision of diaspora, kenosis if you like, in the face of the void, of annihilation and meaninglessness:

> Thus if the post-modern world is in some respects Buddhist in its metaphysics, it is also Christian. There is no substantial individual self; the human realm is a field of communicant intersubjectivity. Becoming incarnate in Christ, God enters this realm and is disseminated through it as bread and wine. He and we both lose centred subjectivity. Thus the last story we tell of our lives ought to be, not a story of the final triumph of monarchical selfhood, but a story of *kenosis*, scattering and dispersal, a self-giving and self-loss that continue, as the hymn says, 'Till death thy endless mercies seal, and make the sacrifice complete'. If we are bold enough to call Good that Friday when darkness fell over the land because God had died in Christ on the cross, then we should be bold enough to call our own night good.[123]

This is a sort of demythologized Hegelian idealism, recalling Hegel's Trinitarian view of God emptying himself into Christ. But this is understood to be a powerful symbol only, rather than an objectively real process in the metaphysics of history.

In *The Long-Legged Fly* (1987) incarnation has come to symbolize the reduction of all meaning to purely human dimensions. There it is shorn of any sure ground, of any referent external to the diversity of human strivings. In part this is a statement of what rebel French philosophers such as Jacques Lacan and recent feminists are telling us—that culture imposes its values on us, that it writes on our bodies in fact, by language. But this is not at all a *fait accompli* for Cupitt. Christianity is also described as particularly (not uniquely) good at remedying the enslavement of desire to culture which he deplores—the reduction of people to unthinking passivity or uncritical obedience in our late twentieth century western culture. Incarnation thus becomes a metaphor for the nature of meaning in the post-modern world:

> The metaphysical metaphor to which we have been led has thus become incarnational. The integral whole-body human being is one in whom flesh and spirit, feeling and meaning, are perfectly conjoined.... It *is* the one person of the Word Incarnate, in whom two logically distinct natures or realms are conjoined 'without confusion, change, division or separation'. So we may read the Chalcedonian Definition as the manifesto of an integral religious humanism (164-65).

Cupitt thus comes ever more explicitly to view Christ as a powerful symbol of something which is true for all of us, recalling Strauss. In *The New Christian Ethics* (1988), illustrating his advocacy of a new ethic of value-creating public action in the world to replace the old Christian eudaemonism of purifying and saving one's own soul, Cupitt is happy to number Jesus in the company of Gandhi, Luther and St. Francis of Assisi,[124] as indeed of ourselves and all who suffer forsakenness and die with him (161). In *Radicals and the Future of the Church* (1989) Cupitt sees Kierkegaard's extreme incarnationalism as close to a world-affirming Buddhism: "To say a paradoxical, intense and heartfelt Yes to divinity-in-transcience is not very far from clinging to the void" (145). Thus he has come to see incarnation in a very weak sense as simply finding the universal in the particular. Cupitt is not, therefore, far from the Zen vision of finding Nirvana in the midst of Samsara.

In none of this, then, is there any goal to history, any scope for Messianism. The whole idea of "the center" is gone. Our religions are just a variety of disruptive spiritualities with Christianity (appropriately purged of patriarchalism, hierarchicalism, etc.) as Cupitt's preferred option. But Buddhism is really much the same. In *Creation Out of Nothing* (1990), Cupitt tells us that we create the world by language, and the creator God is a symbol of this process—ourselves writ large.

What Is a Story? (1991) modulates Cupitt's theme of reality as culturally constructed without remainder into a narrative key; all religions are just stories, and Christianity is no exception. For Cupitt this is the sort of radical implication narrative theologians are too coy to draw out (xiii). Notable here, however, is a greater attention to Christological questions than has been the case in recent years. Cupitt considers why Jesus has proven so attractive a character, why so resilient in history, why so fertile a source for the reimaging he has long undergone in church and in culture. For Cupitt it all comes down to narrative power in the gospels. The anomalous figure they portray has what Cupitt calls a "talismanic quality" which is "ambiguous, transgressive and liberating because it is a story catalyst" (107). Christ, for Cupitt, is thus psychologically like a magically charged boundary-object in children's literature, such as Lewis Carroll's looking glass or C.S. Lewis' wardrobe. This "talismanic quality" of Jesus is identified with "what theology has called his saving activity" (108). Cupitt expects such activity will continue if Jesus is allowed to foster as many new interpretations as people desire, apart from the psychologically death-dealing, power-saturated master narratives he thinks have long been preferred by the tradition.

No longer for Cupitt, then, is there any nature of things, any history, or room for dogmatism of any sort. We must learn that thriving is possible in an eternal present without hankering after any further progress nor any deeper certainty. In these conditions Christianity is just one way among many, Jesus one teacher among many, Christ one symbol among many. Many are good, none are best. Without absolutes there can be no talk of uniqueness or finality.[125]

GEORGE A. LINDBECK

George Lindbeck is an American Lutheran ecumenical theologian, an observer at the Second Vatican Council and now Pitkin Professor of Historical Theology at Yale University. It was he who coined the term "postliberal" in *The Nature of Doctrine: Religion and Theology in a Postliberal Age* (1984), thus labeling an interesting new mix of conservative and progressive which has emerged in American Protestant theology and Christian ethics.[126] David Tracy correctly observes that Lindbeck has really written two books—the

first on the nature of doctrine (Lindbeck's typology proved instructive in establishing my own, as mentioned in the Introduction,
above) and the second advocating his post-liberal theology.[127] It is
both a piece of religious studies, applying philosophical anthropology and sociology to the workings of doctrine, and a thinly veiled
polemic against Tracy-style liberal-revisionist theology.[128] Lindbeck's
book strongly advocates a new way of approaching theology in an
increasingly post-Christian and post-modern world—pragmatist,
antifoundational, intratextual and almost sectarian in its denial that a
public domain for theology survives.[129] Yet the program is nonetheless designed for wide appeal. Conservatives are courted by the possibility of maintaining exclusivist and ontological claims, while liberals are courted with offers of successes greater than their own in
making Christianity more intelligible, or at least more appealing, to
the wider society.

Lindbeck labels traditional, conservative doctrine as "cognitive-
propositional" and liberal approaches as "experiential-expressivist."
So conservatives have revealed propositions while for liberals doctrine is expressive of deeper, pre-reflective religious experience
(Lindbeck does recognize something of a blend of these approaches
in Rahner and Lonergan) (24-25). His own preferred option is "cultural-linguistic." This differs from the "cognitive-propositional" approach according to which propositional truth is found at the level of
doctrine. Instead doctrine is only grammar, the deepest accessible
truth residing at the level of ordinary religious language (69).

Lindbeck rejects the liberal prioritizing of personal experience
over religious language first identified in Schleiermacher.[130] Consequently he will tolerate no Hick-style "Copernican Revolution," according to which the different religions constitute different reifications of selfsame fundamental human insights or experiences (23).
For Lindbeck, different religions *produce* the divergent depth experiences normally associated with them rather than simply *expressing*
them (41).

In his third chapter, "Many Religions and the One True Faith,"
Lindbeck points out the difficulty of establishing the unsurpassable
truth of any given religion from the liberal, "experiential-expressivist" standpoint. As in the case of determining what is "most beautiful" or "reddest," "when truth is understood in terms of symbolic

efficacy it is a variable quality without any logically intrinsic upper limit" (50). Certainly, unsurpassability can be argued in a weaker sense—that a religion may be currently unsurpassed while remaining in principle surpassable. In this connection Lindbeck cites Maurice Wiles' "expressivist" view that earliest Christianity conceived of Jesus' finality no differently to this; it served only to express their faith that he would remain unsurpassed in the light of the imminent parousia (50). Once that eschatological expectation passed, however, a propositional or ontological view of Jesus' finality replaced it at Nicaea and Chalcedon. Wiles rejects this; Lindbeck does not. Lindbeck's own cultural-linguistic approach is supposed to *allow* such claims (to keep the "cognitive-propositionalists" happy) without *enforcing* them (to keep the "experiential-expressivists" happy, too—especially, one supposes, those who are pluralistically-minded).

Lindbeck provides an illustration of this tolerance in attempting to show how a claim for salvation by Christ alone might be rendered compatible with his "cultural-linguistic" view (believing that the wider acceptance of his program demands this be possible) (55ff). He invokes a (typically Lutheran) *fides ex auditu* approach— faith comes from what has been heard (i.e. gospel preaching)— adapted to mean that one can only come to faith through participation in the language and "culture" of those who confess Jesus Christ. As such exposure is unlikely in this life for many adherents of other religions, Lindbeck proposes that nothing in his view substantially precludes its being possible *post mortem*. In *this* life, so he would have it, Christians dialogue with, learn from and help the adherents of other religions. They certainly should not deny the validity and worth of the beliefs of these others with any inclusivist talk. Adherents of the other religions are simply not Christians, anonymous or otherwise, and, according to Lindbeck, this must be seen as God's will. What is more, Christians need not speak as if they *already* possess all truth in Jesus Christ. They can opt rather for a version of the traditional eschatological option according to which Christians see only "in part" and cannot thereby view themselves as unduly favored above the other religions in this present life. Such a view prevents the sort of Christian boasting and superiority which Lindbeck thinks has bedeviled religious dialogue in the past (59). As for the *next* life, however, there Christians will know "full" salvation and non-Christians will also have a chance to hear the gospel and find a saving faith in Jesus Christ. So, for Lindbeck, might the *solus Christus* view of salvation be preserved at least as plausibly (or implausibly) as in the expressivist, "anonymous Christians" case (63). This, then, is how Lindbeck deals with the religions issue: the liberals are matched, and the conservatives are (allegedly) placated, while the advocates of mutual regard and dialogue among the religions are supposedly denied nothing. It seems to me, however, that Lindbeck has apparently found it necessary to reinvent a favorite medieval doctrine, that of purgatory, to provide for the post-mortem religious education he deems needful. This will be too high a price for many, no doubt, if preserving "Christian essentials" is his aim.[131]

Next I consider Lindbeck's "cultural-linguistic" approach to Nicene and Chalcedonian Christological orthodoxy. Following Bernard Lonergan he believes the rules for talking about Jesus came first as regulative principles, as in Tertullian's *Regula Fidei*, with propositional theology following later.[132] There are three rules Lindbeck thinks were involved: 1) the monotheistic principle, 2) an historical specificity to the life of Jesus; and 3) "Christological maximalism." This last rule entails that "every possible importance is to be ascribed to Jesus that is not inconsistent with the first rules" and it is based upon "the central Christian conviction that Jesus Christ is the highest possible clue... within the space-time world of human experience to God..."(94).[133] For Lindbeck the New Testament and patristic eras were filled with the pressure of these three rules, with the cognitively least dissonant response to them becoming Catholic orthodoxy (94, 5): "What guided development, one might say, was the avoidance of cognitive dissonance rather than positive collective desires" (110 n.10). Note, however, that all Lindbeck claims is the centrality of Jesus Christ for *Christians only*, as coded in certain rules.

What are the ontological implications of Lindbeck's post-liberal program? Timothy Jackson blames Lindbeck's "relative insousiance about ontological truth claims" for the upset he has caused to many.[134] Alister McGrath mentions Lindbeck's persistent Wittgensteinian reserve over the external referent of doctrinal statements and labels him an instrumentalist—one for whom theories relate to phenomena and perceptions but not to what is "out there" in the real world.[135] Stephen Williams notes how narrative, according to Lindbeck's theory, does not require the existence of the agent it renders.[136] Lindbeck certainly does find ontology to be superfluous, claiming to pursue the "linguistic" rather than the "metaphysical" dimension of faith (106). Nevertheless he will not definitely rule out the possibility of ontological reference for faith, as McGrath and Williams rightly point out. Essentially, though, he understands faithfulness solely in terms of "intratextuality"—the one Christ, as is the case with the only "God," is rendered by the canonical narratives of the New Testament. Lindbeck needs to be quoted at length on this crucial point:

> If the literary character of the story of Jesus, for example, is that of utilizing, as realistic narratives do, the interaction of purpose and circumstance to render the identity description of an agent, then it is *Jesus' identity* as thus rendered, not his historicity, existential significance, or metaphysical status, which is the literal and theologically controlling meaning of the tale. The implications of the story for determining the metaphysical status, or existential significance, or historical career of Jesus Christ may have varying degrees of theological importance, but they are not determinative. The believer, so an intratextual approach would maintain, is not told primarily to be conformed to a reconstructed Jesus of History (as Hans Küng maintains), nor to a metaphysical Christ of faith (as in much of the propositionalist tradition), nor to an abba experience of God (as for Schillebeeckx), nor to an agapeic way of being in the world (as for David Tracy), but he or she is rather to be conformed to the Jesus Christ depicted in the narrative. An intratextual reading tries to derive the interpretive framework that designates the theologically controlling sense from the literary structure of the text itself.... Further, it is possible to specify the primary function of the canonical narrative (which is also the function of many of its most important component stories from the Pentateuch to the Gospels). It is 'to render a character... offer an identity description of an agent' namely God. It does this, not by telling what God is in and for himself, but by accounts of the interaction of

his deeds and purposes with those of creatures in their
ever-changing circumstances. These accounts reach their
climax, in what the Gospels say of the risen, ascended,
and ever-present Jesus Christ whose identity as the di-
vine-human agent is unsubstitutably enacted in the stories of Jesus of Nazareth. The climax, however, is logically inseparable from what preceeds it. The Jesus of the
Gospels is the Son of the God of Abraham, Isaac, and
Jacob in the same strong sense that the Hamlet of Shakespeare's play is Prince of Denmark. In both cases, the
title with its reference to the wider context irreplaceably
rather than contingently identifies the bearer of the name
(120-21).[137]

Thus ontological concerns about God and Christ are far from primary for Lindbeck. It is, in effect, the Christ of faith that matters, the
Christ of the gospel story.

What is more, Lindbeck would have Christians mold themselves and conform their world to this story; *it* is their primary reality
and their identity must come to "dwell within it."[138] So it is that the
typically post-liberal nexus with sectarianism emerges; Christians
must learn to "speak their own language" and maintain their distinctiveness amid the wider society. While the ethicists Stanley Hauerwas and John Howard Yoder, who vigorously champion similar
views, have their roots in more sectarian traditions of the reformation's radical left-wing, Lindbeck the Lutheran thinks an "intentional
community" approach will suffice, with Christian identity shored up
in it, perhaps, by membership in "cell groups" (78).

Thus Lindbeck does advocate some "sociological sectarianism," and in a way clearly intended to challenge the accommodating
spirit of liberal "experiential-expressivists"—those he sees as eager
to translate their Christianity into the current, culturally dominant
mindset. But it is not just because he dislikes it that Lindbeck rejects
the liberal program of translating Christianity into the modern idiom;
he also believes it will no longer work:

As modern culture moves ever farther away from its religious roots, these translations become more strained,

complex, and obscure to the uninitiated. Relativism increases and foundational appeals to universal structures of thought, experience, or *Existenz* lose their persuasiveness. Tillich communicated to a wide range of intellectuals a generation ago, but it is doubtful that his numerous liberal successors could now match his record even if they had his talent. Scholarly nontheologians who want to understand religion are concerned with how religions work for their adherents, not with their credibility. Their interest, one might say, is in descriptive rather than apologetic intelligibility. The result, paradoxically, is that a postliberal approach, with its commitment to intratextual description, may well have interdisciplinary advantages, while liberal theology, with its apologetic focus on making religion more widely credible, seems increasingly to be a nineteenth-century enclave in a twentieth-century milieu (130).

Clearly, therefore, "Lindbeck's antifoundationalism puts in question the traditional ways of appealing to an 'inner' self and its experiences for apologetic purposes."[139] As William C. Placher describes it, he "pursues apologetics . . . only on *an ad* hoc basis, looking for common ground with a given conversation partner but not assuming some universally acceptable standard of rationality."[140] Thus, corresponding to his anti-foundationalism over the historical Jesus, preferring the Christ of the Gospel narratives, Lindbeck eschews any foundational appeal to the human condition. There are as many "human conditions," according to this view, as there are languages and cultures.[141]

As regards the living-out of Christian commitment in this environment, Lindbeck seeks to make a virtue out of a necessity. Beyond the liberal path of apologetics tuned by modernity—a path he tells us now leads to a dead end—Lindbeck's "higher way" might indeed prove more appealing. What the world needs now, he argues, are strong communities to challenge the harmful effects of modernity through dwelling in quite alternative narrative realities. An interesting implication is that claims of uniqueness and unsurpassability, already deemed possible in principle within the program, may even prove necessary nowadays:

It is at least an open question whether any religion will have the requisite toughness for this demanding task unless it at some point makes the claim that it is significantly different and unsurpassably true; and it is easier for a religion to advance this claim if it is interpreted in cultural-linguistic rather than experiential-expressive terms. Thus it may well be that postliberal theologies are more applicable than liberal ones to the needs of the future (127).

If offense is the best form of defense, then, perhaps irrelevance might be the best form of relevance for Lindbeck's post-Christian Christianity![142]

Lindbeck obviously believes he has avoided relativism and fideism, but this is not David Tracy's perception, who sees both at work in the "cultural-linguistic" program: "Lindbeck's substantive theological position is a methodologically sophisticated version of Barthian confessionalism. The hands may be the hands of Wittgenstein and Geertz but the voice is the voice of Karl Barth."[143] Thus despite the potential radical implications of his approach as regards ontology and the objective existence of God, of Christian unsurpassability along with the uniqueness and finality of Christ, Lindbeck's undertaking can also cut in the direction of extreme theological conservatism, metaphysical realism, etc. So despite sharing the postmodern agenda with Cupitt, Lindbeck shares none of Cupitt's desire to wield Ockham's razor at metaphysics or to enter upon a Foucault-style ideology-critique of religious conservatism. All in all, post-liberals would appear to be the most flexible (shifty?) "complete relativists" in theology.[144]

Apart from the consistency of his program, however, one must also ask whether Lindbeck does justice to those with whom he takes issue. In particular, he has been strongly criticized for his assessment of liberal theology—that which he terms "experiential expressivism." It is my contention that Lindbeck has sold short the possibilities of liberal theology—of what David Tracy calls "the noble correlative enterprise."[145] I would want to argue that faith, despite Lindbeck and his sole dependence on narrative, is not incompatible with liberal theological apologetics. I mention, too, Tracy's denial that Lindbeck's "experiential expressivists" are today's liberals—adding that a hermeneutically sensitive dialectical approach *has* grown up among those Tracy calls "revisionists" since the 1960s, and that this omission undermines Lindbeck's charges.

I dispute the apparent incompatibility between apologetics and any meaningful participation in the Christian narrative, as Lindbeck would have it. First, it does not seem to me that apologetics across the centuries has ever sufficed for the inculcation of belief; as Aquinas knew, for instance, the "five ways" could not stand alone as the basis of belief apart from faith in God. This leads to a second point—my conviction that apologetics is part of a faith response for the intellectually disposed believer. Apologetics and liberal-style argument are part of "entering into the story," if you like, akin to translation; the story must be brought close to readily accessible categories and cast in explicable form before it can have any force to "grab" someone. Having said that, it is certainly true that the experience of being caught up in any conversion of perspective, such as coming to faith in Jesus Christ as unique and final, is "all of a piece"—it is not built up and argued into being through clear steps, only then to "grab" one with existential force once one is entirely convinced. Rather, it involves a shift in outlook and sensibility as a whole.[146] Nevertheless, my point remains that evidence, argument and apologetic *may* have a crucial role to play in such moving of an individual toward the paradigm shift of "conversion," which is also the case in scientific discovery (as is amply attested).

The argument is taken further by David Tracy, who appreciates the hermeneutical sophistication to be found in today's liberal theology. The attempt to correlate experience with language characteristic of Anglo-American philosophy in the tradition of empiricism and pragmatism has led liberal theology beyond the traditionally heavily realist empiricist views of experience as unmediated, on the one hand, and the essentially non-realist "romantic expressivist" views of language on the other. The resultant "critical realist" epistemology is common nowadays in liberal theology. And this, says Tracy, is what Lindbeck fails to recognize.[147] It is this new trend to which Tracy points throughout the present field of liberal theology, with Gilkey going beyond Tillich in this regard, Metz and Küng beyond Rahner, and Tracy himself beyond Bernard Lonergan—there is no doubt that liberal theologians like these have actively taken into account that muddying of anthropological waters characteristic of the humanities today with its post-modern emphasis on cultural diversity.[148]

In Part IV we have met historical skepticism, cultural relativism and attitudes to the world religions ranging from Kantian phenomenalism to radical post-Kantian linguistic naturalism. There are strong currents of liberal foundationalism in all those considered up until Knitter, who led the discussion in a more thoroughgoing radical direction. Yet such radical criticism was not ultimately found to preclude the insights of liberal theology, as the critical discussions of the approaches to relativism touching on both Nineham and Lindbeck have sought to show. Exploring the possibilities this realization allows will be my task in the Conclusion of this study, to follow.

CONCLUSION

This study of recent Christology has been undertaken with an eye to all the methodological coordinates and major preoccupations of contemporary theology as a whole. While the issue at the forefront of these investigations has been the uniqueness and finality of Jesus, nevertheless all today's key issues of Christology in particular and theological method in general have been regularly encountered and much discussed.

Certain major convictions have emerged about the material covered—that liberal-style recourse to experience is fiendishly difficult to excise from theology, that what Jesus of Nazareth actually did is important, and that the various forms of radical skepticism and pluralism now emerging as a force in mainstream theology can be difficult to sustain—they were challenged in discussions of Nineham and Lindbeck in Part IV, and were even seen to fall over on their own, as was the case when veiled liberal theologies were identified among the "religious pluralists."

In contemporary Christology, then, so in theology as a whole: a method of critical correlation, linking widely-agreed-upon elements of human experience on the one hand and the Christian story of Jesus and his God on the other, has emerged as a potential survivor in the attenuated theological conditions of today. This is the approach we find in David Tracy, for instance, whose insights were employed in response to Torrance and Lindbeck. Such an approach does not capitulate to the charms of neo-conservative post-liberalism, nor to the full-blown conservatisms considered in Part I; neither does it sacrifice post-modern insights, as is the case with idealist theology (too overconfident nowadays) and with less methodologically

279

sophisticated liberal options (here I think of Küng rather than Schillebeeckx).

It remains to glean some additional insights from among the cases considered—about the cumulative nature of conviction about Jesus, and the role of Christian experience shaped by narrative participation (these insights address the whole context of faith today, and not just Christology). First, however, it is important to review the critical path which has led my discussion from one part to the next. This will further clarify various of these methodological issues, and so allow the proper framing of a question that simply cannot be avoided at the end of a study such as this: taking account of strong arguments from the "radical" group, what sort of case might still be made for Jesus' uniqueness and finality today?

Concerning the "conservative" writers in Part I, I suggested that insufficient conscious attention had been given to human recipients of the revelation which was heavily relied upon there.[1] Despite many disclaimers, however, some recognition of such a meeting point *was* identified (regardless, for instance, of Moltmann's refusal to identify hope as a human quality apart from its origin in Old Testament revelation). It was discerned in the role of intuition evident in Torrance's work, and in the softening of his hard-line epistemology undertaken by MacKinnon and Gunton. It was also recognized in the *actual* role of human experience for Frei. In all of this, then, the role of the "receiver" in the process of revelation was recognized, despite explicit denials.

In Part II, discussing theologies there termed "idealist," a human meeting point was very much in evidence, as was a focus on the historical Jesus not found in Part I (though Moltmann claims such a focus). This emphasis upon the human condition is central for Rahner's "transcendental anthropology" and for Pannenberg's view of humanity as essentially historical, as open to the world, and as oriented to a future belonging to the risen Jesus Christ. Both of these writers owe a debt to Heidegger's existentialism in their understanding of our human condition as incomplete yet able to strive toward fulfillment.

For both of them, however, the correlation of human experience with what can be known historically of Jesus' life is situated in a much larger drama. For Rahner, it is a matter of divine revelation taking place through God's Word encountering "hearers of the Word." For Pannenberg, revelation takes place through the entire historical process, though it is pre-figured in its fullness through the proleptic event of Jesus' resurrection. Despite elements suggestive of a theology "from below," therefore, overarching metaphysical structures such as these in which humanity and revelation are blended together show that the bold syntheses of Rahner and Pannenberg remain essentially theologies "from above."

But while the human meeting point for a revelation of Jesus' uniqueness which remains unacknowledged in Part I was indeed found among those canvased in Part II, nevertheless the link to Jesus' person was not thought to have been adequately established there; Rahner and Kasper, for instance, made claims for the historical Jesus which were not found to be adequately supported. Nor was there sufficient awareness found of the inroads post-modernity has made into our understanding of human persons—Rahner does not exhibit adequate sensitivity in this area, though Pannenberg shows far more awareness of historical and cultural diversity. The human person and the historical Jesus had a supporting role for the "idealist" writers, then, but ultimately these elements did not carry the argument. Concerns were also expressed about the way belief in Jesus arises and is maintained, with Rahner found to be unclear in his talk of Jesus' cosmic impact, and Pannenberg giving insufficient attention to the experience of Christians.

The "liberal" theologians of Part III, however, sought to base Christologies more or less entirely on a correlation between the human condition and the historical Jesus. The post-modern challenges to notions of a consistent human condition were not always recognized, though; Schoonenberg and Küng (at the time of *On Being a Christian*) are not particularly interested in the challenge of cultural relativism, and while Robinson acknowledges the fact of human diversity and the loss of absolutes characteristic of our present situation in the west, it was left for Schillebeeckx to most thoroughly examine the issue. His discussion of anthropological constants represents a search for a human constant in the midst of cultural diversity, with the fact of suffering deemed to be primary. But it was never made entirely clear just *why* Jesus was the unique answer to the human dilemma and not another, though Robinson and Küng did attempt comparisons between Jesus, Christianity and other religions. In addition, the uniqueness and finality cases offered by the "liberal" writers turned out to be far more cumulative than is normally recognized. Consider, for example, the usual claim that Schillebeeckx's case for Jesus' uniqueness hinges on the "abba relationship"—while this is true, it is by no means the whole story. For Schillebeeckx and Küng, in particular, the resurrection and impact of Jesus (so strongly related that they are almost synonymous) provide a necessary confirmation of the deep correlation between Jesus and human need upon which their cases depend.

Part IV introduced those who deny any meaningful dependence on the historical Jesus or the human condition, rejecting Jesus' uniqueness and finality. The approach of the "religious pluralists," as seen from Hick and Cantwell Smith, was suspected of harboring veiled Christocentrisms, however, while it was suggested that Knitter's "complimentary uniqueness" case presumed too much compatibility between the religions, even though it avoided the syncretism of the other "religious pluralists." Cultural relativism, to which Nineham and Lindbeck devoted by far the closest methodological attention among those studied, was recognized for the problem it poses for "liberal" theology, challenging use of the human condition as a stable pole of theological discourse. Yet these charges were not reckoned to be terminal either; the fact of human communication across linguistic and cultural barriers was invoked as a reliable pointer toward a significant level of human commonality. Against Lindbeck an additional charge was made—that he had misconstrued the nature of liberal theology in the period of interest covered by this study. It was suggested that those dealt with in Part III did *not* absolutize religious feeling and pious human interiority, making these the basis of theological truth claims, as Lindbeck thought the "experiential expressivists" were doing. While some liberals do this, earning for themselves very sharp and insightful censure from Lindbeck, nevertheless this is not what we find in Schillebeeckx, say, who more than anyone in Part III (except perhaps James Mackey, who is cited with Küng in the notes) offers a great deal of hermeneutical sophistication in tempering his claims for human nature as theologically foundational without abandoning these claims. This is what David Tracy calls "revisionist theology"[2]—it is liberal theology but it has heeded the post-modern challenges, producing a "leaner," more hermeneutically sophisticated liberal variant with a critical realist epistemology. It is not an untroubled "conservative" theology based on revelation, nor is it heavily "idealist," but then neither does it flee the field of public discourse leaving theology in the hands of complete relativists and non-realists like Don Cupitt, who have cheerfully abandoned all foundationalism.[3]

Such a position involves argument and apologetic while recognizing that watertight rational proof is not possible—that the intuitive, participatory element of which Lindbeck, Frei and Ritschl make much, and to which most others studied here allude, is also important. So it seems that liberal-style apologetic and post-liberal emphases on narrative, praxis and participation are not incompatible after all, but must together be present in any uniqueness case which seeks to avoid the various pitfalls addressed in this study. What is more, the outline of such a case is already present if we look carefully at what most of the writers considered in this study actually *do*—if we look to the *entirety* of the arguments they offer.

One thing that is clear about *every* case for Jesus' uniqueness and finality treated in this study is that it has been a *cumulative* case. This is true whether the theologian offering it admits this or not. Despite Moltmann's overriding emphasis on the revelation of hope, or Pannenberg's reliance on the objectivity of Jesus' resurrection, or Küng's single-minded conviction that Christ is the unique answer to our modern human dilemma, there are other dimensions to their arguments which are equally important, as we have seen. The following are the apparently unavoidable elements.

Very important and widespread throughout those treated in this study is a focus on Jesus' historically particular person—that he was more than an idea which might be found anywhere.[4] The role of the human condition, stated explicitly as in Parts II and III or implicitly, as here and there in Part I (even among the "religious pluralists" of Part IV), is another unavoidable component of Christology in the period of interest. But, then, so too is the recognition that post-modern concerns have blurred the human condition—this insight was found among those studied in every part, but its particularly strong exponents among the non-"radical" group are Moltmann, Pannenberg and Schillebeeckx. Along with this goes the idea that Jesus and our conceptions of humanity are mutually interacting—that Jesus is not simply our human ideal writ large.[5] Rather, our human needs determine what we make of Jesus, while at the same time our encounter with Jesus redefines our understanding of humanity. This last point was important for every complexion of theologian studied—for Moltmann, Torrance, Gunton, Rahner, Pannenberg, Schillebeeckx and Küng.

Also important was the role of Jesus' impact in supporting the case for his uniqueness and finality. It was not just his historical person or the sublime way in which he addressed the human condition that made him unique, but the fact that believers ancient and modern have been so "bowled over" by him that the confession of his uniqueness and finality arises spontaneously and irresistibly. This subjective element may not suit scholarly tastes—indeed, it has not consciously appealed to many who have been examined in this study. Yet none of them have escaped it, despite claims to the contrary. One would be justified in surmising, therefore, that *no argument can* be offered for Jesus' uniqueness and finality which manages to excise all such subjectivity in favor of a "knockdown proof." Anyway, a strong, realistic, publicly accessible case with a clearly acknowledged subjective element is to my mind a stronger case than one which claims complete objectivity but convinces few if any—except, one supposes, those subjectively disposed for one reason or another to accept it.

It is among the "liberal" theologians of Part III that we see all the above-mentioned features of such a case most fully and consistently deployed. There we find the historical particularity of Jesus' person as a major plank of theology, along with the needs and condition of humanity appreciated as being dialogically related to Jesus' person (albeit tempered by a post-modern awareness of cultural relativism). We also find a recognition that Jesus is not declared to be unique and final on the strength of his historical past alone, but that the experience of Christ risen is an important component of Christian claims for Jesus as uniquely fulfilling the human condition. I have suggested that contemporary experience on the part of Jesus' followers is a component of these resurrection claims, as we saw to be the case throughout our discussion of the "liberal" writers (Schillebeeckx and Küng in particular). It is "liberal" theology like this, I suggest, which comes closest to the only type of case for Jesus' uniqueness and finality that might have some credibility today.

But the weaknesses of the various "liberal" options have also been noted, so that something more is called for over and above the options of Part III. That which is required involves no less than a Christology fully aware of the post-modern situation, and fully "revisionist" in the way David Tracy intends.

There *is* a type of Christology today which offers the sort of cumulative case outlined above, but which explicates the true nature of Christian belief in Jesus' uniqueness and finality more fully than the "liberal" writers do. It adds to the emphases of liberal theology an even deeper awareness that "participation in the story" of Jesus Christ by faith is essential to the birth and maintenance of true conviction. And so it is related to the narrative emphases of Frei and Ritschl, which they share with Lindbeck. But the "story" of Jesus is not presented as a closed world into which one enters as through Alice's looking glass or C.S. Lewis' wardrobe, as it appears to be for these post-liberal theorists. Instead, a correlation between the human experience of Christians and the facts ascertainable about Jesus is admitted, but also a sense that the whole "Christ event" involves participation in it, including contemporary Christian experience and reflection. All these factors need to be present together, with no single element dominating.

This sort of hermeneutically sophisticated "liberal" theology echoes the Ignatian vision of serious engagement with the world, on the one hand, and self-abandonment to the Christian story on the other. For Jesuits, this ideal is approached through a life of discipleship where one "lives the story" by trying to follow the way of Jesus Christ through engagement in the contemporary world. And, indeed, it is among current Jesuit writers that the sort of cumulative case described above is very well expressed. We have met such a dual emphasis already in the Jesuit Schoonenberg, but the role of experience and participation is not spelled out. Jon Sobrino and Juan Luis Segundo go further in their liberation-inspired Christologies, with quite self-conscious discussions about the Christology of Ignatius Loyola's *Spiritual Exercises*. For both, the meaning of Christ is found in the Christian's engagement in present reality, with Segundo offering a range of testimonies to the various faces of this engagement through history in his five-volume series *Jesus of Nazareth: Yesterday and Today* (1984-1988)—from St. Paul to Ignatius Loyola to a modern Jesuit, Teilhard de Chardin.[6] But, as is the case with liberation theology in general, the historical Jesus is forever blurred together with the imperative to know and enter his story, which in turn is aimed at furthering the cause of liberation. In addition, Sobrino and Segundo repeat liberation theology's tendency to offer a socio-economic approach to our human condition in the spirit of Marx—an approach often criticized for its lack of comprehensiveness. So while the participatory, non-cognitive element which certainly appears to be an inevitable component of any case for Jesus' uniqueness and finality is present in abundance, nevertheless the human condition and the historical Jesus, two other key aspects, are somewhat underplayed in these theologies (despite conscious attempts to include them).[7] This is not the case, however, with another Jesuit, Frans Jozef van Beeck—a Dutch-American formerly of Boston College, and now a theology professor at Loyola University in Chicago. His emphasis on the importance of contemporary Christian experience was invoked in the critique of Pannenberg in Chapter 5 above. So to a brief discussion of van Beeck's major work, *Christ Proclaimed: Christology as Rhetoric* (1979), we now turn.[8]

Basically, van Beeck offers an inclusive logos Christology in which Jesus paradigmatically discloses the depths of reality and of human personhood in terms of openness and relatedness. The joint witnesses to this, for van Beeck, are the historical Jesus as disclosed by the new quest, on the one hand, and the testimony of those who are won over by the story of Jesus and enabled to plumb with him depths of human freedom and openness, on the other. This is a "liberal" position like those of Part III, but it constitutes an improvement by offering all the elements of the widely emergent cumulative case which was identified, above.

Van Beeck recognizes that there is a dialectical relationship between the figure of Jesus and the human condition; human concerns illuminate the figure of Jesus, while the figure of Jesus transforms those human realities which are "brought to him." Indeed, for van Beeck the human concerns which are brought to Jesus have become our names for him (146)—a claim he supports with a study of

Christological titles. He believes that surrendered to Jesus our humanity is not only affirmed but also transformed, purified—no longer is there the stifling conformity of a generic human nature which excludes and dehumanizes all who fall short of the ideal and so are left out (368).

A prominent insight of van Beeck is that being caught up in the story of Jesus is necessary for fully appreciating it, as is no doubt true of any other story (the essence of which is unable to be conveyed entirely objectively and propositionally). As the "new quest" shows how Jesus' uniqueness was never established by recourse to foundational historical events alone, but always in the light of his impact upon interpreters (256-57), so too the resurrection is solidly linked by van Beeck with Christian experience ancient and modern: "The resurrection must...be viewed," he writes, "not as an event subsequent to Jesus' life, passion and burial, but as the living presence of Jesus Christ in the Spirit, represented in and behind the personal commitment of the witnesses" (259).

Van Beeck goes much further than anyone in Part III above, in tracing the nature of this impact. While narrative means are used by Frei and Ritschl, as by Lindbeck, these are deployed in the shadow and spirit of Barth, providing an entrée to what is an essentially private world of revelation. This is not the case with Schillebeeckx, however—the most hermeneutically self-conscious and sophisticated of the "liberal" writers considered. And it is not true for van Beeck, who insists on referring to Jesus' history and to human experience as well as to Christian conviction (though the latter, too, is no less open to public scrutiny for not being universally held).[9]

The inclusive logos theology of van Beeck is predicated on his assurance that our world in general and humans in particular are open and relational from top to bottom, and that this is the fundamental metaphysical state of things (there are strong echoes of Teilhard and Rahner, two earlier Jesuits, in van Beeck's thinking here). Insofar as Jesus is the one who most embodies and personalizes this metaphysical truth, van Beeck refers to him as the logos in person: "Jesus' divinity is identical with his attitude of total receptivity" (418). Elsewhere, van Beeck actually defines the logos as "the man Jesus" irreducibility to his own concrete individuality, in virtue of his being absolutely related to God" (454).

The inclusive element is very important for van Beeck, for whom Jesus' uniqueness and finality affirms everything worthwhile in human experience and forecloses on nothing—it is an inclusive uniqueness. This is asserted in the face of any aggressive attempt to establish Jesus' uniqueness and finality by objective means of whatever sort, and especially the approach which compares Jesus with other religious founders. Although van Beeck does not name names, we recall that such an approach was found in Part III, above, in the work of Robinson and Küng—the latter being far more insistent. Whether or not one could ever make such a comparison effectively and with wide appeal is one thing,[10] but for van Beeck it should not be attempted in the first place.

And so it is, all of a sudden, that van Beeck brings our discussion up short. His essentially ethical concern to avoid aggression and exclusivism in Christology represents a rare meta-critical discussion among the non-"radical" theologies addressed in this study. It is highly ironic that the theologian thought here to offer the optimum account of Jesus' uniqueness and finality available in the period of interest should also be the one who resolutely refuses to insist upon that outcome. This represents a further instance of van Beeck bringing together emphases from the "liberal" and the "radical" groups— the latter, and especially the "religious pluralists," having a commendable commitment to redressing past excesses of exclusivism.[11]

This conviction is based ultimately on the praxis of Jesus himself, who van Beeck sees as someone open to everything human and to all people, rejecting nothing and no one—someone who refused to assert himself, or be the basis of others' drive to power or certainty. So any insistence upon Jesus' uniqueness and finality ought to be abandoned "for Jesus' sake," and for the world—clearly people and their needs come first, for van Beeck, as for his praxis-oriented Jesuit brothers Sobrino and Segundo. Any insecure need to establish Jesus' uniqueness and finality is not compatible with this, he argues. I quote van Beeck at length here to illustrate the point (384).

> Such aggressive defenses of Christ's uniqueness are little more than expressions of the type of Christianity that has forsaken the *imitatio Christi* in order to set itself up as a power, a cause at odds with other causes. Most declara-

tions of the "Jesus-and-not-the-Buddha" type are neither about Jesus nor about the Buddha, but are feeble-faithed Christians' attempts at defending themselves. The same applies to much intra-church discussion of the uniqueness of Jesus Christ; many strong affirmations of Christ's divinity are feeble believers' attempts at safeguarding, not doctrine, but themselves, against understandable doubts and legitimate questions. Such defensive affirmations lack the sympathy and compassion of Christ. True *magisterium*, whether of the official or of the unofficial variety, must as a rule be patient and hospitable, in imitation of Christ, the Man for Others. The christological confession is meant to draw people to Christ; it is not meant to sound like the monotonous, never-ending clang of a hammer of heretics forged, once and for all, at Nicaea in 325 A.D.

Van Beeck is quietly confident that "the Word is doing its work," then, without help from hyper-orthodox bullies nervously seeking to discredit "the opposition."[12] His rejection of a certain "high Christology" for Christ's sake further illustrates his point.

Under the cover of a defense of the divinity of Jesus, the Eternal Word Incarnate, traditional christology often engaged in aggressive self-defense; in insisting on the glory of Jesus, it often involved itself in self-glorification. No wonder, then, that it has become possible, on the part of some of the disenchanted, to speak of "christolatry," and that Christianity has been depicted as an inevitably aggressive and even murderous religion, because it is neurotically committed to the defense of the divinity of a man who did not consider equality with God a matter of snatching, and who died like a lamb, without so much as opening his mouth (511)....A high christology easily becomes a high and mighty christology, one that functions as the family ideology of a church that wages war, colludes or negotiates with the intellectual powers that be, or ensconces itself in the fortress of past deliverances. Such

a christology has lost the way, and the cries of the poor
and the suffering and the searching go unheeded (513).

What we have in van Beeck, then, is a liberal theology quite
public in its attention to the historical Jesus and to the human condition, but also quite post-modern—and this in at least three ways.
First, it is post-modern in its awareness that different periods and
places will give rise to different Christologies; second, there is its rejection of "logocentrism" and any possibility that complete rational
proof or closure can be had in matters of this complexity; third, it is
post-modern in its ideology critique of intemperate, insistent claims
for Jesus' uniqueness and finality on grounds that such arguments
demean and exclude others in the name of a man who excluded no
one—such ideology critique is post-modern in the spirit of the critical theorists, as earlier of Marx and Nietzsche with their recognition
that claims for truth are often corrupted by power.

As to the logical status of van Beeck's position, the form of argument he offers is a "cumulative case," as was indicated earlier.
Such cases are not totally convincing in the way that mathematical
proofs are (by definition) convincing, but they are nonetheless widespread in supporting convictions relating to matters of any complexity. Recent studies show that such cases are the very stuff of religious
certainty.[13]

I propose to end this study of Jesus' uniqueness and finality in
late twentieth century theology with the warnings and reassurances
of van Beeck very much in mind—that "the cause of Jesus," if you
will, is not furthered by aggressive defenses of his uniqueness and finality. Even without proof and compelling argument, though certainly not in the absence of such argument as appropriate, belief in the
uniqueness and finality of Jesus will continue to arise for those who
find themselves drawn to his person and to his church. To those who
seek to follow Jesus as his disciples, as the great modern disciple Albert Schweitzer put it, "He will reveal himself in the toils, the con-
flicts, the sufferings which they shall pass through in His fellowship,
and, as an ineffable mystery, they shall learn in their own experience
Who He is."[14]

As I prefaced this study with some imagery of the sea, in a quote from Walt Whitman, so I end it with some more sea imagery—in this case from the fifteenth century Spanish ballad *El Conde Arnaldos*. In so doing I borrow an extended quote from van Beeck, with which he ends his own study. As it seemed to him, so it seems to me—only in the way that knowledge and belief is understood in this ballad do people *really* come to know and believe in Jesus Christ, regardless of whatever arguments for his uniqueness and finality may or may not have presented themselves (and we have met very many arguments and counter-arguments in this study of Christology from the 1960s to the 1990s); "Words will come to those Churches and those Christians that are united with Jesus Christ," writes van Beeck, "and united with him in his love for the world. No new knowledge without participation in the experience." But although van Beeck's insight is totally up-to-the-minute in current theology, superseding even the recent distinction between liberal and post-liberal, nevertheless it is an ancient insight, as is evident with reference to the ballad as he presents it (574-75).

> On the morning of the feast of Saint John, Count Arnaldos rides out to hunt, hawk on gauntlet. He looks up and there, on the smooth sea, he sees a galleon sailing landward. Its sails are made of silk, its mast is cedarwood, and the sailor at the helm sings a song so entrancing that the sea and the wind are calmed, the fish of the deep are called to the surface, and the birds alight on the rigging. Count Arnaldos, struck by the sight and the music, speaks up. In his words we can hear the yearning of all humanity for words of knowledge to control experience:

> > 'For the sake of God, our maker!'
> >   (Count Arnaldos' cry was strong)—
> > 'Old man, let me be partaker
> >   In the secret of thy song!'

> > > '*Por Dios te ruego, marinero.*
> > > *digasme ora ese cantar.*'

The answer comes. What it says is that only those will
know who join in the venture—in its risks and in its
rewards:

> 'Count Arnaldos, Count Arnaldos!
>   Hearts I read and thoughts I know;—
> Wouldst thou learn the ocean secret,
>   In our galley thou must go.'

> *'Yo no digo, esta canción,*
> *sino a quien conmigo va.'*

NOTES

INTRODUCTION

[1] A short, informative statement about the history of Jesus' uniqueness and finality as an issue, and its departure at the enlightenment from the realm of the obvious, is offered by Bruce Marshall in the Introduction to his study *Christology in Conflict* (1987) 1-10.

[2] A number of overview works have appeared, mostly in the journal literature, addressing various aspects of recent Christology. They will be encountered here and there throughout the study. The only one consciously focusing on the question of Jesus' uniqueness and finality, however, is that of Klaus Reinhardt, "In What Way is Jesus Christ Unique?" (1974), which is modest in its aims and by now rather out of date.

[3] Edward Schillebeeckx, *Church* (1990) 235.

[4] Langdon Gilkey, "Plurality and Its Theological Implications" (1987) 39, 40. To this scenario we might add the loss of confidence felt by Americans in their first experience of losing a war—and against Asians!

[5] Wilfred Cantwell Smith, "The Christian in a Religiously Plural World" (1961) 111-112.

[6] George Lindbeck, *The Nature of Doctrine* (1984) 130.

[7] See e.g. Clifford Geertz, *The Interpretation of Cultures* (New York: Basic Books, 1973); especially the essays "Thick Description: Toward an Interpretive Theory of Culture," 4-30, and "Religion as a Cultural System," 87-125.

[8] See Ludwig Wittgenstein, *Philosophical Investigations* (Oxford: Basil Blackwell, 1953). For the interaction between anthropology

and philosophy of language as related to these matters, see two essays by Peter Winch, "Understanding a Primitive Society" in *Ethics
and Action* (London: Routledge & Kegan Paul, 1972) 8-49, and
"Language, Belief and Relativism" in H.D. Lewis (ed.), *Contemporary British Philosophy: Personal Statements* (London: George
Allen & Unwin, 1976) 322-337.

[9] For fine introductions to these subjects, see Vincent Descombes,
Modern French Philosophy (1979) (Cambridge: Cambridge Univer-
sity Press, 1980), Richard Harland, *Superstructuralism: The Philoso-
phy of Structuralism and Post-Structuralism* (New Accents Series;
London: Methuen, 1987) and Terry Eagleton, *Literary Theory: An
Introduction* (Oxford: Basil Blackwell, 1983).

[10] Very useful and wide-ranging here is Paul Rabinow (ed.), *The
Foucault Reader: An Introduction to Foucault's Thought* (London:
Penguin, 1984).

[11] Social factors evident in America, Australia and elsewhere in
the west are the boom in immigration and the press toward a form of
multi-culturalism, and the collapse of former economic certainties
with an attendant social cost, as western societies must redefine their
ethics of work and their notions of the meaning of life beyond the era
of full employment and in an environment of urban decay. My lifetime has also seen the decline of shared moral values, the rise and
valorization of alternative lifestyle options, the pressure to redefine
sex-roles, the universal assimilation of the fact of human diversity
through a ubiquitous electronic media, and other relativizing trends.

[12] I have written elsewhere about theologies conceived within the
environment of post-modernity; see my two articles "Radical Theology, Postmodernity and Christian Life in the Void," *The Heythrop
Journal* 32 (1991) 62-71, and "All This, and God Too? Postmodern
Alternatives to Don Cupitt," *The Heythrop Journal* 33 (1992) 267-
282.

[13] Dietrich Ritschl, for instance, laments the departure of German
Protestant theology from its former exegetical and hermeneutical
strengths since 1965, and its fragmentation into socio-political and
ethical concerns, on the one hand, and militant conservatism on the
other; see his essay "How I See German Theology" in Stephen Sykes
(ed.), *England and Germany* (1982) 131-145, 136.

[14] McIntyre, *The Shape of Christology* (1966) 9-10.

[15] See Austin P. Flannery (ed.), *Documents of Vatican II* (Grand Rapids: Eerdmans, 1975) 750-765.

[16] Reinhardt, "In What Way is Jesus Christ Unique?" (1974) 343.

[17] Fiorenza, "Christology after Vatican II" (1980) 81; the author also provides useful comments about the "Spanish Jesuits" and their neo-scholastic theology, which provided a mainstay of seminary instruction in theology up to the 1950s.

[18] Morgan, "Historical Criticism and Christology" (1982) 80. Another useful contribution to this subject by Morgan is his essay *"Non Angli sed Angeli*: Some Anglican Reactions to German Gospel Criticism," in Stephen Sykes & Derek Holmes (eds.), *New Studies in Theology 1* (London: Duckworth, 1980) 1-30.

[19] Albert Schweitzer, *The Quest of the Historical Jesus* (1906/1968).

[20] See e.g. Rudolf Bultmann's programmatic essay, written during World War II, entitled "New Testament and Mythology," in Hans Werner Bartsch (ed.), *Kerygma and Myth: A Theological Debate* (1948) (London: SPCK, 1954); see also the discussion of "Existence and the Christ," in Paul Tillich, *Systematic Theology* Vol. 2 (1957) (London: SCM, 1978).

[21] R.G. Collingwood, *The Idea of History* (Oxford: Clarendon, 1946).

[22] See Käsemann's essay "The Problem of the Historical Jesus," in *Essays on New Testament Themes* (Studies in Biblical Theology, 41; London: SCM, 1964) 15-47; see also James M. Robinson, *A New Quest of the Historical Jesus* (London: SCM, 1959) and the important rejoinder by Van A. Harvey and Schubert Ogden, "How New is the 'New Quest of the Historical Jesus'?" in C.E. Braaten & R.A. Harrisville (eds.), *The Historical Jesus and the Kerygmatic Christ* (Nashville: Abingdon, 1964) 197-242.

More recently, what has putatively been called a "third quest" has emerged with a new methodological point of departure, looking to the first century Palestinian environment (of which we know far more than the nineteenth century scholars, thanks in large part to the discovery of the Dead Sea Scrolls and the Nag Hammadi library); no longer is the only acceptable access to the historical Jesus given by excluding features of the gospel accounts found to be in common with norms of the time—it is not necessarily good history to retain only the novel and the distinctive, as if Jesus were not a first century Jew. E.P. Sanders, in *Jesus and Judaism* (London: SCM, 1985), is a pioneer in this movement (though far too skeptical for some). See also Anthony Harvey, *Jesus and the Constraints of History* (London: Duckworth, 1982) and the new "lives of Jesus" now emerging from the United States; see John P. Meier, *A Marginal Jew: Rethinking the Historical Jesus,* Vol. 1: The Roots of the Problem and the Person (Anchor Bible Reference Library; New York: Doubleday, 1991) and John Dominic Crossan, *The Historical Jesus: The Life of a Mediterranean Jewish Peasant* (San Francisco: Harper & Row, 1991).

[23] Brown, *Continental Philosophy and Modern Theology* (1987) 58.

[24] As Colin Gunton points out in *Yesterday and Today* (1982) 172.

[25] On kenotic Christology see e.g. Donald Dawe, "A Fresh Look at the Kenotic Christologies," *Scottish Journal of Theology* 15 (1962) 337-349; John Macquarrie, "Kenoticism Reconsidered," *Theology* 77 (1974) 115-124; S.W. Sykes, "The Strange Persistence of Kenotic Christology," in Alistair Kee & Eugene T. Long (eds.), *Being and Truth: Essays in Honour of John Macquarrie* (London: SCM, 1986) 349-375; and James Kenny, "Fullness in Emptiness: The Development of a Russian Spiritual Vision," in Matthew Fox (ed.), *Western Spirituality: Historical Roots, Ecumenical Routes* (Santa Fe: Bear & Co., 1981) 343-368. Some examples of present day kenotic Christologies are Geddes MacGregor, *He Who Lets Us Be: A Theology of Love* (New York: Seabury, 1975); Lucien Richard, *A Kenotic Christology: In the Humanity of Jesus the Christ, The Compassion of Our God* (Lanham: University Press of America, 1982); Richard Sturch, *The Word and the Christ: An Essay in Analytic Christology* (Oxford: Clarendon, 1991); and the classic example, for me, showing the total loyalty of the movement to Chalcedonian orthodoxy at all costs (which in this case are considerable), in Thomas V. Morris, *The Logic of God Incarnate* (1986).

[26] The only major theologian from the period of interest not discussed here is Hans Urs von Balthasar. This prolific, highly cultured, difficult though immensely stimulating "spiritual theologian" is now being discovered by a wider audience since his death in 1988. In the period of interest he has contributed Christological reflections in his *Theo-Drama: Theological Dramatic Theory,* Vol. III. *Dramatis Personae: Persons in Christ* (1978) (San Francisco: Ignatius, 1992) 59-

262; also useful for an overview is his little book *My Work: In Retro-spect* (San Francisco: Ignatius [Communio Books] 1990). See also a fine, new study of his work by John O'Donnell, *Hans Urs Von Balthasar* (Outstanding Christian Thinkers Series; London: Geoffrey Chapman, 1992).

The work of von Balthasar finds many resonances with others throughout this study, in particular with the *theologia crucis* of Molt-mann, gleaned through a deep engagement with Luther and Barth, and the anti-Kantian epistemologies of direct contact with reality which we find in Torrance, MacKinnon and Gunton. Von Balthasar also recalls the narrative emphases of Frei and Ritschl, for he is com-mitted to the realm of the aesthetic and the mystical as revelationally significant. This is a particular instance of von Balthasar's Catholic regard for the world and human experience as revelatory, which is expressed in a sense that that which is directly revealed perfects the natural. But this Thomistic insight does not make von Balthasar a friend of Rahner, whom he believes has sold out the church's claims to direct revelation by his openness to Christ's presence everywhere in the doctrine of "Anonymous Christianity." For von Balthasar, rev-elation is not in any correlation between elements "from below" and "from above," as it is for Rahner and Schoonenberg, say, but rather in the completion of natural theology by revealed theology—he uses the image of a keystone lowered "from above" to complete an arch built up "from below."

Von Balthasar is a doyen of conservative Roman Catholics for re-sisting what they see as the assimilation of the post-Vatican II church to the modern world. While his writings are very fine, nevertheless they ultimately strike me as in-house meditations on revealed truth which do not sufficiently engage the questions raised by historical Jesus studies or the drive to link revelation and salvation with human experience that we find in the other Roman Catholic writers studied. As an ex-Jesuit, and a champion of Ignatian spirituality, von Bal-thasar could have been discussed alongside van Beeck in the Conclu-sion of this study, but he does not match the theological publicness of van Beeck who, despite the hermeneutic of participation he adopts, retains a strong apologetic concern.

[27] Gustav Aulén, *Christus Victor: A Historical Study of the Three Main Types of the Atonement* (London: SPCK, 1931).

[28] H. Richard Niebuhr, *Christ and Culture* (New York: Harper & Row [Harper Torchbooks] 1951).

[29] Peter Berger, The *Heretical Imperative* (New York: Doubleday, 1979).

[30] George Lindbeck, *The Nature of Doctrine* (1984). The "reductive" option of Berger has lost its reductive edge since he wrote, becoming more "religious" and less "secular." The breach between God and the world introduced by Barth's denial of natural theology (a breach only closed at the single point of Jesus' incarnation) developed into the absent God and the entirely secular world of the "death of God" theologians and their "reductive" option to which Berger refers. Drawing on Wittgenstein, linguistics and the findings of cultural anthropology about the closed nature of cultural and linguistic worlds, however, the post-liberal movement in American theology, in tandem with the insights of narrative theology, has produced a variant of Berger's "reductive" option—instead of removing God from the world and then celebrating secularity, the post-liberals remove the whole world of Christian discourse from the wider world, making it a self-authenticating "language game" of its own (though they claim that this allows an even more effective influence in the world because the church becomes an intentional community able to attract and lead by example). There will be further discussion of Lindbeck and the postliberal option in Part IV and the Conclusion.

[31] This distinction has been used by Cupitt, himself a "radical" Christian atheist, since *Only Human* (1985).

[32] David Tracy, *Blessed Rage for Order* (1975) Ch. 2. Tracy's views are involved in the critical discussion of cultural relativism in Part IV.

[33] Charles Davis, *Christ and the World Religions* (1970).

[34] Alan Race, *Christians and Religious Pluralism* (1983).

[35] Paul F. Knitter, *No Other Name?* (1985). Similar to Knitter's typology is that of J. Peter Schineller in a fine study which draws out the ecclesial implications of these positions. In his paper "Christ and the Church" (1976) Schineller offers four positions which he terms "Ecclesiocentric universe, exclusive Christology" (*extra ecclesiam, nula salis*), "Christocentric universe, inclusive Christology" (Jesus and the church are the constitutive but not the exclusive ways of salvation, or else Jesus is the savior of those outside the church, as in

Rahner), "Theocentric universe, normative Christology" (Jesus and the church are the normative but not the constitutive ways of salvation), and "Theocentric universe, non-normative Christology" (the pluralist option with Jesus as one of many ways to salvation).

[36] Avery Dulles, "Contemporary Approaches to Christology" (1976).

[37] Cited (without reference) in 'Tricia Blombery, *God Through Human Eyes: Report from the Combined Churches Survey For Faith and Mission* (Sydney: Christian Research Association, 1989) 38.

[38] George Rupp, *Christologies and Cultures* (1974).

[39] Similarities are identified between Bultmann and Anselm (both "Transactional"), and between Irenaeus and Schleiermacher, who are separated by Aulén but put into the same "realist-processive" bracket by Rupp. As for differences, the straight individual and psychological approaches (in the "nominalist-processive" camp), on the one hand, and the more objective redemptive process envisioned by Schleiermacher (in the "realist-processive" group), on the other, show a distinction which Aulén did not make—he conflated both approaches under his "subjectivist" rubric.

[40] Note that the uses of words like "liberal," "conservative," "idealist," etc., as defined according to my typology, are distinguished from more general uses of such terms by the use of quotation marks.

[41] Some have called the work of Rahner and Pannenberg theology "from below," referring to the role of history and the parameters of human being found there. But while this is certainly true, these elements are subsumed into overarching wholes whether revelational or ontological, on which account I prefer to call theirs theologies "from above."

PART I: CONSERVATIVE

[1] Pauline *theologia crucis* is seldom clearer than in 1 Cor 1:18-25; see also e.g. Günther Bornkamm, *Paul* (1969, ET 1971) (London: Hodder & Stoughton, 1975) 120-56; Rudolf Bultmann, *Theology of the New Testament*, Vol. 1 (1948) (London: SCM, 1952) Ch. 5. On Luther's version see e.g. Alister McGrath, *Luther's Theology of the Cross* (Oxford: Basil Blackwell, 1985). The emphasis on God's hid-

denness in *theologia crucis* also influenced the rise of "death of God" thinking in Protestant philosophical theology, beginning with Hegel.

[2] Moltmann, *The Church in the Power of the Spirit* (1977) 226-42.

[3] See Moltmann's critique of liberation theology for denying its European paternity in "An Open Letter to José Míguez Bonino" (1976).

[4] Dorothee Sölle, who taught at Union Seminary in New York and is now "retired" as a political activist in Hamburg, offers a different eschatological perspective, and one with which Moltmann takes issue. In *Christ the Representative* (1967), Sölle opposes the conservative Protestantism whereby Christ "substitutes" for us before God to win our salvation (e.g. Barth), as well as any promethean theology underplaying the extent of human dependence and need for representation before God (e.g. Albrecht Ritschl). She wishes to maintain humanity's responsibility for its own salvation, too, and to deny that humans are substitutable (in the face of contemporary utilitarianism). So her Christ is a representative, not a substitute, who also represents God to humanity. Her "theism" has the hidden God of *theologia crucis*, recalling 1960s' death of God ideas, with "Jesus the representative of the absent God who vindicates God's cause because God himself does not intervene" (Reinhardt, "In What Way Is Jesus Christ Unique?" [1974] 353).

For our purposes the point is that the finality of Sölle's Jesus is provisional; he does not replace humans' need to become God's representatives and take their own stand. But in days of God's eclipse and of existential uncertainty her Jesus does reveal both "God and man." Note, too, that as with Moltmann the historical Jesus is not such an issue for Sölle, who normally confuses the historical Jesus with the Christ of the gospels.

Moltmann, while applauding Sölle's eschatological perspective, opposes her Christology which he thinks too "low" and functional, with an ultimately superfluous Christ (*The Crucified God* [1974] 262-66). Moltmann's objections reflect the supremacy of Irenaeus over Anselm in his thought, with Christ as part of God's eternal plan of creation and redemption and not merely an antidote for sin. And the objections also reflect his conviction that Jesus has an eternal place in the Trinitarian history of God with the world (ibid. 265).

Sölle's Christ is modalistic and has no place of his own in God's eternal plan, says Moltmann, for whom Jesus "does not make himself superfluous like an employment agency, but so to speak founds a new firm" (ibid. 263). Moltmann also denies that all must ultimately do *just* what Christ has done. Rather, what Christ has done as forerunner *changes the nature of the journey for all who follow*: "Christ experiences death and hell in solitude. His followers experience it in his company" (ibid. 263).

⁵ Barth's impact on Moltmann came via the pervasive influence of his teachers Otto Weber, Hans Iwand (who also brought Hegel's influence to bear on Moltmann according to Bauckham, "Jürgen Moltmann" [1989] 294) and Ernst Wolf, but was by no means conveyed uncritically (Morse, "Jürgen Moltmann" [1984] 662). According to Moltmann scholar Richard Bauckham, the Dutch "apostolate theology" of A.A. van Ruler and J.C. Hoekendijk gained Moltmann his eschatological sense of the church's mission as properly directed toward the coming kingdom of God, while from Wolf he also developed his concerns about social ethics and the necessity of church involvement in secular society (Bauckham, ibid. 293, 4).

⁶ See e.g. Moltmann's "Foreword" to M. Douglas Meeks, *Origins of the Theology of Hope* (1974) and Moltmann, *The Crucified God* (1974) 1.

⁷ Bauckham, "Jürgen Moltmann" (1989) 293, 4.

⁸ Küng, *The Incarnation of God* (1987) 555. Meeks' early study of Moltmann has been accused of missing the impact of Whitehead's process thought (McWilliams, *The Passion of God* [1985] 48 n.25) but, despite the usual incompatibility of neo-orthodoxy with any such theology, nevertheless Moltmann does become increasingly panentheistic, culminating in his recent emphasis on the cosmic Christ in *The Way of Jesus Christ* (1990). Also, Moltmann's attempt to "Christianize the idea of God" in *The Trinity and the Kingdom of God* (1981) displays conscious eastern orthodox influence with its understanding of salvation in terms of deification—of being taken-up into the being of God (e.g. Macquarrie, *Jesus Christ in Modern Thought* [1990] 323, 24). One intention of that book is an attempt to redress the Church's "great schism" of 1054 over the *filioque* clause in the Nicene Creed. Moltmann is also concerned to overcome an even greater schism—that between Christianity and Judaism.

⁹ Morse, "Jürgen Moltmann" (1984) 665; Moltmann, *The Way of Jesus Christ* (1990) 379 n.3.

¹⁰ Macquarrie, *Twentieth-Century Religious Thought,* 4th ed. (1988) 395.

¹¹ Meeks, *Origins of the Theology of Hope* (1974) 11.

¹² Macquarrie, op. cit. As well as Marxists like Bloch and the Frankfurt school (concerning questions of hope), Jewish theologians such as Franz Rosenzweig and Abraham Heschel have also made their impact here (Bauckham, "Jürgen Moltmann" [1989] 294).

¹³ Meeks, op. cit. 3.

¹⁴ In his discussion of the conservative Karl Barth, Moltmann affirms Barth's critique of natural theology while muting Barth's commitment to the *full* revelation of God in Jesus Christ. Moltmann's God is less present in the world than Barth's—not in the death of God sense but in the sense of an as-yet-to-be-realized future (Macquarrie, *Jesus Christ in Modern Thought* [1990] 327).

To this is coupled a critique of metaphysical theism. For Parmenides of Elea (5th century BCE), and then in Plato and his heirs, Being is complete and static with "no future." Philosophical theology indebted to this tradition understands revelation in terms of an unveiling of the abiding reality. Not so with Moltmann, however, for whom "Ousia is revealed only as Parousia" (Morse, "Jürgen Moltmann" [1984] 668-69). For Moltmann, therefore, the self-revelation of Barth's God will collapse into the noetic unveiling of Parmenides' God unless the future element is maintained (58, 228). As David Kelsey observes, "His stress on the unfinishedness of Jesus' identity distinguishes Moltmann from Barth" (Kelsey, *The Uses of Scripture in Recent Theology* [1975] 55). Moltmann thus wishes to replace "a God of epiphanies" (and incarnational religion) with "a God of the promise" (43, 84-85).

¹⁵ For Bultmann the God question is the question of humanity coming to itself, of achieving Heidegger's "authentic existence"—a process of continual decision facilitated and empowered by proclamation of the kerygma. Thus God emerges, in the scientifically closed weave of a Kantian universe, as the requirement for understanding human interiority aright, albeit in light of the gospel. For Moltmann this constitutes "an advanced, deepened and reshaped form of the only proof of God left over by Kant—the moral proof of

God supplied by practical reason" (61). For Bultmann the kerygmatic Christ is unique and final agent of the necessary human transformation, though such restricting of salvation's scope is rejected as dogmatically narrow-minded by Schubert Ogden in his important study *Christ Without Myth* (1962).

[16] Moltmann, *Theology Today* (1988) 16.

[17] Ibid. 86.

[18] Bultmann's reduction of theology to anthropological scope is reversed by Moltmann, whose vision is cosmological. And eschatology is retrieved from the margins of theology, to which Bultmann's program of demythologizing relegated it as a dispensable vestige of first century thinking. For Moltmann, no reduction of Christ's eschatological reality to dimensions of the present is to be tolerated: "Christ did not rise into the Spirit or the kerygma, but into the as yet undetermined future ahead of us which is pointed to by the tendencies of the Spirit and the proclamations of the kerygma" (212).

What Moltmann opposes here are ultimately stoic notions that the present is all that matters, that true Christianity is "not concerned for the morrow" (the rediscovery of realized eschatology owes something to the Johannine studies of C.H. Dodd). In Bultmann's hands eschatology is demythologized entirely into the present as a constant kerygmatic call to decide for authentic existence. Moltmann, however, has no time for any Protestantism which declares salvation in Christ to be already established "once for all" and *extra me*, nor for a cultic Christianity which declares everything to be present and available in the liturgy (158). Such "mysticism of the present moment" recalls for Moltmann the mystery cults, and the Greek desire for an eternal present (155ff). But it is untrue to the manifest imperfection of things in both world and church, and it is not compatible with Moltmann's wayfaring God of the exodus and the resurrection: "The believer is not set at the high noon of life, but at the dawn of a new day at the point where night and day, things passing and things to come, grapple with each other" (31). Hope for Moltmann (as for Bloch, though differently attained) is essential for bearing "the cross of the present"; without it there is only the way of descent into hell which Danté signed "Abandon hope, all ye who enter here" (31-32).

[19] See e.g. Giovanni Garbini, *History and Ideology in Ancient Israel* (1986) (London: SCM, 1988), who argues that so little of any

certainty can be known apart from the Old Testament text itself that the grand "histories of Israel" (e.g. John Bright, Martin Noth) must now be seen as largely pious fictions. The historicity of the patriarchal narratives, and of such figures as Moses and Abraham, has long been widely questioned.

[20] No liberal theologian would see things this way. One thinks of Peter Berger, for instance, seeking to identify what he called "signals of transcendence" in a secular world, and finding the presence of hope to be one of them, expressing a deep conviction that the severe constraints under which humanity so often labors will not ultimately defeat us (Berger, *A Rumour of Angels* [1971] Ch. 3, 66-96). Moltmann would agree, but would ground hope in the promise rather than in any such human faculty or "natural theology." According to Moltmann forward-looking history and the sense of hope it incorporates did not occur to the Greeks, with Thucydides exemplifying for him their lack of a sense of change and newness (259). Instead, as Moltmann reads it, the messianic idea itself generated forward-looking history among the Hebrews, and the Greeks discovered it from them (261). Similarly the messianic idea has had an enormous influence in more recent times, with secular messianism written all over the philosophy of history since Herder (262). And the twelfth century Cistercian abbot from Calabria, Joachim of Fioré, with his three eras of history culminating in an age of the spirit, has inspired nineteenth century history since Lessing (262). Moltmann thus believes that Old Testament ideas of divine promise have issued in a worldwide looking to the future and a linear understanding of history: "The promise which announces the *eschaton,* and in which the *eschaton* announces itself, is the motive power, the mainspring, the driving force and the torture of history" (165).

This distinction between Hebrew and Greek perceptions of time and space is a commonplace of the biblical theology movement (see e.g. Thorlief Boman, *Hebrew Thought Compared With Greek* [London: SCM, 1960] 168ff. And there can be little doubt about the bible's formative role in the emergence of western culture, including its historical sensibilities. But this is not merely a matter of comparative anthropology or the history of ideas, as a liberal theologian might think; for Moltmann such an insight is really built on revealed truth. As was the case with natural theology and human authenticity, then, so too is it the case with western historical sensibilities: for Moltmann they all reflect the impact of God's promise and are not naturally occurring.

21 Macquarrie, *Jesus Christ in Modern Thought* (1990) 322-23.

22 It seems clear that the principle John Hick calls "eschatological verification" is at work here. This was a challenge to logical positivism's attempt at declaring religious language meaningless by claiming that "properly scientific" observation (one of two allowable forms of meaningfulness according to the so-called "verification principle," the other being logical necessity, effectively tautology, in statements) will be possible to observers present in the eschaton. If there is no "afterlife," however, this will not be falsified, allowing only verification. Thus Moltmann could, if he wished, establish the meaningfulness of his ideas to mockers imbued with the spirit of positivism; see Hick's now classic article, "Theology and Verification," *Theology Today* 17 (1960) 12-31, reprinted in Basil Mitchell (ed.), *The Philosophy of Religion* (Oxford Readings in Philosophy; Oxford: Oxford University Press, 1971) 53-71.

23 Macquarrie, *Jesus Christ in Modern Thought* (1990) 321.

24 This is a most interesting admonition. Liberal theology might far more readily claim the high ground of public accessibility in such a discussion, denying that conservative approaches rest on anything but fideism. And some post-liberal theologians are happy to embrace a particularist stance content merely to "tell their own story" amid today's pluralistic conditions without further recourse to apologetic (which is the perennial preoccupation of liberal theology). This difference of opinion is exhibited in the work of George Lindbeck (to be considered in Part IV, below) and in the plea of David Tracy that Lindbeck not surrender the long-standing Christian traditions of natural theology and public confirmability (this is Tracy's constant burden—see particularly Part 1 of his major work *The Analogical Imagination* [1981]; see also his essay "Lindbeck's New Program for Theology" [1985]).

Moltmann shows his proximity to "radical" theology, such as Lindbeck's post-liberalism, in disallowing liberal theology the broadly explanatory power it has long claimed. This is also in keeping with critiques offered by the "historical skeptics" considered in Part IV, who deny that any unequivocal consensus can be arrived at entailing Jesus' uniqueness or finality; there just isn't the historical evidence, they say, amongst other things.

[25] The only way we might excuse Moltmann such apparent obscurantism is to recall the place of "eschatological verification" in his epistemology, and recognize the future confirmability-in-principle of his claims. But this is perhaps to be over-generous, as he makes no such invocation at this point in his argument.

[26] This is a dialectical rather than an analogical approach, according to which God is not discerned in the fulfillments claimed and the continuities experienced by fallen humanity. Thus Moltmann has no time for any "Greek-speaking God" of idealism who constitutes the acme of human insight and sensibility: "In the human search for the good, the true and the beautiful, the crucified Christ was not a valuable aesthetic symbol" (33). God is not identified by analogies from earth to heaven, then, but in sorrow, grief and absence, and through a "crucifying knowledge." But by "putting us in our place" such an approach also sets us free; as Luther wrote, this involves "making us true men instead of unhappy and proud Gods" (212). So, for Moltmann, "faith in which the cross of Christ holds sway... sets at naught the divinity for which we perversely strive and restores the despised weakness of the flesh which we have perversely abandoned" (213). Bourgeois religion cannot bear such bluntness and brutal ugliness, he says, and so it is that the "theologian of glory" *hates* the cross and passion, despite his religiousness. God is not found in the familiar, the like, the lovable, according to this vision, but—and herein the heart of the good news Moltmann offers in this book—God is found in the unlike, among the ugly and unlovable making them beautiful and lovable by loving them, and among the damned as alone constituting their salvation. This clearly flies in the face of any natural theology, be it scholastic or liberal, but it is the only way Moltmann can live with what he sees to be the terror of history (278).

One who overestimates the *explicit* incarnationalism in *The Crucified God* is Brian Hebblethwaite; see "The Moral and Religious Value of the Incarnation" (1979) 97-98.

[27] Braaten, "A Trinitarian Theology of the Cross" (1976) 115 (italics mine).

[28] It has been suggested that there is *implicit* incarnationalism and even speculative metaphysics (of a decidedly "Greek" stamp) in this

notion of God present in the suffering of Jesus: see Zimany, "Molt-mann's Crucified God" (1977) 51; Braaten, art. cit. 119. But this is to overlook Moltmann's careful repudiation of Luther's recourse to the *communicatio idiomatum* and two-nature incarnationalism in his ren-dering of God's "death in Christ," just as it discounts the pains Molt-mann takes over distinguishing the suffering of the Father (grief) from that of the Son (death, abandonment) in the cross of Jesus (243).

[29] Note that "the punishing God of Calvinism" (Macquarrie, *Twen-tieth-Century Religious Thought*, 4th ed. [1988] 395) remains for Moltmann in his insistence that Jesus is abandoned by God. Indeed this is quite normative; for him the central question becomes "Who is God in the cross of the Christ who is abandoned by God?" (4). Macquarrie expresses doubt, however, that God could be said to suf-fer in Jesus when he is, at the same time, the God who has just aban-doned Jesus. Would it not be soteriologically sufficient for Jesus sim-ply to *feel* abandoned by God, thereby entering no less fully into the travail of "Godforsaken" humanity? (Macquarrie, *Jesus Christ in Modern Thought* [1990] 323). Schillebeeckx makes a similar criti-cism; see *Christ* (1980) 728.

Moltmann obviously wishes to say that God is present to human suffering not in immanence and incarnate sharing, as an idealist or liberal might have it (present incognito, if you like) but, rather, as one *genuinely* absent—genuinely sovereign and distant to the point of actually *abandoning* those he loves, while at the same time *dialec-tically* present and thus able to save. Such presence demands faith to perceive it, just as it demands internal (in fact, Trinitarian) differenti-ation within the Godhead to bring it off. While constituting a piece of necessary dogmatic baggage for the reformed Moltmann, neverthe-less one must admit that such a dialectical understanding does pro-tect against confusing the divine persons more readily than does a more immanentist conception of divine suffering. And so a highly social Trinitarianism, and an "essential" rather than merely "econom-ic" one (as Trinitarian thought often is among liberal theologians), is Moltmann's answer to the God question.

[30] Moltmann does allow a question about the historicity of Jesus' passion predictions (127), and employs the historical-critical insight that embarrassing material about Jesus is more probably authentic than an invention of early Christians (137). At the same time, howev-

er, he can leave completely unquestioned the authenticity of Jesus' sermon on the mount (128), his parables and forgiveness of sins (121). And having said at one point how the historical Jesus is important (85) Moltmann immediately proceeds to focus on the Christological titles, nearly all of which are commonly thought to have been placed on Jesus' lips by the evangelists. So where Jesus' life and ministry matter at all it appears to be Jesus-figures of the Gospels rather than the historical Jesus of scholarly reconstruction upon which Moltmann relies (e.g. 105-06).

[31] Zimany, "Moltmann's Crucified God" (1977) 52.

[32] Bauckham, "Jürgen Moltmann" (1989) 309.

[33] Ibid. 296.

[34] Cook, *The Jesus of Faith* (1981) 181.

[35] So while this book is Moltmann's most kenotic, nevertheless the motive here is not speculative, as kenotic Christology frequently is and has been (see the discussion in the Introduction).

[36] The potentially forlorn and defeatist strain in Spanish-influenced Christology and Christ-mysticism is discussed in Saúl Trinidad, "Christology, *Conquista*, Colonization" and George Casalis, "Jesus—Neither Abject Lord nor Heavenly Monarch," both in José Míguez Bonino (ed.), *Faces of Jesus* (1984), 49-65 and 72-76 respectively.

[37] Moltmann especially rejects modalistic tendencies characteristic of western Trinitarianism. These he links to the Platonists' distinction between idea and appearance (158) and to enlightenment "individualism" with its bias toward the single subject—divine for Barth, human for Schleiermacher and Rahner (139-47) (this recalls Moltmann's discussion in *Theology of Hope* about the transcendental subjectivity of God versus that of "man," and the need to overcome this false conservative/liberal dichotomy). The only way beyond undervaluing the divine persons by the "philosophical" expedient of grounding their unity in some pre-Trinitarian "divine substance" is, for Moltmann, a return to "biblical" thinking about God's unity. This he prefers to understand in eschatological terms, as we have seen. A post-modern (13-19) and non-patriarchal solution is sought. God the powerful individual, "disposer supreme" (192-202), is replaced by a God of internal relationships yet ever bound salvifically to the world and history. Thus John Damascene's doctrine of *perichoresis* (mutual

indwelling) is invoked by Moltmann to do what notions of "substance" could not, and therein he also overcomes a western predeliction for separating the economic and the immanent Trinity—his God is *in his deepest nature* related and outgoing. There is no question for Moltmann that this might only be a model of something more deeply veiled (149-58); he rejects the much vaunted "mystery of God" in favor of a quite "open," visible eschatological process of cosmic "deification" which the Father is effecting through the Son in the Spirit. This is what Moltmann's God now *is*, and the overtones of a process understanding will not be missed in his formulation.

[38] Moltmann is unconvincing in his distinction between the Logos who relates the Son to the world and to God, on the one hand, and the Spirit who relates the Father to the world through the Son on the other (108). Nor is it clear how Son and Spirit are properly to be distinguished in creating the world, as Moltmann sees it (redolent of Origen's emanationist ideas), and in bringing the world back into God. Dogmatic pressure to distinguish what others more liberal are happy to identify is obviously very great on Moltmann, and here I have in mind advocates of an "inspiration Christology," such as Geoffrey Lampe, or a "Logos Christology" such as that offered by John A. T. Robinson or Piet Schoonenberg (see Robinson, *The Human Face of God* [1973]; Schoonenberg, *The Christ* [1974] and the discussion in Chapter 7). In such a way might Moltmann mount just as effective attacks on the divine aseity (which he disavows) *without* giving the impression of being unable to clearly distinguish the Spirit from the Logos in association with the Son.

One cannot help thinking that Moltmann, despite his serious advocacy of a social Trinity in the face of western modalism, has nevertheless managed to commit the modalist's mistake of "confusing the persons" (though of course Moltmann has not "divided the substance"—he has denied the notion of substance altogether). Note, too, that it is difficult to conceive the Spirit, as envisioned by Moltmann, in any way suggesting a separate person; it appears far more like a process.

[39] Moltmann extends this to include both the confidence of Jesus' high priestly prayer (95-96) (which, incidentally, many critical biblical scholars would happily call a piece of Johannine composition) and his genuine despair and abandonment in the garden of Gethse-

mane and at the cross (79) (again, not accounts free of historical doubtfulness).

[40] See Nineham's "Epilogue" (1977), and the discussion of his and others' views on this matter in Part IV.

I also note that the anti-idealist Moltmann, so keen to avoid a dehistoricizing of Jesus in *The Crucified God*, has difficulty establishing a necessary connection between the Son of God and the person of Jesus. All he says about the Son is in the form of expounded dogma supported by scripture quotation, while Jesus is simply declared to be that Son. Such fideism is "worsened," if you will, by Moltmann's assurance that his theology enshrines Jesus' history.

[41] Another anti-liberal preoccupation is Moltmann's aforementioned post-modern conviction that modern Christology tuned to some "human condition," effectively relating to individuals and their interiority alone, ignores the social and political underpinnings of all such bourgeois subjectivity, tending thereby toward quietistic "culture Protestantism" (63-64).

[42] See e.g. Raymond Brown, *The Birth of the Messiah: A Commentary on the Infancy Narratives in Matthew and Luke* (Garden City, NY: Image, 1977) 160-61.

[43] He now describes this in terms of avoiding the distinction between theology "from above" and theology "from below" (69).

[44] This last insight is drawn from Conzelmann, and Moltmann further doffs his cap to the new quest by observing that community reminiscence about Jesus on the one hand and Easter proclamation on the other could not have been too different, otherwise one would have collapsed (141). But this is yet another isolated and underutilized critical insight.

[45] Of course this also means judgment for the world, but Moltmann does not see this in dread terms. It will not be a *dies irae*, he suggests (335), but a *dies pacifica*. This also represents a further consequence of Moltmann's departure from primarily individualistic, privatistic notions of salvation. The mystical element comes from Moltmann's belief that all suffering is taken up into God in the suffering of Jesus—through Jesus' participation in all the orders of being, human, historical and natural, all of which will be taken up in his resurrection (259). Such a post-modern understanding involves a decidedly non-Cartesian, non-spiritualistic, linguistic and relational

view of human beings and their eternal reward. This reward Molt-mann envisages in bodily terms as involving all human generations and eras, as redemptive of history's travail, as part of a recreated natural environment, and even as fully sexual (262).

Taking this embodied vision to some logical conclusions, however, one wonders which species in the new creation one will "enjoy on toast," what age bracket in human life will be deemed optimal for our reappearance or, for that matter, with respect to which culture, language and historical period will culturally, linguistically and historically constrained human beings be situated?

[46] This exercise in fine-tuning resurrection belief is perhaps motivated by Moltmann's recognition that no hard and fast evidence for a bodily resurrection exists (contra Pannenberg), that such belief is historically *sui generis* (Barth) and not accessible to analogy (Troeltsch); and so emphasis shifts to the resurrection appearances, which are more historically definite (216). But when was Moltmann ever tempted to state any explicit dependence of his views on church experience, ancient or modern?—he prefers dogmatic assertion or biblical literalism over any such "modernism."

If Moltmann wishes to view resurrection as a process of nature's redemption, though, would it not be appropriate to expect a transformation of Jesus' corpse as the first fruits? This should especially be the case in the light of Moltmann's insistence that Jesus was linked to the cosmos' various orders of existence through his body (259) (cf. Colin Gunton, *Yesterday and Today* [1983] on the nature of miracles as a sign that the creation's bondage to decay is over [132]).

[47] John Polkinghorne would agree, assessing liberal Christologies in the light of Jesus' apparent power to transform tragic, fallen lives: "An evolutionary view of Jesus as the "new emergent" in creation fails that test, for what hope could such a figure provide for us who have not emerged?"; see *Science and Creation* (1988) 92; see also Kasper, *Jesus the Christ* (1976) 223-24. Teilhard's classic work is *The Phenomenon of Man* (1955, ET 1959) (London: Collins [Fount], 1977).

[48] Rouner, "Theology of Religions in Recent Protestant Theology" (1986) 114.

[49] Here Moltmann favors what Hick and Knitter's symposium *The Myth of Christian Uniqueness* (Part III) calls "the ethico-practical

bridge" to dialogue, as Hans Küng also favors in his writings on religious peace as the necessary precursor to world peace; see Küng, *Christianity and the World Religions* (1987), *Global Responsibility: In Search of a New World Ethic* (1990) (London: SCM, 1991) and the discussion of his views in Chapter 8.

[50] Pawlikowski, *Christ in the Light of the Christian-Jewish Dialogue* (1982) 42-44.

[51] Moltmann, *The Crucified God* (1974) 102.

[52] The problem here is that Christianity so conceived constitutes a fuller realization of "God's plan" than does the religion of Israel. As Roy Eckhardt rightly grasps, in Moltmann "the Church *does* constitute the practical replacement of Israel in the work of salvation. The Church remains...the (round-about) instrument of the salvation of Israel" (Eckardt, "Jürgen Moltmann, the Jewish People, and the Holocaust" *Journal of the American Academy of Religion* 44 [1976] 689, cited in Pawlikowski, op. cit. 46). Moltmann thus constructs a picture of Judaism which, although distinguished Jewish advocates such as Moses Maimonides and Martin Buber can be found to support it (3), many or even most Jews might well reject. It is also the case that, hard as Moltmann might try, he cannot erase the common New Testament conviction that Judaism is superseded by Christianity (one need only think of the Lucan writings, especially the infancy narrative, and the letter to the Hebrews). Those well-intentioned souls who seek to deny this element in the New Testament are not ultimately convincing, I fear: see e.g. Clark M. Williamson and Ronald J. Allen, *Interpreting Difficult Texts: Anti-Judaism and Christian Preaching* (London: SCM; Philadelphia: Trinity Press International, 1989).

[53] Cf. Bauckham, "Jürgen Moltmann" (1989) 309.

[54] McGrath, *The Making of Modern German Christology* (1986) 193.

[55] An interesting assessment of Moltmann's political radicalism as not particularly radical is offered by the English priest/economist Ronald Preston: "One route is to denounce the many evils of today from the perspective of an ideal expression of the kingdom of God in the world, and then arrive at a few very tepid proposals when it comes to recommending some action to deal with the enormities

which they have denounced. We have an example of this in Moltmann, who has been criticized (with others) by the liberation theologians for it"; see *Religion and the Ambiguities of Capitalism* (1991)
130. In his Scott Holland lectures Canon Preston observes: "In practice when one asks what such theologians want us to do it turns out
to be surprisingly conventional, in spite of all the talk of revolutionary newness. It amounts to what one might call a progressive liberal
or radical stance"; see *Church and Society in the Late Twentieth Century* (1983) 108.

[56] Bauckham, art. cit. 308; McGrath, ibid.

[57] Eberhard Jüngel, a Lutheran pastor and fellow professor of Systematic Theology at Tübingen, provides an interesting neo-orthodox
comparison with Moltmann. His work is difficult, as anyone who has
labored through his representative volume *God as the Mystery of the
World* (1983) will testify. In it Jüngel dialogues closely with philosophical traditions back to the pre-Socratics, with contemporary hermeneutics (Fuchs, Ricoeur) and with German theology, though all to the exclusion of Anglo-American debates and their analytic agendum.

Jüngel, like Moltmann, joined the post-war German revival of
Luther's *theologia crucis* and developed his own theology as an East
German in the context of oppressive, militant Stalinism (for autobio-
graphical reflections see Jüngel, "Toward the Heart of the Matter"
[1991]). Jüngel is, however, methodologically tighter and more consistent than Moltmann. The following indications of his abiding concerns follow the excellent survey in J.B. Webster, "Eberhard Jüngel"
(1989).

Jüngel shares Moltmann's distaste for the anthropological parameters of liberal, enlightenment theology. As today's preeminent interpreter of his teacher Karl Barth, he offers instead a theological realism with human God-talk most truly constituted by God's self-
identification with the crucified Jesus Christ. And, like Moltmann,
Jüngel asserts his "death of God" convictions in the face of traditional theism and its atheistic shadow (96). Of so prioritizing God's self-
disclosure over the human perception favored by liberals, Jüngel
himself says in his aforementioned biographical essay "The Augustinian *interior intimo meo* ('nearer than I am to myself') became
something of a hermeneutical key" (231).

As with Moltmann, Christology is central to the entire program rather than separate and explicit. Jüngel sees the cross as central to understanding who Christ is, and this is illuminated by the resurrection which, as with Moltmann in *The Crucified God*, is a divine confirmation of the dark way of the cross. Jüngel is sensitive to the nature of gospel narratives as testimonies composed from resurrection faith, and so he does not "flirt with the historical Jesus" in an attempt to gain evidence of his divinity, as the less hermeneutically sensitive Moltmann does in more recent work. Jüngel begins from the resurrection, in which Jesus is now seen to be *enhypostatic* in the logos, then looks back to the Jesus of history whom he deduces must thus have been *anhypostatic*, the kingdom of God providing the center of his life.

As for God, Jüngel shares Moltmann's *theopaschite* leanings, following Barth by recasting divine sovereignty in terms of suffering love. For Jüngel, as for Moltmann, Trinitarian dogma puts gospel narratives in conceptual form. Jüngel's anthropology is centered on the cross as is his theism, with Christ revealing *and enabling* a true humanity inaccessible apart from divine grace operating through him. Jüngel and Moltmann both reverse the traditional order of natural theology, with "the true nature of nature" only evident in the light of revelation: "God is the "mystery of the world" because his self-communication is that which brings about the renewal of that world by disclosing its possibilities" (Webster, art. cit. 103; cf. Moltmann on present, natural "parables" of the eschatological future in *Theology of Hope*, Ch. 5. and *The Crucified God*, Chs. 7 & 8).

Jüngel's is no theology of hope, however. As with Barth his Jesus is already revealed to be unique and final—a conclusion Moltmann cannot fully credit in advance of the eschaton. But Jüngel's is clearly a "conservative" position, as is Moltmann's, in its rejection of the historical Jesus and human condition as primary evidence for Jesus' uniqueness and finality, and with its commitment to the divinely revealed nature of Trinitarian and Christological orthodoxy (despite a greater hermeneutical sensitivity than Moltmann over the differences between Pauline theology, gospel narratives and their later dogmatic elaboration).

[58] In claiming this I support David Tracy's suggestion that any "revisionist theology" today must take aboard the negative insights of

neo-orthodoxy. Tracy believes these insights constitute a sobering influence within the broader, enlightenment enterprise. Thus he eschews any predictable and superior liberal disdain; see *Blessed Rage for Order* (1988) 27-31, 33.

[59] The strictness of Torrance's realism, unparalleled in modern theology, perhaps accounts for his meager reception among theologians interested in science but inclined to the "softer" approaches; see Daniel Hardy, "Thomas F. Torrance" (1989) 82.

[60] Torrance is unlike Moltmann in his unbroken commitment to the tradition and to credal orthodoxy, believing, too, that the best insights of the ancient Catholic faith are preserved in the central themes of Reformed theology. This was evident when, in his recent patristic study, *The Trinitarian Faith*, he chose for a subtitle, *The Evangelical Theology of the Ancient Catholic Church* (Edinburgh: T & T Clark, 1988).

[61] Torrance is not the straight Calvinist or Barthian many think, however. As Torrance scholar Daniel Hardy puts it: "Neither Calvin nor Barth as such attracts Torrance. He is attracted by the possibility for theology which their approaches exemplify, the possibility of a *scientific theology*. For Calvin maintained just that, in contrast to medieval thought. He saw that knowledge was objectively derived from God as 'active,' 'through modes of knowing imposed on us from the nature of God and from his self manifestation through the Word.' ... The great virtue of Barth, as Torrance sees it, was that he recalled theology from 'Calvinism,' that logicized version of Calvin which is so frequently mistaken for Calvin's own position, to the recognition that knowledge of God comes by the free and graceful activity of God in a dynamic 'analogy of grace'" (Hardy, "Thomas F. Torrance" [1989] 74-75).

[62] Ibid. 72, 77.

[63] Torrance, *God and Rationality* (1971) 10. The English theoretical physicist, priest and theologian, John Polkinghorne, in his *Science and Creation* (1988), agrees with Torrance's insistence that *true* science is done under the pressure of its object, and often counter-intuitively. He cites unlikely conclusions from modern physics that *none* welcomed initially, nor supported out of hand, findings which defy explanation in terms of forces such as social convention, existing paradigms etc., as fixed upon by "soft" interpreters of science.

The best recent example, I think, is that of "parity non-conserva-
tion," or "left handedness," in the spin of subatomic particles. This
imbalance offends against our sense that "nature likes pairs," as well
as aesthetic sensibilities concerning balance, evenness and proportion. It just isn't "common sense." But, nevertheless, the hypothesis
is supported by evidence (in, say, the spin of electrons produced in
the beta decay of Cobalt-60), and it allowed physicists Lee and Yang
to effect a considerable classificatory simplification of the hitherto
confusing "soup" of newly discovered particles with their many
properties (88).

Polkinghorne recognizes that notions such as the hypostatic union
and the uniqueness of Christ strike many today as similarly counter-
intuitive, but he has been taught by his physics to expect that reality
is often like that. He thinks that such ideas *do* force themselves upon
theology in the manner Torrance suggests. And they offer a richer
appreciation of Christian redemptive mysteries than do the more
"common sense" liberal alternatives of evolutionary and inspiration
Christologies (92).

[64] Torrance has no time for popularizers in either science or theology who, he believes, muffle the impact of serious work by their un-
detected biases (Torrance, *God and Rationality* [1971] 117-18). This
is an *intolerably* elitist position, however—as if the greatest scientists have not refused to relinquish old paradigms, as Einstein the in-
veterate determinist refused to do in the face of growing evidence for
quantum indeterminacy, and as if many "serious" theologians are not
lifelong representatives (prisoners?) of a particular school of thought.

[65] Ibid. 52-53. These are more disclosive, presumably, than questions addressed to lower levels of organization or perception such as
those of the reductionist "masters of suspicion"—Feuerbach, Marx,
Durkheim and Freud.

[66] Ibid. 19. Indispensable for the serious inquirer is an attitude of
repentance, says Torrance, referring to that "suspension of belief"
and willingness to be challenged by evidence deemed characteristic
of good scientific method. Here we see the impact of Michael
Polanyi who, more than any other, has influenced Torrance's thought
on these matters (that Torrance's theology is shaped by Polanyi's
philosophy of science is established by Colin Weightman in his doctoral dissertation *Theology in a Polanyian Universe* [1991]). As

Polanyi himself would have it, "Those who listen sympathetically will discover for themselves what they would otherwise never have understood. Such an acceptance is a heuristic process, a self-modifying act, and to this extent a conversion" (Michael Polanyi, *Personal Knowledge* [London: Routledge & Kegan Paul, 1958] 151; cited in Torrance, *God and Rationality* [1971] 204). And as in science, so too in matters Christian—the Reformed Torrance will admit of fallen people understanding the gospel only if they have undergone a conversion in their deep habits of mind (Torrance, ibid. 72). The believer is thus grasped by God and responds in an appropriate act of "understanding" (ibid. 22). This is grounded in Calvin's reading of justification, according to Torrance, which doctrine "remains the most powerful statement of objectivity in theology" (ibid. 68).

Calvin appears to fall between the "forensic" understanding of justification as "imputed" in Luther and the "imparted" justification (really a part of sanctification) of Tridentine orthodoxy (Calvin's catechism pictured justification as imparting participation in Christ's righteousness to those for whom union with Christ had already been established [ibid. 64]). For our purposes, however, this means that the justified are the only ones who have been enabled to see aright in theological matters. But these are surely the *elect*, according to Calvin, and none but the elect. I have more to say about the implications of this arbitrary restriction in my critique of Torrance.

⁶⁷ Ibid. 54. The manner of thinking which Torrance favors is identified with that of the Greek fathers who, between the third and sixth centuries, struggled to bring a realism linking empirical and theoretical in classical theology. In establishing credal orthodoxy these fathers strike Torrance as exemplary in letting go many emphases of Hellenistic thought, and thus allowing the gospel to "create its own philosophy" (we must not uncritically claim that the *homoousion* and other aspects of their vision can be entirely cashed out in the common coin of the then philosophical environment; see e.g. C.N. Cochrane, *Christianity and Classical Culture: A Study of Thought and Action from Augustus to Augustine* [Oxford: Clarendon Press, 1944]).

But this spirit was not to last. A dualism separating idea and appearance came to dominate medieval theology through influences from the Platonic/Aristotelian tradition of Augustinianism upon

Thomism (i.e. as medieval "realism"), and on Roman Catholic theology today. This Augustinian-sponsored dualism also influenced modern phenomenalism via Kant, with subsequent dualistic phenomenology constituting another major influence on recent Roman Catholic theology (see Torrance, "Theological Realism" [1982] 173; it would be nice to have had a posited connection between Augustine and Newton explained here, but Torrance is often light on such specifics). Torrance blames William of Ockham for providing another precursor to contemporary theological subjectivism in the shift to considering "authorial intention" in the interpretation of texts, thus interposing subjectivity and obscuring the object. He believes this turn to interiority and "oblique intention" was cemented by Erasmus, while Calvin and Luther maintained the objectivity of earlier recourse to "direct intention" (see Torrance, op. cit. 36-37).

But the main inspiration for this favored interrogative thinking in theology is ascribed to Calvin—the father of modern theology according to Torrance. Calvin (the lawyer) applied to theology and scripture the Ciceronian question-and-answer approach which was brought forward into Renaissance law by Laurentius Valla (who himself employed it in biblical interpretation). This spirit came to influence science via Calvin's impact on Francis Bacon, thinks Torrance, and from science the effect worked back upon theology and scripture through Spinoza. Thus *interrogatio* (active, deductive interrogation) came to replace the inductive spirit of medieval *quaestio* in tandem with the rise of Reformed theology (ibid. 33-35).

Apart from this, however, it is from the dogged scientific realism of Einstein and the Scots physicist James Clerk Maxwell (whose six justly famous differential equations, in the 1860s, cemented the link between electrical and magnetic phenomena by establishing the electromagnetic field) and from Polanyi's philosophy of science that Torrance takes his bearings.

[68] Torrance, op. cit. 139.

[69] Ibid. 140. In this sense humanity is the pinnacle, even the priest of creation. But Torrance makes no theological mileage from this in the manner of evolutionary Christologies "from below" such as that of Teilhard de Chardin.

[70] Ibid. 201. Despite his distaste for any dualism in epistemology, depriving the "subject" of direct access to the "object," nevertheless

Torrance appears to maintain his own version of dualism in ontology: "The rejection of radical dualism...must not be taken to imply the advocacy of any oneness or even any proportion between God and the world, but rather the rejection of a deistic disjunction between them" (ibid. 71). Thus Torrance rejects the tradition, stemming from Origen, that God endows creation with his own rationality. Instead he favours the idea of a separate, created rationality as understood in the alternative tradition of Anselm, Duns Scotus, Pascal and Barth (ibid. 64-65; in Anselm, the Word of God as *Suprema Veritas* or *Ratio Veritas* is different from and greater than the *veritatis* or *rationes* of our own understanding, though God is only known through them [ibid. 170]). In the absence of a natural link, therefore, the link Torrance does admit is one opened by the Holy Spirit to human spirits, and constantly in need of being maintained by the Holy Spirit (ibid. 171, 180).

This "fontal rationality," "presupposed in the created rationalities of nature explored through the natural sciences," not only impinges upon scientists but upon Christians as well—as the power under which they fall in Jesus Christ (ibid. 96, 45). Torrance cannot conceive of any meaningful inquiry apart from a recognition of this "higher rationality": "when we...ask the question as to ultimate rationality, to be agnostic would be an act of sheer irrationality, for it would mean that our reason was being loosed from its bond with the source of rational being" (ibid. 97). Indeed, he believes that thus being grasped is so real for the Christian that no doubting can intrude, readily concluding that "God is the most certain and compelling fact in all knowledge" (ibid. 98).

One thing we can say with certainty is that Torrance does *not* see God as any Tillichian "Ground of Being"; rather, his God holds the world in Being without any necessary connection to it. It is as if a *form* of analogy links God and the world, but it is a perpetually driven one that would collapse if God "let it go." His God is, ultimately, a hidden God, as we also find to be the case for Moltmann and for the Reformation ancestors he and Torrance share.

[71] To understand Torrance's disdain for liberal theology, we must further understand his unwillingness to support modern disjunctions between inquirer and object of inquiry which underlie it. Torrance sees in field theory a link between all things otherwise understood to

be disjoined, and in quantum mechanics he finds the notion of the participating observer. The need for *a priori* notions like space, time and causality to order our experience is denied, too, in contravention of Kant. Here he relies on Einstein. According to the theory of general relativity, space is curved by the presence of matter, with gravitational forces understood as merely another way of talking about relative movement of objects within the geometry of a curved space-time continuum. Thus Einstein could declare that geometry has become a natural science, inextricable from the actual dynamics of material interaction in a way forever fusing the spatial with the temporal *and the conceptual* (ibid. 6-7, 100; also *Space, Time and Incarnation* [1969] 58).

Behind these approaches Torrance identifies the empiricism characterizing Newton and deism, with Locke's doctrine of "representative perception" seen to revive a yet older medieval idea of "images in the middle." This refers to "ways of thinking through the medium of images and ideas that intervened between the mind and reality... *objecta mentis*... which rendered the relation... between sign and thing signified *oblique*" (Torrance, "Theological Realism" [1982] 174). But, for Torrance, "Since it is impossible from within appearances to determine their relation to any alleged reality beyond them, Hume's scepticism was well nigh unavoidable" (art. cit. 174). Torrance opposes this widespread belief in an underlying mechanistic disjunction between ourselves and the world. It is a disjunction, too, which was "vigorously rejected by the great scientists of our time... by Planck and Einstein" but which "has taken a long time to die, for it has received a strange anachronistic extension to its life in linguistic and existentialist philosophy and not least in corresponding types of theology which have their roots in Kantian dualism between phenomena and noumena, or in Lessing's 'ugly ditch' between accidental truths of history and necessary truths of reason" (art. cit. 175).

[72] Torrance, *God and Rationality* (1971) 62.

[73] This manifests that classic Protestant turn from Christ's person to his work, which risks separating the work of salvation from Jesus' historical person entirely (*God and Rationality* [1971] 63, 121). It is the liability of all idealist solutions, emerging also among those to be considered in Part II.

[74] Torrance, *God and Rationality* (1971) 109, 120-21.

[75] There is a big difference, says Torrance, between Luther's talk of Christ's work *pro me*—objective, historically independent, based on God's gracious justifying act—and this *pro me* in the hands of Bultmann, for whom justification has become mere justifying faith (ibid. 59, 121) cashable in no surer form than the unreliable coin of personal existential decision.

[76] Ibid. 109.

[77] Torrance, *Space, Time and Incarnation* (1969) 61. An implication of dualism in its medieval form was that biblical interpretation became content with allegorical and typological exegesis (Torrance, "Theological Realism" [1982] 194 n.6). This is just what has returned in the "form criticism" practiced by Bultmann, in which the mindset of early Christian communities is thought to provide the referent for the texts, rather than any historical events they might describe. This spirit continues in "redaction criticism"; this is not discussed by Torrance in the works consulted but it, too, looks for its referent in the minds of Jesus' later interpreters (in this case, those of the evangelists) rather than in the events themselves.

[78] London: SCM, 1963.

[79] Torrance, *God and Rationality* (1971) 31, 4.

[80] Ibid. 40-41.

[81] Ibid. 51.

[82] Ibid. 40. Robinson's Christology is discussed in Chapter 7.

[83] Ibid. 55.

[84] Torrance, "Theological Realism" (1982) 176.

[85] Ibid. 188. The volumes of Schillebeeckx considered by Torrance include, *Revelation and Theology, 2: The Concept of Truth and Theological Renewal* (London, Sheed & Ward, 1968).

[86] Ibid. 182.

[87] Ibid. 176-77.

[88] Ibid. 186-87 (italics mine). In the same context Torrance mentions Bernard Lonergan, an influential modern writer on theological method, as turning "from objective structures in reality to *subjective structures in man's rational self-consciousness*" (ibid. 195 n.25) (italics mine). This he sees as the standard current Roman Catholic strategy, mentioning also other transcendental Thomists such as Blondel, Márèchale and their offspring Karl Rahner (ibid. 176; see the discussion of Rahner's Christology in Chapter 4).

322   Is Jesus Unique?

[89] This denial of Cartesian subjectivism and its consequent theological appeal to the interiority of some "human condition" is postmodern in its way, as Hans Küng declares to be the case with Karl Barth, thus identified as the first post-modern theologian (Küng, "Karl Barth and the Postmodern Paradigm" [1988]). We could likewise call Torrance post-modern, as Moltmann was so labeled (though Moltmann is committed to forms of *self-styled* post-modern philosophy, unlike Torrance).

[90] Torrance, *Space, Time and Incarnation* (1969) 62. The Thomistic alternative was to "leave the lid off," as in the fathers, whereby Christ retained his throne of the universe while incarnate on earth. Luther's alternative solution involved extending Jesus' humanity to include aspects of his divinity by the *communicatio idiomatum* (ibid.).

[91] This reached its logical conclusion, for Torrance, with Kant's reduction of the "receptacle" into which God was emptied to the dimensions of our own heads. This he opposes for the way it courted subjectivism and, thus, uncertainty in subsequent liberal theology (ibid. 62).

[92] Torrance, *God and Rationality* (1971) 164 (italics mine).

[93] Torrance, *Space, Time and Incarnation* (1969) 53.

[94] Torrance, *God and Rationality* (1971) 144.

[95] Torrance, "Theological Realism" (1982) 85, 89-90.

[96] See e.g. John Knox, *The Humanity and Divinity of Christ* (1978) 113-16; Maurice Wiles, "Myth in Theology" (1977) 161; many others considered in this study tacitly admit that resurrection involves Christian experience, as we shall see.

[97] Torrance, *God and Rationality* (1971) 64. Note that the same trend is found in modern liberal writings which claim to keep something like the work of Christ while sacrificing his person, as with the recourse to functional Christology in Hick (ed.), *The Myth of God Incarnate* (1977).

[98] Ibid. 168.

[99] Ibid. 180.

[100] Ibid. 145 (italics mine).

[101] Ibid. 143.

[102] Ibid. 145; cf. n.4, above.

[103] Ibid. 145.

[104] See Baillie, *God Was in Christ: An Essay on Incarnation and Atonement* (1948, 2nd ed. 1956) (London: Faber & Faber, 1961).

[105] Torrance, op. cit. 68-69.

[106] Ibid. 145; cf. *Space, Time and Incarnation* (1969) 66.

[107] Fermat's Principle in optical theory establishes how light, when traversing a range of different media, always seeks that path which minimizes the time of its passage. It allows the refractive indices of materials to be derived.

[108] Ibid. 146.

[109] Ibid. 149. This is also true of Calvin. We have seen how Moltmann reinterprets this Reformed tradition.

[110] And so, one supposes, Torrance would welcome the historical-critical agenda up to a point; recall that Barth did so, although chiefly for its negative effect in removing any possibility that the truths of God in Christ could be established historically.

[111] Ibid. 186; cf. 185, where the Holy Spirit emerges as guarantor. Elsewhere, however, Torrance seems to be saying that the risen Christ himself oversaw apostles in preparing their gospels, so that "the Word *which He put into their mouth*...became the controlled unfolding of his own revelation within the mind and language of the apostolic foundation" (ibid. 152, italics mine). Thus it is, against Bultmann and his school, that Torrance declares the kerygma to rest on revelation by God through Christ in the Spirit rather than in any reflection by early Christians. I would say, however, that this revelatory, post-Easter Jesus is a far cry from the one who eschewed messianic and divine honors in (three out of four of) the very gospels which Torrance has him "revealing" to the apostles. And have we not seen Torrance elsewhere identify *the Holy Spirit* as mediating between the Word (in Christ) and our minds, rather than Christ himself? (see above, referring to ibid. 168).

[112] This again falls short of that recourse to the historical Jesus characterizing liberal Christologies.

[113] Ibid. 143-44.

[114] Ibid. 65-66, 150-51.

[115] See e.g. John Dominic Crossan, *In Parables* (New York: Harper & Row, 1973); Dan Otto Via, *The Parables: Their Literary and Existential Dimension* (Philadelphia: Fortress, 1967); Sallie McFague TeSelle, *Speaking in Parables* (Philadelphia: Fortress,

1975); Norman Perrin, "The Modern Interpretation of the Parables of Jesus and the Problem of Hermeneutics" *Interpretation* 25 (1971) 131-48; and the use made of such approaches for understanding the idea of revelation by David Tracy, *Blessed Rage for Order* (1988) Ch. 6, 119-45.

[116] *God and Rationality* (1971) 65-66, 150-51, 203.

[117] In advancing from subatomic particles through cellular organisms to animal populations and human beings, the science deemed appropriate to each level is regarded as progressively *softer*, from physics through the levels of biology to social science. Humanities is normally considered to be "off the scale" in such considerations!

Torrance admits that different levels are present in reality which are accessible to different levels of inquiry (*God and Rationality* [1971] 52-53)—including the theological—but he does not draw the obvious conclusion that different blends of objectivity and subjectivity are appropriate for these different levels.

[118] Weightman, *Theology in a Polanyian Universe* (1991) 332-33.

[119] Bell's Theorem proves the incompatibility of Einstein's "hidden variables" with any statistical interpretation of Quantum mechanics. Earlier, Einstein, Podolsky and Rosen had devised a thought-experiment (the famous EPR Experiment) to undermine any probabilistic interpretation: consider two photons with (necessarily) opposite spins produced in the same event and diverging at the speed of light. Measuring the spin of one would collapse the wave-function of their joint system (linked forever, say the probabilists) and so "force" the other particle to disclose its (opposite) spin, though it be separated from its partner at potentially enormous distances. This would, however, call for a communication between the particles which would need to travel at greater than the speed of light—an impossibility according to Einstein's theory of Special Relativity. This *reductio ad absurdum* result was meant to illustrate the impossibility of viewing all a system's states as indeterminate prior to their measurement. But recent attempts to actually perform something like this experiment appear to establish that such "non-local" action at a distance is indeed possible, therein adding weight to the probabilistic explanation. Details of this exciting process can be found in Ch. 10 of what is perhaps the most reliable and readable of the popular introductions to

Quantum mechanics; see John Gribbin, *In Search of Schrödinger's Cat: Quantum Physics and Reality* (London: Corgi, 1984).

[120] At the level of more ordinary reality, beyond observable quantum effects, the determinacy of classical physics has never ceased to apply. But in the light of Chaos Theory this supposed simplicity is now seen to belie a reality full of complex instability. The "linearity" (smoothness, simple continuity) of most classical solutions (even for systems traditionally thought to be simple, like pendulums) is now seen to be painfully naive in the face of nature's complexity, reflecting the tidying tendencies of our minds rather than the actual complexities of nature.

Thus the determinism Torrance holds dear can now be seen as a culturally driven imposition on the evidence—even at the level of ordinary experience. And this is the very thing he condemns.

There is a balancing consideration revealed by Chaos Theory, however, involving the discovery of deep order and recurring patterns—called "strange attractors"—concealed within the dynamics of chaotic systems. The well known "Mandelbrot Set" provides a visual entrée to this deep order (these are color computer graphics representing, in abstract graphical form, certain characteristics of the system's dynamics).

For popular introductions to Chaos Theory, see James Gleick, *Chaos: Making a New Science* (London: Sphere Books [Cardinal], 1988) (which is good on the movement's history and for biographical insights about its founders) and Ian Stewart, *Does God Play Dice? The Mathematics of Chaos* (London: Penguin, 1990) (which endeavors to explain more of the theory).

[121] This is referred to as "the collapse of the wavefunction": a photon strikes a fluorescent screen and apparently loses its wavelike properties, appearing thus as a particle.

[122] Polkinghorne, however, thinks it has become more compelling, criticizing Capra's reliance on "bootstrap" theories popular in the mid-1970s (making much of the fundamental interchangeability and the "Shiva-like" creation and destruction of all fundamental particles from nothingness in the "vacuum field") in favor of the now more widely accepted view that, despite indeterminacy, there *are* fundamental particles such as quarks and gluons (cf. the deep order Chaos

Theory is finding in disordered systems); see Capra, *The Tao of Physics* (UK: Fontana [Flamingo], 1976) and Polkinghorne's comments in *Science and Creation* (1988), 93-94; see also his *One World: The Interaction of Science and Theology* (London: SPCK, 1986).

¹²³ To be sure, Torrance insists on publicness in that he opposes theological subjectivism. But this is the publicness of an essentially private revelation.

¹²⁴ See e.g. the classic treatment in Rudolf Otto, *The Idea of the Holy* (1917, ET 1923) (London: Oxford University Press, 1958).

¹²⁵ See e.g. Peter Berger, *A Rumour of Angels* (1971); John Bowker, *The Sense of God* (Oxford: Clarendon, 1973) and David Tracy, *The Analogical Imagination* (1981), who insists upon the public accountability of theology.

¹²⁶ I am indebted here to Ian Barbour's Gifford Lectures, *Religion in an Age of Science,* Vol. 1 (1990), where similar processes of verification and falsification are identified at work in both science and religion, including the pressure to change paradigms. A paradigm approach is also found in Maurice Wiles, *The Remaking of Christian Doctrine* (1974) as in Hans Küng and David Tracy, *Paradigm Change in Theology* (1989). On this dialogical understanding of the relationship between theory and experiment, see Barbour's Ch. 2, "Models and Paradigms," esp. Fig. 1 on p. 32.

¹²⁷ This issue is also raised by the work of another Scottish presbyterian, Lesslie Newbigin (a former bishop of Madras in the Church of South India, where he championed inter-religious dialogue). In a contribution to the English "myth debate" he shares Torrance's desire that theology resist the liberal retreat into subjectivism. His Jesus is the decisive clue for understanding history, without whom it makes no overall sense and we are left as subjects adrift in vast uncharted seas. A consequence of having no such sense of a meaning and purpose to history is identified by Newbigin in the way eastern religions, dedicated to the subject, seek escape from history as from a burdensome flux (Newbigin, "The Centrality of Jesus for History" [1979] 200-01, 202-03). Torrance would ascribe such a sense to pressure from the object. In Newbigin, however, it is declared to be the sort of perspective or assumption from which one views history as a whole and from which investigation can proceed. That would put it

in the category of a theory which guides observation as surely as any scientist is guided by "hunches."

Maurice Wiles, responding to Newbigin, points out that such hunches or working hypotheses must be open to challenge by the object—they must not unduly dominate the proceedings (Wiles, "Comment on Lesslie Newbigin's Essay" [1979] 212-13). Torrance would be forced to agree, given his insistence that theory must bow to the claims of its object. But for Torrance such assumptions or perspectives, as Newbigin identifies them, are anything but early steps in a dialogue leading to insight; they are, rather, the final form of his beliefs about God in Christ and are *not* liable to challenge. And nor are they for Newbigin either, as Alan Race points out: "Newbigin does want to view the Incarnation as a judgement of historical evidence and interpretation, but only in a limited sense. The exercise of critical reflection is confined to the presupposition of Christ's uniqueness and is subordinate to it. If we ask how it is that he knows that the event of Jesus Christ represents God's unique intervention, the answer must be *sola fide*. At this point his position becomes logically invulnerable, and is analogous to the invulnerability of Barth's view of revelation" (Race, *Christians and Religious Pluralism* [1983] 35). Whatever you call this, it is *not* the stuff of open-ended scientific method under the control of objective reality.

Newbigin's views on the issues at hand are all essentially in place with *The Finality of Christ* (1969); for his reactions to the recent pluralist symposium *The Myth of Christian Uniqueness* (1987), edited by John Hick and Paul Knitter, see his "Religion for the Marketplace" (1990). Knitter pairs Newbigin's views on the question of other religions with those of Anglican missionary Bishop Stephen Neill, both of whom soften Barth's exclusivism by allowing revelation and the possibility of salvation within other religions (Knitter, *No Other Name?* [1985] 108-10). Neill's "conservative" views can be found in *The Supremacy of Jesus* [1984] and his essays for that swift, evangelical rejoinder to *The Myth of God Incarnate* (1977) entitled *The Truth of God Incarnate*, Michael Green (ed.) (Grand Rapids: Eerdmans, 1977).

[128] We have seen Torrance oppose the Thomistic idea that human will must play its part in the matter of assent, an idea common in modern theology and not least under the influence of existentialism.

[129] Two of the five points of Calvinism asserted against Arminianism at the Synod of Dort (1618-19).

[130] I would add to these comments about a possible hidden religious influence my suspicion that Torrance's rhetoric of duty, obedience and manliness in submitting to them is quite in keeping with a strict Church of Scotland personal ethic. But, then, any authoritarian system will inculcate such values in its subjects, and admit of no valid way to see things apart from its own. Marxists and feminists are teaching us to deconstruct such lofty claims, however, and to recognize the human "will to power" (Nietzsche) concealed within. As Einstein sought "hidden variables" underlying quantum reality, therefore, so should Torrance be aware that his own views might be similarly determined.

And could there not have been religious influences behind Einstein's fundamental conviction that "God does not play dice," in his Spinozist pantheism and his Jewish respect for the law, which colored his science (though by no means negatively)? That is to say, maybe even Einstein's scientific realism was not entirely free of ideological underpinning, in a manner Torrance's anti-subjectivism would oppose.

[131] This is the strategy adopted by today's liberal apologetics which normally denies the provability, for instance, of claims that God exists, being satisfied to establish their *likelihood* on the basis of commonly agreed criteria (see e.g. Hans Küng, *Does God Exist?* [1980]; David Tracy, *Blessed Rage for Order* [1988]). Certainty must thus be content to abide at the level of existential conviction, without the luxury of exclusive claims to support it.

[132] See Fox, *Original Blessing* (Santa Fe, NM: Bear, 1983); *The Coming of the Cosmic Christ* (1988).

[133] See e.g. the excellent, even-handed treatment offered by the Irish theologian Gabriel Daly, OSA in his *Creation and Redemption* (Theology for a Pilgrim People Series; Dublin: Gill & Macmillan, 1988).

[134] See Torrance, *God and Rationality* (1971) 52.

[135] Gen 3:23-24.

[136] See Ian Barbour, *Religion in an Age of Science* (1990) Part 1, in which possible views are canvased and the critical realist position favored.

[137] See also Schillebeeckx on the nature of revelation in *Christ* (1980) Ch. 1.

[138] MacKinnon, "Substance in Christology" (1972) 292-93.

[139] Oscar Culmann's influential study *The Christology of the New Testament* (1957) (London: SCM, 1959), which studies Jesus from the perspective of Christological titles, typifies this approach (see MacKinnon, "The Relation of the Doctrines of the Incarnation and the Trinity" [1976] 93-94).

[140] MacKinnon, "Substance in Christology" (1972) 299.

[141] Ibid. 298.

[142] Ibid. 298, 299.

[143] Ibid. 292-93, 298 (favoring the ontology of "substance" as tying Christology to Jesus' person in a way that idealist generality cannot); see also MacKinnon, "The Relation of the Doctrines of the Incarnation and the Trinity" (1976) 98 (wherein he wishes to do what Moltmann did, in *The Crucified God* [1974], redefining the absoluteness of God in light of Jesus' cross).

[144] MacKinnon, "The Conflict Between Realism and Idealism" in *Explorations in Theology 5* (1979) 151-65, 203-04; 164.

[145] MacKinnon, "The Relation of the Doctrines of Trinity and Incarnation" (1976) 100.

[146] At one point, however, MacKinnon casts his "theology from above" in a form more in keeping with the approach of Hans Frei. Frei concentrates on the rendering of Jesus' uniqueness in the synoptic gospels. MacKinnon, in his "Prolegomena to Christology" (1982), finds the figure of Jesus (especially as drawn in John's gospel [155]) to possess a "strangeness" suggestive of his incarnate status: "This strangeness may be judged rooted in, and expressive of, the way in which he lives uniquely as the frontier of the familiar and the transcendent, the relative and the absolute, and by so standing, demands that our very conception of both alike be revised" (154). This constitutes an attempt by MacKinnon to explain the mechanism by which the revelation of Jesus' uniqueness and finality is received—it is consistent with the principles of narrative theology (see n. 156, below), but falls short of what Frei attempts.

[147] Here (p. 156) Gunton has in mind MacKinnon's paper, "Substance in Christology" (1972) 294, 297.

[148] Gunton would also agree with the claims of Torrance and MacKinnon that scripture has been misread by "subjective theology." He favors the conclusion of J.D.G. Dunn that the New Testament knows of no historical Jesus apart from developed Christian faith, again forbidding any Kantian chasm between things and what we say about them (83). In this vein Gunton denies that incarnational belief constitutes a later imposition of Greek philosophy on the pristine teaching and example of Jesus, as argued by Harnack and subsequent liberal theology. Unlike the nineteenth century quest of the historical Jesus, the new quest seeks the historical Jesus "in, with and under" the Christ of faith, believing them to be inseparable. But, nevertheless, they remain distinguishable—there is an overplus of interpretation. Gunton does not appear to recognize this (as does Dunn). A more realistic theological use of these insights is to be found, I believe, in "liberal" approaches such as those of Schillebeeckx (Chapter 8) and Mackey (Part III, n.140).

[149] Gunton's musical insights are drawn from Victor Zuckerkandle, *Sound and Symbol: Music and the External World* (London: Routledge & Kegan Paul, 1956).

[150] It may even be the case that Gunton has abandoned the virgin birth, as Moltmann did, in his assertion: "If Jesus is to be fully part of space and time as a human being, then indeed he must be part of the genetic process that is human birth and life" (*Yesterday and Today* [1983] 126).

[151] Gunton has also written on the atonement, in *The Actuality of Atonement: A Study of Metaphor, Rationality and the Christian Tradition* (Edinburgh: T & T Clark, 1988). Another recent study of that topic (and in the fideist spirit identified in this section) is provided by an Oxford Baptist, Paul Fiddes, in *Past Event and Present Salvation: The Christian Idea of the Atonement* (London: Darton, Longman & Todd, 1989) where we find echoes of Sölle on Christ as representative, of Torrance on the Spirit communicating *logos* to the Christian, and of Moltmann on the need to reconceive God. Both works are neatly summarized and discussed in Vernon White, *Atonement and Incarnation: An Essay in Universalism and Particularity* (Cambridge: Cambridge University Press, 1991) Ch. 4, 42-50.

[152] Torrance, op. cit. 47.

[153] Hardy, "Thomas F. Torrance" (1989) 78.

¹⁵⁴ Torrance, "Theological Realism" (1982) 192-93 (italics mine).

¹⁵⁵ MacKinnon does begin so to probe, however, in his "Prolegomena to Christology" (1982); see n. 146, above.

¹⁵⁶ Nowadays, "story" is as important a category for theology as was "history" when biblical theology held sway in the 1950s. George Stroup, in the first book-length study of narrative theology, denies that narratives must become the content of theology. But it is coming to be recognized that human identity is tied up in the particular stories of our lives, where formerly we might have looked to abstract essences or to the spirit of historical periods. Supplementing such factors with a new attention to narrative is the aim of this movement, as Metz and Weinrich have pointed out in their discussions of it (Metz, "A Short Apology of Narrative" [1973]; Weinrich, "Narrative Theology" [1973]). Certainly, turning to the particular, to the contingent and the "non-logical," as existentialism and the Freudian revolution do, is part of this. Gabriel Fackre identifies other cultural influences, however, including the imaginative, affective counter-culture and feminist movements which emerged in the 1960s and 1970s to challenge the aggressive rationality of technocratic America, the "hunger for stories" which Harvey Cox identifies as a consequence of the television age, and the way in which "some, responding to the range and depth of modern conflict and historical peril, are drawn to the dramatic structure of narrative as befitting both historic faith and contemporary fact, a usage anticipated in the conflict and victory motif of classical soteriology" (Fackre, "Narrative Theology" [1983] 342).

But there are other reasons why narrative has achieved theological popularity. Stroup discusses the way revelation became the cornerstone of twentieth century theology's attempt to recover from the collapse (due to the European crisis of confidence occasioned by World War I) of nineteenth century liberal Protestantism. He mentions Barth's *Church Dogmatics*, Brunner's *Revelation and History* and H. Richard Niebuhr's *The Meaning of Revelation* as evincing the centrality of this issue in the 1930s and 1940s. But a crisis arose in the wake of neo-orthodox supremacy, when the nature of revelation became unsure (Stroup, *The Promise of Narrative Theology* [1984] 39-40).

By offering narrative as a key for reappropriating revelation, however, Stroup means "not only that a particular literary genre is of decisive importance for Christian theology but that there is a peculiar form of understanding in the appropriation of Christian faith to which theology must attend" (97). He sees revelation as a "collision" between the objective historical givenness of "that series of events that constitutes Israel's covenental history and the life history and personal identity of Jesus of Nazareth as the Christ" and the believer's "own story," for whom to "confess faith in Jesus Christ is to reconstruct that personal identity narrative in the light of the community's *Credo*" (194).

Stroup, by the way, believes that Jesus is *revealed* to be unique in the now accustomed "conservative" manner: "It is Jesus of Nazareth in the uniqueness of his personal identity who reveals the meaning of Christian faith and in so doing establishes the identity of those communities who witness to him" (168). There is some Torrance-style "control by the object" here (one possible means of its outworking is investigated in the discussion of Frei and Ritschl).

Note, however, Stroup's earlier non-exclusivism regarding Jesus' uniqueness—he perceived Jesus as the unique agent of God's grace *for Christians*, while reluctant to make any claims for his *overall* uniqueness; see Stroup's essay, "The "Finality" of Jesus Christ" (1982). This is an approach more in keeping with some of the "religious pluralists" to be considered in Chapter 10.

[157] There is the same gap in MacKinnon's works, discussed above, concerning the mechanism by which these "truths" are appropriated. I note with interest, however, his recourse to literary tragedy (mainly Sophocles and Shakespeare) in explicating the Christian faith, and his recommendation that the gospels be read as tragedies: see "Ethics and Tragedy," in *Explorations in Theology 5* (1979) 182-95, 206; especially p. 194. This is thoroughly in keeping with narrative theology's approach to scripture, and so MacKinnon, too, can be seen as begging the questions such a theology confronts.

As for Gunton, in *Yesterday and Today* (1983), his view of music constituting a constructive matrix linking past, present and future and so redeeming time from its apparent forlorn slavery to decay might also be asserted of liturgy, of games (which draw us into their own time, and hence talk in some recent theology about "the play of God" as a metaphor for creation and redemption), but also of *stories*.

Dietrich Ritschl, whose *Memory and Hope* Gunton favors (82), is a work of narrative theology which investigates the revelatory dynamics of Christianity's story. Like Torrance, Gunton hints at how these dynamics might work, suggesting: "Such solution as is possible must derive from a search for elements of intrinsic intelligibility in the biblical portrayal of Christ, elements that enable us to bring together both time and eternity" (53). But for an examination of how this "intrinsic intelligibility" might actually work, we must follow Frei and Ritschl if we are not to end up in the realm of liberal theology and its hermeneutical claims.

[158] New Haven, CT: Yale University Press, 1974; see the discussion in Placher, "Postliberal Theology" (1989) 118.

[159] Herein is the neo-orthodox spirit of Frei's program revealed. In his critique of accommodating liberal spirits he recalls Barth's critique of culture Protestantism. In addition he joins other post-liberals in their post-modern belief that universally endorsable realities have deserted us. He shares, too, the insights of modern sociology, anthropology and philosophy of language that meaning is tied to discrete language games or *Gestalten*. Thus Geertz and Wittgenstein join Barth in contributing to the patrimony of Frei's thought, as we also find to be the case with Ritschl.

[160] Torrance, "Theological Realism" (1982) 196 n.34.

[161] Similarities between Frei and Moltmann on the necessity of biblical narrative for identifying Jesus are discussed in Kelsey, *The Uses of Scripture in Recent Theology* (1986) 54-55.

[162] Frei believes we are closer to a genuine "Christ figure" in the "whisky priest" of Graham Greene's novel *The Power and the Glory*, but he sees this character more as a disciple than as an outright Christ figure.

Frei also denies that the gospel portrayal of Jesus allows that his humanity could be enhanced by others, as was the case for Greene's "whisky priest" in the time of his imprisonment before execution (81). Might there be exceptions to this in the texts, however? For instance, is Jesus' encounter with the Syrophonecian woman in Mk 7:24-30 an instance where he learned from another person—in this case from a faith as considerable as it was unexpected, as winsome as it was socially unconventional in its expression?

[163] For a discussion of difficulties inherent in the rendering of literary Christ figures see Stewart Sutherland, *God, Jesus and Belief: The Legacy of Theism* (Oxford: Basil Blackwell, 1984) 150-62.

[164] As Collingwood states, "When a man thinks historically, he has before him certain documents or relics of the past. His business is to discover what the past was which has left these relics behind it"; see *The Idea of History* (Oxford: Clarendon, 1946) 282.

[165] This criticism of post-liberal theology is echoed by Alister McGrath in his Bampton Lectures *The Genesis of Doctrine* (1990), in rejoinder to Lindbeck, *The Nature of Doctrine* (1984). There, McGrath denies that the genesis of beliefs can be ignored in the way Lindbeck (and Frei) suggest.

[166] Herein Ritschl demonstrates the strange affinity which exists between conservatives and radicals where both have abandoned liberal-style apologetics as unworkable. He is influenced by the same Anglo-American philosophical tradition, characterized by Wittgensteinian notions of "meaning as use not reference," as are George Lindbeck and others to be considered among the "radical" group in Part IV (this emphasis is particularly clear in Ritschl's more recent work *The Logic of Theology* [1986] to which reference is made throughout this section).

[167] The church in this dispensation became a mediator of traffic between God and the individual which led either to an overemphasis on the institutional church (Roman Catholic) or to an underemphasis (spiritualistic anti-church secular Protestantism) (120-21, 124).

[168] It is interesting that Ritschl (and Frei, for that matter) makes so much of the *Christus praesens* where others are content to talk of Christ's presence in terms of the Holy Spirit and of the Spirit's witness to Christ. We have seen such emphasis on the Spirit grow in importance for Moltmann, but Ritschl's similarities with his fellow German do not extend this far. This is doubly interesting, however, given Moltmann's interest in Greek Orthodox theology, especially since *The Trinity and the Kingdom of God* (1983), because Ritschl's *denial* of this emphasis is also inspired by Eastern Orthodox thinking. Another issue is also worth mentioning. In *The Logic of Theology* Ritschl approves Eastern Orthodox rejection of the *filioque* clause on grounds that processions of *both* the Son and the Spirit from the Father emphasize the *distinction* of the second and third persons

rather than their *virtual interchangeability*, as in a "more western" approach to the question of Jesus' presence. Accordingly, activity outside the church and apart from Christ can more readily be ascribed to the Spirit. This recognition is identified by Ritschl in Russian piety and, one supposes, in the also mentioned willingness of Anglicans nowadays to relinquish the *filioque* clause (163).

One thus realizes why Ritschl can operate without a Logos Christology. His God is active outside the church and throughout the world in the Spirit, rather than as the Logos, and so God's presence everywhere in general can be spoken of in different terms than can God's more obviously Christological presence in and for the church (cf. the discussion of spirit vs. logos approaches in Part III, n.29).

[169] This is the burden of Schubert Ogden's critique in his excellent study of Bultmann, *Christ Without Myth* (New York: Collins, 1962).

[170] One suspects that to all subjective human dilemmas and uncertainties Ritschl would offer the balm of his psychotherapy; it appears not to be the business of theology, as he conceives it, to minister in this direct, personal and "medicinal" way.

[171] Ritschl also expresses a liking for the work of D.M. MacKinnon who, as we have seen, shares this particular concern.

[172] This may seem a strange state of affairs from one far more committed to the Anglo-American agenda in philosophy than is the average Germanic theologian, but it is not the empiricist element in this tradition which Ritschl holds dear. Instead it is the Wittgensteinian element. According to the theory of language games thus entailed, meaning can indeed be restricted to such logical and linguistic islands in the stream of collective meaningfulness.

[173] This problem is not adequately resolved in *The Logic of Theology* (1984). There, Ritschl explicitly works back from the church's experience of God's presence in Jesus to the resurrection and, eventually, the incarnation. He feels, too, that the doctrine of the incarnation is a mistake, as is also generally the case for Moltmann. Moltmann traces the retrojection of Easter faith ever earlier, too, believing that this process produced, in turn, the incarnation, virgin birth and, eventually, the pre-existence of Jesus; see *The Way of Jesus Christ* (1990) 77-78.

[174] His position is in sympathy with an Anglican-style *lex orandi, lex credendi* approach and (like Barth and Torrance) he owes much

to the Greek fathers. According to their "spiritual" or "mystical" theology, metaphysics was the handmaid of prayer and worship so that "The notion of an ontic description of trans-intelligible realities outside of faith, i.e. outside the framework of *worship*, had no legitimate place in the thinking of the Greek Fathers, nor in later Eastern Orthodoxy" (*Memory and Hope* [1967] 86). For Ritschl, then, ontology must always stay close to doxology if it is to avoid ossification and remain meaningful (ibid. 87).

[175] We recall a similar too-easy willingness to confuse the Jesus of history with the Jesus of gospel portrayal in the works of Moltmann.

PART II: IDEALIST

[1] *Schriften zur Theologie*, 16 vols., 1954-84.

[2] An excellent introduction to the life and thought of this fascinating man is that of Rahner's former pupil and long-time friend Herbert Vorgrimler, *Understanding Karl Rahner* (1986), in which the close connection of Rahner's life and spirituality to his theology is a major theme. A good, short overview article is that of Anne Carr, "Karl Rahner" (1984). Also useful, though less balanced and insightful than Carr's piece, is J.A. DiNoia, "Karl Rahner" (1989).

[3] See e.g. Rahner, "Ignatian Mysticism of Joy in the World" (1975) 313-17.

[4] See e.g. Vorgrimler, *Understanding Karl Rahner* (1986) 29-31.

[5] McCool, "Introduction: Rahner's Philosophical Theology," in *A Rahner Reader* (1975) xiii-xxviii, xix.

[6] See Rahner, *Mein Problem—Karl Rahner antwortet jungen Menschen* (Freiburg, 1982), cited in Vorgrimler, op. cit. 29.

[7] A brief correspondence from this period reproduced by Vorgrimler (op. cit. 141-84) is most instructive and interesting in this regard.

[8] Metz, "Karl Rahner—ein theologisches Leben," 43-57, 55; in *Unterbrechungen. Theologisch-politische Perspektiven und Profile* (Gütersloh, 1981), cited by Vorgrimler, op. cit. 37.

[9] Rahner also founded, edited and contributed to the series *Quaestiones Disputatae*, appearing from 1958. His editorial work extended to cover the *Lexicon für Theologie und Kirche* (1955-67), the *Handbuch der Pastoraltheologie* (1964-72), the theological encyclopedia

Sacramentum Mundi (1967-69), and a single-volume *Dictionary of Theology* (*Kleine Theologische Wörterbuch*, 10th ed., with Herbert Vorgrimler, 1976). For these bibliographical details I am indebted to DiNoia, "Karl Rahner" (1989) 186-87.

[10] Rahner, *Foundations of Christian Faith* (1978) 19.

[11] Carr, "Karl Rahner" (1984) 520-21.

[12] DiNoia, "Karl Rahner" (1989) 200.

[13] Key ideas and figures in neo-Thomism are discussed in, e.g., Macquarrie, *Twentieth-Century Religious Thought* (1981) 278-90. For aspects of the revival of Christology in Roman Catholic thought since 1950 see e.g. Grillmeier, "The Figure of Christ in Roman Catholic Theology Today" (1965). Macquarrie cites a complaint of Rahner, relevant here, that textbooks of Catholic dogma published in 1950 were hardly distinguishable from textbooks of 1750, despite the shattering events of those two centuries (*Jesus Christ in Modern Thought* [1990] 303).

[14] Vorgrimler, *Understanding Karl Rahner* (1986) 55.

[15] DiNola, "Karl Rahner" (1989) 193-94 is helpful here. Not all Counter-Reformation thought has overlooked St. Thomas at this point, however; one thinks, for instance, of the Tridentine doctrine of justification as including elements of sanctification—of incorporation into the divine life—in contradistinction to the (Augustinian) disjoining of nature and grace evident in Luther's sundering of justification from sanctification.

[16] This was the mark of Roman Catholic modernism—to emphasize a unity between experience of self and experience of God. Mary Hines points out, however, that Rahner steers a path between the "immanentism" of which modernists were accused and the "extrinsicist" anti-modernist reaction which tended to see doctrines as falling fully-formed from heaven (Hines, *The Transformation of Dogma* [1989] 3-4, 7). By the same token, Rahner is Christocentric but not, like Barth, in a manner excluding the human subject, as Anne Carr notes ("Karl Rahner" [1984] 527).

Indeed, Rahner is ever careful to affirm the utter gratuity of revelation along with Augustine and the reformers. So his philosophical theology is anything but subjectivistic, as Tullio Citrino points out: "The methodological centrality assigned to the human person as starting point is accompanied by an assertion that the human person

must take as his focus of attention an initiative which he cannot produce nor deduce and which is not at his disposal" (Citrino, "The
Principle of 'Christocentrism' and Its Role in Fundamental Theology" [1982] 175).

[17] Rahner is also influenced by Hegel's belief that matter and spirit
are not disjoined—indeed, all idealism involves the marriage of
mind and matter (and so is the opposite of empiricism). Hegel's
basic idea about Absolute Being needing "the other" to express itself
is also evident in Rahner's Christology, with Jesus as both God's ultimate self-expression and humanity's ultimate response. There is
also the influence here of Schleiermacher on humanity's sense and
taste for the infinite (as pointed out e.g. in Macquarrie, *Jesus Christ
in Modern Thought* [1990] 304).

[18] In the influential fifth volume of *Le Point de départ de la Meta-
physique* (studied closely by Rahner while a theological student)
Márèchal argued "that if Kant's transcendental reflection on human
knowledge is applied consistently, it leads to metaphysical realism
and not to critical idealism, as Kant had mistakenly supposed" (Mc-
Cool, "Introduction: Rahner's Philosophical Theology," in *A Rahner
Reader* [1975] xiii).

Via Maurice Blondel and Pierre Rousselot, Márèchal took up
Fichte's revision of Kantian epistemology, and this influenced Rahner—Kant's separation of speculative reason from practical reason
had relegated God to the realm of practical reason along with other
"regulative" ideas, whereas Fichte saw a fundamental orientation to
the absolute as constitutive of all *speculative* thought and perception,
so that God is a dimension of *all* knowing and not speculatively
"surplus to requirements" as in Kant's epistemology. So it was that
Rahner recovered Aquinas' link between nature and supernature, between natural human knowing and knowledge of God—the drive of
Aquinas' "active human intellect" toward the infinity of God—from
the abyss of Kantian agnosticism. Márèchal thus taught Rahner that
the metaphysics of human knowing and the metaphysics of finite and
infinite reality are linked, so that transcendental reflection on human
knowing opens up the knowledge of God (ibid. xiii-xvi).

As in Aquinas and Kant, the starting point for Rahner's speculative metaphysical knowledge is in the ordinary, sensible world of
human experience. So ordinary human knowledge is linked to sacred

knowledge for Rahner, contrary to the position of Augustine and his Protestant followers such as Luther, Pascal, Barth and Moltmann, though, in accord with this same tradition, Rahner does not believe God can simply be "read off" from an examination of the world—the "hidden God" is also a major feature of this most Germanic theology (as pointed out e.g. in Newlands, "G.M. Newlands on *The Myth of God Incarnate*" [1980] 191). The *potentia obedientialis* of Aquinas becomes for Rahner a constitutive human openness to the revelatory word which makes its address to us from the horizon of human experience (Macquarrie, *Jesus Christ in Modern Thought* [1990] 304-05).

[19] DiNoia, "Karl Rahner" (1989) 191. From the time of his earliest writings Rahner was also impressed by Bonaventure's synthesis of theology with philosophy and spirituality, for whom God's self-expression in the Word grounds all intelligibility, coupling natural and supernatural knowledge. McCool points out a link between "the Augustinian and Dionysian mysticism which undergirds Bonaventure's *The Mind's Road to God* and the German philosophical tradition to which both Hegel and Heidegger belong" (McCool, "Introduction: Karl Rahner's Philosophical Theology" [1975] xxii, cf. xx)—a tradition in which Rahner clearly stood.

It has also been pointed out that Rahner's philosophical anthropology owes much to Ignatian teaching on prayer—especially, one suspects, the discipline of the progression from meditation on concrete images to contemplation which is characteristic of retreats based on Ignatius' *Spiritual Exercises*. Late in life, Rahner even admitted that "The spirituality of Ignatius himself which we shared in through the practice of prayer and a religious formation has become more significant for me than all learned philosophy and theology inside and outside the order" (P. Imhof and H. Biallowons [eds.], *Karl Rahner im Gespräch*, Vol. II [Munich, 1983] 51; cited in Vorgrimler, *Understanding Karl Rahner* [1986] 57).

[20] McCool, "Introduction: Rahner's Philosophical Theology," in *A Rahner Reader* (1975) xvii.

[21] Ibid. Rahner is like Rudolf Bultmann in his attention to Heidegger on pre-understanding, but Bultmann exhibits more Kantian agnosticism regarding the being of God than Rahner. Bultmann is also far more loath to depend upon the historical Jesus than Rahner, just as he rigorously avoids the cosmological dimension that Rahner (like

Teilhard) is more than happy to court (as pointed out e.g. in Molt-mann, *Theology Today* [1988] 75).

²² For the development of Rahner's thought (which has not under-gone sufficient drastic changes to detain us here) see the study by John McDermott, "The Christologies of Karl Rahner" I & II (1986).

²³ Two of Rahner's Heideggerian terms bear mention at this point—"existential" and "existentiell." An "existential," for Rahner, is an ontological part of human nature, like historicity, or dependency. It is simply something which is there, and about which we have no choice. "Existentiell," on the other hand, refers to the free actualiza-tion of something which is already there (16).

²⁴ Indeed, Rahner believes that the traditional proofs for God's ex-istence are merely reflections upon our transcendental orientation (52)—"they mediate a reflexive awareness of the fact that man al-ways and inevitably has to do with God in his intellectual and spiri-tual existence, whether he reflects upon it or not, and whether he freely accepts it or not" (69).

²⁵ Carr, "Karl Rahner" (1984) 523 (this is also the case for Heideg-ger). Of this universal bestowal of grace Rahner writes, "This tran-scendental moment in revelation is a modification of our transcen-dental consciousness produced permanently by God in grace. But such a modification is really an original and permanent element in our consciousness as the basic and original luminosity of our exis-tence" (149). Thus Aquinas' view that "grace perfects nature" be-comes, for Rahner, belief in a divine spark implanted in all of us (one wonders whether Eckhardt and the other Rhineland mystics have had an influence here). There appears to be some lack of clarity in this, however, occasioned perhaps by Rahner's desire to avoid pitfalls such as any too-simple neo-scholastic distinction between nature and grace. Rahner seems to resolve matters by dividing the ontological constitution of persons into "nature" in the abstract, on the one hand, and "historical nature" on the other. Both this lack of clarity and this proposed solution are evident in Rahner's claim that "It makes no difference ... to what extent and in what sense this ontological orien-tation (*desiderium*) towards immediacy to God belongs to man's 'na-ture' in the abstract, or to his historical nature as elevated in grace by the supernatural existential. This latter, however, belongs to his basic ontological constitution" (298).

²⁶ Macquarrie does identify Rahner with Troeltsch's religious *a priori* (*Jesus Christ in Modern Thought* [1991] 304), but this is too simplistic, I fear—after all, we have just seen Rahner deny any *sui generis* and unambiguous experience of God (e.g. 54).

²⁷ Rahner has a deep respect for human freedom, understanding it as intended by God. As Vorgrimler notes, "he sought to show that in the process of a life a human being 'makes' something of himself or herself which will remain for ever—because no one, not even God, can undo what human beings have done in freedom" (*Understanding Karl Rahner* [1986] 15). Clearly, this respect is incompatible with any salvific universalism irresistibly impressed upon persons by God.

²⁸ Here Rahner would find himself in complete disagreement with the theology of Thomas Torrance, which was discussed in Ch. 2, above.

²⁹ This notion of "Anonymous Christianity," for which Rahner is justly famous, will be discussed more fully once Rahner's views on the universal scope of Christ's work have been stated and the way thus prepared.

³⁰ Rahner is also like Moltmann in understanding God along highly Trinitarian lines (136). This he believes necessary if the abiding mystery and yet the salvific closeness of God is to be expressed aright. Rahner also writes of God "becoming himself" in and through the other, also identifying a "death of God" dimension (Hegel) in the incarnation (305). Rahner declares that "He who is not subject to change in himself can *himself* be subject to change *in something else*" (220), in a quite self-consciously kenotic understanding of God (222; see also, Pannenberg, *Jesus—God and Man* [1968] 317-22, who praises Rahner among contemporary advocates of kenoticism, but critically nonetheless). Rahner is thus willing to surrender divine immutability, though not so readily as Moltmann.

Rahner's God has come very near to the God of process theism, then, with something like an unchanging "primordial nature" and a mutable "consequent nature." Thus it is understandable that David Tracy could write, concerning the Rahner of the *Foundations*, that "By the time of his summary volume...Rahner had become something like an anonymous process theologian" (Tracy, "Kenosis, Sunyata and Trinity" [1990] 138). Note, however, that the guarantee of success Rahner gives to the cosmic process as a whole on account of Jesus Christ is incompatible with that open-endedness ascribed to cosmic history by at least some process theologians (as pointed out in Carmody & Carmody, "Christology in Karl Rahner's Evolutionary World View" [1980] 202).

[31] On the whole issue see also e.g. Hübner, "Evolution in Different Theological Traditions"; Daecke, "Putting an End to Selection and Completing Evolution"; and Schmitz-Moormann, "Teilhard de Chardin's View of Evolution" in S. Anderson and A. Peacocke (eds.) *Evolution and Creation: A European Perspective* (Aarhus, Denmark: Aarhus University Press, 1987) pp. 106-12, 153-61 and 162-69 respectively.

[32] See n. 50, below, about Rahner and Moltmann on "hope."

[33] This is the issue taken-up by the "historical skeptics," to be discussed in Chapter 9—those who believe there is inadequate historical evidence for ascribing any uniqueness to Jesus. Rahner offers a more detailed discussion of these matters in his essay, "Remarks on the Importance of the History of Jesus for Catholic Dogmatics" (1975). His argument here corresponds with that of Peter Carnley in "The Poverty of Historical Skepticism" (1972).

[34] Cf. Rahner, "The Position of Christology in the Church Between Exegesis and Dogmatics" (1974) 198-99.

[35] An interesting feature here is how Rahner (with characteristic deftness and "Jesuitical subtlety") seeks to justify Jesus' erroneous belief about the imminent coming of God's kingdom. This Rahner took to be an instance of Jesus' deep, unspoken and implicit closeness to God, his radical heeding of God's commands, though nevertheless expressed erroneously at the verbal and explicit level (250). He adds a further interesting dimension to this argument by claiming that Jesus' imminent expectation of God's kingdom meant that he appreciated his own finality in expecting no one else from God to come after him (253).

[36] Rahner, "Dogmatic Reflections on the Knowledge and Self-Consciousness of Christ" (1966).

[37] Ibid. 203.

[38] Such approaches lead to Nestorianism, or else to consequences equal in oddness to anything split-brain research has uncovered. Here I am thinking of Thomas V. Morris, a recent advocate of such

views—*The Logic of God Incarnate* (1986). Morris' Jesus appears to have two minds.

Rahner is seen at his radical best in this discussion, dismissing the accretions of Roman Catholic dogma and Thomism by attending to scripture and to modern questions. Interestingly, Rahner has escaped major censure from Rome, unlike Congar, Küng, Schillebeeckx, Curran, Boff, Drewermann, Fox and many others. "Indeed, I would conjecture," writes A.T. Hanson, "that only his remarkable skill in using traditional language in an untraditional sense has prevented him from being summoned before the same array of inquisitors that has already confronted the unfortunate Schillebeeckx. For all intents and purposes Karl Rahner may be said to present a doctrine of the mode of the incarnation that goes as far as the most extreme version of Nestorianism known to the ancients" (Hanson, *The Image of the Invisible God* [1982] 12).

I cannot think why this charge of Nestorianism would be leveled against Rahner without considerable qualification. While it is true Rahner's Jesus knows far more of his supposed divine status than any Jesus to be met in Part III, for instance, nevertheless Rahner is frequently at pains to point out just how continuous is Jesus' self-understanding with ordinary human knowing under the horizon of divine mystery. Considering Rahner's frequent reference to the hypostatic union (part of the ancient church's response to Nestorianism) it is not obvious that Hanson's charge is altogether fair, though he is certainly correct that Rahner has pushed the limits of "theological obedience" in the name of bringing dogma before the bar of theology and scripture.

[39] Rahner, "Dogmatic Reflections on the Knowledge and Self-Consciousness of Christ" (1966) 211.

[40] Ibid. 212.

[41] John McDermott, "The Christologies of Karl Rahner" (1986) 118-19.

[42] Rahner, "The Position of Christology in the Church Between Exegesis and Dogmatics" (1974) 202; cf. *Foundations of Christian Faith* (1978) 245-46.

[43] There is a marked difference, for instance, between the approach of Rahner to Jesus' history and that of Schillebeeckx, whose two massive volumes dedicated to this very undertaking are dis-

cussed in Ch. 8, below. Though Rahner gives evidence of some familiarity with the world of contemporary exegesis throughout the *Foundations*, he usually does little more than acknowledge it in passing, with none of the close engagement we find in Schillebeeckx (or in Pannenberg, for that matter). And this is because his beliefs about Jesus are really grounded in his philosophical theology—only the earthly doings of Jesus and the extent of Jesus' self-understanding are significantly challenged by exegetical doubt, according to Rahner, and not too much; the other component of Jesus' uniqueness and finality in his system is, as we have seen, the conviction that the meshed dynamic of divine offer and human response requires a high point, and this for all sorts of philosophical reasons entirely divorced from the historical Jesus.

⁴⁴ Rahner, "The Position of Christology in the Church Between Exegesis and Dogmatics" (1974) 201.

⁴⁵ Fiorenza, "Christology After Vatican II" (1980) 85 n.31. This is an unavoidable criticism. The closest Rahner has come to any real engagement of this sort is in *A New Christology* (1980), authored jointly with the New Testament scholar Wilhelm Thüsing. But Rahner gives the briefest Introduction only, reiterating his theology, while leaving the engagement of theology with exegesis to Thüsing.

⁴⁶ For a variation on this argument in support of resurrection belief itself see Rahner, "The Position of Christology in the Church Between Exegesis and Dogmatics" (1974) 213.

⁴⁷ Krieg, "The Crucified in Rahner's Theology" (1983/4) 158-61.

⁴⁸ Nevertheless, this does place Rahner in opposition to the approach characteristic of those in Part III—a "Christology from above" remains to balance his "Christology from below," but both the "Christology from above" *and* the more metaphysical aspects of Rahner's "Christology from below" are deemed unnecessary among the "liberals" discussed in Part III.

⁴⁹ This Rahner identifies with the dawn of our present historical epoch—that period characterized by unparalleled human freedom and responsibility, "that realm of history which man has opened for himself... a realm of time, almost ahistorical again, in which man will exist in a nature which has finally been made subject to him" (169). Note, however, that Rahner sees the modern world in which we live, in its key elements, as extending right back into the time of

Jesus—indeed, perhaps as far back as Jaspers' "axial" eighth century BCE. "Therefore," claims Rahner, "the single and final fundamental caesura in secular history and the final, fundamental caesura in the history of salvation and revelation occur in the same historical moment of transition, even if this moment lasts several thousand years" (170).

We note, too, that there is nothing general about what Rahner sees in Jesus, as there is in a D.F. Strauss, say, for whom Jesus merely lays bare the state of *all* human beings. For Rahner, this forgets that "historicity and personhood must not be reduced to the level of nature, to the level of what is given always and everywhere" (218). The Christ is no Straussian myth, then—Rahner is very insistent on maintaining the strict event-character of Jesus' life, his historical happenedness, and his particularity too (this is true in the sense that Rahner's Jesus is a human being, but he does not go as far as does Schillebeeckx in understanding Jesus as a particular human *individual* [as pointed out in Macquarrie, *Jesus Christ in Modern Thought* {1990} 308]).

It is important to note here that this is *not* the view we will encounter in the early works of Don Cupitt in Chapter 11—the view that Jesus' teaching renders universal what was only local or provisional formerly (which is to say that Jesus just happens to be the teacher, in a long line of teachers, thanks to whom an age-old message has at last been cast in a form which all can understand and receive). Rahner, on the contrary, is careful to focus on Jesus' *person* and not merely on his teaching, nor solely on anything he did. His Jesus is final as God's universal offer of himself incarnate, and not merely as a man who taught something-or-other in a definitive and uniquely effective or accessible way. At the end of the day, then, Rahner's is still a "Christology from above," though he does *use* "Christology from below" to explicate and "ground" his "Christology from above."

Nor does he believe, as some do (such as contributors to *The Myth of God Incarnate*), that one can have function without ontology in Christology—Jesus can only do what he did because he was who he was, according to Rahner, though he does think those holding more functional, less ontological positions are implicit believers in the incarnation anyway, even though they do not know it (227; this is perhaps intended to support fellow theologians such as Küng and Schillebeeckx whose belief in this regard has been questioned; see e.g. Peter Hebblethwaite, *The New Inquisition* [1980]).

[50] As with Moltmann there is a "hope" dimension here, though hope is differently accounted for by the two writers; for Moltmann it is the product of revelation via the Old and New Testaments while for Rahner it is part of the "supernatural existential," and so it is effectively as good as a part of the human condition. But, like Moltmann, Rahner is loath to see everything definitively finished and wound up in the incarnation—history is not over! Thus he has none of the realized eschatology of which Moltmann has provided so searching a critique. But Rahner does see in Jesus Christ the real irreversibility of a process which, nevertheless, leaves the future open for each individual (299). Moltmann holds to this irreversibility himself though, as was evident in Ch. 1, above, he was not always ready to admit what we might call his "closet finality."

[51] Rahner has come to depend more on the resurrection and less on the incarnation in his Christology, and also less on the empty tomb. He came to see the tomb and the appearances as secondary explanations, the primary experience of the resurrection being identified with convictions among the disciples that Jesus is now part of God's glory—an experience which, Rahner suggests, is accessible to all Christians (Galvin, "The Resurrection of Jesus in Contemporary Catholic Systematics" [1979] 125-30). So, for Rahner, resurrection simply "means the final and definitive salvation of a concrete human existence by God" (266) as it did for Jesus, and as Christians hope it will for them, too.

[52] Rahner, "Experiencing Easter" (1971) 164.

[53] Ibid. 164-66; cf. *Foundations of Christian Faith* (1978) 268-69.

[54] Rahner, "Christology Today," in *A New Christology* (1980) 3-17, 13.

[55] We see here an unwillingness to rest content with the focus of credal orthodoxy upon the death (and birth) of Jesus as alone providing the justification for ascriptions of uniqueness; like many other theologians in this study's period of interest, Rahner insists that the *life* of Jesus must also be taken into account and recognized as extraordinary; see e.g. the treatment of Jesus as "social person" and not just "eschatological person" in Moltmann, *The Way of Jesus Christ*

(1990) 136-50 (discussed in Ch. 1, above), as well as everyone in Part III.

[56] Vorgrimler, *Understanding Karl Rahner* (1986) 111.

[57] Knitter, *No Other Name?* (1985) 127. Of course, Rahner believes that the religions find their fulfillment in Christianity, and are only provisional until the mind of Christ is sufficiently formed in the culture nurturing each religion that its adherents can understand the gospel "each in their own tongue" (is there an echo here of strategies employed in the great Jesuit missions of the 16th to the 18th centuries?). Thus, like Hans Küng, Rahner sees the religions as ordinary ways of salvation and Christianity as the "extraordinary way" (ibid. 128).

[58] Rahner's classic article here is "Christianity and the Non-Christian Religions" (1966). His "Anonymous Christians" position typifies the "inclusive" approaches canvased in standard overviews of Christian responses to the world religions (see Race, *Christians and Religious Pluralism* [1983]; D'Costa, *Theology and Religious Pluralism* [1986]; Knitter, *No Other Name?* [1985] and e.g. Schineller, "Christ and the Church" [1976] for such typologies). This approach has won widespread support in Roman Catholicism fostered, no doubt, by the tolerant spirit of Vatican II's "Declaration on the Relation of the Church to the Non-Christian Religions" (*Nostra Aetate;* see Flannery [ed.] *Documents of Vatican II* [Grand Rapids, MI: Eerdmans, 1975] 738-42).

Some other Roman Catholics with an "inclusive," "anonymous Christians" perspective, but who undertake an actual search for Christ within the weave of the other religions (which Rahner himself never pursued) are: Panikkar, *The Unknown Christ of Hinduism* (1964) and articles too numerous to begin mentioning (Panikkar, incidentally, has of late moved in the direction of the "pluralist" position, to be discussed in Chapter 10: see his essay, "The Jordan, the Tiber and the Ganges" [1987]; but Panikkar "hedges his bets" over this issue, and so has not decisively "crossed the Rubicon" [as this embrace of "pluralism" is often now called]); Bühlmann, *The Coming of the Third Church* (1977) (Rahner called this the best Catholic book of the year in 1973) and *All Have the Same God* (1979); Davis, *Christ and the World Religions* (1971); Hillman, *The Wider Ecumenism* (1968), "Towards the Catholicization of the Church" (1974) and "Evangelization in a Wider Ecumenism" (1975); Rossano, "Christ's Lordship and Religious Pluralism in Roman Catholic Perspective" (with Responses and a Reply) (1981); Schlette, *Towards a Theology of Religions* (1966); and Moloney, "African Christology" (1987)—see also Schreiter, "The Anonymous Christian and Christianity" (1978) and a splendid collection of essays edited by him entitled *Faces of Jesus in Africa* (Maryknoll, NY: Orbis, 1991).

⁵⁹ Rahner, "One Mediator and Many Mediations" (1972) 177, 178-79. This has a flavor we would nowadays associate with new-age writing. I am thinking, for instance, of the homespun new-age wisdom of Brian Swimme, *The Universe Is a Green Dragon: A Cosmic Creation Story* (1984) (London: Penguin [Arkana], 1991). This volume is dedicated to Thomas Berry, and it is interesting how creation theologians like Berry and Matthew Fox, no doubt influenced by Rahnerian ideas omnipresent in Roman Catholic thought since the council, have "gone new-age" themselves in their emphasis on the interconnectedness of all reality (in keeping with contemporary scientific cosmology, social science and linguistics too, of course).

⁶⁰ Marshall, *Christology in Conflict* (1987) 41 (cf. the difference between Moltmann and Sölle on this matter; see n. 4 in Part I, above).

⁶¹ John McDermott, "The Christologies of Karl Rahner" (1986) 115.

⁶² Cf. Pannenberg's discussion of Rahner on this point (whom he does not consider to be sufficiently eschatological in his ascription of ultimacy to Jesus Christ) in *Jesus—God and Man* (1968) 387-88.

⁶³ See eg. Vorgrimler, *Understanding Karl Rahner* (1986) 125-30.

⁶⁴ Ibid. 122-23.

⁶⁵ Ibid. 121-22.

⁶⁶ Ibid. 124.

⁶⁷ Carr, "Karl Rahner" (1984) 539.

⁶⁸ Moltmann, *Theology Today* (1988) 67-78.

⁶⁹ Moltmann, *The Way of Jesus Christ* (1990), discussed in Ch. 1, above.

⁷⁰ Ibid. 297-301; cf. the discussion in Ch. 1, above.

⁷¹ See e.g. Krieg, "The Crucified in Rahner's Christology" (1983/4) 160-61; Inbody, "Rahner's Christology" (1982) 309-10; John McDermott, "The Christologies of Karl Rahner" (1986): I 117,

II 315, 319, 323; and, especially, the Yale doctoral thesis of Bruce
Marshall published as *Christology in Conflict: The Identity of a Saviour in Rahner and Barth* (1987), devoted (through endless reiterations!) to this single issue. Rahner himself admits the difficulty in his
essay "Christology Today" in *A New Christology* (1980) 8.

[72] Marshall, *Christology in Conflict* (1987) 117.

[73] The Preface clearly indicates that this is a Yale-style piece; Frei
is obviously much revered by Marshall. For a discussion of post-liberal vs. liberal, Yale vs. Chicago, etc., see the section on George A.
Lindbeck in Chapter 11.

[74] See the original quotation footnoted at n.143 in Part IV, below.

[75] Marshall, op. cit. 145-46. A similar criticism is found in Metz,
Faith in History and Society (New York: Seabury, 1980), which is
sympathetic to the narrative theological agenda and understands
Jesus as identified through New Testament narrative—this is discussed in Krieg, "The Crucified in Rahner's Christology" (1983/4)
163-64. For comments on narrative theology, see n.156 in Part I,
above.

[76] Marshall, op. cit. 149.

[77] See e.g. Inbody, "Rahner's Christology" (1982) 301-06; DiNoia,
"Karl Rahner" (1989) 201; Marshall, *Christology in Conflict* (1987)
119, 148, 149.

[78] Perhaps recalling Paul Klee's painting *"Vergesslicher Engel"* of
1939.

[79] Kerr, *Theology after Wittgenstein* (1986) 14.

[80] Rahner, *Foundations of Christian Faith* (1978) 169.

[81] Cited (without reference) in Neuhaus, "Wolfhart Pannenberg"
(1969) 12.

[82] Pannenberg, "God's Presence in History" (1981) 94.

[83] Pannenberg's doctoral dissertation at Heidelberg, published in
1954, considered *Die Prädestinationslehre des Duns Skotus*, while
his *Habilitationsschrift* probed the role of analogy in western thought
up to Thomas Aquinas (Schwöbel, "Wolfhart Pannenberg" [1989]
257).

[84] Pannenberg, "God's Presence in History" (1981) 95.

[85] Ibid.

[86] Carl Braaten observes that "Pannenberg dusted off an old leaf
from German idealism, particularly that of Hegel, who advanced the

idea that only the totality of reality as history comprises the self-communication of the divine" (Braaten, "Wolfhart Pannenberg" [1984] 642).

[87] Ibid 643. This existentialist assessment of the human person is also taken up in Pannenberg's use of Heidegger, which extends beyond his thoughts on the priority of the future. According to Philip Clayton, "(Heidegger's) analysis of individual human existence in terms of modes of being-in-the-world, everydayness, thrownness, and projection has played a central role in Pannenberg's anthropological writings, perhaps less noticeably in *What Is Man?* but certainly very clearly in the recent anthropology" (Clayton, "Anticipation and Theological Method" [1988] 135 n.24).

[88] Dilthey expressed his conviction thus: "One would have to wait for the end of a life and, in the hour of death, survey the whole and ascertain the relation between the whole and its parts. One would have to wait for the end of history to have all the material necessary to determine its meaning" (Dilthey, *Gesammelte Schriften* [Leipzig: B.G. Tuebner, 1927] 7:233; excerpted in *Dilthey: Selected Writings*, ed. and trans. H.P. Rickman [Cambridge: Cambridge University Press, 1976] 236; cited in Clayton, "Anticipation and Theological Method" [1988] 134).

[89] For Pannenberg it is not at the point of death that the definitive word can be spoken about a life—this depends upon its subsequent, ongoing re-evaluation by those who come after (Sartre). The only horizon broad enough to allow an *absolute* interpretation is the eschatological horizon, according to Pannenberg, for whom "Only a final future, a place beyond history... could provide a totality... unsurpassable by any further history. In short, philosophical considerations themselves lead to a concept of universal history which can only be fully grasped from a theological—more specifically, an eschatological—perspective"; see Clayton, "Anticipation and Theological Method" (1988) 134-35.

[90] Neuhaus, "Wolfhart Pannenberg" (1969) 48.

[91] There had arisen in mid-century German theology an impasse between the revelatory positivism of Barth and his conservative followers, on the one hand, and the existentially-driven program of demythologization of Bultmann and his liberal followers on the other. Pannenberg had learned much at Heidelberg from Gerhardt von Rad

on the transmission of Old Testament traditions, from Günther Bornkamm on the importance of the historical Jesus (then making his reappearance in theology after a half-century absence) and from Hans von Campenhausen on the need for a theological interpretation of church history (Schwöbel, "Wolfhart Pannenberg" [1989] 258); Pannenberg and his confreres felt that the divergence between biblical studies, church history and systematic theology needed to be overcome in a new synthesis.

The original five were Pannenberg himself (systematic theology), Rolf Rendtorff and Klaus Koch (Old Testament) with Ulrich Wilckens and Dietrich Rössler (New Testament). They were later joined by the church historian Martin Elze and the social ethicist Trutz Rendtorff.

[92] In the light of geology, evolutionary biology, astrophysics, quantum mechanics and sub-atomic physics the natural cosmos must nowadays be understood in terms of constant flux and, hence, "historically." The static cosmos of the Greeks has gone forever, replaced by a true "natural *history*." A theology like that of Rahner, and more particularly of Teilhard, combines cosmic focus with historical teleology—these dimensions need no longer be seen as mutually exclusive.

[93] This is really saying, however, that the success and broad appeal of Christianity, especially the powers of assimilation it showed in encompassing classical and subsequent cultural forms, assures its favoured place in divine revelation. And this is essentially the point Hans Küng expressed with far less recourse to ontology and philosophy of history in his *On Being a Christian* (ET 1976). There, in considering the challenge of the world religions, Küng argued that Christianity is best suited to surviving in today's experience of western cultural hegemony. This pragmatic consideration is advanced, albeit most eirenically, as an argument for the ultimacy of Christianity (Küng, *On Being a Christian* [1984] 110-12). So, too, with Pannenberg; basically, he is affirmed in his belief about the ultimacy of Christ because, as he sees it, Christianity has carried all before it (Pannenberg quite specifically makes this point elsewhere, declaring that western [Christian] culture, grounded in the biblical command for humanity to "have dominion," is more powerful than both Buddhist detachment and Islamic resignation; see *What Is Man?* [1972] 125, cf. 135).

⁹⁴ See e.g. Don Cupitt, *Creation out of Nothing* (1990), *What Is a Story?* (1991) and *The Time Being* (1992).

⁹⁵ Elsewhere Pannenberg writes: "Human nature ... is no ... given and invariable structure, but has a history. More precisely, human nature *is* the history of the realization of human destiny" (*Human Nature, Election, and History* [1977] 24). Thus he combines his sense of the historical variety of human nature with the emphasis on the appearance of true human nature in the resurrection (known proleptically in Jesus) which is more fully discussed in *Jesus—God and Man.*

⁹⁶ Having established a fundamental openness to the infinite as constitutive of the human person (à la Rahner), Pannenberg suggests that Jesus expressed this fundamental openness precisely in *not* becoming an end in himself, so that God's vindication of Jesus' self-abandoning path by the resurrection confirmed that in him religion was freed from thraldom to the finite (39).

⁹⁷ But if God reveals this universal horizon as a preferred framework for humanity to understand God, then one wonders whether revelation is not perspectival and interpretative after all, contrary to Pannenberg's claims. For he does see this life-giving historical perspective as a direct input from God into human thinking, albeit through the events of history. And although we have considered how interpretation is included à la Collingwood into Pannenberg's system despite his denial that revelation consists in any attitude toward the facts apart from the facts themselves, nevertheless such *gnosis* is effectively what we find in Pannenberg's biblically driven historicism.

Pannenberg never claims a purely natural knowledge of God, however. This is evident in a recent comment, recalling Rahner: "... dissatisfaction with the finite can take the form of the question of God only on the condition of a knowledge of God that is gained elsewhere" (*Systematic Theology*, Vol. 1 [1991] 116).

⁹⁸ The way to resolve the apparent impasse of circularity between hope as a feature of the human condition supporting resurrection belief and hope as a part of that unified human condition first prefigured by and imagined as a result of resurrection belief is to go back to Pannenberg's reliance upon Jewish apocalyptic expectation. We see in this "divine longing" the source of both the hope which longs

and the resurrection for which it longs. One commentator refers to Pannenberg's paradoxical position as a "natural theology of resurrection"; see Clarke, "Current Christologies" (1979) 38.

⁹⁹ Raymond Brown disagrees with this assessment suggesting that, while natural generation involves a new person, virginal conception implies a pre-existent person, with the result that virginal conception and pre-existence are not incompatible: see Brown, *The Virginal Conception and Bodily Resurrection of Jesus* (Mahwah, NJ: Paulist, 1973) 43 n.58. Schoonenberg, too, denies any incompatibility between the virginal conception and pre-existence of Jesus, claiming that Luke 1:35 does not deny any prior sonship to Jesus; see *The Christ* (1974) 54.

¹⁰⁰ Like Moltmann, Pannenberg chooses a starting point which allows him quite a liberal stance on issues of historicity in the gospels over which others would balk, and this from two sometime doyens of the conservatives. Pannenberg can do this because he sees everything as following upon the resurrection. As Avery Dulles put it, "By concentrating revelation in the one event of Jesus' resurrection, Pannenberg can dispense himself from having to defend anything else as revelation. He can freely admit that the non-Christian religions are distorted, that the Old Testament abounds in legend and myth, that Jesus himself was unoriginal and confused, and that the miracles attributed to the prophets and to Jesus lack probative force"; see Dulles, "Pannenberg on Revelation and Faith" (1988) 175.

¹⁰¹ Also notable is Pannenberg's critique of "logos Christology," rejected as an unviable option in the face of a contemporary scientific world view. Such theology disregards history, complains Pannenberg, both by failing to understand the world in historical terms in its preference for a static Greek conception of an eternal order, and by insufficient reference to the actual life of Jesus: "One is often astounded," he writes, "at the way these theologians know how to say everything about Jesus' divinity without reference to the historical Jesus" (165). In both cases, it is with reference to the end of history revealed in advance that Pannenberg defines the uniqueness and finality of Jesus, rather than in terms of any "unchangeable ultimate ground of the phenomenal order" (165). Only thus is the world created through Jesus—in the light of its *end*, rather than in its beginning or its ongoing life (169).

To this Pannenberg adds a most incisive observation about the place of logos ideas in ancient thought having no obvious parallel in the world as conceived by recent science: "A contemporary analogy to the apologists' Logos Christology perhaps would have to look something like this: Jesus Christ would be conceived as the embodiment of Einstein's theory or of some other inclusive physical law" (166). But this would be to step outside the Platonic or stoic ideas which the apologists took aboard.

Pannenberg is latterly more positive about this sort of thing, however, coming to view the field theories of science "as approximations to the metaphysical reality of the all-pervading spiritual field of God's creative presence in the universe" (*An Introduction to Systematic Theology* [1991] 47). The beginnings of this re-evaluation, however, are to be found in the Postscript to the fifth German edition of *Jesus—God and Man*, discussed in n.106 below.

[102] This is the case more generally, too, in cultures outside Israel (207), though Pannenberg argues that the true nature of our deepest hopes and their fulfillment is not always consciously known by us (meaning, no doubt, that there is an element of anonymity in Jesus' winning the salvation of humanity at large) (206-07).

[103] The inclusivity of Jesus' death, and the loneliness of the Christian's own death as mitigated by union with the complete forsakenness of Jesus' death (263), is an aspect of Pannenberg's thought strongly redolent of Dorothee Sölle; see n. 4 in Part I, above.

It should be noted that Pannenberg came to regret this identification of a religion of law with Judaism, reassessing Judaism as redeemable if it were only to recognize the error of those who condemned Jesus and see in him and his resurrection the proper fulfillment of Israel's religion (*The Apostles' Creed* [1972] viii, 83-84).

Elsewhere, while welcoming new historical critical insights into "the Jewishness of Jesus," Pannenberg nevertheless expresses a wish that the challenge of Jesus to the Judaism of his day be recognized for what it was, denying any too-simple identification of Jesus with typical Jewish attitudes (*An Introduction to Systematic Theology* [1991] 63).

Moltmann was so solicitous to affirm Judaism he seemed unable to see that he was asserting the ultimacy of Christ, in advance of the eschaton, despite claims to the contrary (as we saw in our discussion in Ch. 1, above). Pannenberg, however, exhibits no such hesitation. Otherwise, however, he is in basic agreement with Moltmann on this issue, believing that in Christ the eschatological hope of Israel is brought before the nations.

[104] Of late, Pannenberg has made even more of such factors in accounting for Jesus' uniqueness. He refers to the character of Jesus' teaching, his intimacy with God and his obedience to God (*An Introduction to Systematic Theology* [1991] 58-60). Nevertheless, the adoptionist tone of Pannenberg's Christology remains—factors such as these never stand on their own for Pannenberg, but are always dependent upon their confirmation in Jesus' resurrection.

[105] Pannenberg adds a last twist to this argument, however. Instead of leaving us with the paradoxical assertion of Jesus' oneness with God throughout his life which is, nevertheless, ambiguous to an observer apart from its confirmation in the resurrection, Pannenberg adds that Jesus' embracing of the cross "set the purity of his mission free from all ambiguity" (364). But surely one cannot comment on the purity of motive involved in a willingness to die, as in many other areas of life, apart from knowing what was going on in the mind of the subject. It is naive of Pannenberg to claim that such sacrifice as Jesus displays at Calvary is proof positive that his motives were pure; given his willingness to court skepticism and recognize ambiguity with reference to other facts of Jesus' life, he must recognize that dying for a cause is by no means an unambiguous act. Motives crucial for properly understanding any death can seldom be read just from the facts—if they could, the work of homicide detectives would be immeasurably easier! We do not know with historical certainty how Jesus died; the occasionally canvased possibilities that Jesus died with curses on his lips, not blessings, and that he just might have been dragged reluctantly to the cross, would render his death profoundly ambiguous.

The only way to avoid such ambiguity, given the lack of hard historical evidence which Pannenberg admits, is by positing something about Jesus' private self-understanding. But this very type of recourse is one we have seen Pannenberg reject elsewhere, claiming that only Jesus' acts will reveal depths such as these. But where are we left if historical doubt clouds these acts, as it does here? Perhaps it would have been better, then, if Pannenberg had remained with resurrection and retrospectivity rather than taking a last grab at the historical certainties and unambiguous actions he otherwise refuses to pursue.

[106] In the Postscript to the fifth German edition of the book, in response to various criticisms, Pannenberg recasts his opposition to logos thinking by asserting that Jesus and his life coincides with the logos itself, rather than merely expressing it; Jesus' particular history actually *is* the clue to the meaning of events, rather than merely providing clues to some deeper meaning (this recalls the emphasis upon Jesus' *actual* life story, rather than simply seeing that story as an instance of something else—this approach we met in the work of Frei and Ritschl, discussed in Part I, above). Thus Pannenberg claims that he has laid the foundations for a new, historically and eschatologically ordered logos Christology (409).

More recently, Pannenberg has begun to emphasize that the universal activity of the Son of God, incarnate only in Jesus, was "at the same time ... at work in the whole creation and especially in the life of human beings created in the image of God" (*An Introduction to Systematic Theology* [1991] 65).

[107] Pannenberg, "Toward a Theology of the History of Religions" (1971) 74.

[108] Ibid. 100.

[109] This is identified as Pannenberg's unswerving perspective on the religions in Braaten, "The Place of Christianity among the World Religions" (1988) 300.

[110] Ibid. 94; this parallels insights into the birth of the idea of religion found in the classic study by Wilfred Cantwell Smith, *The Meaning and End of Religion* (1964).

[111] Ibid. 115.

[112] Pannenberg, "Religious Pluralism and Conflicting Truth Claims" (1990) 97.

[113] Ibid. 99.

[114] Ibid. 100. Pannenberg's inclusivist position is made even more explicit in another recent source: "It does not necessarily deny salvation to members of other cultures and religious traditions, but it certainly claims that if those persons will obtain salvation it will be through the grace of Jesus Christ whom perhaps they do not even know; it will not be through the power of their own religion" (*Introduction to Systematic Theology* [1991] 54).

[115] We would do well, at a point where their positions are in agreement, to compare Pannenberg's understanding of the uniqueness and finality of Jesus with that of Carl Braaten. This American Lutheran professor of Systematic Theology is also a member of the school of hope, though closer to Pannenberg than to Moltmann. Braaten, like Pannenberg, seeks from Moltmann a more thorough grounding in the historical Jesus, believing Moltmann to be more speculative than he will admit (Braaten, "A Trinitarian Theology of the Cross" [1976]). Unlike Pannenberg, however, Braaten sees Jesus as Lord of life and hence as Logos of the original creation (Braaten, "The Lordship of Christ in Modern Theology" [1965] 267; cf. his anti-liberal sentiments on pp. 262 and 264).

On the matter of world religions, Braaten rejects evangelical exclusivism and the pluralist solution in favor of what we might call an "eschatological inclusivism." He admits that salvation is present "phenomenologically" in the freedoms accessible through other religions as well as in secular movements of liberation, but salvation for the New Testament is in terms of victory over death wrought by God in Jesus Christ (Braaten, "Who Do We Say That He Is?" [1980] 24-26). There is, however, some presence of Christ in the other religions, just as there is in the Old Testament. But here Braaten's theology of hope comes in; he argues, despite all these assertions about Christ's ultimacy, that nothing is given definitively and finally: "We have a universal hope in Christ, not a universal gnosis" ("Who Do We Say That He Is?" [1980] 29). Thus the uniqueness of Christ is seen, strictly, to be "unproved"; it is still being worked out, despite being glimpsed proleptically in the resurrection (here Braaten is very close to Pannenberg).

This view of salvation as an appropriate category *for Christianity only* is found also in Kenneth Surin, "Revelation, Salvation, the Uniqueness of Christ and Other Religions" (1983); see n. 131 in Part IV.

[116] Ibid. 103. Rouner describes this position of Pannenberg, in common with that of Cobb and Moltmann, as *"nonrelativistic* without being inclusive" (Rouner, "Theology of Religions in Recent Protestant Theology" [1986] 113). Neuhaus finds in this refusal by Pannenberg to trim Christianity's claims neither audacity nor triumphalism but only "a decent respect for truth" (Neuhaus, "Theolo-

gy for Church and Polis" [1988] 235). Nevertheless we see just how redolent of Barth is Pannenberg's assessment of the religions vis-à-vis Christianity; it is not Christianity that is ultimate, he argues (the scandal of particularity cuts across the failings of Christianity as of all religions); it is only Christ, and not any religion, which is ultimate. To this conviction of Barth, however, Pannenberg adds from the school of hope the concern that Christ is only *provisionally* ultimate (though, as we discovered to be the case with Moltmann, no other "contender for the title" is foreseen).

For his own part Pannenberg sees his position as compatible with a deep respect for and tolerance toward adherents of the world religions. But he would think it impudent to require of Christians a sacrifice of their belief that Christ alone is savior, apart from which conviction he does not believe there can be any Christian belief (*An Introduction to Systematic Theology* [1991] 54-55).

¹¹⁷ Pannenberg, "Toward a Theology of the History of Religions" (ET 1971) 118.

¹¹⁸ Pannenberg, "Religious Pluralism and Conflicting Truth Claims" (1990) 103; cf. 106 n.28.

¹¹⁹ A useful survey of this critical literature is provided in Grenz, "The Appraisal of Pannenberg" (1988).

¹²⁰ In a sense, Pannenberg is claiming something quite different than Moltmann in his theological anthropology. Moltmann thought the bible accounted for the origin of historical thinking, which then disseminated to the world. I wonder if such thinking could equally well be seen to have arisen in the normal course of human growth to greater understanding, thereafter becoming the preferred vehicle for conceiving God and the world. Pannenberg wishes to say, on the one hand, that the biblical understanding (of history, say) best reflects the human condition and, on the other hand, that revelation through events has given rise *both* to the natural perceptions of humans and to the biblical insights. *This means that biblical witness and human condition have a common root for Pannenberg, where Moltmann was content to ascribe priority to the bible in neo-orthodox manner.*

Like Moltmann, Pannenberg has emphasized the cultural dissemination and wide subsequent influence of the biblical ideas, but he has not achieved this by denying any appeal to the human condition as religiously disclosive apart from the biblical ideas. Perhaps we might

say that for Pannenberg the bible best expresses or brings into focus
that which is more generally true about humanity. This is not to understand such revelation as lying in the interpretation of facts rather
than in the facts themselves (while Pannenberg forbids this as a general principle he allows it with reference to historical events, after
Collingwood, as we have seen). Rather, concerning his apparently
symbiotic link between the general human condition (as with Rahner, say) and the primacy of biblical categories (as with Moltmann,
say), I think it most likely that Pannenberg finds something like a
general revelation in the human condition which scripture optimally
explicates according to apocalyptic categories. This is not to say that
all revelation is in scripture, as with Moltmann, but that scripture is a
witness.

[121] See Pannenberg, *Jesus—God and Man* (1968) 66.

[122] As for the claim that his Christology is "from below," Pannenberg is criticized by Segundo for rushing too quickly from Jesus' life
to draw conclusions about dimensions "from above." Segundo wishes to "rescue Jesus from the grip of theology" (not a new project by
any means), believing that any genuine theology "from below" will
not rush to embrace themes of traditional theology "from above,"
such as incarnationalism, as does Pannenberg; see Segundo, *Jesus of
Nazareth Yesterday and Today,* Vol. II: *The Historical Jesus of the
Synoptics* (1985) 30; see also the discussion of Segundo in the Conclusion.

[123] O'Collins, *What Are They Saying About Jesus?* (1983) 11.

[124] Wiles points out, too, that Pannenberg begins from only one
possible historical reconstruction of Jesus' message, believing it to
focus upon the immanence of the general resurrection (Wiles,
"Christology in an Age of Historical Studies" [1979] 21). Given the
centrality of Jesus' resurrection for Pannenberg's whole assessment,
however, such a reconstruction of Jesus' message may be prejudiced
by the desired outcome.

In addition, even if this reconstruction favored by Pannenberg *is*
what the gospel writers were ascribing to Jesus it would still be as
much the retrojection of resurrection belief into the life of Jesus as
is otherwise typical of the gospel accounts. If everything else the
earliest church came to say about Jesus in its developing Christology was an outgrowth and elaboration of resurrection belief, as Pan-

nenberg claims, then this reconstruction of Jesus' acts and message cannot be free of such influence too; after all, the realization that the gospel accounts of Jesus' deeds and teachings are just as theologically colored as the accounts of his birth or of his pre-existence is a commonplace of New Testament studies. So this claim that Jesus' deeds and message are somehow supportive of Pannenberg's claims overlooks the fact that Jesus' portrayal in the gospels is already colored by resurrection faith, and thus such recourse cannot be declared free of tautology.

[125] Cobb, "Pannenberg and Process Theology" (1988) 70. Further, Cobb thinks that Pannenberg's findings concerning the human person are not neutral and objectively available to all inquirers but that *different* conclusions are rendered possible, for instance, by seeing all things as cohering in God as Pannenberg does. Thus Cobb believes a level of confessional thinking remains, so that Pannenberg is not entirely neutral (ibid. 64-66). The same could be said for Pannenberg's favoring of the historical, the eschatological and the apocalyptic as premier categories for understanding humanity—that others would look elsewhere for their key concepts is all the evidence needed to show that Pannenberg's reading of the human condition is by no means obvious or value-neutral.

[126] Burhenn, "Pannenberg's Argument for the Historicity of the Resurrection" (1972) 377-78.

[127] See e.g. Kerr, *Theology after Wittgenstein* (1986) 14, and the discussion earlier in Chapter 4.

[128] As with Moltmann, such claims about a revelational basis for theological anthropology are hard to establish. Just as Moltmann's claims to ground the concept of history in revelation were questioned, so too can the Jewish apocalyptic ideas to which Pannenberg ascribes revealed status be understood as the natural product of a particular intellectual and cultural milieu. According to Geyer, "a general anthropological situation is required to guarantee the validity of the historical intellectual structure of the late Jewish apocalyptic... making the resurrection of Jesus, as the declared basis of Christian faith, subject to the historical confirmation of an inherent structural principle in human life, existing independently" (Geyer, "The Resurrection of Jesus Christ" [1968] 131). Here, too, the general anthropological principle required to support a particular belief is

recognized as being more sectional or more perspectival than Pannenberg would allow.

[129] Wiles, "Christology in an Age of Historical Studies" (1979) 21.

[130] As we saw in our discussion of *What is Man?* Pannenberg asserts the relevance of this apocalyptic world to our own world through Rahner-style arguments for a fundamental human openness to the future and hope beyond death. Also, he argues that resurrection of the dead better suits the appreciation of human life as a psychosomatic unity which is being recovered in contemporary thought. Pannenberg's favored perspective was assessed earlier in this discussion as reflecting only one among many options in recent anthropology, and hence as less than compelling.

[131] Burhenn, "Pannenberg's Argument for the Historicity of the Resurrection" (1979) 377-79.

[132] Clayton, "Anticipation and Theological Method" (1988) 141-42.

[133] Burhenn, art. cit., 378.

[134] Grenz, "The Appraisal of Pannenberg" (1988) 44.

[135] See e.g. C.F. Evans, *Resurrection in the New Testament* (Naperville, Il: A.R. Allenson, 1970) 180; as cited in Grenz, art. cit. 44.

[136] Dietrich Rössler, *Gesetz und Geschichte: Untersuchungen Zür Theologie der Jüdischen Apokalyptic und der Pharisäischen Orthodoxie* (Neukirchen, 1960); see McGrath, *The Making of Modern German Christology* (1986) 168.

[137] Carnley, *The Shape of Resurrection Belief* (1987) 90, 81-83.

[138] Ibid. 90-91; see Pannenberg, *Jesus—God and Man* (1968) 99-100.

[139] Pannenberg, *Jesus—God and Man* (1968) 89.

[140] Carnley, op. cit. 85. An alternative solution within the school of hope is that of Jürgen Moltmann, for whom there is nothing provable in the resurrection of Jesus. Though he agrees with Pannenberg that the end is shown proleptically in Jesus, nevertheless Moltmann sees his conviction lying in the realm of faith and hope and not in the knowledge of facts, as is the case for Pannenberg with his claims for historical certainty (Moltmann, *The Crucified God* [1974] 172-73).

[141] See e.g. Pannenberg, *Jesus—God and Man* (1968) 107, 109; "Religious Pluralism and Conflicting Truth Claims" (1990) 103; cf. 106 n.28.

[142] Grenz, "The Appraisal of Pannenberg" (1988) 23.

[143] Althaus, "Offenbarung als Geschichte und Glaube: Bemerkungen zu W. Pannenberg's Begriff der Offenbarung" *Theologische Literaturzeitung* 87 (1962) 321-30; cited in McGrath, *The Making of Modern German Christology* (1986) 177.

[144] Dulles, "Pannenberg on Revelation and Faith" (1988) 179. Pannenberg goes some way to admitting this wider dependence in his elevation of late Jewish apocalyptic to privileged status, but he does not allow it to stand alone as revelatory in its own right—it depends on the resurrection of Jesus to justify it. As we have seen, this apocalyptic world view is claimed by Pannenberg to correspond optimally with the human condition as he understands it, but this too is only confirmed in the resurrection.

[145] See Gunton, *Yesterday and Today* (1983) 24-26.

[146] Van Beeck, *Christ Proclaimed* (1979) 317.

[147] Pannenberg, *Jesus—God and Man* (1968) 27; cited in van Beeck, op. cit. 314.

[148] Van Beeck, op. cit. 315. Perhaps Pannenberg, the great contemporary theological supporter of scientific rationality, is very *unscientific* in overlooking the experience of Christians throughout the ages—they are the *obvious* experimental subjects for testing the truth of Christian claims, as every critic of the church insists (and this despite Pannenberg's occasional recourse to a pragmatist style of argument).

To this, by the way, one might add the little observation that Pannenberg's view of the resurrection as historical event is cast in an unfalsifiable form. This is the case, as has been suggested, because the resurrection is shored up by faith rather than fact in Pannenberg's thought. So it is a matter of interpretation after all, not least in the light of present Christian experience (as van Beeck has highlighted).

[149] Van Beeck, op. cit. 322.

[150] Pannenberg is not wholly insensitive to these insights, however; see e.g. the essay "Eucharistic Piety—A New Experience of Christian Community," in his *Christian Spirituality and Sacramental Community* (1984) 31-49. I hasten to add that van Beeck is not entirely dependent on narrative, worship and participation for his Christology—there is a strong liberal apologetic dimension, too.

Thus he escapes the critique of Ritschl, offered in Chapter 3. See the discussion of van Beeck in the Conclusion.

[151] Macquarrie, "The Concept of a Christ Event" (1981) 69-80. The impact of Jesus upon his followers is a major component of the uniqueness claims to be considered in Part III.

[152] Johnson, "The Ongoing Christology of Wolfhart Pannenberg" (1982) 245.

[153] Van Beeck, *Christ Proclaimed* (1979) 323.

[154] Schwöbel, "Wolfhart Pannenberg" (1989) 284.

[155] Neuhaus, "Theology for Church and Polis" (1988) 238.

[156] Clayton, "Anticipation and Theological Method" (1988) 131. This overturns the normal scientific view of causality by an idealist-inspired prioritizing of the whole over the part both conceptually and causally; see Ford, "The Nature and Power of the Future" (1988) 82-83.

[157] Nichols, "Walter Kasper and his Theological Programme" (1986) 16.

[158] Another linked to this school is Hans Küng, but Kasper and others think he has overbalanced with his focus on the historical Jesus, at the expense of the Christ who meets Christians in the church's life and teaching. On this movement as a whole see e.g. Klinger, "Tübingen School," in Karl Rahner et al. (eds.), *Sacramentum Mundi,* Vol. 6 (New York: Herder & Herder, 1970) and Burchtaell, "Drey, Möhler and the Catholic School of Tübingen," in Ninian Smart et al. (eds.), *Nineteenth Century Religious Thought in the West,* Vol. 2 (Cambridge: Cambridge University Press, 1985) 111-39.

[159] Kasper's *Habilitationsschrift,* tendered at Tübingen in 1964, was written on *Das Absolut in der Geschichte: Philosophie und Theologie der Geschichte in der Spätphilosophie Schellings* (Mainz, 1965).

Through Schelling the grand idealist view of history had its last major engagement with Christianity, and took its last convincing stand in the face of challenges from the young Hegelians, the early existentialists and Nietzsche. Faced by the growing loss of confidence in Hegel's attempt to bind the Absolute to history, Schelling came to see this link in an act of transcendental reflection toward something standing *altogether outside* the dialectical process which

Hegel had sought to map. But Schelling's "negative philosophy" could never yield up a conception of this Absolute that showed it *truly* absolute, and not merely a product of the mind's own reflection. Thus he came to the view that the Absolute needed to be freely revealed to humanity in the context of history, and thus he understood Jesus Christ.

Kasper seeks no firmer foundation than this recognition, based on faith and hope. He rejects, for instance, the transcendental speculations of Rahner, who wishes to establish a firmer grounding for humanity's link to the Absolute. Herein lay the failure of Hegel and the early Schelling, according to Kasper. But, then, the effective severing of ties to history by Barth (in favor of revelation) clears a way to the later Protestant linking of God to the realm of human subjectivity (Tillich and Bultmann), which is no improvement. Kasper's emphasis on faith and hiddenness, showing his Protestant sympathies, also puts him out of step with another Protestant, Wolfhart Pannenberg, who thinks history far more straightforward.

For an excellent discussion of Kasper vis-à-vis Schelling and this range of current theological opinion (a discussion to which I am indebted for these insights) see Loewe, "The New Catholic Tübingen Theology of Walter Kasper" (1980) 32-34, 36-38, 41-42.

[160] Kasper begins with a critical overview of current Christologies. He is not convinced that they achieve what they set out to achieve, which is to affirm the universal and ultimate significance of Jesus Christ as the one in whom the human yearning for freedom and liberation is definitively answered.

Kasper declares himself dissatisfied with anthropological approaches (18). He points out that, given how poor are we in western culture at accounting for the single and the particular, "Christology [becomes] a mere vehicle, function, cypher, symbol, interpretament and, ultimately, a particular instance of anthropology" (47). He sees Rahner as a great example of an approach he thinks cannot answer Strauss' question as to why the reality found in Christ should be restricted to only one historical instance (51-52). In particular, he rejects the overarching evolutionary perspective found in Rahner and Teilhard. Rather than Christ revealing any obvious meaning to the evolutionary process as a whole, sufficient to hold contrary evidences of meaninglessness and futility at bay, Kasper believes the best we can hope for is an unambiguous sign in history—"Are you he who is to come, or shall we look for another?" (Mt 11:3) (58). Here it appears that Kasper is closer to the qualified certainties of the school of hope (though, as we have noted in our discussions of Moltmann and Pannenberg, the commitment to the uniqueness and finality of Jesus found there remains a very strong one). Note, however, that Kasper also criticizes the universal historical perspective of Moltmann and Pannenberg as reducing theology to philosophy (17-18). The type of Jesus-centered theology emerging as a result of the new quest is also questioned for its inability to show why Jesus should be accorded special status (19).

[161] Clarke, "Current Christologies" (1979) 447.

[162] Regarding the ancient problem of Athens vs. Jerusalem, Loewe offers the following interpretation of Kasper's views on the relationship between theology and Philosophy: "Philosophy is of itself impotent, and no conception of the Absolute at which philosophy arrives can be simply identified with the God of revelation. On the other hand, the opposition between philosophy and theology has a dialectical character. The experience of the failure of philosophy can provide an opening for revelation, and the meaningfulness of revelation can be articulated in philosophical terms. But no single philosophical system can be canonized, for this would tend both to reduce theology to philosophy and, given the historicity of philosophy, to render theology obsolete" (Loewe, "The New Catholic Tübingen Theology of Walter Kasper" [1980] 39-40).

[163] Brian McDermott, "Roman Catholic Christology" (1980) 340.

[164] See p. 70. It is in this context that Kasper allows reference to Jesus' "abba relationship." He believes Jesus was not interested in himself at all, with the implication that those who concentrate on Jesus' self-consciousness are fundamentally wrongheaded, but that we can nevertheless find in this term "abba," at once fond and formal, an indication of how Jesus viewed God, if not himself (79-80).

The accounts of Jesus' miracles in the New Testament are understood to rest on a firm base of history, though Kasper recognizes that they are highly elaborated (89-90). He sees them as isolated signs of the new creation coming into being in Jesus' person (96). Kasper sees Jesus as implicitly confirming his status as the bringer of God's kingdom by putting himself above Moses and the law, and as exhibiting a filial obedience to God that came to be translated after his death into an understanding of Jesus as God's Son—"What Jesus lived before Easter ontically is after Easter expressed ontologically" (110).

165 Galvin, "The Resurrection of Jesus in Contemporary Catholic Systematics" (1979) 132.

166 Rosato, "Spirit Christology" (1977) 439.

167 Kasper is most dissatisfied with the various alternatives to hand in current theology for understanding the resurrection. He rejects Bultmann's attempt to see it as merely a faith perspective on the cross, just as he rejects reliance upon the need of human freedom and hope for a definitive confirming instance which he finds in Rahner, Pannenberg and Moltmann (133-36) (now and again Kasper overestimates the dependence of Moltmann and Pannenberg on a phenomenology of hope, as he does here, failing to recognize the recourse to revelation characterising their eschatologically-oriented theologies).

168 We would do well at this point to note similarities between Walter Kasper and the Australian Jesuit Gerald O'Collins, currently Professor at Rome's Pontifical Gregorian University. O'Collins is found to be in agreement with Kasper (and Pannenberg) that the resurrection is foundational for Christology, and that it means the new creation has dawned through Jesus in the Spirit (cf. Kasper). But he does not believe the resurrection is an historical event, as against Pannenberg; it is not an "event" in this world strictly speaking but, rather, an event of the new creation. Nor does O'Collins follow Pannenberg in his restriction of "proof" for Jesus' resurrection to events of the past—like Kasper, O'Collins sees the church's experiences as providing crucial evidence, from the resurrection appearances to the testimonies of Christians today.

O'Collins is closer to Rahner than Kasper over the historical Jesus; he declares the historical Jesus to be important, contra Bultmann, but he is less concerned with the detail of Jesus' ministry than Kasper. But, then, he is closer to Kasper than Rahner over the contribution of any overarching philosophical system, preferring to depend on revelation (through the resurrection) rather than high ontology (see his various books on the resurrection, e.g. *The Easter Jesus* [1973]; *Jesus Risen* [1987]). O'Collins' perspective on Jesus' uniqueness and finality in the light of the religions follows the "anonymous

Christians" approach of Vatican II and Rahner (see e.g. the chapter entitled "Christ and Non-Christians" in his *Fundamental Theology* [1981] 114-29).

[169] Like Rahner, Kasper understands Jesus' divine Sonship in light of his human obedience to God and, like Pannenberg and Moltmann, he declares Jesus' eternal Sonship (protology) as a necessary consequence of what was revealed at the resurrection (eschatology) (175). All this he sees as part of a new understanding of God which dawned in the life of Jesus—an understanding which found expression in Trinitarian doctrine. With Rahner, and denying Schoonenberg, Kasper argues for an essential link between the inner-divine Trinity and the "economic Trinity" predicated upon the church's experience of salvation by God through Christ in the Spirit—the latter necessarily relying upon the former (181-83). Again, like Rahner, Kasper sees in Jesus the final coming-to-itself of humanity, and so he believes that all people participate in this achievement *anonymously* (185-88). Yet, unlike Rahner and others, Kasper wishes to hold firm Jesus' historical particularity, as we have seen—he seeks thereby to avoid a slide into that complete secularism which requires nothing of anyone and blesses the status quo (189-90).

[170] This is also a solidarity with the dead and the victims of history, which is how Kasper understands notions of Jesus' descent into hell (223-24). Here he is in agreement with Moltmann in his criticism of evolutionary Christologies, claiming that they offer no redress for those who fall by the wayside (see the discussion in Ch. 1, above, referring to Moltmann, *The Way of Jesus Christ* [1990] 297), with which I take issue in a discussion footnoted at n. 70, above.

[171] Kasper is at pains to emphasize that the divine initiative and the response of creation are both needed for this to take place, and that both are present in the career and person of Jesus (230). He is happy with the *pneuma/sarx* distinction found in New Testament Christologies, then, which evolved into an abstract formula involving two natures at Chalcedon (237). This is a distinction characteristic of all people, he thinks, though it has received "its specific form, plenitude and perfection" in Jesus (247).

[172] Brian McDermott, "Roman Catholic Christology" (1980) 341.

[173] See Lampe, *God as Spirit* (1977) and the discussion at n. 29 in the notes for Part III.

[174] Given the equality of the Logos, thus expressed, in the divine economy of Jesus' life, the description of Kasper's approach as a "Spirit Christology" is perhaps overenthusiastic; in reality, it appears all he is doing is asserting the unique influence of God in Jesus' life and person in a manner similar to Rahner and Schoonenberg (to be discussed shortly). What is notable, however, is the advance on Pannenberg's solution this represents—Pannenberg, criticized by van Beeck and others for failing to recognize the importance of contemporary Christian experience, was thought too rationalistic in basing Jesus' uniqueness and finality on historical fact alone, albeit the "fact" of Jesus' resurrection.

[175] Rosato, "Spirit Christology" (1977) 443.

[176] Where Kasper diverges most thoroughly from Pannenberg, of course, is in his sense of the ambiguity of history and the unprovability of God—in a way, he is in this sense truer to Luther than the Lutheran Pannenberg. Both Kasper and Pannenberg avoid any crass extrinsicism, whereby some events are "divine" and others purely "secular." Where they apparently differ, though, is in the importance accorded to interpretation. Pannenberg *claims* not to identify revelation with interpretation, whereas for Kasper "Historical facts constitute at most signs for faith, ambiguous in themselves and requiring clarification from the word of revelation" (Loewe, "The New Catholic Tübingen Theology of Walter Kasper" [1980] 41-42). We have seen, of course, that Pannenberg attempts to collapse event and interpretation in the manner of Dilthey and that, in all probability, the resurrection itself is an interpretation of subsequent facts for Pannenberg (the faith of the early church, mostly) rather than an historical event pure and simple. So he and Kasper may not be so different here, despite Pannenberg's claims—it seems that the Spirit and the experience of the church, rendered explicit in Kasper, are also components of Pannenberg's system, albeit overlooked.

[177] Gerald McCool, *Catholic Theology in the Nineteenth Century: The Quest for a Unitary Method* (New York, 1977); cited in Loewe, "The New Tübingen Theology of Walter Kasper" (1980) 31.

[178] Kuschel, *Born Before all Time?* (1992) 454-55.

[179] Krieg, *Story-Shaped Christology* (1988) 48.

Part III: Liberal

¹ See Pannenberg, *Jesus—God and Man* (1968) 161-63. For a thorough historical discussion see e.g. George Maloney, *The Cosmic Christ: From Paul to Teilhard* (New York: Sheed & Ward, 1968).

² See Pujdak, "Schoonenberg's Christology in Context" (1979) 1, and the extensive bibliographical information about this phenomenon in the footnotes to be found there.

³ Schoonenberg's argument here is, basically, that a model exists to help us conceive such action of God, that this model is validated by its association with Thomas Aquinas, and that a scriptural development toward such a conception is discernible, especially in the book of Wisdom. The natural analogy he advances is that of the person inhabiting his or her own body and causing bodily movements which are, nevertheless, entirely explicable at the level of the biochemical processes through which they take place (for more on this this model in the "Dutch Christology" see Robert North, "Soul-Body Unity and God-Man Unity" [1969]).

⁴ This conviction that humans cannot achieve their goal within their own powers, unlike animals, is drawn from Aristotle and Aquinas; it is a view wholly in tune with that of Rahner (and Teilhard).

⁵ It ought to be added that this seamless presence of God in history does not present itself apart from the need for interpretation. Here Schoonenberg is at his farthest from Pannenberg, who believes that God's action within the events of history is accessible at the level of reason, and especially in the light of events comprising Jesus' resurrection. Not so with Schoonenberg, however, for whom divine action in history only becomes revelation through the action of God's Spirit in interpreting it (46-47).

⁶ Schoonenberg believes the Chalcedonian concept of "nature," and of two different natures coexisting, renders the one person of Jesus inexplicable in our day. In addition it fails to explain how God and the human Jesus interacted, nor does it account for the link between soteriology and Christology to which Christian theology is always driven (62-65).

⁷ Herein lies a fascinating dimension of Schoonenberg's thought. He does not believe the Logos is a "Person" prior to the incarnation,

and thus he does not believe God is Triune prior to the revelation of the Father through the Son in Jesus. In Schoonenberg's view, writes Pujdak, "it is only through becoming man that the Word achieved a special and distinct relation as *person* to the Father" (Pujdak, "Schoonenberg's Christology in Context" [1979] 14). As Reinhardt points out, this means that "the divine Logos, who first operates as an impersonal divine force in history, becomes in the man Jesus of Nazareth a person, the second person of the Trinity. It follows from this that God's Trinity does not simply originate in God's eternal essence but from the Logos' being human, from his becoming a person in the man Jesus" (Reinhardt, "In What Way Is Jesus Christ Unique?" [1974] 362).

Such an understanding calls for a sundering of the economic from the immanent Trinity, such as Karl Rahner was at pains to deny. To be sure, Schoonenberg does believe that the God met in Jesus Christ is Triune, but he expresses agnosticism about the inner being of God apart from this revelation (82).

Herein we see Schoonenberg's considerable sympathy for process theology at work. He is happy with the idea of God changing and surprising us, finding compatibilities here with Aquinas (85n.): "I myself am convinced that the idea of God becoming triune through his salvific self-communications is possible," he writes (86n.). The long footnote stretching across pp. 82-86 in *The Christ* sets out the dependence of Schoonenberg on such process ideas (which have also influenced Robinson).

[8] Schoonenberg believes in the bodily resurrection of Jesus, but in a most unconventional and oblique way. He distinguishes between Jesus' body and his corpse, effectively denying that a resurrection of Jesus' body calls for any reanimation of his corpse (172).

In other respects, Schoonenberg recalls Rahner on the resurrected body of Christ present in the church and its sacraments (on the analogy of the extension of our bodily identity evident through the individual stamp we put on our dress and on our homes, as well as the merging which takes place between persons in love). He also recalls Bultmann in his understanding of the resurrection as laying bare the depth-dimension of Jesus' cross, though he ascribes this perspective to John's gospel primarily (169-72).

[9] Schoonenberg's writings on the non-Christian religions further indicate his commitment to the uniqueness and finality of Jesus, though in a manner closer to the conclusions of Hans Küng than those of Karl Rahner. Rather than the anonymous savior of all, as he is for Rahner, Schoonenberg's Christ, as he is for Küng, stands as norm and critical standard among the religions (through which the omnipresent Logos and Spirit work salvation); see Schoonenberg, "The Church and Non-Christian Religions" (1966).

[10] Schoonenberg further discusses the role of the Spirit, offering a sympathetic critique of charismatic claims, in "Baptism with the Holy Spirit" (1974). Schoonenberg's influence on his fellow Jesuit, Frans Jozef van Beeck (who is discussed in the Conclusion to this study), is clear, though van Beeck attends far more fully to the questions of hermeneutics, explicating the nature of this impact far more thoroughly.

[11] This report of the Sacred Congregation for the Doctrine of the Faith, dated 8 March 1972 and entitled "Safeguarding Belief In the Incarnation and Trinity," is reprinted in *La Osservatore Romano* and elsewhere. This reference is from *The Catholic Mind* (70, #1264) June 1972, 61-64; 62. A range of other critical material is footnoted in Pujdak, "Schoonenberg's Christology in Context" (1979) 14-15.

[12] Milet, *God or Christ?* (1981) 195. Milet also labels Robinson a death of God theologian (103), which is just not right (although, like Schoonenberg, Robinson does offer a positive theological assessment of secularity).

[13] Lonergan, "Christology Today" (1985) 95.

[14] See Kasper, *The Christ* (1976) 181, who argues that, on the matter of God's inner life, Schoonenberg is modalistic rather than agnostic, as claimed. This dismissal by Kasper is cited as evidence that German theology failed to understand the importance of Schoonenberg in the 1970s; see Cooke, "Horizons on Christology in the Seventies" (1979) 205.

[15] Cook, *The Jesus of Faith* (1981) 139.

[16] A standard feature of such conservative critique, of course, is too strongly identifying the object of belief with one's own favored formulation of that belief. In this case, the conservative critics of Schoonenberg forget that the Chalcedonian Definition is only *an in-*

terpretation of Jesus, albeit a classic one rightly deserving ongoing attention. Schoonenberg seeks to examine it in the light of other equally authoritative interpretations from the New Testament in the context of current thought forms in order to best interpret the one who stands behind and above all such formulae. Such definitions, dogmas, etc. can hardly be exhaustive, nor should their proper objective be obscured through their use as polemical devices, both of which unsavory outcomes are courted by such conservatives. It should be remembered that the creeds were regulative rather than entirely prescriptive in their day, and thus they best function now.

[17] Mondin, "New Trends in Christology" (1974) 61.

[18] Other theologians with a Logos perspective must face the same question. Suffice it briefly to mention one of them, the former Dominican and now Episcopalian priest Matthew Fox. From reading his eclectic, stimulating, timely (though rather "Aquarian") creation theology, one would not think that the uniqueness of Jesus would occur to Fox, thinking perhaps that he might find his place closest to that occupied by Hick and Cantwell Smith in my Chapter 10. But this is not the case, apparently, for he unaccountably retains reference to Jesus' resurrection and so, presumably, wishes to see him as in some way unique among those who express "the cosmic Christ"; see *The Coming of the Cosmic Christ* (1988) 140-41.

[19] Much can be learned about the man, and his understanding of God's action in the world, from his last sermon at Trinity College, entitled "Learning from Cancer"; see *Where Three Ways Meet: Last Essays and Sermons* (London: SCM, 1987) 189-94.

[20] London: SCM, 1963—constantly reprinted.

[21] Born in 1919 into a considerable clerical dynasty, and as close to the heart of Anglican tradition as one might get (the cathedral close at Canterbury), Robinson inherited from the scholar-parsons among his forebears both a love for the ecclesiastical institution, its worship, scripture and tradition, and a liberal-minded, reforming zeal typical of the nineteenth century English church. After a classics education in Cambridge and then theological study to doctoral level while an ordinand at Westcott House, Robinson was ordained to a Bristol curacy. There followed an appointment at Wells Theological College, and a period of liturgical creativity as Dean of Clare College, Cambridge, before his decade as Suffragan Bishop of Wool-

wich in South London. After this Robinson returned to his Cambridge beginnings as Dean of Trinity, the largest and wealthiest college. While in that appointment he traveled and lectured widely, concentrated on New Testament studies mostly, was passed over for academic and ecclesiastical preferment, and finally made a brave death.

Influential in both the Church of England and the wider world of theology, Robinson has already rated a full-length biography; see Eric James, *A Life of Bishop John A.T. Robinson: Scholar, Pastor, Prophet* (London: Collins, 1987); cf. James' short biographical note in Alistair Kee's study of Robinson's thought, *The Roots of Christian Freedom* (1988) xi-xvi.

[22] The main source for Robinson's "panentheism" is *Exploration into God* (London: SCM, 1967); for the history of this now widespread revision of theism see John Macquarrie's Gifford lectures for 1983-84, published as *In Search of Deity: An Essay in Dialectical Theism* (London: SCM, 1984).

[23] He recognizes that every age has its own Christological emphasis and that Christological answers must be correlated with the spirit of every age (though not uncritically subsumed under it, as he believes was the case with the nineteenth century lives of Jesus) (15-16).

[24] Robinson was highly influenced by the personalist philosophy of Martin Buber, with its emphasis upon the human condition as fundamentally relational; it is a commonplace that all Robinson's theology is present in nucé in the doctoral thesis he wrote on Buber: see his *Thou Who Art: The notion of personality and its relation to Christian theology with particular reference to (a) the contemporary "I-Thou" philosophy; (b) the doctrines of the Trinity and the Person of Christ* (unpublished PhD Dissertation, University of Cambridge, 1945).

[25] Robinson quotes Wisdom 7:1-6, in which Solomon describes the origin of every king through the natural processes of sex and procreation (the second of which is normally ascribed to Mary, but not the first). So when Jesus says that "a greater than Solomon is here" (Mt 12:42//Lk 11:31), Robinson wonders whether denying sexuality and the natural helps account for that greatness, particularly when Jesus himself sees the beauty of nature surpassing that of "Solomon in all his glory" (Mt 6:28-29//Lk 12:27) (141-42).

[26] Robinson also seeks to show that the birth of Jesus from an ir-regular union would have been "strikingly in line with the pattern of the divine good pleasure in choosing to raise children of promise" (62) from the adulterous wife of Hosea; see also his "Hosea and the Virgin Birth" (1984).

He also insists that Jesus was a sexual being, as are all humans, airing the possibility (originating elsewhere) that Jesus might have experienced an erection when, as the gospels have it, a woman wiped his feet with her hair in what could only be described as a sexually charged moment (64).

It is the *relationality* of Jesus that Robinson seeks to retain with such suggestions. He is concerned that even allegedly radical por-trayals of Jesus' person fail to present this relationality. A good ex-ample he uses is that of Italian Marxist Pier Paulo Pasolini in his justly famous film *The Gospel According to St. Matthew*, whose oth-erwise controversial Jesus-figure strides impassively through the world touching others while remaining untouched by them (65).

[27] There are problems with this phenomenology of Christological faith, however, not least its "high failure rate"—many simply do not see these depths in Jesus, from the time when "his own people re-ceived him not" to our own just-as-skeptical present.

[28] Colin Gunton quite erroneously numbers Robinson among those perpetrating this version of degree Christology; but the "de-gree" to which Robinson refers concerns Jesus' mediation of God's presence, and *not* his human attainments (see Gunton, *Yesterday and Today* [1983] 15-16).

[29] There are a number of other writers whose views are basically the same as Robinson's, mostly Anglo-American influenced and An-glican. Throughout *The Human Face of God* Robinson quotes John Knox and Norman Pittenger. Knox favorably mentions Robinson and Pittenger, too, in *The Humanity and Divinity of Christ* (1967)—there he has Jesus uniquely incarnating the Logos, which we know through the resurrection and experience in the church (Knox was a Protestant Bultmannian but has since become an Anglo-Catholic priest). Pit-tenger, another Anglo-Catholic, made his major contribution to Chris-tology before the period of interest in this study; for a more recent Christological text, however, see *Catholic Faith in a Process Per-spective* (1981) Ch. 9, "A Process Christology," where Pittenger's

views are similar to those of Robinson, and Jesus is the fullest representation of God in the world. For the uniqueness of Jesus in Pittenger's thought, discussed alongside that of Robinson, see a section entitled "Christologies from the Side of Man" in H.E.W. Turner, *Jesus the Christ* (1976); see also Jerry K. Robbins, "The Finality of Christ in the Theology of Norman Pittenger" (1989).

Eugene TeSelle criticizes the Christocentrism of the Christian tradition in an historical study which also offers a logos perspective on Jesus as one who does not exhaust the Word of God, but whose uniqueness nevertheless consists "in being the touchstone by which other responses are judged, the achievement by which their deficiencies are overcome, the centre of gravity around which they cluster"; see *Christ in Context* (1975) 164.

A variant on the logos approach of Robinson is the "Inspiration Christology" of G.W.H. Lampe, *God as Spirit* (1977). In a patristic study Lampe disclaims the making of an hypostasis of the Logos where initially a divine action was meant. He goes on to conceive God as Spirit, disclaiming any essential Trinitarianism and, most importantly for our purposes, understanding Jesus not as the one who most embodies the Logos but, rather, the one who most fully expresses and enables others to express God the Spirit. Robinson declares that his own position is very similar to that of Lampe, and does not disagree with what he sees to be simply the transposing of a Logos-Son Christology into a Spirit one (Robinson, *Truth Is Two-Eyed* [1979] 115-16). But he does prefer to stick with ideas of incarnation and sonship, as against the writers of *The Myth of God Incarnate* (Hick ed. 1977), as such ideas best emphasize the humanity of Jesus which is so important for his Christology (Robinson, ibid. 116). Cf. Ritschl's solution: see Part I, n. 168, above.

[30] As Robinson puts it elsewhere, "Jesus is unique because he alone of all mankind of whom we have any external evidence or internal experience was truly normal ... [he] lived in a relationship to God and his fellow men in which we are all called to live but fail to live"; see "What Future for a Unique Christ?" (1987) 11.

[31] Regarding access to to the historical Jesus, Robinson is convinced that a high (though functional) Christology was quickly in place in earliest Christianity. Such a functional Christology, because it is "high," can then hold its own against the less functional, more

ontological Christologies of the patristic era which Robinson fears will suppress the humanity of Jesus in search of some allegedly "higher" Christology. So despite his willingness to demythologize the New Testament after Bultmann and John Knox, Robinson is quite confident that Jesus' person, self-understanding and impact upon his contemporaries was much as it is portrayed there.

[32] Robinson, "Need Jesus Have Been Perfect?" (1972) 46.

[33] Cf. Peter Carnley, "The Poverty of Historical Scepticism" (1972).

[34] Robinson thinks the tradition of the empty tomb to be early and genuine—why would (legally inadmissible) female witnesses have been invented, he asks, if the point of the story was to put off doubters? But Robinson does not see a "physical" resurrection as proved thereby (132).

[35] The nature of the appearances is greater than that of purely private, subjective illusion, according to Robinson (who points out that Paul is not overreliant on his own "visions"). But they must have been shared psychic experiences involving encounter with Jesus which were taken to be true if a faith could grow up from them, eventually becoming independent: "In form, these appearances should probably be classified as 'objectively projected' hallucination, not essentially different from other such phenomena. But they would have signified 'resurrection' (as opposed to the temporary survival of an individual loved one) only if in content a radically new spiritual awareness had communicated itself through them" (130).

While arguing for the possibility of divine action in the resurrection of Jesus without any tear in the veil of normalcy and historical ambiguity, nevertheless Robinson does not wish to be a dogmatic positivist. He raises the interesting possibility that the disappearance of Jesus' body could have involved natural processes, albeit ones better understood in the east than in the modern west. The instance he provides is of certain Buddhist holy men whose bodies allegedly fade away to nails and hair within days, through some hitherto unexplained transmutation of matter into energy in those who have achieved higher than normal levels of psychic advancement (139 n.157) (here Robinson cites a 1953 report recounted by Chögyam Trungpa in *Born in Tibet* [London: Allen & Unwin, 1966] 95f. The particular case was not unique in the locality, according to the guru who informed Trungpa's immediate source—note, however, that this report was already third-hand when it came to Trungpa).

Surely, however, any ascription of such spiritual power to a purely human Jesus would put him so far beyond normal abilities that the notion of shared humanity could not be maintained, which is what Robinson wishes to avoid at all costs.

³⁶ "Christ," according to Robinson, "stands for whatever reveals, mediates, embodies the invisible, timeless mystery of *Theos* in the finite" ("What Future for a Unique Christ?" [1987] 13-14)—this wider sphere of reference is evident in his conviction that the profoundest insights into the Christ today are to be found in psychology, art and drama; see *The Human Face of God* (1973) 241.

His mention here of "the Christ who will be" is a rare bit of future eschatology in Robinson; it is not normally a feature of his decidedly non-eschatological Christology. However, he does augment his claim that the Christ is larger than Jesus by comparing the parousia Christ, Tennyson's "Christ who is to be," with the historical Jesus; see Robinson *Truth Is Two-Eyed* (1979) 125, 129.

³⁷ Robinson is "not persuaded that it is possible to remain indifferent to the findings of the historian on how Jesus understood himself, nor that an ultimate scepticism is either tolerable or necessary"; see "The Last Tabu?" (1984) 158-59. He charts Jesus' vocational course from its beginnings among the disciples of John the Baptist, through a time of disaffection and conversion when he came to conceive his role in terms of liberation rather than judgment, until at last he found his identity in the Isaianic servant songs (*The Human Face of God* [1973] 82-83). Regarding the paucity of New Testament material about his self-consciousness, Robinson believes that Jesus' own reticence is at fault. Nevertheless, he trusts the fourth gospel as historically faithful in its portrayal of Jesus as ever conscious of a special calling from the Father (art. cit. 164-65).

³⁸ Robinson, "What Future for a Unique Christ?" (1987) 15.

³⁹ This recourse to Jesus' psychology is the subject of much popular writing nowadays in the realm of spirituality. Of Jesus, Jung himself writes: "The most important of the symbolical statements about Christ are those which reveal the attributes of the [archetypal] hero's life: improbable origin, divine father, hazardous birth, rescue in the nick of time, precocious development, conquest of the mother and of

death, miraculous deeds, a tragic, early end, symbolically significant manner of death, post-mortem effects (reappearances, signs and marvels, etc."; see C.G. Jung, "A Psychological Approach to the Dogma of the Trinity," in *The Collected Works,* Vol. 11: *Psychology and Religion: West and East* (London: Routledge & Kegan Paul, 1958) 154-55. This illustrates Jung's reductionist understanding of the Christ as an intra-psychological reality, recognizable in the figure of Jesus and in others. Such a view is very influential, and many Christian interpreters of Jung do not maintain the uniqueness of Jesus, as does Robinson, while those who do maintain it frequently offer little reason for their decision. On the Jungian understanding of religion in general, see the convenient overview of approaches in Knitter, *No Other Name?* (1985) Ch. 4, "Common Psychic Origin," pp. 55-71. For an overview of specifically Christian understandings informed by depth psychology in this way, see Bernard J. Tyrrell SJ, *Christotherapy II: The Fasting and Feasting Heart* (Mahwah, NJ: Paulist, 1982) Ch. 5, "Principles and Methods of a Spiritual-Psychological Synthesis," in which all the major writers are mentioned. A good, "sensible" introduction to the whole field of Jung and Christianity (by an Anglican Cowley Father) is Christopher Bryant, SSJE, *Jung and the Christian Way* (London: Darton, Longman & Todd, 1983). Theorists of the increasingly popular enneagram have also written on Jesus; see Robert J. Nagosek CSC, *Nine Portraits of Jesus: Discovering Jesus Through the Enneagram* (Denville, NJ: Dimension, 1987) (surely, however, to ascribe all nine types to Jesus, or to see him as coming to incorporate all of them, is to deny his human particularity; the human task, according to enneagram theory, is to redeem the flaws of one's own type, rather than range over all the types—Robinson certainly does not deny that Jesus had only one personality type, just as he would have had only one blood type; see *The Human Face of God* [1973] 69).

⁴⁰ Robinson, "What Future for a Unique Christ?" (1987) 15-16. Robinson points out that it is not just the life of Jesus which convinces him of this, but the experience of "the *Totus Christus* filling and reconciling the entire cosmos" which integrates and incorporates "more of my experience than any other focal figures or archetypal images"; ibid. 14-15. Hans Küng is the only other writer considered in this study who attempts this sort of comparison.

[41] This issue is the subject of Robinson's book *Truth Is Two-Eyed* (1979) in which he discusses Hindu and western Christian ideas about the absolute, in conversation with Indian Christian theologians, opting as he does elsewhere for the latter.

[42] At this point an early study by Leonardo Boff bears mention. In *Jesus Christ Liberator* (1972/78) the then Franciscan priest from Brazil offered what amounts to a logos Christology with a strong interest in Jesus' historical person and his praxis in an attempt to move Christology beyond dogmatic formulae and make of it a critical, liberating discourse. Since the first edition of that work emerged in 1972 Boff has become an outspoken ecclesial critic; he was silenced by the Vatican, and has now resigned his priests' orders.

Like Rahner, Schoonenberg and Robinson he supports the "anonymous Christians" view of Christian inclusivism, echoing also the thought of Pannenberg on Christ as the fullness of the eschaton encountered proleptically. Like Schoonenberg and Robinson he does not rely on the virgin birth or the physical resurrection, offering a fine "demythologizing" of these doctrines (though his ecclesial conservatism, at the time of the first edition, prevents him from being too explicit).

In the manner of Schoonenberg and Robinson, not to mention Rahner and Teilhard, Boff regards Jesus as the highest human person and, as such, the Logos incarnate. This he supports with reference to the figure of Jesus in the gospels (with liberation theologians it is never quite the historical Jesus, as we shall further consider in the Conclusion, below). Boff's Jesus was a person "of extraordinary good sense and sound reason" and, more than that, a reformer, liberator, brother and archetype. The human condition as Boff sees it involves a utopian element uniquely realized in Jesus' praxis and resurrection. He also emphasizes the social over the personal, in a manner typical of Marx and liberation theology, and this he also finds reflected in Jesus' praxis.

The Epilogue, included in the 1978 edition during a safer period in Brazilian political life, far more thoroughly reflects a specific Latin American agenda in theology with its disdain for Christological speculation. This trend is evident in Boff's *Passion of Christ, Passion of the World* (1987) and in his books on the church (*Church, Charism and Power: Liberation Theology and the Institutional*

Church [1981] [London: SCM, 1985] and *Ecclesiogenesis: The Base Communities Reinvent the Church* [1977] [Maryknoll, NY: Orbis; London: Collins, 1986]), but this is not the case in the 1972 edition of *Jesus Christ Liberator*. There we have little of the distinctive voice of liberation theology but only "a rather contemporary Christology derivative from Europe but applicable to Latin America" (Cook, "Jesus From the Other Side of History" [1983] 269). The liberation theologians Jon Sobrino, SJ and Juan Luis Segundo, SJ will be considered in the Conclusion among a small group of writers who offer alternatives to the typology under consideration in this study, but in *Jesus Christ Liberator* Boff is not sufficiently different from others in the mainstream to warrant separate treatment alongside Sobrino and Segundo.

[43] See e.g. C.G. Jung *Collected Works*, Vol. 9, Part 1: *Archetypes and the Collective Unconscious* (Bollingen Series XX: New York, 1959). This trend to which I refer offers a Logos theology in modern dress with a decidedly eastern flavor, and hence its popularity in the less existentialist, more holistic and "new-age" revival of "spirituality" now sweeping mainstream churches in the west (cf. n. 39, above). Robinson would have shuddered, I am sure, to be numbered with this company, but at the end of the day his English empiricist and rationalist bent and his theology "from below" do not preserve him from venturing as much into popular psychology as he does elsewhere into metaphysics.

[44] This inversion of the more usual priority in English theology (radical exegesis/conservative theology, which is discussed in Cupitt, "A Sense of History" [1986]), confuses many who seek to understand Robinson.

[45] See e.g. the (obvious but nonetheless telling) criticisms to this effect in Richard, *What Are They Saying About Christianity and the World Religions?* (1981) 26; and Butterworth, "Bishop Robinson and Christology" (1975) 81ff. Butterworth thinks Robinson should make more of the *faith* of Jesus, but it appears that this is just what he *has* done with his emphasis on Jesus' response to God, along with his consequent self-consciousness and its psychological implications. Surely the question is: Has Robinson employed enough historical inquiry to substantiate his historical claims regarding this, or any other, aspect of the historical Jesus? Recall that Schoonenberg was more

explicit in his attention to Jesus' faith—James P. Mackey, among the major writers mentioned in this study, makes a similar emphasis (see n. 140 below), as do Boff and Sobrino.

This failure really to address the historical Jesus as claimed is frequently made in this study, with only Edward Schillebeeckx escaping it from a large field. But it is a valid criticism—one which the "historical skeptics" (see Chapter 9) wield mercilessly. Robinson simply does not establish that the Jesus he finds in the New Testament is any different from the Christ figure he reads off the surface of the text—nor do Küng and the liberation theologians, nor Moltmann and Rahner, nor nearly everyone else writing Christology in the last thirty years, despite the advances in historical Jesus research which many of them claim to employ.

⁴⁶ Robinson read *The Christ* after he finished *The Human Face of God*; he is particularly taken with the "enhypostasia of the Word" as Schoonenberg employs it, finding himself in considerable agreement. Nevertheless Robinson thinks he goes further than the Dutchman (109 n.44). One area in which this is certainly the case is in his unwillingness to back away from adoptionism, whereas Schoonenberg at least *claims* to avoid it (*The Christ* [1974] 93).

⁴⁷ Despite his avowed sympathies for Antioch, Robinson is also a representative of Alexandria with his emphasis upon the Logos.

⁴⁸ To be sure, Robinson has given the resurrection a more central place in his Christology than Schoonenberg, which could halt any slide toward relativism by providing him with something objective to hold onto. But the resurrection is also primarily a matter of present experience for Robinson, as we have seen. It is not that this is a bad thing, of course—Pannenberg was criticized, above, for *failing* to link the resurrection to contemporary experience. But in a case such as this, making far fewer demands upon revelation and the metaphysics of history than Pannenberg's, any hedge against falling into relativism would have helped.

⁴⁹ Meier, "Jesus among the Theologians: 1. Küng and Schillebeeckx" (1990) 36.

⁵⁰ See Kennedy, *Schillebeeckx* (1993) 17; see also Schillebeeckx's engaging essay "Dominican Spirituality" (1983).

⁵¹ Schreiter, "Edward Schillebeeckx" (1984) 626. In this spirit Schillebeeckx has never claimed any absolute certainty to ground

Christian belief (in the manner of Pannenberg, say). He learned from De Petter a view of experience as richer than reason and concept, and an appreciation of "mystery" as an unavoidable component of theology; see Schreiter, "Edward Schillebeeckx" (1989) 157-58; cf. Kennedy, *Schillebeeckx* (1993) 39-40.

[52] Schreiter sees the latter theme as the *leitmotif* of Schillebeeckx' work, though I think the God-world connection represents a more central preoccupation, of which the apologetic task is a subset; see Schreiter (1989) 630.

[53] This emphasis on *ressourcement*, on extensive historical study (*ad fontes*, "back to the sources") rather than the speculative approach of the formerly dominant Neo-Thomism, drove the first phase of renewal in twentieth century Roman Catholic theology, influencing profoundly the Second Vatican Council.

[54] Chenu supervised Schillebeeckx's doctoral thesis, published in revised form in 1952 as *De Sacramentele Heilseconomie*. Chenu was a medieval historian; it was from his book *Une Ecole de Théologie: Le Saulchoir* (1937) that Schillebeeckx drew his central conviction that dogma is shown up by the history of theology to be secondary— events and faith come first, and formularies second. "For our purposes," concludes Philip Kennedy, "this is an interesting position because it reflects the same standpoint as De Petter. Through Chenu and De Petter... Schillebeeckx was stimulated to relativize theology conceived as a conceptual system, and to place theological reflection in a historical (Chenu) and human-experiential context (De Petter)"; see Kennedy, *Schillebeeckx* (1993) 22.

[55] Meier draws attention to the highly internationalist flavor of Schillebeeckx's historical critical program, drawing as it does on German, English, Scandinavian and French exegesis; see "Jesus among the Theologians: 1. Küng and Schillebeeckx" (1990) 42.

[56] Schillebeeckx writes: "What was visible in Christ has now passed over into the sacraments of the Church"; see *Christ the Sacrament of Encounter with God* (1966) 54.

[57] Kennedy, *Schillebeeckx* (1993) 3.

[58] Founded at the University of Frankfurt in 1923, the Institute for Social Research (in exile in New York through the Nazi years), the "Frankfurt school," advocates a perpetual critical stance in the face of ideology (in particular that of Soviet Marxism with its positivism

and crude materialism) which can oppress and alienate, and hence the interest of Schillebeeckx. They also offer a critique of technocracy and mass society which has influenced the new left, and hence their interest for Hans Küng. Their theory, drawing on the early writings of Marx which they reclaim, denies that there is any value-neutral ideology or language. For an overall placing of the movement, see e.g. Terry Eagleton, *Ideology: An Introduction* (London, New York: Verso, 1991); easy access to key texts is to be found in Andrew Arato & Eike Gebhardt (eds.), *The Essential Frankfurt School Reader* (New York: Urizen, 1978).

[59] Krieg points out that Schillebeeckx is also influenced by the Frankfurt school in looking to the specific and unique features of Jesus' life rather than his life in the abstract—as subsumed under general principles of existence; see *Story-Shaped Christology* (1988) 71.

[60] It is worth noting that Schillebeeckx spent the early years of his life, and the early years of his priesthood, in a country under military occupation by an invader; as Moltmann's war experience colored his theology, so one suspects Schillebeeckx was similarly influenced in his thinking about suffering and his suspicion about idealist views of historical progress.

[61] Kennedy, *Schillebeeckx* (1993) 43. "Schillebeeckx's philosophical turnabout," according to Kennedy (127), "was an exchange of an aprioristic epistemology for an *a posteriori* theory of knowledge ... (in which) ... knowledge of reality arises in the first place in the concept of action or praxis, and in a secondary step, becomes explicitly accounted for in a process of speculation."

[62] Ramisch, "The Debate Concerning the "Historical Jesus" in the Christology of Schillebeeckx" (1984) 32-33.

[63] In addition to critical theory, Schillebeeckx was also studying Ian Ramsey, Ludwig Wittgenstein and others from the Anglo-American school of linguistic philosophy.

[64] Ibid. 31.

[65] For a detailed summary of Schillebeeckx's early work, in the context of an overall assessment of his Christology, see Scheffczyk, "Christology in the Context of Experience" (1984) 383-93.

[66] Macquarrie, *Jesus Christ in Modern Thought* (1990) 308.

[67] London: SCM, 1981.

[68] London: SCM, 1985.

[69] Details of Schillebeeckx's life story are drawn largely from overview articles by Robert Schreiter, both titled "Edward Schillebeeckx" (1984 and 1989), and from discussions in Kennedy, *Schillebeeckx* (1993). For details of his encounter with the Sacred Congregation for the Doctrine of the Faith, see the racy account by ex-Jesuit, journalist and professional Vatican-watcher Peter Hebblethwaite, in *The New Inquisition* (1980); see also Kuschel, *Born Before All Time?* (1992) 477-82. Part of Schillebeeckx's response to his accusers, as well as to the academic critics of his two big Jesus books, is found in his *Interim Report* (1980).

[70] Schreiter, "Edward Schillebeeckx" (1984) 635.

[71] Kennedy, *Schillebeeckx* (1993) 118.

[72] Kerr, "The One Who Got Away" (1993) 1300 (this is a review of Kennedy's book).

[73] Macquarrie, *Jesus Christ in Modern Thought* (1990) 308.

[74] This awareness of kerygmatic diversity provides the critical backbone of Schillebeeckx's historical program. He allows no single, primitive Jerusalem kerygma which later diversified (84), nor does he accept the Pauline "Easter kerygma" as central or original, as its subsequent prominence in the canon might indicate (110-11). Rather, he finds diverse interpretations of Jesus from the start, interacting in a complex fashion (84). Schillebeeckx embraces the approach of James Robinson and Helmut Koester in identifying four "trajectories" through earliest Christianity, all of which arise from a particular dimension of Jesus' life and person, so that all of them contain historical material (see James M. Robinson and Helmut Koester, *Trajectories Through Early Christianity* [Philadelphia: Fortress, 1971]). Confident that Jesus proclaimed the imminent reign of God, Schillebeeckx sees the *"Maranatha"* or *"Parousia"* Christology emerging, according to which Jesus is the Lord of the future who brings the approaching salvation and judgment (408). Recognizing the historical core around which the miracle tradition coalesced, while admitting the overstatement and inflation characterizing its historical elaboration, Schillebeeckx further discerns a *Theos Anér* trajectory, according to which Jesus is a divine miracle worker (this tradition was suppressed in the developing canon) (423-29). On the basis of Jesus' use of wisdom sayings and proverbs Schillebeeckx also sees a "Wisdom"

Christology arising, according to which Jesus is the incarnate bringer
and teacher of pre-existent wisdom (a trend to which St. Paul is hostile, fearing degeneration of the gospel into a mystery religion) (432).
Lastly, Schillebeeckx mentions the "Easter Christologies" which
came to dominate the gospels and Paul's epistles. This interpretation
of Jesus as the crucified and risen one appeals to Schillebeeckx as
preserving Jesus' truly human mode of existence better than the previous two, according to which Jesus can appear as a veiled God
(433-36). None of these traditions can be neglected, however, in arriving at an accurate historical appreciation of Jesus. What they all
have in common, Schillebeeckx emphasises, is the fact that Jesus *in
person* is focally important.

[75] This confidence represents a major difference between Schillebeeckx and more "suspicious" theologians, such as Dennis Nineham
and John Bowden, numbered among the "historical skeptics" in
Chapter 9. As one person might see a glass of water as half empty
and another see it as half full, so the evidence about Jesus is variously evaluated. Why this difference? Certainly in Schillebeeckx's case
no adequate Christology can be had apart from what can be historically known about Jesus, for his historically particular life and doings provide the locus of revelation, despite the recognized importance of later interpretation. For the "historical skeptics" of Chapter
9, however, as was the case for Bultmann and Tillich, this is not as
important; for them the Christ of faith as experienced by those finding new life in the church is primary.

[76] The criteria of authenticity employed by Schillebeeckx in his
uncovering of the historical Jesus do not include "negative criteria,"
because he believes such exclusion of familiar Jewish background
material robs Jesus of his context—he denies that originality is as
important as those would have it who employ this criterion (90). The
"positive criteria" he uses include and combine the following features: a) the incorporation willy-nilly by redactors of elements which
do not fit in—these could represent revered traditions (91-92); b) the
dual irreducibility criterion of Bultmann and Conzelmann, though
used positively (whereby anything which cannot be accounted for in
terms of Jewish thinking or later Church belief is to be deemed authentic) (93-94); c) cross section, whereby elements found in a range
of places in the New Testament are probably authentic (though

Schillebeeckx does not hold to the inverse of this, that single attestation renders historicity unlikely) (95); d) consistency of content, in terms of the relation of parts to the evolving whole (96); and e) the "execution" criterion, according to which the fact that Jesus annoyed people enough to warrant execution must tell us something about what he did (97). It is noteworthy that Schillebeeckx rejects the search for Aramaisms or Palestinian local color; nor does he believe distinctiveness is a primary criterion for evaluating the authenticity of parables (98-99). He does not trust "but I say to you" statements as necessarily historical, but he does accept the "abba" usage, though not every time (100).

[77] A similar reality is testified to in the other kerygmatic trajectories (those without explicit Easter faith), though he admits that the resurrection kerygma may have grown to prominence in the canonical process because it aptly articulated what the others were trying to say (396).

[78] Schillebeeckx notes the pre-Pauline antiquity of the Peter tradition in claiming this, also making much of Peter's designation as "the rock" and such other fragments as Luke 22:32: "Simon—when you have turned again, strengthen my disciples" (389).

[79] Cf. Schillebeeckx, *Interim Report* (1980) 79. Philip Kennedy is more insistent than I think is justifiable concerning Schillebeeckx's commitment to the corporeality of Jesus' resurrection; see *Schillebeeckx* (1993) 116.

[80] On p. 48 in *Jesus*, Schillebeeckx offers a discussion similar to that offered by Nineham in his "New Testament Interpretation in an Historical Age" (1976) 155, emphasizing the difference between ancient and modern worldviews: see the reference at Part IV, n. 16, below. But Schillebeeckx thinks such differences, while real, do not preclude talk of the human condition, or of the continuity across history of the selfsame Christian experience.

[81] This is similar to the stance of David Tracy; see *Plurality and Ambiguity* (1987).

[82] Schillebeeckx also allows that Jesus himself has made a contribution to any adequate definition of the human. So Schillebeeckx is not simply seeking to fit Jesus to what can already be known about the human, as if that were all there is to it. Rather, he sees Jesus as questioning our idea of normal humanity (630). But it remains un-

clear whether this is a matter of "qualitative" distinction or merely "quantitative"—Jesus cannot be allowed to skew the definition of what it is to be human too much, or else he cannot be seen to have fulfilled or completed our humanity in any meaningful way. So at worst such claims are misleading, while at best they are simply restating in other terms the claim that Jesus fulfills our human condition.

[83] There is a place carved out here for the ecclesial institution in the life of the world, seen as an essential outworking of Jesus' salvific work. This is in keeping with Schillebeeckx's early writing on the Church's sacraments as liberating encounters with the living Christ; see *Christ the Sacrament of Encounter with God* (1963). He makes more of the institutional component of human salvation in his next book *Christ* (1979).

[84] To this Schillebeeckx adds a touch of *theologia crucis*, asserting that Jesus' cross is "the definitive and supreme revelation of God," at which point Jesus "reached the lowest depths of the human condition, and at the same time lived through his inviolable affinity with God" (651). "This belonging to God in an anti-Godly situation," Schillebeeckx claims, "serves to effect our salvation" (652).

[85] To make sure we have not slipped too enthusiastically into a theology "from below," forgetting the theory of immanent divine action and revelation through the events and faith interpretation of Jesus' life (including the resurrection) which he has sought to keep before us throughout the book, Schillebeeckx concludes his discussion with a high claim for God's definitive action in Jesus. "Deeper than the *Abba* experience... and its ground," he writes, "is the Word of God, the self-communication of the Father. This signifies some such thing as a 'hypostatic identification' without *anhypostasis*: this man, Jesus, within the human confines of a (psychologically and ontologically) personal-cum-human mode of being, is identical with the Son... the 'Second Person' coming to self-consciousness and shared humanity in Jesus" (666).

Kuschel wishes that Schillebeeckx had avoided this too-fragmentary attempt at Christological synthesis offered at the end of *Jesus*, pointing out that Schillebeeckx subsequently retreated from such attempts at blending biblical and patristic notions, preferring to stick with biblical ones in *Christ* and in his *Interim Report*; see Kuschel, *Born Before All Time?* (1992) 470-77.

⁸⁶ This call for an ethic of worldwide responsibility is more thoroughly worked out by Hans Küng; see his *Global Responsibility* (1991).

⁸⁷ What he does offer here, however, is a long discussion of suffering as it is understood in a variety of cultures and time frames. Its sheer universality and ubiquity, and the frequency with which non-dualistic responses have been conceived within the world religions and major philosophies, indicate to Schillebeeckx that there is a reasonably uniform phenomenon of human suffering admitting of a universal solution (which he finds in the Christ event). In compressed fashion (672-723) Schillebeeckx addresses suffering as it has been understood in the world religions as well as among the Greeks and Romans. He rejects attempts by Stoics and by enlightenment thinkers before Voltaire and Kant to rationalize suffering theoretically (704), affirming instead the Marxist drive to overturn it. Apart from the spirituality of suffering which has grown to prominence in some expressions of Christianity, a spirituality he condemns, Schillebeeckx favors what he takes to be the central Christian message about suffering: Christianity offers "no dualism, no dolorism, no theories about illusion—suffering is suffering and inhuman—however, there is more, namely God, as he shows himself in Jesus Christ" (699). Schillebeeckx will make no peace with suffering, allowing it no place within an acceptable Christian worldview—this he has learned from the Frankfurt school and their critical theory. Nor does he naively claim that suffering has been overcome, and in this he echoes Moltmann's skeptical assessment of our human lot. "For in our history," he writes, "I know redemption only in fragments which are experienced personally and collectively; in which, however, Jesus remains the critical and productive promise of an indefinable definitive future salvation. Nowhere do I see signs of an 'objectively completed' redemption" (25).

⁸⁸ When Schillebeeckx embraces Levinas' point that "I-thou" is inadequate without a "he," without society, might he be seeking to broaden the highly personalist philosophy favored by Pope John Paul II, from whose conservative pontificate we might expect him to have developed some critical distance?

⁸⁹ To be sure, the uniqueness and finality of Jesus is unverifiable, though Schillebeeckx is at greater pains in this volume to insist that

more than the rhetoric of faith is at work in Christian uniqueness claims. And the truth will be known fully only at the end of history—this is a refinement of Schillebeeckx's earlier commitment to eschatological verification (174), recalling Pannenberg's appeal to Dilthey over our inability to make thorough historical assessments in advance of history's end (i.e. when all the facts are in). This truth must be available to some extent in advance, if it is to remain believable. Schillebeeckx thus revisits his earlier claims that the experienced efficacy of the power of Christ from God, and evidence that it is taken seriously in the church, are necessary precursors to the acceptance of that belief—that it really *does* work in the concrete, that it is not merely an abstract idea (168, 173).

[90] Such universal action is a matter of particular emphasis in this book, in which the action of God outside the Church is highlighted. "Salvation from God," writes Schillebeeckx, recalling Rahner, "comes first of all in the worldly reality of history, and not primarily in the consciousness of believers who are aware of it" (12). For Schillebeeckx this is why the church is necessary—to bring this depth dimension of history to light: "Churches are the places where salvation from God is thematized or put into words, confessed explicitly, proclaimed prophetically and celebrated liturgically" (13). This involves the claim that salvation history is nothing but the history of human liberation, though it is not always recognized as such.

[91] In his *Interim Report* (1980) Schillebeeckx recalls the arguments for Jesus' uniqueness offered by Karl Rahner in describing Jesus as "the man in whom the task of creation has been successfully accomplished" (111). Elsewhere in the book he writes, "In the last resort Jesus, whom we may call God's only beloved Son, is also a human being just like you and me—except that he is even more human" (139). This point about Jesus' humanity being "fuller" than everyone else's is implicit in the two big Jesus books, but nowhere as explicit as it is here.

[92] Schillebeeckx, "Answer" (to the CDF) (1977) 150-51.

[93] Meier, "Jesus among the Theologians: 1. Küng and Schillebeeckx" (1990) 40-41. Meier affirms Schillebeeckx over the choice of historical criteria used in his investigations, including the rejection of a search for Aramaisms underlying the gospel texts (as in Jeremias and Matthew Black) and unquestioned reliance on the historicity of

parables, which were not as uncommon in Jewish usage as some have thought. Schillebeeckx is also praised for insisting that Jesus' offensiveness, sufficient to have him killed by his enemies, must be allowed as an element of any valid historical reconstruction (Meier believes "historical Jesuses" are often too non-threatening to account for this) (ibid. 42-43). Schillebeeckx is also praised for his recognition of Christological plurality in the New Testament, while retaining his "truly Catholic" link between the Jesus of history and the Christ of faith (ibid. 44-45).

[94] Ibid. 45.

[95] Schreiter, "Schillebeeckx" (1989) 161.

[96] With regard to the Q document Meier is far more skeptical than Schillebeeckx about what can be known. He dismisses the "Q community" hypothesis, upon which aspects of Schillebeeckx's argument depend (based as it is upon the reconstructions of Siegfried Schulz), as "an academic phantom, for there is no solid empirical evidence that such a community with such a limited kerygma ever existed"; see Meier, art. cit. 46.

Schillebeeckx appears to rely on the Q document to provide a "high," early Christology which does not rely upon the resurrection (Küng, "How Does One Do Christian Theology?" [1988] 114); in this he is like Robinson, whose hypothesis concerning the priority of John's gospel appears to serve a similar purpose in declaring a high, ontological Christology to have been in place at an early date.

As for the Christological titles as they appear in Schillebeeckx's study, Meier is suspicious that the *theos anér* figure as it emerges from the radical Marcan studies of Theodor Weeden is too rare among first century references to miracle workers to bear the weight Schillebeeckx places on it. The pivotal image for Schillebeeckx is, of course, Jesus as eschatological prophet, but the prominence of this figure is also disputed by Meier. He argues that this is not an important image in first century Judaism, basing his claims here on a study by Richard Horsley, "Like One of the Prophets of Old: Two Types of Popular Prophets at the Time of Jesus," *Catholic Biblical Quarterly* 47 (1985) 435-63, esp. 437-43; see Meier, art. cit. 45-46.

[97] See n. 22 to the Introduction, above, in which various titles are listed.

[98] Schillebeeckx, *Interim Report* (1980) 2.

[99] O'Collins, *What Are They Saying About Jesus?* (1983) 59.

[100] Ruether, *To Change the World* (1981) 2.

[101] Nevertheless, such a reading is not thought to fit into a New Testament world colored by apocalyptic and other forms of pre-modern thought. "I seriously doubt," writes Dupré, "whether the early Christians understood the *metanoia* as a summons to structural changes in society" (Dupré, "Experience and Interpretation" [1982] 51). The extent to which Schillebeeckx is as bad at this point as Dupré would have it is questionable, however. So, for instance, in *Christ* (563) Schillebeeckx recognizes just how strange is this idea of social transformation in the New Testament world, though he believes that it is incipient and will develop further. St. Paul's attitude to the institution of slavery in the Epistle to Philemon is the instance Schillebeeckx offers of an incipient early Christian social critique.

[102] Richard, *What Are They Saying About Christianity and the World Religions?* (1981) 61.

[103] Kennedy, *Schillebeeckx* (1993) 117.

[104] What of the resurrection in Schillebeeckx's program? The trend among critics is to find Schillebeeckx's project lacking in this area. John P. Meier, Gerald O'Collins, James Mackey and John Macquarrie all wonder what *event* would have been necessary to spark off the conversion experience which, according to Schillebeeckx, swept up Peter and the other disciples after the death of Jesus—"The whole thing sounds too much like an academic consensus reached after discussion in a German university seminar," concludes Meier (Meier, "Jesus among the Theologians: 1. Küng and Schillebeeckx" [1990] 46; see also O'Collins, *What Are They Saying About Jesus?* [1983] 61; Mackey, *Modern Theology* [1987] 69-70; Macquarrie, *Jesus Christ in Modern Thought* [1990] 311-12). This recalls the critique of Pannenberg from Chapter 5, where the roots of his resurrection belief were questioned (though in Pannenberg's case the challenge was more pointed, given his insistence that the resurrection was an historical event, rather than a meta-historical reality as claimed by Schillebeeckx).

[105] This criticism is leveled in Vandervelde, "Creation and Cross in the Christology of Edward Schillebeeckx" (1983) and Fackre, "Bones Strong and Weak in the Skeletal Structure of Schillebeeckx's Christology" (1984).

It has been argued that lostness and alienation, guilt and despair have been lit upon by existentialists as characteristic of humanity, while in reality they may only be characteristic of depressed post-war Europeans, and so deserving of no wider recognition than the cultural orbit of these existentialists themselves. Nevertheless there does seem to be something more fundamental than suffering in human life. Schillebeeckx admits this by listing the anthropological constants which fix humanity in an embodied, historical, social world, with suffering construed as something of a secondary phenomenon, in the sense that it results from the breakdown of the anthropological constants, which are the primary determinants of human being. I would think, however, that suffering is really a *tertiary* phenomenon, with the fact and circumstances of the breakdown of these primary anthropological constants constituting the secondary phenomenon. So things like guilt and alienation are thus rendered explicable with reference to Schillebeeckx's identification of the fundamental human norms they undermine, so that only through such secondary human realities as guilt and alienation does suffering arise. But it is a less fundamental reality, tertiary rather than secondary, and certainly not primary.

Schillebeeckx is steeped in the resistance to suffering characteristic of the critical theory which he prizes so highly. This recognition supports his resistance to the traditional Catholic mysticism of suffering which so devalues both the natural, created, limited state of humans in the world (which he seeks to affirm, as is evident through his choice of anthropological constants) and the actual life of Jesus, which he wishes also to affirm in the light of those who rush either to the cross or the resurrection to find a center to the variegate New Testament witness. Yet one can avoid these pitfalls without feeling one must avoid Jesus' death—after all, we have seen Jürgen Moltmann walk this particular tightrope.

[106] Ramisch, "The Debate Concerning the Historical Jesus in the Christology of Edward Schillebeeckx" (1984) 46.

[107] This is the criticism offered by John Galvin in his essay "The Death of Jesus in the Theology of Edward Schillebeeckx" (1983/4).

[108] This difference is in spite of Küng's own favorable assessment of Schillebeeckx's program as being largely in step with his own; see Küng, "How Does One Do Christian Theology?" (1988).

[109] Richard, *What Are They Saying About Christianity and the World Religions?* (1981) 42.

[110] A number of the biographical details in the following pages are drawn from two overview articles: Swidler, "Hans Küng" (1984), especially 710-17; and Jeanrond, "Hans Küng" (1989) 164-72.

[111] *Justification, la doctrine de Karl Barth et une réflexion catholique*, a thesis completed under Louis Bouyer and published in Switzerland by von Balthasar (who later joined Küng's virulent conservative opponents) in 1957. It is available in English as *Justification: The Doctrine of Karl Barth and a Catholic Reflection* (ET 1964) (London: Search, 1968).

[112] Küng, *The Church* (1967) (London: Search, 1968); *Infallible: An Enquiry* (1970, ET 1971) (London: Collins, 1972).

[113] Details of the Küng controversy are to be found in Peter Hebblethwaite, *The New Inquisition?* (1980), including the text of Küng's hurried appeal (163-65). This appeal was considered at Castelgandolfo after Christmas in 1979 in the presence of Pope John Paul II and Küng's ordinary, Bishop Moser of Rottenburg, despite whose offices it was rejected (Küng had no cardinals to support him, as on previous occasions). The account of Küng's battle with Rome is more thorough in the article "Hans Küng" by Swidler (1984), who draws on his book *Küng in Conflict* (New York: Doubleday, 1981) (which, in addition, reproduces a large amount of the key documentation).

[114] Swidler, "Hans Küng" (1984) 721-22.

[115] Jeanrond, "Hans Küng" (1989) 171.

[116] Küng, "Theology on the Way to a New Paradigm: Reflections on My Own Career" (1988) 187-88.

[117] The strong dependence of Küng on the thought of Hegel is evident from the large study of Hegel's thought entitled *The Incarnation of God* (1970, ET 1987) in which the nature of God is reconceived along more panentheistic lines (this theme, set out particularly in Ch. 8 of the book, forms the major plank of Küng's response to modern atheism in *Does God Exist?*). This eighth chapter, "Prolegomena to a Future Christology" (497-508), also contains the Christological outline which Küng follows in *On Being a Christian*.

[118] This understanding undergirds an approach which is in the widest sense "ecumenical," for Küng's constant desire is to find agreement between positions and persons formerly thought to be ir-

394 IS JESUS UNIQUE?

reconcilably opposed. Latterly, this abiding preoccupation has been enhanced by Küng's struggle for peace and justice, in particular through the fostering of inter-religious peace and understanding; see e.g. *Christianity and the World Religions* (1985) and *Global Responsibility* (1990), as well as the new series of books on particular world religions now beginning to emerge.

[119] Küng, art. cit. 199.

[120] Ibid. 193.

[121] He does not see suffering as a total evil, recognizing (as one must if one is realistic) that persons can mature through suffering with the right help (579). This is an insight that Schillebeeckx is reluctant to admit, perhaps because it implies that suffering is attitudinal, and hence not as primary as he suggests; see my observations in n. 105, above, about the non-centrality of suffering.

[122] Küng is not without post-enlightenment insight, however; he recognizes, for instance, that tradition and diverse cultural experience have a part to play in molding the human (540-41), in the same way that human religious experience is only mediated through the concrete world of the religions (96). Nevertheless, Küng stands for the "late modern" rather than "post-modern" reading of the present cultural situation in the west, insofar as he admits of no radical deconstruction of the self in the light of historical and cultural diversity, nor of any post-historical flight from the quest for overarching meaning. With this platform, however (no doubt the most reasonable in the face of dilletantish claims for total deconstruction of everything coming from an extensive, radical post-modern lobby in the humanities), goes Küng's failure to deeply engage with the radical pluralists and post-modern atheists in his apologetic work *Does God Exist?* (1976), which was its greatest weakness.

[123] Jesus' particular freedom was a theme in 1960s' secular theology. Käsemann emphasized the freedom of Jesus from the law and religious constraint (offering a spirituality, however, which verges on non-ecclesial Christian individualism); see *Jesus Means Freedom* (1968) (London, SCM; Philadelphia, Fortress, 1969); see also Paul van Buren, *The Secular Meaning of the Gospel* (New York: Macmillan, 1963).

[124] Regarding historical access to Jesus, Küng opts for a middle ground between credulity and hypercritical skepticism, describing "the *Jesus tradition* historically as *relatively reliable*" (157). Not

only do we know comparably more about the historical Jesus than we do about the founders of the Asian religions, according to Küng, but there was less of a gap between the events and their incorporation in texts than was the case concerning other religions and their founders (147). In addition he points out that the texts are very well attested, with the Dead Sea Scrolls confirming most ancient extant manuscripts (147-48).

Küng declares important various criteria of historicity (though we will be led to question just how important they really are for him, whose approach is nowhere near as careful in this regard as that of Schillebeeckx). He affirms the criterion of dissimilarity while recognizing the danger of severing Jesus from his environment (158). He shies away from an overdependence on authentic Jesus material, too, believing that the interpretative portraits provided by the evangelists may be just as disclosive of the real Jesus (159). It occurs to me that this might be at the root of his failing to offer reasons for historical claims concerning Jesus: in effect he is overriding the usual criteria of historicity with this conviction that everything in the gospels might be just as good historically. Such an approach will not guarantee accuracy at the level of fine detail, but it will allow access to the *ipsissima vox* of Jesus if not the *ipsissima verba*: he believes we can still have access to "the peculiar forms of behaviour, the typical basic trends, the clearly dominating factors" (159). He is skeptical of focusing on Jesus' titles, even that of the Son of Man (290), while maintaining that even the eschewing of titles tells us something about the history of Jesus while heightening the mystery of his person (291). In this he is in agreement with Schillebeeckx, with whom he also employs the "execution criterion" whereby Jesus' behavior had to be sufficiently radical and disruptive for people to have become murderously angry with him (291). Yet unlike Schillebeeckx he values Jesus' "I say to you" formulae, thinking them to be authentic and distinctive (317).

[125] As for miracles, Küng thinks them unlikely and makes belief in them optional. Clearly, they do not contribute to his argument for Jesus' uniqueness and finality. This is true for the virginal conception of Jesus (453-55), as for the healing and nature miracles, though Küng does believe that there were healings of psychosomatic disorders (230) and in historical remembrances behind the nature miracle accounts

(231). Overall, however, all accounts of miracles provide indications rather than proofs—Küng quotes John, for whom it is better not to have seen, and yet believe (237). Although he is no liberal reductionist, nevertheless Küng is rationalistically motivated touching this issue.

[126] Küng is clear in *On Being a Christian* that other religions can be affirmed without being believed, and that their adherents are saved, if at all, *in spite* of their beliefs rather than through them: "They will be saved, not because of, but in spite of polytheism, magic, human sacrifice, forces of nature. They will be saved, not because of, but in spite of all untruth and superstition" (104). He is also well known for his opinion that Asian religions are unable to survive and give spiritual leadership in a world increasingly embracing the linear historical understanding of history, change and progress which has its paternity and proper home in the world of Judaeo-Christian experience; modern technological civilization and eastern ideas of the unreality of the world are simply incompatible, according to Küng (108). Küng sees the world religions as fatally sunk in "unhistoricity, circular thinking, fatalism, unworldliness, pessimism, passivity, caste spirit, social disinterestedness" (Knitter, *No Other Name?* [1985] 133). Thus Küng seeks a path between arrogant absolutism and weak eclecticism, "claiming for Christianity *not exclusiveness, but certainly uniqueness*" (112).

[127] Küng's attitudes toward the world religions have shifted somewhat since *On Being a Christian*. I have discussed this elsewhere: see my article "Hans Küng and the World Religions: The Emergence of a Pluralist" (1989). Rather than revisit this same ground at any length, I will briefly sketch the more recent developments. The move away from his position in *On Being a Christian*, in which Küng taught that Christ was norm and critical standard among the religions, has been toward a position which I call "modified pragmatism" whereby religions are assessed according to their basic humanity, then the extent to which they are in touch with their own essence and origins—their consistency—after which come intra-religious criteria, which are binding within each particular religion (see Küng, "What Is True Religion?" [1987], also "Is There One True Religion?" [1988]). This shift struck me when I wrote the article (in 1987) as a declaration that Küng had indeed "crossed the Rubicon" and embraced a pluralist position, as Knitter had challenged him to

do (see Knitter, "Hans Küng's Theological Rubicon" [1987]), for this new threefold criteriology clearly meant that the normativity of Christ for all religions had been surrendered, becoming no more than a "normativity for Christians" such as we will find in the work of John Hick. Alan Race disagreed with my assessment, however (see Race's letter to the editor in *Theology* 92 (1989) 296-97), with Küng himself muddying the waters in a 1989 article in which a clear position is quite indiscernible (see Küng, "Ecumenism and Truth" [1989]). Whatever his position, however, Küng maintains his willingness to compare religions and his readiness to declare one better than another on humanitarian grounds, as well as on grounds of consistency. This is bold and distinctive in the face of those who fear offending anyone in the pluralistic marketplace; Küng has not abandoned this method, even though his criteria for religious truth have broadened somewhat (becoming less Christocentric) since *On Being a Christian*.

[128] A close summary of Küng's views is found in Galvin, "The Resurrection of Jesus in Contemporary Catholic Systematics" (1979) 132-33.

[129] It goes without saying that Küng declares the empty tomb tradition to be secondary and supportive of the appearance tradition, offering no "proof" (364-66). But he does not dwell on the experiences and the faith which *preceded* the appearances, as does Schillebeeckx, whom we saw declaring the appearances secondary (nor, by the way, does he accept with Schillebeeckx the possibility of an early cult at the tomb of Jesus [342]).

[130] Küng has been criticized, essentially, for committing the genetic fallacy by looking for the essence of Christianity purely in its origins with the historical Jesus (Chirico, "Hans Küng's Christology" [1979] 265-68; cf. the denial that history gives privileged access to Jesus, above and beyond that offered through faith, which is found in O'Collins, *What Are They Saying About Jesus?* [1983] 77). Küng's assessment of the resurrection as containing no additional revelation beyond that available in Jesus' life is also criticized (ibid. 268-70). The former criticism recalls that of van Beeck, directed at the excessive historicism of Pannenberg (which we encountered in Chapter 5) in favor of more space being given to contemporary Christian experience. To be fair to Küng, however, it is by no means merely the his-

torical Jesus upon which his uniqueness case rests but also the unique impact of Jesus, which is clearly a matter of contemporary experience. As for the non-revelational nature of the resurrection, this is surely a matter of hair-splitting; Küng's point is that the resurrection is a radicalizing of belief in God and Christ, rather than an addition to it, but he nowhere denies that the resurrection is not separate and in addition to the life of Jesus, as Bultmann does. We might say that the resurrection, for Küng, is the *medium* through which Jesus' uniqueness is revealed, rather than the content of that revelation.

[131] Ruether, *To Change the World* (1981) 2-3.

[132] Cf. O'Collins, *What Are They Saying About Jesus?* (1983) 25.

[133] Meier, "Jesus among the Theologians: 1. Küng and Schillebeeckx" (1990) 36-38. Meier also accuses Küng of inconsistency in linking the historical Jesus with the Christ of faith—while claiming that this is what he does, Küng's focus upon historical reconstruction behind the text gives the lie to his formal position here (ibid. 39). Yet the effective failure of Küng to make this distinction in practice has been noted. Meier is not convinced that Küng has brought off what he takes to be an attempted higher synthesis of faith and reason in his joint reliance on the Christ of faith and the Jesus of the new quest: "the marriage of Bornkamm's Jesus to post-Vatican II theology remains a shotgun wedding" (ibid. 40).

[134] Knitter, "World Religions and the Finality of Christ" (1981) esp. 204-05; cf. his comparison of Jesus with the Buddha in Knitter, "Horizons on Christianity's New Dialogue with Buddhism" *Horizons* 8 (1981) 40-61, in which (57) he refers to Roy C. Amore, *Two Masters, One Message: The Lives and Teachings of Gautama and Jesus* (Nashville, TN: Abingdon, 1978). These views are discussed by William M. Thompson in his survey volume *The Jesus Debate* (1985) 386-88, who himself offers a strange kenotic view of Jesus' uniqueness as real but hidden (388-94)—a cross between Knitter's "complementary uniqueness" (see the discussion in Chapter 10) and the "eschatological uniqueness" case of Moltmann. Knitter's point is echoed in Hick, "Jesus and the World Religions" (1977) 176.

[135] Tracy, *Blessed Rage for Order* (1988) 234 n.94.

[136] O'Collins, *What Are They Saying About Jesus?* (1983) 38. Recall that Robinson is the only other writer discussed in this study who attempts such a comparison.

¹³⁷ Richard, *What Are They Saying About Christianity and the World Religions?* (1981) 43.

¹³⁸ Meier, "Jesus among the Theologians: 1. Küng and Schillebeeckx" (1990) 38. The books in question are, of course, Bornkamm, *Jesus of Nazareth* (1956, 3rd ed. 1959, ET 1960) (London: Hodder & Stoughton, 1973), and Käsemann, *Jesus Means Freedom* (1968) (London: SCM, 1969).

¹³⁹ Chirico, "Hans Küng's Christology" (1979) 256; cf. Meier, art. cit. 37, who makes a similar concession despite his own major criticisms.

¹⁴⁰ British Roman Catholic theologian James P. Mackey (a laicized priest who is now Professor and Dean in the Protestant divinity faculty at the University of Edinburgh), in *Jesus the Man and the Myth* (1979), builds his uniqueness case on Jesus' impact, rooted in his special person and work.

Mackey begins with a strong case for the historical Jesus' accessibility through the myth of Jesus Christ (Ch. 1), arguing that history and myth are uniquely powerful tools of human knowing (cf. his *Modern Theology* [1987] on Gadamer concerning the role of tradition in forming identity [14-18]). Mackey finds in the myth of Jesus Christ a unique balm for the human person, the nature of which he conceives in primarily Heideggerian terms (though incorporating the ideas of Merleau-Ponty on "bodily knowing"). These ideas (which are further developed by Jacques Lacan and Julia Kristeva) provide a powerful hedge against the total cultural relativism of post-modernity, though they are not to be found in either Schillebeeckx or Küng. Mackey finds a stable human condition disclosed in recurring transcultural images of varying depth related to universal experiences of embodiedness and embededness within the structures of the natural; writes Mackey, "We all need to breathe, and to eat and drink, and to practice some form of hygiene, no matter how elementary, and to breed, and to maintain some form of regularity in the internal relationships that exist between ourselves and our fellow humans and the good earth we all share.... A great variety of images originates in these vital ties ... and because of recurring patterns that are so widespread, these images acquire a certain universality of meaning despite the particularity of their concrete details" (*Jesus the Man and the Myth*, 77; cf. *Modern Theology*, 11-14). Here the existential emphasis on guilt and abandonment, enslavement and powerlessness which were absent from Schillebeeckx are to be found: "the symbols which are used to express the significance of Jesus' death...are all powerfully evocative of the fragile and decaying side of our experience of life" (ibid. 80).

For Mackey, these images are focused in the person of Jesus because that person is a living reality of Christian experience (this is how he interprets the resurrection). Drawing upon the exegesis of James D.G. Dunn (*Jesus and the Spirit* [London: SCM, 1975]) and Ingo Hermann (*Kyrios und Pneuma* [Munich: Kösel, 1961]) Mackey interprets the resurrection in even more experiential and vocational terms than did either Schillebeeckx or Küng, understanding the risen Christ, as in St. Paul primarily, as the very Spirit of God. This reality Christians experience not "by any physical seeing or touching of the bodily Jesus...but by the experience of his power in our lives which these [New Testament] writers so vividly described long ago, and which can alone convince us today that Jesus lives and reigns" (ibid. 112). So without any dependence on miracles as proof (ibid. 154ff) Mackey declares the resurrection to be the experience of life as a whole and other people as a gift, in the same way that they were for Jesus—this Mackey clearly sees in Jesus' parables, table fellowship, good works and "deeds of power" (whatever they were), and in his own faith. The sheer forcefulness of this faith as it is both experienced now by Christians and recovered from historical research into Jesus' person marks Jesus out as quantitatively stronger and more impressive than others: "Most of us prove to be of little or no significance for others principally because our own identities are dispersed and fluctuating. They are due more to accident than to design....On the contrary, there are those who gradually forge such a strong identity for themselves that even death seals their identity with its own awful finality. The identity of Jesus which makes him of such supreme significance for others was forged by...his obedience, and what we understand as his faith" (ibid. 258-9).

It is conceivable, however, that a relativist like Knitter could incorporate all Mackey has said about Jesus into his own scheme of merely "complementary uniqueness" (see the discussion of Knitter in Chapter 10).

PART IV: RADICAL

[1] Preston, "Need Dr. Nineham Be So Negative?" (1979) 276.

[2] Nineham, *Saint Mark* (1969) 49 n. *.

[3] Morgan, "Historical Criticism and Christology" (1982) 80.

[4] Nineham, "What Happened to the New Reformation?" (1988) 153.

[5] Cupitt, "A Sense of History" (1986) 365-66.

[6] Nineham, *The Use and Abuse of the Bible* (1976) 223.

[7] Ibid. 235.

[8] Rodwell, "Relativism in Science and Theology" (1979) 216.

[9] See the first draft of Hick's essay in *The Myth of God Incarnate*, as Nineham reports in his "Epilogue" (1977) 187.

[10] Cf. Carnley, "The Poverty of Historical Scepticism" (1972).

[11] Nineham, "New Testament Interpretation in an Historical Age" (1976) 147ff.

[12] Nineham, *The Use and Abuse of the Bible* (1976) 10-11. He identifies the discovery of this problem with German idealists and romantics like Goethe and Spengler and notions of a *Zeitgeist* or a *Volksgeist* (ibid. 15ff). His favorite exponent of such views is Ernst Troeltsch, for whom culture forms *eine Totalität*, while from our own century he mentions the anthropological insights of Malinowski concerning Trobriand Islanders and those of Evans-Pritchard gleaned among the Azande (see n. 11, above).

[13] Cf. Mackey on "bodily knowing"; see n. 140 in Part III.

[14] Nineham, *The Use and Abuse of the Bible* (1976) 6; "New Testament Interpretation in an Historical Age" (1976) 148; "Individual Essay" (1976) 81.

[15] Nineham, e.g. *The Use and Abuse of the Bible* (1976) 101.

[16] Nineham, e.g. "New Testament Interpretation in an Historical Age" (1976) 155.

[17] Nineham, *The Use and Abuse of the Bible* (1976) 116-17; "Individual Essay" (1976) 80; "God Incarnate: Why 'Myth'?" (1979) 45-46.

[18] Nineham, *The Use and Abuse of the Bible* (1976) 32-33.

[19] Ibid. Ch. 2.

[20] Nineham, *Saint Mark* (1969) 43-48.

[21] Ibid. 20.

[22] Ibid. 21, 23.

²³ Nineham, *The Use and Abuse of the Bible* (1976) 187-88.

²⁴ Ibid. 164, 162; cf. Wiles, "Looking into the Sun" (1969) 156; Young, "A Cloud of Witnesses" (1977) 40-41.

²⁵ Ibid. 109ff.

²⁶ Ibid. 28.

²⁷ Nineham, "Individual Essay" (1976) 84.

²⁸ Nineham, "New Testament Interpretation in an Historical Age" (1976) 164.

²⁹ Nineham, *The Use and Abuse of the Bible* (1976) 168-69.

³⁰ Nineham, "Individual Essay" (1976) 78-79.

³¹ Nineham, "Schweitzer Revisited" (1977) 119.

³² Nineham, "Response" to David L. Edwards (1989) 302.

³³ Nineham, *The Use and Abuse of the Bible* (1976) 174, 220; "History and the Gospel" (1977) 88.

³⁴ Nineham, "God Incarnate: Why 'Myth'?" (1979) 64.

³⁵ Nineham, "Individual Essay" (1976) 79.

³⁶ Nineham, *The Use and Abuse of the Bible* (1976) 196; "New Testament Interpretation in an Historical Age" (1976) 162-63; *Explorations in Theology 1* (1977) 4-5; "What Happened to the New Reformation?" (1988) passim; "Individual Essay" (1976) 87-88.

³⁷ Barton admits, however, that while some features of human life have changed a lot over time, like our western notions of love in general since romantic, sexual love arose in the middle ages, certain other things have remained more or less the same, such as our experience of guilt in the west from St. Paul to St. Augustine (108). Although Barton does not do so, it would be possible to argue for a deep, more general invariance once the fact of such invariance in particular instances has been admitted.

³⁸ The incommensurability of world-views is often illustrated by "Wittgensteinian pictures" like the duck-rabbit, or the one in which a perceiver sees either two opposed faces on a white background or else a chalice on a black background. These instances are not conclusive, however, for the simple reason that once one has seen the picture in both ways one can then switch more or less at will thereafter, thus showing that one participates in both world-views (193). And although it has been pointed out that only one of the two perceptions is ever available at once, so that one must switch between them in successive instances of consciousness, nevertheless the perceiver *can*

have access to both worlds. The fact that only a temporal delay is involved perhaps illustrates that the relativist problem, while real, is only a minor one.

[39] Edwards, *Tradition and Truth* (1989) 199.

[40] Newlands, "G.M. Newlands on *The Myth of God Incarnate*" (1980) 190.

[41] I will confine myself to this, as little is added by the more recent dialogue in Edwards' book *Tradition and Truth* (1989) 169-90, 291-96.

[42] Looking to the history of Jesus to establish his uniqueness is blamed on doctrinal necessity in a post-metaphysical age and declared historically bankrupt by another radical English priest, Graham Shaw, in his attack upon authoritarianism and manipulativeness in the church (largely a New Testament study—and published by Bowden!) entitled *The Cost of Authority* (1983) 273-74.

[43] Sanders, in his seminal work *Jesus and Judaism* (London: SCM, 1985), challenges the new quest and subsequent use of the bible in recent theology. He presents Jesus as an apocalyptic prophet, albeit friendly to Jewish law and religion, and not the religious reformer and advocate of freedom favored by the major scholarly (and popular) consensus.

[44] Oxford: Clarendon, 1964.

[45] See e.g. Pelikan, *Jesus Through the Centuries* (1985); Cupitt, "One Jesus, Many Christs" (1972).

[46] Thiessen—London: SCM & Philadelphia: Fortress, 1979; Toynbee—London: SCM, 2nd ed. 1982.

[47] Their close similarity is especially evident from Wiles, "Christology in an Age of Historical Studies" (1979).

[48] Brown, *Continental Philosophy and Modern Theology* (1987) 61.

[49] Prusak, "The Son of Man Came Eating and Drinking" (1980) 5.

[50] Wiles, "Christian Doctrine in the 1960s" (1970).

[51] Wiles' article is criticized for demonstrating puzzlement over the full force of theologies of the word: see Stephen Sykes, "Germany and England" (1982) 162 n.4. In most other places, however, Wiles seems to appreciate not only the traditional Anglican emphasis on the incarnation and the *person* of Christ but also the Protestant emphasis on redemption and the *work* of Christ, thereby drawing the sting of Sykes' criticism.

[52] Wiles, "Does Christology Rest on a Mistake?" (1972) 8; cf. John A.T. Robinson's "two stories" view in *The Human Face of God* (1973) 114-25; also Frances Young, "A Cloud of Witnesses" (1977) 31ff.

[53] Wiles, *The Remaking of Christian Doctrine* (1974) Chs. 3, 4; 41-82.

[54] Wiles invokes 2 Cor. 5:16b here: "even though we once regarded Christ from a human point of view, we regard him thus no longer."

[55] Prusak, "The Son of Man Came Eating and Drinking" (1980) 4-5.

[56] Wiles, "A Survey of Issues in The Myth Debate" (1979) 10-11.

[57] Wiles, "Christian Theology in an Age of Religious Studies" (1979) 40. For other instances of the view that Christ provides all religions with a necessary insight into God, cf. Tadsen, *Jesus Christ in the World Theology of Wilfred Cantwell Smith* (1986) 212, and Knitter, *No Other Name?* (1985) 222.

[58] Gerrish, "Friedrich Schleiermacher" (1985), III.2; 136-40.

[59] Bowden, *Jesus* (1988) 158.

[60] One might add that writers such as Moltmann and Pannenberg, emphasizing eschatology, have their own way of dealing with this problem. They acknowledge that the unique disclosure of God in history cannot be discerned before the end of history, therein admitting the "hidden God" agnosticism they share with Wiles. Their way around this impasse, to see in the resurrection of Jesus a proleptic foretaste of the revelatory ending to history, would not please Wiles at all, however, who as I have said would no doubt find it to be unsustainable, fideistic and unaware of the contribution of Christian experience rendering such claims circular.

[61] Cf. Wiles and Robinson; see references at n. 52 above.

[62] Cf. Nineham and Wiles; see references at n. 24 above.

[63] Young, "Incarnation and Atonement" (1979) 102.

[64] Young, *Sacrifice and the Death of Christ* (1975) 130,1.

[65] Note, too, A.O. Dyson and his small book *Who Is Jesus Christ?* (1969). The tenor of the examination is set by existentialism, but the narrow focus of "Christ alone" in Bultmann's prescription for authentic existence is rejected. As with Ogden and Buri, Dyson believes that the call to responsible personhood cannot be limited exclusively to Jesus. Nor, with Jaspers, does he wish to commit the error of treating the historically contingent (the Christ-

ian myth) as universally true (eg. 70, 104-05). Also, like Teilhard (and Wiles and Young), Dyson does not wish to limit God's action to specific events.

Dyson does not go all the way with Teilhard, however, and posit Christ as center or else high-point of the process: "That there are other witnesses and signposts is beyond dispute. Whether and in what sense Jesus has a pre-eminent place among these I feel unable to say. Nevertheless, and in no spirit of exclusiveness, I find that this personal, concrete, and therefore vulnerable witness constrains me to risk now a "huge and *totally human* hope" that we and our world, in our present reality and in our future possibility, are dwelling and growing in nothing less than the divine milieu" (120).

[66] See e.g. Twiss, "The Philosophy of Religious Pluralism" (1990).

[67] Edwards, *Tradition and Truth* (1989) 242.

[68] D'Costa, *John Hick's Theology of Religions* (1987) 162.

[69] See the now classic treatment of religion as an illicitly reified category in Cantwell Smith, *The Meaning and End of Religion* (1969).

[70] Twiss, "The Philosophy of Religious Pluralism" (1990) 567.

[71] Ibid. 567.

[72] Hick, "The Christology of D.M. Baillie" (1958).

[73] Gillis, "John Hick's Christology" (1988). Hick provides personal statements retracing his overall development in the Introduction to *God Has Many Names* (1980) and in "Pluralism and the Reality of the Transcendent" (1981).

[74] London: Faber & Faber, 1948.

[75] Hick, *Faith and Knowledge* (Ithaca, NY: Cornell University Press, 2nd ed. 1966) 216 (cited by Gillis, 42, 57).

[76] Ibid. (cited by Gillis, 42).

[77] London: SCM, 1968 (cited by Gillis, 43).

[78] Reprinted in Hick, *God and the Universe of Faiths* (London: Macmillan, 1973) 148-64 (cited by Gillis, 44, 57).

[79] *Expository Times* 64 (1972) 36-39 (cited by Gillis, 47, 57).

[80] *Modern Churchman* 18, nos. 1-2 (1974) 8-17 (cited by Gillis, 57).

[81] *Reform*, Oct. 1974, 18-19 (cited in Lipner, "The Uniqueness of Christ" [1975] 359, 360).

[82] Gillis, 57 (corrected).

[83] Hick, "Reply to Edwards" (1989) 308-09.

[84] Baillie, *God Was in Christ* (1948) (London: Faber & Faber, 2nd ed. 1961) 117; Lampe, *God as Spirit* (1977) 12 (both cited in Hick, "An Inspiration Christology" [1988] 21).

[85] 1902, rev. ed. 1929; Richmond, VA: John Knox, 1971.

[86] Hick, "The Non-Absoluteness of Christianity" (1987) 16; see also Sarah Coakley's fuller treatment of Troeltsch's development in *Christ Without Absolutes: A Study of the Christology of Ernst Troeltsch* (Oxford: Clarendon, 1988) Ch. 1; cf. 114-15.

[87] Rouner, "Theology of Religions in Recent Protestant Theology" (1986) 110; see also the detailed historical treatment of this theme in Jean Milet, *God or Christ?* (1981).

[88] Ruth Page, of the Edinburgh Divinity Faculty, has recently offered a discussion of Jesus' uniqueness and finality drawing on and indeed echoing views from Hick's recent book, *An Interpretation of Religion*. Her interesting Christology *The Incarnation of Freedom and Love* (1991) exhibits everything "historical skeptics" and "religious pluralists" have taught about historical skepticism and cultural relativism. Her treatment is in terms of the process/logos ideas to which Hick is partial, with Jesus deemed crucially important for Christians though by no means the only "incarnation of freedom and love." Page admits that "the universality of Christ has to be affirmed if he is believed in any way to encapsulate the character of the infinite God in relation to humanity."...Anyone may come to God through Christ. But to say "anyone may come" is very different from saying "everyone must come," and to affirm the uniqueness and finality of Jesus Christ within the Christian tradition, even with its universal horizon, is not to affirm that Jesus Christ must be unique and final for those in other religions of the world" (165, 166). It is noteworthy that full-length Christologies like this can now be written— of considerable religious seriousness and by no means "radically dismissive" of church and tradition, yet requiring so few of the supports deemed needful by "conservative" and "liberal" writers and able to do without Jesus' uniqueness and finality.

[89] See e.g. Hick's debate with a newly "out of the closet" (and out of the priesthood) atheist in Michael Goulder and John Hick, *Why Believe in God?* (London: SCM, 1983).

⁹⁰ Gilkey, "A Theological Voyage with Wilfred Cantwell Smith" (1981) 302.

⁹¹ Race, *Christians and Religious Pluralism* (1983) 101.

⁹² Tadsen, *Jesus Christ in the World Theology of Wilfred Cantwell Smith* (1986) 370, citing a private letter from Cantwell Smith of 29 March 1982.

⁹³ Ibid. 162.

⁹⁴ This indicates a preference for "colloquy" rather than "dialogue," which for Cantwell Smith is a less self-obsessed undertaking. This is made explicit in *Towards a World Theology* (1981) 192-93.

⁹⁵ Almond, "Wilfred Cantwell Smith as Theologian of Religions" (1983) 338.

⁹⁶ Ibid. 336-37; see also e.g. Cantwell Smith, *Towards a World Theology* (1981) 184, 85.

⁹⁷ Gilkey, "A Theological Voyage with Wilfred Cantwell Smith" (1981) 300.

⁹⁸ Hughes, *Wilfred Cantwell Smith* (1986) especially 90-97.

⁹⁹ Ibid. 96.

¹⁰⁰ Cantwell Smith, *Towards a World Theology* (1981) 68-69.

¹⁰¹ Ibid. 102-03.

¹⁰² Tadsen, *Jesus Christ in the World Theology of Wilfred Cantwell Smith* (1986) 225, 229, where she mentions Cantwell Smith, *Belief and History* (Charlottesville, VA: University Press of Virginia, 1977) 88-89.

¹⁰³ Ibid. 184.

¹⁰⁴ Ibid. 184; citing Cantwell Smith, "Can Religions be True or False?" in *Questions of Religious Truth* (New York: Charles Scribner's Sons, 1967) 65-95; 91, 92.

¹⁰⁵ Tadsen, *Jesus Christ in the World Theology of Wilfred Cantwell Smith* (1986) 212.

¹⁰⁶ Also bearing mention is Alan Race, a priest in the Church of England whose pluralist perspective appears in his survey volume *Christians and Religious Pluralism: Patterns in the Christian Theology of Religions* (1983). As for his overall perspective on religious diversity, "It is the belief that there is not one, but a number of spheres of saving contact between God and man. God's revealing and redeeming activity has elicited response in a number of culturally conditioned ways throughout history. Each response is partial, in-

complete, unique; but they are related to each other in that they represent different culturally focused perceptions of the one ultimate divine reality. This is also sometimes called pluralism, and is the expression preferred in the present work" (77-78).

Race's argument is two-pronged. He establishes his pluralist position and then produces an "action Christology" compatible with it.

As for the pluralism, Race begins by postulating a single object of religious experience, albeit variously embodied in and only accessible through different religious traditions (e.g. p. 139). Here is familiar ground for both Hick and Cantwell Smith. But, with Troeltsch, Race sees each religion as a complete *Weltanschauung* (80) and this leads to difficulties in determining "truth value" between the religions. For Race it will be chiefly within dialogue, such as that characterizing the Christian ecumenical movement, "where evaluation of the different images of God can take place" (87). But no ultimate truths are thought to be accessible by that or any other path: "Final unity of belief can only be eschatological, that is, located in the being of God himself" (87). This last insight is ascribed to the later Troeltsch and, of course, it recalls Hick's notion of "eschatological verification" (90).

To these convictions about religious pluralism Race brings an action Christology envisaging Jesus' incarnation in moral terms, as God's "love in action": "Jesus was incarnate in that he embodied not only a profound human response to God, that openness to God necessary for the life of faith, but also the turning of God towards man in his distress and need of salvation" (133).

Race deprives the Jesus thus conceived of his traditional uniqueness, however, by employing a qualification already encountered with Cantwell Smith. He refuses to speak of divine action except in terms of human responses to it: "The objectivity lies in the relativity of what is being offered through the event, and the subjectivity lies in the realization that until we respond, the offer remains of no consequence" (129). This allows Race to see Jesus as objectively important, but not objectively unique. Indeed, he is only subjectively so: "Jesus is decisive, not because he is the focus for all the light everywhere revealed in the world, but for the vision he has brought in one cultural setting" (135-36). Thus Race is saved from the liberal conclusions, in terms of Jesus' uniqueness, of his liberal-style "action

Christology"; Jesus is the unique focus of God's action only to those for whom he is its channel—only for Christians.

Finally, note how Race stands vis à vis my foundational criteria of the historical Jesus and the human condition. He believes there is enough consensus among subscribers to the new quest for confidence in Christology that "the gap between 'history' and 'faith' is not intolerable" (124); clearly, like Hick, Race believes the historical Jesus to have been an impressive enough figure to stand behind gospel portrayals of the Christ of faith. As for the human condition, Race hangs much on religious experience (as does Hick, though not exclusively). Nevertheless he believes with Ninian Smart that the phenomenology of religious experience cannot establish the existence of a common ground of human experience and certainly not that of a truth toward which all such phenomena point (85).

So Race, like Hick and Cantwell Smith, is a liberal at heart. All depend upon the religious disclosivity of the human condition, while Hick and Race depend to a degree upon the historical Jesus. Certainly, none of them are confident that such liberal foundations will establish the uniqueness and finality of Jesus. One might say that although they begin as liberals all three end up as radical pluralists.

[107] Gilkey, "A Theological Voyage with Wilfred Cantwell Smith" (1981) 304.

[108] See e.g. Knitter's review article, "Making Sense of the Many" (1989) 206; this is also D'Costa's major criticism in *Theology and Religious Pluralism* (1986).

[109] Nor is Hick able to convince us that the Theravada Buddhist avoidance of theism has been adequately catered for by simply renaming his conception of God as "the real." Such a step calls to mind Tillich's "ground of being," which might sound universal and inclusive but in reality has its roots deep in western religious soil—in the Rhineland mystics, Jacob Boehme and in later German idealism.

[110] Heim, *Is Christ the Only Way?* (1985) 21-23.

[111] As classically charted in Cantwell Smith, *The Meaning and End of Religion* (1962).

[112] Hick, *God and the Universe of Faiths* (1977) 140.

[113] Tracy, *Blessed Rage for Order* (1988) 121, 2; who, in turn, derives this insight from Ian Ramsey, *Religious Language: An Empirical Placing of Theological Phrases* (London: SCM, 1957), Part 1.

[114] Knitter, *No Other Name?* (1985) 222. There is no "Christocentricity problem" with the pluralistic theism of Knitter, as was suggested in the case of Cantwell Smith.

[115] A number of Knitter's insights, including this one about the role of dialogue, are found also in Henri Maurier, "The Christian Theology of the Non-Christian Religions" (1976). He argues that it is in dialogue that the differing absolute beliefs of the religions are to be assessed beyond anyone's claims to superiority and in a spirit of witness rather than proselytism. Note, however, that Maurier explicitly rejects the position presenting "Jesus as divine because *totally human*" (73) for overidentifying the human and the divine rather than seeing these different realities as only properly linked in the hypostatic union. Surely no surer sign of belief in Jesus' uniqueness exists than claiming he constitutes a hypostatic union! But, then, Maurier will not assert this belief when confronted by the other religions.

Ignace Puthiadam follows Maurier. In his article "Christian Faith and Life in a World of Religious Pluralism" (1980) he speaks about the absoluteness of Jesus Christ (106), the hypostatic union (108) and Jesus' resurrection (111); but he too refuses to see the absolute claims of other religions as disproved thereby.

Such views would label both these writers as relativists like Race, if not closet conservatives, but for their claiming the possibility that inter-religious dialogue might clear the matter up. Either way they do indeed appear to be the pluralists Knitter thinks them to be, in *No Other Name?* (1985) 259 n.97; see also Knitter, "Catholic Theology of Religions at a Crossroads" (1986) 107. But while surrendering the uniqueness of Jesus these two Roman Catholic priests certainly keep sufficient hints of a high Christology that they would survive, if necessary, any challenge to their orthodoxy from the magisterium. As a married layman, however, it may be assumed that Knitter is "safe."

[116] This is a perspective found elsewhere. The Asian style of liberation theology finds a good representative in the Sri Lankan Jesuit and sponsor of Buddhist-Christian dialogue, Aloysius Pieris. His approach recognizes the dual challenge felt by Asian Christians, of grave and widespread poverty combined with the absolute minority status of Christianity (3%). For Pieris the religions all express a deep revolutionary urge and their focus is soteriology: see Pieris, "The Place of Non-Christian Religions" (1983); also "Speaking of the Son

of God" (1982). Christ is not a unique center of this salvific reality—the Buddha, for instance, is seen as equally good; see Pieris, "The Buddha and The Christ" (1987). Recall that the desire to foster justice and world peace has recently driven Hans Küng in the same direction; see Chapter 8.

The liberation theme has also drawn many feminist theologians to similar radical Christological conclusions. Rosemary Radford Ruether in *Sexism and God Talk* (1983) writes as a Christian feminist and activist who enlists Jesus for her cause. So she reads the historical Jesus far more politically than all but the liberation theologians do. There is no question of any uniqueness or finality for her Jesus, who only embodies a message; Mary Snyder, in *The Christology of Rosemary Radford Ruether* (1988), identifies Ruether's position with that of Knitter's "complimentary uniqueness" (85). "Only twice does Ruether specifically use the word 'unique' in relation to Jesus," writes Snyder. "According to her, the statement 'Jesus is the Christ' makes sense only insofar as it is an affirmation that is '...paradigmatic for the structure of human existence and not something unique about Jesus.' In light of this I would argue that Ruether does not support traditional claims for the uniqueness and finality of Jesus, either an exclusive or inclusive uniqueness" (84). The quote used by Snyder here is from Ruether, "Messiah of Israel and the Cosmic Christ: A Study of the Development of Christology in Judaism and Early Christianity" (unpublished manuscript, Washington, DC: 1971).

Virginia Ramey Mollenkott moves away from her evangelical beginnings with the radical work *Godding: Human Responsibility and the Bible* (New York: Crossroad, 1987). Mollenkott sees people (of all faiths) as incarnators of God—"godders"—but she retains a special liking for Jesus. In a now familiar way Mollenkott equivocates, suggesting that Jesus' life has "created a union between the divine and human natures" (*Godding* 78) while elsewhere denying any such Christocentrism in favor of a theocentrism we all incarnate (*Godding* 7, 10). Indeed, Mollenkott declares that the Christian focus on Christ in theology and worship is parochial—what matters is the cause of liberation and unity with other faiths; see Mollenkott, "Letter to the Editor," *Journal of Feminist Studies in Religion* 2 no. 2 (1986) 107-09; 108 (see Barbara Smith's doctoral dissertation *Options in Contemporary Feminist Christology* [1989] especially 99-100).

The self-confessed lesbian, Episcopalian priest/theologian and member of the (in)famous "Philadelphia 11," Carter Heyward, completes this picture. She understands the divine as creative, relational and "justice making" power incarnated by all people in the holiness of their embodiment. But some people—Mother Teresa, Sojourner Truth and Martin Luther King for instance, as well as Jesus—are powerful foci. She rejects a Jesus-only, Chalcedonian view of the incarnation. Indeed Heyward echoes the concern of Ruether and other feminist theologians that a lone, male savior is an enemy of the feminist cause. For Heyward, Jesus' human life and his praxis of liberation serve as a metaphor of incarnation for us. Her primary attention is to the Marcan story but it is unclear if the historical Jesus or the Christ of Marcan redaction is intended. The only reason Jesus provides the focus for Heyward's approach to the liberation issue is apparently his traditional importance for Christians. In assessing this in her aforementioned thesis, however, Barbara Smith labels such an attitude simply as nostalgia. Heyward makes these points in her book *Our Passion for Justice: Images of Power, Sexuality and Liberation* (New York: Pilgrim, 1984), discussed by Smith op. cit., especially 236-41.

While remaining a Christian, the Japanese-American feminist Rita Nakashima Brock, in *Journeys by Heart* (1991), opposes all exclusivism as patriarchal. Recalling Ruether, she understands Jesus (especially the Marcan Jesus) as instancing an upwelling of liberation and human wholeness which she calls "Christa/Community." "Jesus is like the whitecap on a wave," she writes; "Jesus' power lies with the great swells of the ocean without which the white foam is not brought to visibility" (105-06). Brock's is an inclusive logos Christology with a "female logos" like that of Ruether—a liberating *sophia*.

[117] Such an undertaking is not altogether novel. Of the four styles Eric J. Sharpe has identified in Christian-Hindu dialogue, Knitter's favoured approach comes closest to what Sharpe calls "secular dialogue," "aiming solely at the recognition of joint concern and the need for joint secular action"; see Sharpe, "The Goals of Inter-Religious Dialogue" in John Hick (ed.) *Truth and Dialogue: The Relationship between World Religions* (London: Sheldon, 1974) 77-95; 85.

[118] Like Knitter, Race emphasises the importance of religious traditions in *mediating* the experiential basis of religion; one cannot get

beyond or below the traditions as easily as Hick and Cantwell Smith would have it. The plurality of traditions, for Race, will always "obscure" the transcendent—at least this side of the eschaton. So any hope there might be of establishing some priority among the religions would depend on dialogue—here, too, Knitter and Race are in agreement.

They differ, however, over the issue of relativism. Race believes all the traditions give access to "God," and indeed he is less willing to allow judgment between traditions than the other pluralists. Thus he is more of a relativist than Hick or Cantwell Smith. Knitter's view is of course quite the opposite. He understands each tradition as representing not the whole but only a part of the whole. Thus there is no relativism, as the religions do not all claim to be giving access to the same thing (cf. Kenneth Surin in n. 131, below). Also dialogue, as Knitter envisages it, provides more scope for critical comparison among the religions than in Race's vision.

[119] This paragraph about Cupitt's earlier views on Jesus' finality is taken from my study *Atheist Priest?* (1988) 22-23.

[120] Another minimal claim for Jesus' uniqueness is made by another English atheist priest (but one who resigned his orders) in the person of Michael Goulder. In his essay "Jesus, the Man of Universal Destiny" (1977) he likens Jesus to other figures such as Winston Churchill who caught up in their own persons the yearnings and hopes of an era. This does not allow for any necessary uniqueness, however, and amounts to a claim that Jesus was special, a great figure, which few would wish to deny.

In commenting upon this idea, suffice it to say that there is little evidence that the "man of sorrows" was widely appreciated or followed apart from the birth of faith in his person among Christians. It is precisely this which must be accounted for, as Schillebeeckx and others considered earlier in this study know full well.

[121] See my *Atheist Priest?* (1988) Ch. 2.

[122] This asserting of Giles Deleuze (desire, freedom) in the face of Jacques Lacan (language/culture, constraint) is Cupitt's project in *The Long-Legged Fly* (1987).

[123] Cupitt, *Life Lines* (1986) 198. The reference to bread and wine recalls Cupitt's own fondness for the eucharist as a symbolic enactment of both our religious context after the death of God and what

414   Is JESUS UNIQUE?

Christians must themselves do by way of self-emptying. Cupitt tells
me that when presiding at the eucharist he begins by bowing to the
altar and ends by bowing to the people—those among whom, symbolically speaking, God has decentered and dispersed himself in the
blessed sacrament.

[124] Cupitt, *The New Christian Ethics* (1988) 95, 123, 158 respectively. Note that Cupitt is occasionally still very critical of what developed Christianity has made of the figure of Jesus. And a strong
trace of old-style liberal contempt for St. Paul as the first offender remains (68ff). Graham Shaw in *The Cost of Authority* (1983) is invoked for support here (see n. 42, above).

[125] Similar views are expressed by the American a/theologian
Mark C. Taylor, Professor of Religion at Williams College, in his
book *Erring* (1984). The denial of any fixed meaning in texts, the refusal to ground the signifying process in any "transcendental signified" (Derrida) apart from merely aimless writing itself—this is the
post-structuralist call which Taylor links to death of God theology.
Meaning is gone, as the objective existence of God is gone. And this
is symbolized by the incarnation myth in Christianity. As Taylor puts
it, "Radical christology is *thoroughly* incarnational—the divine '*is*'
the incarnate word.... Incarnation *irrevocably* erases the disembodied logos and inscribes a word that becomes the script enacted in the
infinite play of interpretation (103).... Incarnation, therefore, is not a
once-and-for-all event, restricted to a specific time and place and
limited to a particular individual.... God is what word means, and
word is what 'God' means" (104). All that we see here, however, is a
radical Christian finding Christian symbols to be useful tools in cultural criticism. No absolute claims about Jesus or Christianity are entailed.

[126] On post-liberal theology as a Yale (vs. Chicago) phenomenon
see Placher, "Postliberal Theology" (1989) 115ff; also e.g. the critique of Lindbeck by a current Chicago professor in Tracy, "Lindbeck's New Program for Theology" (1985).

[127] Tracy, "Lindbeck's New Program for Theology" (1985) 462.

[128] Michalson, "The Response to Lindbeck" (1988) 110.

[129] A comparison with another leading American theologian is also
apposite here. Langdon Gilkey has now retired from his chair at the
Chicago Divinity School. In his paper "Plurality and Its Theological

Implications" (1987) he rejects any Hick-style theocentrism as sundering the undividedness of religious symbol-systems. He sees each of these as a *Gestalt*, such that a doctrine like that of "God" cannot be excerpted and then set up *in vacuo* as a universal for all religions. Gilkey allows no universal standpoint at the price of such abstractions (41), thus exhibiting a major post-modern insight. He then wishes to find a vision of Christianity which is normative but not exclusive, lamenting his own former Christian inclusivism as parochial and inadequate to the situation (42).

Yet Gilkey feels that some capacity for discrimination remains necessary lest the many evils perpetrated under the aegis of religion go unmet. Thus he advocates an absolute commitment on the part of Christians to their own vision where it is just and liberating, coupled with a recognition of its complete relativity. For Gilkey this pushes and lures us into the middle of a maze we can still barely enter intellectually; but "what to reflection is a contradiction, to praxis is a workable dialectic" (47).

In the final analysis, however, Gilkey cannot leave behind a Tillichian God-beyond-God as an absolute ground of meaning (this step is also taken, despite his having otherwise embraced the challenges of post-modernity, by the Tillichian former death-of-God theologian Thomas J.J. Altizer, who claims to identify similar views in Derrida; see Altizer, "History as Apocalypse" in Altizer et al., *Deconstruction and Theology* [New York: Crossroad, 1982] 147-77). To be sure, this is a "God" as remote as possible beyond good and evil and thus in keeping with Tillich's vision of God as "Being" constantly overcoming dialectical non-Being within his own person (Paul Tillich, *Systematic Theology*, Vol. 1 [1951] [London: SCM, 1978] 189). This God-only-relatively-manifest-as-God is then seen as variously represented among the religions. Gilkey suggests that "possibly a series of manifestations can co-exist on the same level but with genuine validity" (48).

And there is only the slightest hint of the uniqueness of Jesus, in Gilkey's talk of divine agape being Christological (50). This agape is revealed in Christ (with a hint, perhaps, that its expression there might be normative) but also in Bodhisattvas, etc. But since nothing is expressly stated about a unique Jesus, however, it appears probable Gilkey has abandoned the doctrine.

Thus Gilkey has illustrated a halfway attempt at reconciling his Christian vision with the post-modern challenge. In so doing, however, he has been forced to dress up confusion and dissembling as dialectic, passing off an inability to surrender his "ground of being" and its consequent ethical norms as the sort of paradox praxis demands. Thus Gilkey—the Chicago man, the Tillichian—has not really moved toward the Yale-style alternative of Lindbeck, preferring still "the one" to "the many."

[130] Alister McGrath denies this connection with Schleiermacher who, he argues, refers to a specifically *Christian* type of experience which is corporate not private, specific not general: "The delicate interplay between language and experience suggested by Schleiermacher does not appear to be vulnerable to Lindbeck's critique, and does not even appear to fall within its scope"; see *The Genesis of Doctrine* (1990) 25-26.

[131] Kenneth Surin argues that one can preserve the same claims for the sole salvific efficacy of Christ without locating salvation only after death. Influenced by English philosophy and theology that is skeptical about the conceivability of life after death, Surin opts for a perspective which he thinks is more faithful to central Christian insights. He understands the Christian reality to be co-extensive with all creation while focused in Jesus Christ, yet in so claiming he makes no recourse to inclusivism. For Surin, Lindbeck fails to appreciate the radical incommensurability of the religions as much as he claims. Surin thinks it more faithful to the Christian vision to leave the salvation question open. For all of this see Surin, "Many Religions and the One True Faith" (1988). Elsewhere, he advocates a non-triumphalistic exclusivism since only Christianity claims, and thus deserves, to be treated as a religion of salvation; see Surin, "Revelation, Salvation, the Uniqueness of Christ and Other Religions" (1983).

[132] For Alister McGrath, Lindbeck overlooks the fact that Athanasius bases the regulative function of the *homoousion* on its substantive content—the ontology preceding any grammatical, regulative function; see McGrath, *The Genesis of Doctrine* (1990) 29. Stephen Williams denies that Lonergan offers a regulative theory as Lindbeck suggests; see "Lindbeck's Regulative Christology" (1988) 174. The primary citations Williams uses are from that portion of Lonergan's

NOTES 417

De Deo Trino (1964) translated into English as *The Way to Nicaea.*
Page numbers are given but no publication details.

[133] According to an experiential-expressivist view, Trinitarian doctrine gives voice to deep human experiences. One example which
comes to mind is Raimundo Panikkar, for whom the doctrine expresses a deep threefoldness in religious awareness throughout all
cultures (see *The Trinity and the Religious Experience of Man*
[Maryknoll, NY: Orbis; London: Darton, Longman & Todd, 1973]).
Similarly, for the Church of England Doctrine Commission, Trinitarian doctrine captures the allegedly threefold contours of Christian
experience at prayer (see the report *We Believe in God* [London:
Church House, 1987]).

It has been suggested that an adequate "Christological maximalism" entails Jesus' Trinitarian divinity, thus entailing ontological
claims: see Stephen Williams, "Lindbeck's Regulative Christology"
(1988) 184. One wonders, however, if this can be had without compromising Jesus' humanity and risking docetism.

[134] Timothy Jackson, "Against Grammar" *Religious Studies Review* 11 (1985) 241 (cited in Michalson, "The Response to Lindbeck" [1988] 111).

[135] McGrath, *The Genesis of Doctrine* (1990) 31-32. McGrath
draws attention to the problems raised by instrumentalism in the philosophy of science. He also suggests that the (mediated) history of
Jesus should be seen as the proximate external referent of doctrinal
statements in Christology. All in Part III would agree. And of course
we might ask why Jesus is so important to have caused all the concern—the question of the origin of our doctrines upon which Mc-
Grath bases his critique of Lindbeck.

[136] Stephen Williams, "Lindbeck's Regulative Christology" (1988)
182-83.

[137] Lindbeck is indebted here to Kelsey, *The Uses of Scripture in
Recent Theology* (1975). Kelsey shares with Lindbeck a place in "the
Yale school." We recall Frei in this connection also, along with Marshall's critique of Rahner. A similar point is made by another post-
liberal, Stanley Hauerwas, in his essay, "Jesus: The Story of the
Kingdom" (1981). There, Jesus as known in the New Testament *is
himself* the kingdom of God and his story *is itself* a social ethic.

Hauerwas rejects liberal attempts to abstract a "moral" from the story of Jesus—the *whole* story must be taken *in toto*. Hauerwas does not, however, adequately distinguish the historical Jesus from the Christ of faith met in the narrative. This is a problem encountered in another group involved with social ethics, the liberation theologians.

Just because God is rendered as a character in the narrative, however, does not preclude God's objective existence. Lindbeck would allow this and David Tracy would argue for it. God has even been understood as *establishing* his reality in this way—expressly through the mechanisms of human imagination and its role in producing such sacred narrative; see e.g. Dale Patrick, *The Rendering of God in the Old Testament* (Overtures in Biblical Theology Series; Philadelphia: Fortress, 1981). This notion is also found in much narrative theology; see e.g. Terrence W. Tilley, *Story Theology* (Wilmington, DE: Michael Glazier, 1985).

[138] If the story is the prime reality, then the low status of the historical Jesus in Lindbeck's program is explained. But what brought the story itself into being? For Alister McGrath, Lindbeck has illicitly leapfrogged questions of the origin and development of doctrine in his haste to discuss its nature. McGrath seeks to redress this imbalance, naming his Bampton lectures in which he attempted this *The Genesis of Doctrine* (1990). If the historical person of Jesus and a spirit of "Christological maximalism" are crucial Christian basics, as Lindbeck tells us, then surely some claim for the historical Jesus and his impact on earliest Christianity is entailed. As McGrath puts it, "Lindbeck's insistence upon the primacy of... 'language, doctrine, liturgies and modes of action' raises the unanswered question of how these primary data may be accounted for" (28). McGrath is convinced that "this grand retreat from history reduces doctrine to little more than a grammar of an ahistorical language... which—like Melchizedek—has no origins" (34).

[139] Michalson, "The Response to Lindbeck" (1988) 114.

[140] Placher, "Postliberal Theology" (1989) 117.

[141] William C. Placher offers some background observations about this in his essay, "Revisionist and Postliberal Theologies" (1985) 402. There he writes, "Part of the debate here concerns the way one thinks about a human self. Frei, Lindbeck and Kelsey have all been influenced by Gilbert Ryle's arguments that our true self is not some-

thing distinct and separate from our speech and action. Revisionist theologians often draw on models from idealism and its heirs which put more emphasis on the interiority of the true self, so that speech and action can at most only *manifest* who one really is."

[142] How does Lindbeck address the question of truth in religions if they can only be properly understood intratextually? It transpires that he views religions as paradigms, with reasonableness largely a function of their interpretative, assimilative powers (131). If on its own terms a religion helps us make the most coherent sense out of experience then it is true for us.

[143] Tracy, "Lindbeck's New Program for Theology" (1985) 465.

[144] Two American Mennonites—a denomination well represented among postliberals—also offer similar views. A recent short "proto-systematics" in this tradition has been provided by the American church historian Daniel Liechty in his *Theology in Postliberal Perspective* (1990). Actually, however, he maintains much of the liberal agenda, preferring the historical Jesus to the accretions which were added to form the Christ of faith (a figure which, according to Liechty, has long blessed oppression, exclusivism, etc.). To this traditional, nineteenth century liberal argument Liechty adds relativist views on the uniqueness of Jesus: "Those who have experienced the present-future kingdom of freedom and mutuality at table fellowship with those of other belief systems are not likely to feel much urgency in defending the uniqueness of their Christ" (58).

The Harvard professor Gordon D. Kaufman has also moved to a similar position. In his paper "Religious Diversity, Historical Consciousness and Christian Theology" (1987) it is world peace which now demands the surrender of former absolutisms and exclusivisms, especially religious ones, in the face of a "nuclear eschatalogy." Thus the present pluralistic situation demands acceptance of the many ways of being human. Communities which disagree must nonetheless be willing to dialogue (4). Kaufman explicitly disavows any liberal recourse to an "essential oneness" shared by all human beings as the basis for such dialogue, however—"A universal frame of orientation for human understanding and life is no more available to us than is a universal language" (5). Typically post-modern, he warns that the symbolic, the linguistic and conceptual cannot be milked for any common essence.

So, too, are the religions seen to be simply a range of human inventions in response to human experience as understood from the perspectives of different times and places: "Humans created and developed the various religious traditions, thus giving life the variant meanings it has come to have" (7). Kaufman's message to Christians, in consequence, is that such critical historical consciousness can free the church from its need to make absolute dogmatic claims as formerly. Kaufman values religion, but its truths can now be understood simply as normative for its members rather than absolute in any more substantial way.

Christ remains one of the central, inescapable Christian "categories" for Kaufman, but here is no question of any wider relevance; he is that figure from human history who is believed by Christians to reveal or define, on the one hand, who or what God really is, and, on the other hand, that in which true humanity consists. The historical figure of Jesus Christ thus gives concreteness and specificity to the understanding of both God and humanity, in this way significantly shaping these central symbols that define what is normative for orienting human existence in Christian terms (11).

[145] Tracy, "Lindbeck's New Program for Theology" (1985) 465. Cf. McGrath's criticism of Lindbeck for underrating the sophistication of Schleiermacher's recourse to experience; see n. 130, above.

[146] This is pointed out by Placher in his essay, "Revisionist and Postliberal Theologies and the Public Character of Theology" (1985) 414.

[147] Tracy, art. cit. 463-65.

[148] Tracy, art. cit. 468. Tracy also points here to the way today's best liberal theology refuses to identify a common core in the religions, as Hick continues to do.

Conclusion

[1] The need for some such meeting point, as classically asserted by Brunner against Barth in the earlier generation of neo-orthodox thinking, was resisted by the writers considered in Ch. 1 as it had been resisted by Barth; see e.g. *Natural Theology: Comprising "Na-*

ture and Grace" by Professor Dr. Emil Brunner and the reply "No!" by Dr. Karl Barth with an Introduction by John Baillie (London: Geoffrey Bles [Centenary] 1946).

[2] See Tracy, *Blessed Rage for Order* (1975) Ch. 2.

[3] Compare Cupitt's most original offering on this topic, *The Long-Legged Fly* (1987), with David Tracy's defense of a "revisionist theology" against such claims, as in his study *Plurality and Ambiguity* (1987).

[4] I mention in passing one current Christology which seeks to maintain the uniqueness and finality of Christ while severing the link to Jesus' historical person and denying any uniform human condition, though without any recourse to revelational positivism. It is that offered by the American Methodist and process theologian John Cobb, in his book *Christ in a Pluralistic Age* (1975). Cobb finds in Christ a uniquely powerful focus of the divine drive toward transformation in the world, though his attention to the historical Jesus is slight compared to the "liberal" theologians, and he admits of no human condition in the light of post-modern challenges. Cobb goes beyond Wiles, who wished to see the presence of God smoothly distributed throughout the whole world process without being focused anywhere, though Cobb finds in Christ a symbol for the entirety of this presence. It is not a *genuine* case for Jesus' uniqueness and finality, however, establishing no adequate links to Jesus' historical person, nor to any constants of human experience, and hence to the public world. It thus appears as an ungrounded speculative preference, like the preference of Lindbeck and the post-liberals for Christianity despite their denial of any apologetic.

[5] Such a "Feuerbachian Christ," if you like, is what Don Cupitt offers in his essay "One Jesus, Many Christs" (1972).

[6] See Segundo, Vols. 3, 4 and 5, entitled *The Humanist Christology of Paul* (1986), *The Christ of the Ignatian Exercises* (1987) and *An Evolutionary Approach to Jesus of Nazareth* (1988).

[7] In Sobrino's *Christology at the Crossroads* (1978), from someone who narrowly escaped joining the recent Jesuit martyrs of El Salvador, there is a relatively rare emphasis on the faith of Jesus as undergirding his praxis, and as providing resources for the liberating struggle in oppressive Latin American conditions. For Segundo, the

first of his series *Jesus of Nazareth: Yesterday and Today*, entitled *Faith and Ideologies* (1984), is a polemic against religious readings of the human condition of the sort David Tracy offers in *Blessed Rage for Order* (1975), along with other recent Roman Catholic apologists; essentially, Segundo rejects the notion of a transcultural human condition (related to God and disclosed through the fact of fundamental trust, as Tracy would have it), opting rather for a Marxist-inspired view of human life as dominated by economic and political forces. He fears that a religious interpretation of basic human drives and needs will divert attention from the kingdom of God and the press for liberation toward a pious and innocuous interiorizing of the message of Jesus. Segundo supports his case with a highly political reading of Jesus and his motivations, which is expanded in his second volume *The Historical Jesus of the Synoptics* (1985).

It is clear that Sobrino and Segundo give inadequate attention to the historical Jesus debate as it is properly understood in serious New Testament study—this is pointed out fairly scathingly by John P. Meier (whose views about this issue as it concerned Schillebeeckx and Küng were important in Ch. 8) in his essay "Jesus among the Theologians: II. Sobrino and Segundo" (1990). But both Jesuits see the meaning and uniqueness and finality of Christ not simply as ends in themselves but in terms of the transformation of the world when an ever-expanding Christ event engages new situations with the challenge of liberation. Furthermore, that engagement involves the catching-up of the believer into the story and into current events, understood as an actual participation in the Christ event. The Ignatian quality here is discussed in Sobrino's Appendix, "The Christ of the Ignatian Exercises" (pp. 396-424), in which praxis is seen very much as a precursor to right Christology—doing precedes knowing, for Sobrino, in a self-consciously Ignatian spirituality of "contemplation in action" cast in a key familiar from liberation theology.

⁸ There are similarities here with Monika Hellwig (who like van Beeck was influenced by Schoonenberg) and Peter Hodgson, with whom van Beeck himself claims affinity. See e.g. Hellwig, *Jesus the Compassion of God: New Perspectives on the Tradition of Christianity* (Theology and Life Series, 9; Collegeville, MN: Michael Glazier [Liturgical Press], 1983) and her essays, "The Uniqueness of Jesus in

Christian Tradition," in Thomas F. McFadden (ed.), *Does Jesus Make a Difference?* (New York: Seabury, 1974) 81-98 and "Christology in the Wider Ecumenism," in Gavin D'Costa (ed.), *Christian Uniqueness Reconsidered* (1990) 107-16. See also Peter Hodgson, *Jesus—Word and Presence* (Philadelphia: Fortress, 1971).

[9] There are also pragmatic criteria at work; van Beeck makes much of the fact that Christian faith and practice can be shown to work in generating appropriate Christian behavior.

[10] Recall the argument of Tracy, picked up at Part III, n. 135, above, that at least a full systematic theology would be necessary to establish such a uniqueness case based, among other things, on much close and detailed analysis of the world religions.

[11] A similar eirenicism, and "inclusive uniqueness," also prevails at the end of another lengthy study (and one considering a related theme); see Kuschel, *Born Before All Time?* (1992) 513.

[12] The attitude of van Beeck here is fully in keeping with some of the most recent developments in the debate over Christianity and the world religions. Without claiming the inclusivist stance of Rahner's "anonymous Christianity" or its cognates (such as Küng's case for Christian superiority in his "Christ as norm and critical standard among the religions" view), on the one hand, or of the (to my mind) now discredited indifferentism of Hick and Cantwell Smith on the other, one can nevertheless affirm Christianity—this can be done without demeaning the other religions, either by calling them inferior or by emasculating them, as Hick and Cantwell Smith do by denying them any fundamental distinctiveness. In other words, one can find a truly post-modern position which respects the fact of human diversity, which shies away from overarching truth claims in an awareness that the age of the knockdown proof is over (if it ever existed), and yet which allows a deep Christian commitment—deepened all the more by acknowledging personal commitment as the way to both deeper understanding *and* to the conversion of others. I find such trends, for instance, in a fine essay by John Milbank entitled "The End of Dialogue" (1990) and in S. Mark Heim's convincing, gently assertive study *Is Christ the Only Way?* (1985); cf. the essays of Kenneth Surin, footnoted at Part IV, n. 131; Pannenberg's essay "Religious Pluralism and Conflicting Truth Claims" (1990), footnoted at

Part II, n. 112, and Moltmann's essay "Is 'Pluralistic Theology' Useful for the Dialogue of World Religions?" the discussion of which is footnoted at Part I, n. 49.

[13] This insight into the nature of religious statements comes from English philosophy of religion with its discussion of verification and falsification, which in turn arose out of the logical positivists' concern to assess the scientific character of religious statements. The important symposium of Anthony Flew, R.M. Hare and Basil Mitchell, "Theology and Falsification" (Anthony Flew and Alasdair MacIntyre [eds.], *New Essays in Philosophical Theology* [London: SCM, 1955] 96-108), recognizes that belief has non-specifiable, subjective elements, and that an empirical approach will never solve religious questions.

In his splendid study *The Justification of Religious Belief* (1973) Mitchell argues that belief in God is only ever a cumulative case—one which is "rational, but does not take the form of a strict proof or argument from probability" (39). This is also the case for theological statements more generally, in the development of scientific or artistic intuition, as in many life situations—a number of bits of evidence and argument are piled up until one finds oneself convinced. This is not irrational or totally subjective, however; the developing case is fully open to criticism, as a whole or piece by piece, but in the end the birth of conviction is supra-rational.

Why, then, is someone disposed to confess Jesus' uniqueness and finality and another not? "In the last analysis," writes David L. Edwards, "one's general approach to complex and ambiguous phenomena seems to depend on whether one is temperamentally inclined to see the constants or the variables. The general debate therefore continues and seems unlikely to end" (*Tradition and Truth* [1989] 200). I cannot help recalling the Polanyian contention of Thomas Torrance at this point, that "reality" imposes its own mode of knowing upon us to which the properly disposed knower will submit. In this instance, it seems apparent that faith in Jesus Christ is an essential component of any claim for his uniqueness, as is evident given the apparent inexcisability of Jesus' impact from any case for his uniqueness.

[14] Albert Schweitzer, *The Quest of the Historical Jesus* (1906, ET 1968) 403.

BIBLIOGRAPHY

The date of first publication is given in parentheses after the title, and that of the first English translation, if one or both differ from the publication date of the textual version consulted.

Almond, Philip, "Wilfred Cantwell Smith as Theologian of Religions," *Harvard Theological Review* 76 (1983) 335-342.

Barbour, Ian, *Religion in an Age of Science*, Vol. 1 (San Francisco: Harper & Row, 1990).

Bauckham, Richard, "Jürgen Moltmann," in David F. Ford (ed.), *The Modern Theologians*, Vol. 1 (1989) 293-310.

Berger, Peter, *A Rumour of Angels: Modern Society and the Rediscovery of the Supernatural* (1969) (Harmondsworth, UK: Penguin [Pelican], 1971).

Boff, Leonardo, *Jesus Christ Liberator: A Critical Christology for Our Time* (1972, rev. ed. & ET, 1978) (London: SPCK, 1980).

———, *Passion of Christ, Passion of the World: The Facts, Their Interpretation, and Their Meaning Yesterday and Today* (1977) (Maryknoll, NY: Orbis, 1987).

Bowden, John, *Jesus: The Unanswered Questions* (London: SCM, 1988).

Braaten, Carl, "A Trinitarian Theology of the Cross," *The Journal of Religion* 56 (1976) 113-121.

———, "The Lordship of Christ in Modern Theology," *Dialog* 4 (1965) 259-267.

———, "The Place of Christianity Among the World Religions: Wolfhart Pannenberg's Theology of Religion and the History of Religions," in Carl Braaten & Philip Clayton (eds.), *The Theology of Wolfhart Pannenberg* (1988) 287-312.

————, "Who Do We Say That He Is? On the Uniqueness and Universality of Jesus Christ," *Missiology* 8 (1980) 13-30.

————, "Wolfhart Pannenberg," in Martin E. Marty & Dean G. Peerman (eds.), *A Handbook of Christian Theologians* (1984) 639-659.

Braaten, Carl and Clayton, Philip (eds.), *The Theology of Wolfhart Pannenberg: Twelve American Critiques* (Minneapolis, MN: Augsburg, 1988).

Brock, Rita Nakashima, *Journeys by Heart: A Christology of Erotic Power* (New York: Crossroad, 1988).

Brown, David, *Continental Philosophy and Modern Theology* (Oxford: Basil Blackwell, 1987).

Bühlmann, Walbert, *All Have the Same God: An Encounter With the Peoples and Religions of Asia* (Slough, UK: St Paul's Publications, 1979).

————, *The Coming of the Third Church* (Maryknoll, NY: Orbis, 1977).

Burhenn, Herbert, "Pannenberg's Argument for the Historicity of the Resurrection," *Journal of the American Academy of Religion* 40 (1972) 368-379.

Butterworth, Robert, "Bishop Robinson and Christology," *Religious Studies* 11 (1975) 73-85.

Cantwell Smith, Wilfred, "Idolatry in Comparative Perspective," in John Hick & Paul F. Knitter (eds.), *The Myth of Christian Uniqueness* (1987) 53-68.

————, "The Christian in a Religiously Plural World," (1961) in *The Faith of Other Men* (New York: Mentor Books, 1965) 105-128.

————, "Theology and the World's Religious History," in Leonard Swidler (ed.), *Toward a Universal Theology of Religion* (1987) 51-72.

————, *The Meaning and End of Religion: A New Approach to the Religious Traditions of Mankind* (1962) (London: SPCK, 2nd ed. 1978).

————, *Towards a World Theology: Faith and the Comparative History of Religion* (Philadelphia: Westminster, 1981).

Carmody, D.L. & Carmody, J.T., "Christology in Karl Rahner's Evolutionary World View," *Religion in Life* 49 (1980) 195-210.

Carnley, Peter, "The Poverty of Historical Scepticism," in S.W. Sykes & J.P. Clayton (eds.), *Christ, Faith and History* (1972) 165-189.

————, *The Shape of Resurrection Belief* (Oxford: Clarendon, 1987).

Carr, Anne, "Karl Rahner," in Martin E. Marty & Dean G. Peerman (eds.), *A Handbook of Christian Theologians* (1984) 519-542.

Chirico, Peter, "Hans Küng's Christology: An Evaluation of its Presuppositions," *Theological Studies* (1979) 256-272.

Citrino, Tullio, "The Principle of 'Christocentrism' and its Role in Fundamental Theology," in René Latourelle & Gerald O'Collins (eds.), *Problems and Perspectives of Fundamental Theology* (Mahwah, NJ: Paulist, 1982) 168-185.

Clarke, Thomas, "Current Christologies," *Worship* 53 (1979) 438-448.

Clayton, Philip, "Anticipation and Theological Method," in Carl Braaten & Philip Clayton (eds.), *The Theology of Wolfhart Pannenberg* (1988) 122-150.

Cobb, John B., "Pannenberg and Process Theology," in Carl Braaten & Philip Clayton (eds.), *The Theology of Wolfhart Pannenberg* (1988) 54-74.

————, *Christ in a Pluralistic Age* (Philadelphia: Westminster, 1975).

Cook, Michael, "Jesus From the Other Side of History: Christology in Latin America," *Theological Studies* 44 (1983) 258-287.

————, *The Jesus of Faith: A Study in Christology* (Theological Inquiries Series; Mahwah, NJ: Paulist, 1981).

Cooke, Bernard, "Horizons on Christology in the Seventies," *Horizons* 6 (1979) 193-217.

Cowdell, Scott, "Hans Küng and World Religions: The Emergence of a Pluralist," *Theology* 92 (1988) 85-92.

————, *Atheist Priest? Don Cupitt and Christianity* (London: SCM, 1988).

Cupitt, Don, "A Sense of History," *Theology* 89 (1986) 362-366.

————, "One Jesus, Many Christs," in S.W. Sykes & J.P. Clayton (eds.), *Christ, Faith and History* (1972) 131-144.

————, "Professor Stanton on Incarnational Language in the New Testament," in Michael Goulder (ed.), *Incarnation and Myth* (1979) 166-169.

————, "The Finality of Christ," *Theology* 78 (1975) 618-628.

————, "The Leap of Reason," *Theology* 78 (1975) 291-302.

————, *Creation Out of Nothing* (London: SCM, 1990).

————, *Jesus and the Gospel of God* (London: Lutterworth, 1979).

————, *Life Lines* (London: SCM, 1986).

————, *Only Human* (London: SCM, 1985).

————, *Radicals and the Future of the Church* (London: SCM, 1989).

————, *Taking Leave of God* (London, SCM, 1980).

————, *The Long-Legged Fly: A Theology of Language and Desire* (London: SCM, 1987).

————, *The New Christian Ethics* (London: SCM, 1988).

————, *The Sea of Faith* (London: BBC, 1984).

————, *The Time Being* (London: SCM, 1992).

————, *The World to Come* (London: SCM, 1982).

————, *What is a Story?* (London: SCM, 1991).

————, *Who Was Jesus?* (with Peter Armstrong) (London: BBC, 1977).

D'Costa, Gavin (ed.), *Christian Uniqueness Reconsidered: The Myth of a Pluralistic Theology of Religions* (Maryknoll, NY: Orbis, 1990).

————, *John Hick's Theology of Religions: A Critical Evaluation* (Lanham, VA: University Press of America, 1987).

————, *Theology and Religious Pluralism* (Oxford: Basil Blackwell, 1986).

Davis, Charles, *Christ and the World Religions* (New York: Herder & Herder, 1971).

DiNoia, J.A., "Karl Rahner," in David F. Ford (ed.), *The Modern Theologians,* Vol. 1 (1989) 183-204.

Dulles, Avery, "Contemporary Approaches to Christology: Analysis and Reflections," *Living Light* 13 (1976) 119-144.

————, "Pannenberg on Revelation and Faith," in Carl Braaten & Philip Clayton (eds.), *The Theology of Wolfhart Pannenberg* (1988) 169-187.

Dupré, Louis, "Experience and Interpretation: A Philosophical Reflection on Schillebeeckx's *Jesus* and *Christ*," *Theological Studies* 43 (1982) 30-51.

Dyson, A.O., *Who is Jesus Christ?* (London: SCM, 1969).

Edwards, David L., *Tradition and Truth: The Challenge of England's Radical Theologians 1962-1989* (London: Hodder & Stoughton, 1989).

Fackre, Gabriel, "Bones Strong and Weak in the Skeletal Structure of Schillebeeckx's Christology," *Journal of Ecumenical Studies* 21 (1984) 248-277.

————, "Narrative Theology: An Overview," *Interpretation* 37 (1983) 340-352.

Fiorenza, Francis Schüssler, "Christology After Vatican II," *The Ecumenist* 18 (1980) 81-89.

Ford, David F. (ed.), *The Modern Theologians: An Introduction to Christian Theology in the Twentieth Century* 2 Vols. (Oxford: Basil Blackwell, 1989).

Ford, Lewis, "The Nature and Power of the Future," in Carl Braaten & Philip Clayton (eds.), *The Theology of Wolfhart Pannenberg* (1988) 75-94.

Fox, Matthew, *The Coming of the Cosmic Christ: The Healing of Mother Earth and the Birth of a Global Renaissance* (1988) (Melbourne: Collins-Dove, 1989).

Frei, Hans, *The Identity of Jesus Christ: The Hermeneutical Bases of Dogmatic Theology* (Philadelphia: Fortress, 1975).

Galvin, John "The Death of Jesus in Contemporary Theology: Systematic Perspectives and Historical Issues," *Horizons* 13 (1986) 239-252.

————, "The Death of Jesus in the Theology of Edward Schillebeeckx," *The Irish Theological Quarterly* 50 (1983/4) 168-180.

————, "The Resurrection of Jesus in Contemporary Catholic Systematics," *The Heythrop Journal* 20 (1979) 123-145.

Gerrish, B.A., "Friedrich Schleiermacher," in Ninian Smart et al. (eds.), *Nineteenth Century Religious Thought in the West,* Vol. 1 (Cambridge: Cambridge University Press, 1985) 123-156.

Geyer, Hans-Georg "The Resurrection of Jesus Christ: A Survey of the Debate in Present Day Theology," in C.F.D. Moule (ed.),

The Significance of the Message of the Resurrection for Faith in Jesus Christ (London: SCM, 1968) 105-135.

Gilkey, Langdon, "A Theological Voyage with Wilfred Cantwell Smith," *Religious Studies Review* 7 (1981) 298-306.

———, "Plurality and its Theological Implications," in John Hick & Paul F. Knitter (eds.), *The Myth of Christian Uniqueness* (1987) 37-50.

Gillis, Chester, "John Hick's Christology," *Bijdragen* 49 (1988) 41-57.

Goulder, Michael, "The Man of Universal Destiny," in John Hick (ed.), *The Myth of God Incarnate* (1977) 48-63.

———, (ed.), *Incarnation and Myth: The Debate Continued* (London: SCM, 1979).

Grenz, Stanley, "The Appraisal of Pannenberg: A Survey of the Literature," in Carl Braaten & Philip Clayton (eds.), *The Theology of Wolfhart Pannenberg* (1988) 19-52.

Grillmeier, Aloys, "The Figure of Christ in Catholic Theology Today," in J. Feiner et al. (eds.), *Theology Today, Vol. 1: The Renewal in Dogma* (Milwaukee, WI: Bruce Publishing, 1965) 66-108.

Gunton, Colin, *Yesterday and Today: A Study of Continuities in Christology* (London: Darton, Longman & Todd, 1983).

Hanson, A.T., *The Image of the Invisible God* (London: SCM, 1982).

Hardy, Daniel, "Thomas F. Torrance," in David F. Ford (ed.), *The Modern Theologians*, Vol. 1 (1989) 71-91.

Hauerwas, Stanley, "Jesus: The Story of the Kingdom," in *A Community of Character* (Notre Dame, IN: Notre Dame University Press, 1981) 36-52, 232-239.

Hebblethwaite, Brian, "The Moral and Religious Value of the Incarnation," in *The Incarnation: Collected Essays in Christology* (Cambridge: Cambridge University Press, 1979) 27-44.

Hebblethwaite, Peter, *The New Inquisition: The Case of Edward Schillebeeckx and Hans Küng* (San Francisco: Harper & Row, 1980).

Heim, S. Mark, *Is Christ the Only Way? Christian Faith in a Pluralistic World* (Valley Forge, PA: Judson, 1985).

Hick, John & Knitter, Paul F. (eds.), *The Myth of Christian Uniqueness* (London: SCM, 1987).

Hick, John, "An Inspiration Christology for a Religiously Plural World," in Stephen T. Davis (ed.), *Encountering Jesus: A Debate on Christology* (Atlanta, GA: John Knox, 1988) 5-22.

————, "Evil and Incarnation," in Michael Goulder (ed.), *Incarnation and Myth* (1979) 77-84.

————, "Jesus and the World Religions," in John Hick (ed.), *The Myth of God Incarnate* (1977) 167-185.

————, "The Christology of D.M. Baillie," *Scottish Journal of Theology* 11 (1958) 1-12.

————, "The Non-Absoluteness of Christianity," in John Hick & Paul F. Knitter (eds.), *The Myth of Christian Uniqueness* (1987) 16-36.

————, (ed.), *The Myth of God Incarnate* (London: SCM, 1977).

————, *An Interpretation of Religion: Human Responses to the Transcendent* (London: Macmillan, 1989).

————, *God and the Universe of Faiths* (1973) (London: Collins [Fount], 1977).

————, *God Has Many Names: Britain's New Religious Pluralism* (London: Macmillan, 1980).

Hillman, Eugene, "Evangelism in a Wider Ecumenism: Theological Grounds for Dialogue With Other Religions," *Journal of Ecumenical Studies* 12 (1975) 1-12.

————, "Towards the Catholicization of the Church," *American Ecclesiastical Review* 168 (1974) 122-134.

————, *The Wider Ecumenism* (New York: Herder & Herder, 1968).

Hines, Mary, *The Transformation of Dogma: An Introduction to Karl Rahner on Doctrine* (Mahwah, NJ: Paulist, 1989).

Hughes, Edward, *Wilfred Cantwell Smith: A Theology for the World* (London: SCM, 1986).

Inbody, Tyron, "Rahner's Christology: A Critical Assessment," *St Luke's Journal of Theology* 25 (1982) 294-310.

Jeanrond, Werner, "Hans Küng," in David F. Ford (ed.), *The Modern Theologians,* Vol. 1 (1989) 164-180.

Johnson, Elizabeth, "The Ongoing Christology of Wolfhart Pannenberg," *Horizons* 9 (1982) 237-250.

Jüngel, Eberhard, "Toward the Heart of the Matter," *The Christian Century* 27 February 1991, 228-233.

————, *God as the Mystery of the World: On the Foundation of the Theology of the Crucified One in the Dispute between Theism and Atheism* (3rd ed. 1977) (Edinburgh: T & T Clark, 1983).

Kasper, Walter, *Jesus the Christ* (1974, ET 1976) (London: Burns & Oates; Mahwah, NJ: Paulist, 1977).

Kaufman, Gordon, "Religious Diversity, Historical Consciousness and Christian Theology," in John Hick & Paul F. Knitter (eds.), *The Myth of Christian Uniqueness* (1987) 3-15.

Kee, Alistair, *The Roots of Christian Freedom: The Theology of John A.T. Robinson* (London: SPCK, 1988).

Kelsey, David, *The Uses of Scripture in Recent Theology* (Philadelphia: Fortress, 1975).

Kennedy, Philip, *Schillebeeckx* (Outstanding Christian Thinkers Series; London: Geoffrey Chapman, 1993).

Kerr, Fergus, "The One Who Got Away," (review of Phillip Kennedy's *Schillebeeckx*) *The Tablet* 9 October 1993, 1299-1300.

————, *Theology After Wittgenstein* (Oxford: Basil Blackwell, 1986).

Knitter, Paul F., "Catholic Theology of Religions at a Crossroads," *Concilium* 183 (1986) 99-107.

————, "Hans Küng's Theological Rubicon," in Leonard Swidler (ed.), *Toward a Universal Theology of Religion* (1987) 224-230.

————, "Making Sense of the Many," *Religious Studies Review* 13 (1989) 204-207.

————, "Toward a Liberation Theology of Religions," in John Hick and Paul F. Knitter (eds.), *The Myth of Christian Uniqueness* (1987) 178-200.

————, "World Religions and the Finality of Christ: A Critique of Hans Küng's *On Being a Christian*," in Richard Rousseau (ed.), *Interreligious Dialogue* (Philadelphia: Ridge Row, 1981) 202-221.

————, *No Other Name? A Critical Survey of Christian Attitudes Toward the World Religions* (Maryknoll, NY: Orbis, 1985).

Knox, John, *The Humanity and Divinity of Christ: A Study of Pattern In Christology* (1967) (Cambridge: Cambridge University Press, 1978).

Krieg, Robert, "The Crucified in Rahner's Christology," *The Irish Theological Quarterly* 50 (1983/4) 151-167.

————, *Story-Shaped Christology: The Role of Narratives in Identifying Jesus Christ* (Theological Inquiries Series; Mahwah, NJ: Paulist, 1988).

Küng, Hans & Tracy, David, *Paradigm Change in Theology: A Symposium for the Future* (Edinburgh: T & T Clark, 1989).

Küng, Hans, "Ecumenism and Truth: The Wider Dialogue," *The Tablet* (28 January 1989) 92-93.

————, "How Does One Do Christian Theology?" in *Theology for the Third Millennium* (1988) 103-122.

————, "Is There One True Religion? An Essay in Establishing Ecumenical Criteria," in *Theology for The Third Millennium* (1988) 227-256.

————, "Karl Barth and the Postmodern Paradigm," in *Theology for the Third Millennium* (1988) 257-284.

————, "Theology on the Way to a New Paradigm: Reflections on My Own Career," in *Theology for the Third Millennium* (1988) 182-206.

————, "What is True Religion? Toward an Ecumenical Criteriology," in Leonard Swidler (ed.), *Toward a Universal Theology of Religion* (1987) 231-250.

————, *Christianity and the World Religions: Paths of Dialogue With Islam, Hinduism and Buddhism* (with Josef van Ess, Heinrich von Stietencron & Heinz Bechert) (1985) (London: Collins, 1987).

————, *Does God Exist? An Answer for Today* (1978) (London: Collins, 1980).

————, *Global Responsibility: In Search of a New World Ethic* (1990) (London: SCM, 1991).

————, *On Being a Christian* (1974, ET 1976) (New York: Doubleday [Image], 1984).

————, *The Incarnation of God: An Introduction to Hegel's Theological Thought as Prolegomena to a Future Christology* (1970) (Edinburgh: T & T Clark, 1987).

————, *Theology for the Third Millennium: An Ecumenical View* (New York: Doubleday, 1988).

Kuschel, Karl-Josef, *Born Before All Time? The Dispute Over Christ's Origin* (1990) (London: SCM, 1992).

Lampe, Geoffrey, *God as Spirit* (1977) (London: SCM, 1983).

Liechty, Daniel, *Theology in Postliberal Perspective* (London: SCM; Philadelphia: Trinity Press International, 1990).

Lindbeck, George, *The Nature of Doctrine: Religion and Theology in a Postliberal Age* (London: SPCK, 1984).

Lipner, J., "Christians and the Uniqueness of Christ," *Scottish Journal of Theology* 28 (1975) 359-368.

Loewe, William, "The New Catholic Tübingen Theology of Walter Kasper," *The Heythrop Journal* 21 (1980) 30-49.

Lonergan, Bernard, "Christology Today: Methodological Reflections," (1975) in Frederick Crowe (ed.), *A Third Collection: Papers by Bernard J. F. Lonergan, S.J.* (Mahwah, NJ: Paulist; London: Geoffrey Chapman, 1985) 74-99.

Mackey, James P., *Jesus The Man and the Myth: A Contemporary Christology* (London: SCM, 1979).

————, *Modern Theology: A Sense of Direction* (Oxford: Oxford University Press [OPUS], 1987).

MacKinnon, D.M., "Ethics and Tragedy," in *Explorations in Theology 5* (London: SCM, 1979) 182-195.

————, "Prolegomena to Christology," *Journal of Theological Studies* 33 (1982) 146-160.

————, "Substance in Christology—A Cross-Bench View," in S.W. Sykes & J.P. Clayton (eds.), *Christ, Faith and History* (1972) 279-300.

————, "The Relation of the Doctrines of the Incarnation and the Trinity," in R. McKinney (ed.), *Creation, Christ and Culture: Studies in Honour of T.F. Torrance* (Edinburgh: T & T Clark, 1976) 92-107.

Macquarrie, John "The Concept of a Christ Event," in A.E. Harvey (ed.), *God Incarnate: Story and Belief* (London: SPCK, 1981) 69-80.

————, *Jesus Christ in Modern Thought* (London: SCM; Philadelphia: Trinity Press International, 1990).

————, *Twentieth-Century Religious Thought* (1963) (London: SCM, 2nd ed. 1981; 4th ed. 1988).

Marshall, Bruce, *Christology in Conflict: The Identity of a Saviour in Rahner and Barth* (Oxford: Basil Blackwell, 1987).

Marty, Martin E. & Peerman, Dean G. (eds.), *A Handbook of Christian Theologians* (Cambridge: Lutterworth, 1984).

Maurier, Henri, "The Christian Theology of the Non-Christian Religions," *Lumen Vitae* 31 (1976) 59-74.

McCool, Gerald (ed.), *A Rahner Reader* (New York: Seabury, 1975).

McDermott, Brian, "Roman Catholic Christology: Two Recurring Themes," *Theological Studies* 41 (1980) 339-367.

McDermott, John, "The Christologies of Karl Rahner," 1 & 2, *Gregorianum* 67 (1986) 87-123, 297-327.

McGrath, Alister, *The Genesis of Doctrine: A Study in the Foundations of Doctrinal Criticism* (Oxford: Basil Blackwell, 1990).

————, *The Making of Modern German Christology: From the Enlightenment to Pannenberg* (Oxford: Basil Blackwell, 1986).

McIntyre, John, *The Shape of Christology* (London: SCM, 1966).

McWilliams, Warren, *The Passion of God: Divine Suffering in Contemporary Protestant Theology* (Macon, GA: Mercer University Press, 1985).

Meeks, M. Douglas, *Origins of the Theology of Hope* (Philadelphia: Fortress, 1976).

Meier, John P., "Jesus among the Theologians: I. Küng and Schillebeeckx," in *The Mission of Christ and His Church* (1990) 33-48.

————, "Jesus among the Theologians: II. Sobrino and Segundo," in *The Mission of Christ and His Church* (1990) 49-69.

————, *The Mission of Christ and His Church: Studies in Christology and Ecclesiology* (Good News Studies Series, 30; Wilmington, DE: Michael Glazier, 1990).

Metz, Johann Baptist, "A Short Apology of Narrative," *Concilium* 85 (1973) 84-96.

Michalson, Gordon, "The Response to Lindbeck," *Modern Theology* 4 (1988) 107-120.

Míguez Bonino, José (ed.), *Faces of Jesus: Latin American Christologies* (1977) (Maryknoll, NY: Orbis, 1984).

Milbank, John, "The End of Dialogue," in Gavin D'Costa (ed.), *Christian Uniqueness Reconsidered* (1990) 174-191.

Milet, Jean, *God or Christ? The Excesses of Christocentricity* (New York: Crossroad, 1981).

Mitchell, Basil, *The Justification of Religious Belief* (London: Macmillan, 1973).

Moloney, Raymond, "African Christology," *Theological Studies* 48 (1987) 505-515.

Moltmann, Jürgen, "An Open Letter to José Míguez Bonino," *Christianity and Crisis* 36 (1976) 57-63.

———, "Is 'Pluralistic Theology' Useful for the Dialogue of World Religions?" in Gavin D'Costa (ed.), *Christian Uniqueness Reconsidered* (1990) 149-156.

———, *The Church in the Power of the Spirit: A Contribution to Messianic Ecclesiology* (1975) (London: SCM, 1977) .

———, *The Crucified God: The Cross of Christ as the Foundation and Criticism of Christian Theology* (1973) (London: SCM, 1974).

———, *The Trinity and the Kingdom of God: The Doctrine of God* (1980) (London: SCM, 1981).

———, *The Way of Jesus Christ: Christology in Messianic Dimensions* (1989) (London: SCM, 1990).

———, *Theology and Joy* (1971) (London: SCM, 1973).

———, *Theology of Hope: On the Ground and Implications of a Christian Eschatology* (1965) (London: SCM, 1967).

———, *Theology Today* (London: SCM, 1988).

Mondin, Battista, "New Trends in Christology," *Biblical Theology Bulletin* 4 (1974) 33-74.

Morgan, Robert, "Historical Criticism and Christology: England and Germany," in Stephen Sykes (ed.), *England and Germany* (1982) 80-112.

Morris, Thomas V., *The Logic of God Incarnate* (Ithaca, NY: Cornell University Press, 1986).

Morse, Christopher, "Jürgen Moltmann," in Martin E. Marty & Dean G. Peerman (eds.), *A Handbook of Christian Theologians* (1984) 660-676.

Neill, Stephen, *The Supremacy of Jesus* (London: Hodder & Stoughton, 1984).

Neuhaus, Richard, "Theology for Church and Polis," in Carl Braaten & Philip Clayton (eds.), *The Theology of Wolfhart Pannenberg* (1988) 226-238.

————, "Wolfhart Pannenberg: Portrait of a Theologian," in Wolfhart Pannenberg, *Theology and the Kingdom of God* (Philadelphia: Fortress, 1969) 9-50.

Newbigin, Lesslie, "Religion for the Marketplace," in Gavin D'Costa (ed.), *Christian Uniqueness Reconsidered* (1990) 135-148.

————, "The Centrality of Jesus for History," in Michael Goulder (ed.), *Incarnation and Myth* (1979) 197-210.

————, *The Finality of Christ* (Richmond, VA: John Knox, 1969).

Newlands, G.M., "GM Newlands on *The Myth of God Incarnate*," in Stephen Sykes and David Holmes (eds.), *New Studies in Theology 1* (London: Paulist, 1980) 181-192.

Nichols, Aidan, "Walter Kasper and his Theological Program," *New Blackfriars* 67 (1986) 16-24.

Nineham, Dennis, "Epilogue," in John Hick (ed.), *The Myth of God Incarnate* (1977) 186-204.

————, "God Incarnate: Why Myth?" in Durstan R. McDonald (ed.), *The Myth/Truth of God Incarnate* (Wilton, CT: Moorehouse-Barlow, 1979), 45-66.

————, "History and the Gospel," in *Explorations in Theology 1* (London: SCM, 1977) 76-91.

————, "Individual Essay," in the Doctrine Commission of the Church of England *Christian Believing* (London: SPCK, 1976) 75-88.

————, "New Testament Interpretation in an Historical Age," in *Explorations in Theology 1* (London: SCM, 1977) 145-165.

————, "Response," in David L. Edwards *Tradition and Truth* (1989) 296-306.

————, "Schweitzer Revisited," *Explorations in Theology 1* (London: SCM, 1977) 112-133.

————, "What Happened to the New Reformation?" in Eric James (ed.), *God's Truth: Essays to Celebrate the Twenty-Fifth Anniversary of* Honest to God (London: SCM, 1988) 152-160.

————, *Saint Mark* (1963) (Harmondsworth, UK: Penguin [Pelican], rev. ed. 1969).

————, *The Use and Abuse of the Bible* (London: SPCK, 1976).

North, Robert, "Soul-Body Unity and God-Man Unity," *Theological Studies* 30 (1969) 27-60.

O'Collins, Gerald, *Fundamental Theology* (London: Darton, Longman & Todd, 1981).

————, *The Easter Jesus* (London: Darton, Longman & Todd, 1973).

————, *Jesus Risen* (London: Darton, Longman & Todd, 1987).

————, *What Are They Saying About Jesus?* (1977) (Mahwah, NJ: Paulist, rev. ed. 1983).

Page, Ruth, *The Incarnation of Freedom and Love* (London: SCM, 1991).

Panikkar, Raimundo, "The Jordan, the Tiber and the Ganges: Three Kairological Moments of Christic Self-Consciousness," in John Hick and Paul F. Knitter (eds.), *The Myth of Christian Uniqueness* (1987) 89-116.

————, *The Unknown Christ of Hinduism* (1964) (London: Darton, Longman & Todd, 1981).

Pannenberg, Wolfhart, "Dogmatic Theses on the Doctrine of Revelation," in Wolfhart Pannenberg (ed.), *Revelation as History* (1962, ET 1968) (London: Macmillan, 1969) 125-158.

————, "God's Presence in History," in James Wall (ed.), *Theologians in Transition* (New York: Crossroad, 1981) 93-99.

————, "Religious Pluralism and Conflicting Truth Claims: The Problem of a Theology of The World Religions," in Gavin D'Costa (ed.), *Christian Uniqueness Reconsidered* (1990) 96-106.

————, "Towards a Theology of the History of the Religions," (1962) in *Basic Questions in Theology*, Vol. 2 (1967) (Philadelphia: Westminster, 1971) 65-118.

————, *An Introduction to Systematic Theology* (Grand Rapids, MI: Eerdmans, 1991).

————, *Christian Spirituality and Sacramental Community* (1983) (London: Darton, Longman & Todd, 1984).

————, *Human Nature, Election and History* (Philadelphia: Westminster, 1977).

————, *Jesus—God and Man* (1964) (London: SCM, 1968).

————, *Systematic Theology*, Vol. 1 (1988) (Grand Rapids, MI: Eerdmans, 1991).

————, *The Apostles' Creed: In The Light of Today's Questions* (London: SCM, 1972).

————, *What is Man? Contemporary Anthropology in Theological Perspective* (1962, rev. ed. 1964, ET 1970) (Philadelphia: Fortress, 1972).

Pawlikowski, John, *Christ in the Light of the Christian-Jewish Dialogue* (Mahwah, NJ: Paulist, 1982).

Pelikan, Jaroslav, *Jesus Through the Centuries: His Place in the History of Culture* (New Haven, CT: Yale University Press, 1985).

Pieris, Aloysius, "Speaking of the Son of God in Non-Christian Cultures, e.g. in Asia," *Concilium* 153 (1982) 65-70.

————, "The Buddha and the Christ: Mediators of Liberation," in John Hick & Paul F. Knitter (eds.), *The Myth of Christian Uniqueness* (1987) 162-177.

————, "The Place of Non-Christian Religions and Cultures in the Evolution of Third World Theology," in V. Fabella and S. Torres (eds.), *Irruption of the Third World: Challenge to Theology* (Maryknoll, NY: Orbis, 1983) 113-139.

Pittenger, Norman, *Catholic Faith in a Process Perspective* (Maryknoll, NY: Orbis, 1981).

Placher, William, "Postliberal Theology," in David F. Ford (ed.), *The Modern Theologians,* Vol. 2 (1989) 115-128.

————, "Revisionist and Postliberal Theologies and the Public Character of Theology," *Thomist* 49 (1985) 392-416.

Polkinghorne, John, *Science and Creation: The Search for Understanding* (London: SPCK, 1988).

Preston, Ronald, "Need Dr Nineham be so Negative?" *Expository Times* 90 (1979) 275-280.

————, *Church and Society in the Late Twentieth Century: The Economic and Political Task* (London: SCM, 1983).

————, *Religion and the Ambiguities of Capitalism* (London: SCM, 1991).

Prusak, Bernard, "The Son of Man Came Eating and Drinking: An Overview of Christological Perspectives on the Incarnation," in F. Eigo and S. Fittipaldi (eds.), *Who Do People Say I Am?* (Proceedings of the Theology Institute of Villanova University, 12; Villanova, PA: Villanova University Press, 1980) 1-46.

Pujdak, Stephen, "Schoonenberg's Christology in Context," in Stephen Pujdak et al., *Sylloge Excerptorum e Dissertationibus, Vol. 50: Ad Gradum Doctoris in Sacra Theologia vel in Iure*

Canonico Consequendum Conscriptis (Louvain, Belgium: Katholieke Universiteit te Leuven, 1979) 338-353.

Puthiadam, Ignace, "Christian Faith and Life in a World of Religious Pluralism," *Concilium* 135 (1980) 99-112.

Race, Alan, *Christians and Religious Pluralism: Patterns in the Christian Theology of Religions* (London: SCM, 1983).

Rahner, Karl, "Christianity and the Non-Christian Religions," in *Theological Investigations 5* (1966) 115-134.

―――, "Christology Today," (1972) in Karl Rahner and Wilhelm Thüsing *A New Christology* (London: Burns & Oates, rev. ed. 1980) 3-17.

―――, "Christology Within an Evolutionary View of the World," in *Theological Investigations 5* (1966) 157-92.

―――, "Dogmatic Reflections on the Knowledge and Self-Consciousness of Christ," in *Theological Investigations 5* (1966) 193-215.

―――, "Experiencing Easter," in *Theological Investigations 7: Further Theology of the Spiritual Life 1* (New York: Herder & Herder, 1971; London: Darton, Longman & Todd, 1971), 159-168.

―――, "Ignatian Mysticism of Joy in the World," (1974) excerpted in Gerald A. McCool (ed.), *A Rahner Reader* (1975) 313-317.

―――, "One Mediator and Many Mediations," in *Theological Investigations 9: Writings of 1965-1967* (London: Darton, Longman & Todd, 1972) 169-184.

―――, "Remarks on the Importance of the History of Jesus for Catholic Dogmatics," in *Theological Investigations 13: Theology, Anthropology, Christology* (London: Darton, Longman & Todd, 1975) 201-212.

―――, "The Position of Christology in the Church Between Exegesis and Dogmatics," in *Theological Investigations 11: Confrontations 1* (London: Darton, Longman & Todd; New York: Seabury, 1974) 185-214.

―――, *Foundations of Christian Faith: An Introduction to the Idea of Christianity* (1976) (London: Darton, Longman & Todd, 1978).

―――, *Theological Investigations 5: Later Writings* (Baltimore, MA: Helicon; London: Darton, Longman & Todd, 1966).

Ramisch, Joseph, "The Debate Concerning the 'Historical Jesus' in the Christology of Schillebeeckx," *Semeia* 30 (1984) 29-48.

Reinhardt, Klaus, "In What Way is Jesus Christ Unique?" *Communio* 1 (1974) 343-64.

Richard, Lucien, *What Are They Saying About Christ and the World Religions?* (Mahwah, NJ: Paulist, 1981).

Ritschl, Dietrich, *Memory and Hope: An Inquiry Concerning the Presence of Christ* (London: Collier-Macmillan, 1967).

————, *The Logic of Theology: A Brief Account of the Relationship Between Basic Concepts in Theology* (1984) (London: SCM, 1986).

Robbins, Jerry K., "The Finality of Christ in the Theology of Norman Pittenger," *Encounter* 50 (1989) 353-366.

Robinson, John, "Hosea and the Virgin Birth," *Theology* 52 (1948) 373-375; expanded in *Twelve More New Testament Studies* (London: SCM, 1984) 1-11.

————, "Need Jesus Have Been Perfect?" in S.W. Sykes & J.P. Clayton (eds.), *Christ, Faith and History* (1972) 39-52.

————, "The Last Tabu: The Self-Consciousness of Jesus," in *Twelve More New Testament Studies* (London: SCM, 1984) 155-170.

————, "What Future for a Unique Christ?" in *Where Three Ways Meet: Last Essays and Sermons* (London: SCM, 1987) 9-17.

————, *The Human Face of God* (London: SCM, 1973).

————, *Truth is Two-Eyed* (London: SCM, 1979).

Rodwell, John, "Relativism in Science and Theology," in Michael Goulder (ed.), *Incarnation and Myth* (1979) 214-223.

Rosato, Philip, "Spirit Christology: Ambiguity and Promise," *Theological Studies* 38 (1977) 423-449.

Rossano, Pietro, "Christ's Lordship and Religious Pluralism in Roman Catholic Perspective," (with responses & reply) in Gerald Anderson & Thomas Stransky (eds.), *Christ's Lordship and Religious Pluralism* (Maryknoll, NY: Orbis, 1981) 96-109, 110-132.

Rouner, Leroy, "Theology of Religions in Recent Protestant Theology," *Concilium* 183 (1986) 108-115.

Ruether, Rosemary Radford, *Sexism and God Talk: Towards a Feminist Theology* (London: SCM, 1983).

————, *To Change The World: Christianity and Cultural Criticism* (London: SCM, 1981).

Rupp, George, *Christologies and Cultures: Toward a Typology of Religious Worldviews* (The Hague: Mouton, 1974).

Scheffczyk, Leo, "Christology in the Context of Experience," *The Thomist* 48 (1984) 383-408.

Schillebeeckx, Edward, "Answer," (to the Sacred Congregation for the Doctrine of Faith) (1977) in Peter Hebblethwaite, *The New Inquisition* (1980) 129-153.

————, "Dominican Spirituality," in *God Among Us: The Gospel Proclaimed* (1982) (London: SCM, 1983) 232-248.

————, *Christ the Sacrament of Encounter With God* (1960) (London: Sheed & Ward, 1963).

————, *Christ: The Christian Experience in the Modern World* (1977) (London: SCM, 1980).

————, *Church: The Human Story of God* (1989) (London: SCM, 1991).

————, *Interim Report on the Books* Jesus *and* Christ (1979) (London: SCM, 1980).

————, *Jesus: An Experiment in Christology* (1974, ET 1979) (London: Collins [Fount] 1983).

Schineller, J.P., "Christ and the Church: A Spectrum of Views," *Theological Studies* 37 (1976) 545-566.

Schlette, Heinz Robert, *Towards a Theology of Religions* (*Questiones Disputatae*; London: Burns & Oates, 1966).

Schoonenberg, Piet, "Baptism with the Holy Spirit," *Concilium* 6 (1984) 20-37.

————, "The Church and Non-Christian Religions," in D. Flanagan (ed.), *The Evolving Church* (Staten Island, NY: Alba Publishing House, 1966) 89-109.

————, *The Christ* (1969, ET 1972) (London: Sheed & Ward, 1974).

Schreiter, Robert, "The Anonymous Christian and Christology," *Missiology* 6 (1978) 29-52.

————, "Edward Schillebeeckx," in David F. Ford (ed.), *The Modern Theologians,* Vol. 1 (1989) 152-163.

————, "Edward Schillebeeckx," in Martin E. Marty & Dean G. Peerman (eds.), *A Handbook of Christian Theologians* (1984) 625-638.

Schweitzer, Albert, *The Quest of the Historical Jesus: A Critical Study of its Progress From Reimarus to Wrede* (1906) (New York: Macmillan [Collier], 1968).

Schwöbel, Christoph, "Wolfhart Pannenberg," in David F. Ford (ed.), *The Modern Theologians,* Vol. 1 (1989) 257-292.

Segundo, Juan Luis *Jesus of Nazareth: Yesterday and Today,* Vol. 1: *Faith and Ideologies* (1982) (Maryknoll, NY: Orbis, 1984).

———, *Jesus of Nazareth: Yesterday and Today,* Vol. 2: *The Historical Jesus of the Synoptics* (1982) (Maryknoll, NY: Orbis, 1985).

———, *Jesus of Nazareth: Yesterday and Today,* Vol. 3: *The Humanist Christology of Paul* (1982) (Maryknoll, NY: Orbis, 1986).

———, *Jesus of Nazareth: Yesterday and Today,* Vol. 4: *The Christ of the Ignatian Exercises* (1982) (Maryknoll, NY: Orbis, 1987).

———, *Jesus of Nazareth: Yesterday and Today,* Vol. 5: *An Evolutionary Approach to Jesus of Nazareth* (1982) (Maryknoll, NY: Orbis, 1988).

Shaw, Graham, *The Cost of Authority: Manipulation and Freedom in the New Testament* (London: SCM, 1983).

Smith, Barbara, *Options in Contemporary Feminist Christology* (Unpublished PhD Dissertation, Boston University Graduate School; Ann Arbor, MI: University Microfilms International, 1989).

Smith, Wilfred Cantwell—see Cantwell Smith, Wilfred.

Snyder, Mary, *The Christology of Rosemary Radford Ruether: A Critical Introduction* (Mystic, CT: Twenty-Third Publications, 1988).

Sobrino, Jon, *Christology at the Crossroads: A Latin American Approach* (1976) (London: SCM, 1978).

Sölle, Dorothee, *Christ the Representative* (1965) (London: SCM, 1967).

Stroup, George, "The 'Finality' of Jesus Christ," *Austin Seminary Bulletin* 97 (1982) 5-13.

———, *The Promise of Narrative Theology* (1981) (London: SCM, 1984).

Surin, Kenneth, "'Many Religions and The One True Faith': An Examination of Lindbeck's Chapter Three," *Modern Theology* 4 (1988) 187-209.

————, "Revelation, Salvation, The Uniqueness of Christ and Other Religions," *Religious Studies* 19 (1983) 323-343.

Swidler, Leonard, "Hans Küng," in Martin E. Marty & Dean G. Peerman (eds.), *A Handbook of Christian Theologians* (1984) 710-726.

————, (ed.), *Toward a Universal Theology of Religion* (Faith Meets Faith Series; Maryknoll, NY: Orbis, 1987).

Sykes, S.W., "Germany and England: An Attempt at Theological Diplomacy," in S.W. Sykes (ed.), *England and Germany* (1982) 146-170.

————, (ed.), *England and Germany: Studies in Theological Diplomacy* (Studies in the Intercultural History of Christianity; Frankfurt: Verlag Peter D. Lang, 1982).

Sykes, S.W. and Clayton, P.J. (eds.), *Christ, Faith and History: Cambridge Studies in Christology* (Cambridge: Cambridge University Press, 1972).

Tadsen, Rose, *Jesus Christ in the World Theology of Wilfred Cantwell Smith* (Unpublished PhD dissertation, University of St. Michael's College, Toronto, 1984; Ann Arbor, MI: University Microfilms International, 1986).

Taylor, Mark, *Erring: A Postmodern A/theology* (Chicago: University of Chicago Press, 1984).

TeSelle, Eugene, *Christ in Context: Divine Purpose and Human Possibility* (Philadelphia: Fortress, 1975).

Thompson, William M., *The Jesus Debate: A Survey and Synthesis* (Mahwah, NJ: Paulist, 1985).

Torrance, Thomas, "Theological Realism," in Brian Hebblethwaite and Stewart Sutherland (eds.), *The Philosophical Frontiers of Christian Theology: Essays Presented to D.M. Mackinnon* (Cambridge: Cambridge University Press, 1982) 169-196.

————, *God and Rationality* (London: Oxford University Press, 1971).

————, *Space, Time and Incarnation* (London: Oxford University Press, 1969).

Tracy, David, "Kenosis, Sunyata and Trinity: A Dialogue With Masao Abe," in John B. Cobb & Christopher Ives (eds.), *The Emptying God: A Buddhist-Jewish-Christian Conversation* (Faith Meets Faith Series; Maryknoll, NY: Orbis, 1990) 135-154.

————, "Lindbeck's New Program for Theology: A Reflection," *The Thomist* 49 (1985) 460-72.

————, *Blessed Rage for Order* (1975) (San Francisco: Harper & Row, 1988).

————, *Plurality and Ambiguity: Hermeneutics, Religion, Hope* (1987) (London: SCM, 1988).

————, *The Analogical Imagination: Christian Theology and the Culture of Pluralism* (London: SCM, 1981).

Turner, H.E.W., *Jesus the Christ* (Oxford: Mowbray, 1976).

Twiss, Sumner B., "The Philosophy of Religious Pluralism: A Critical Appraisal of Hick and his Critics," *Journal of Religion* 70 (1990) 533-368.

Van Beeck, Frans Jozef, *Christ Proclaimed: Christology as Rhetoric* (Theological Inquiries Series; Mahwah, NJ: Paulist, 1979).

Vandervelde, George, "Creation and Cross in the Christology of Edward Schillebeeckx: A Protestant Appraisal," *Journal of Ecumenical Studies* 20 (1983) 257-271.

Vorgrimler, Herbert, *Understanding Karl Rahner: An Introduction To His Life and Thought* (1985) (London: SCM, 1986).

Webster, J.B., "Eberhard Jüngel," in David F. Ford (ed.), *The Modern Theologians*, Vol. 1 (1989) 92-106.

Weightmann, Colin, *Theology in a Polanyian Universe: The Theology of Thomas Torrance* (Unpublished PhD Dissertation, University of Queensland, Department of Studies in Religion, 1991).

Weinrich, Harald, "Narrative Theology," *Concilium* 85 (1973) 46-56.

Wiles, Maurice, "A Survey of the Issues in The Myth Debate," in Michael Goulder (ed.), *Incarnation and Myth* (1979) 1-12.

————, "Christian Doctrine in the 1960s," *Church Quarterly* 2 (1970) 215-221.

————, "Christian Theology in an Age of Religious Studies," in *Explorations in Theology 4* (London: SCM, 1979) 28-40.

————, "Christianity Without Incarnation?" in John Hick (ed.), *The Myth of God Incarnate* (1977) 1-10.

————, "Christology in an Age of Historical Studies," in *Explorations in Theology 4* (London: SCM, 1979) 14-27.

————, "Comment on Lesslie Newbigin's Essay," in Michael Goulder (ed.), *Incarnation and Myth* (1979) 211-213.

————, "Does Christology Rest on a Mistake?" in S.W. Sykes & J.P. Clayton (eds.), *Christ, Faith and History* (1972) 3-12.

————, "Looking into the Sun," (1969) in *Working Papers in Doctrine* (London: SCM, 1976) 148-163.

————, "Myth in Theology," in John Hick (ed.), *The Myth of God Incarnate* (1977) 148-166.

————, "Religious Authority and Divine Action," (1971) in *Working Papers in Doctrine* (London: SCM, 1976) 132-147.

————, *Faith and the Mystery of God* (London: SCM, 1982).

————, *God's Action in the World* (London: SCM, 1986).

————, *The Remaking of Christian Doctrine* (London: SCM, 1974).

Williams, Stephen, "Lindbeck's Regulative Christology," *Modern Theology* 4 (1988) 173-186.

Young, Frances, "A Cloud of Witnesses," in John Hick (ed.), *The Myth of God Incarnate* (1977) 13-47.

————, "Incarnation and Atonement: God Suffered and Died," in Michael Goulder (ed.), *Incarnation and Myth* (1979) 100-103.

————, "The Finality of Christ," in Michael Goulder (ed.), *Incarnation and Myth* (1979) 174-186.

————, *Sacrifice and the Death of Christ* (London: SCM, 1975).

Zimany, Roland, "Moltmann's Crucified God," *Dialog* 16 (Winter 1977) 49-57.

INDEX

References to the principal treatment of a subject are in **boldface.**

ACKNOWLEDGMENTS

The Publisher gratefully acknowledges use of the following excerpts: *Christ: The Experience of Jesus as Lord* by Edward Schillebeeckx. The original Dutch version of the book was published under the title **Gerechtigheid en liefde: Genade en bevrijding** by Uitgeverij H. Nelissen B.V., Bloemendaal, in 1977. Copyright © 1977 by Uitgeverij H. Nelissen B.V., Bloemendaal. English translation copyright © 1980 by The Crossroad Publishing Company. Used with permission of The Crossroad Publishing Company, New York; *Foundations of Christian Faith: An Introduction to the Idea of Christianity*, by Karl Rahner, copyright (1978) by London: Darton, Longman, and Todd, Ltd., originally published by The Seabury Press, copyright © The Seabury Press, Inc., reprinted by permission of HarperCollins Publishers, Inc.; From *On Being a Christian* by Hans Küng. Copyright © by Doubleday, a division of Bantam Doubleday Dell Publishing Group, Inc. Used by permission of Doubleday, a division of Bantam Doubleday Dell Publishing Group, Inc.; excerpts from *Yesterday and Today* by Colin Gunton, copyright © 1983, London: Darton, Longman, & Todd, reprinted by permission; excerpts from *The Way of Jesus Christ: Christology in Messianic Dimensions* by Jürgen Moltmann, English translation copyright © 1990 by Margaret Kohl. Reprinted by permission of HarperCollins Publishers, Inc., with U.K. rights reprinted by permission of SCM Press, Ltd., 9-17 St. Albans Place, London N1 0NZ, England; excerpts from *Jesus: An Experiment in Christology* by Edward Schillebeeckx, copyright © 1974, 1979, 1983, London: HarperCollins Publishers; excerpts from *The Myth of Christian Uniqueness* edited by John Hick and Paul F. Knitter, copyright © 1987 by Orbis Books, Maryknoll, New York, English translation copyright © 1987 by SCM Press, Ltd. London, England; excerpts from *Theology of Hope* by Jürgen Moltmann, English translation copyright © 1968 by SCM Press, Ltd. Reprinted by permission of HarperCollins Publishers Inc.; excerpts from *The Crucified God* by Jürgen Moltmann, English translation copyright © 1974 by SCM Press Ltd. Reprinted by permission of HarperCollins Publishers Inc.; excerpts from *Jesus: God and Man* by Wolfhart Pannenberg, translated by Lewis L. Wilkins and Duane Priebe, copyright © MCMLXVIII The Westminster Press. Used by permission. Excerpts from *Jesus: God and Man* by Wolfhart Pannenberg, copyright © 1968 for English translation rights by SCM Press, London, United States and Canadian rights, Westminister/John Knox Press, Publications Unit of The Presbyterian Church, Louisville, Kentucky; excerpts from *Christology in Conflict: The Identity of a Saviour in Rahner and Barth* by Bruce Marshall, copyright © 1987 by Basil Blackwell, Oxford, England; excerpts reprinted from *The Identity of Jesus Christ* by Hans Frei, copyright © 1975 Fortress Press. Used by permission of Augsburg Fortress; excerpts from *God and Rationality* by Thomas Torrance, copyright © 1971, London: Oxford University Press, reprinted by permission of Oxford University Press. The following excerpts are reprinted by permission of Paulist Press, Mahwah, New Jersey: *Christ Proclaimed: Christology as Rhetoric* (Theological Inquiries Series) by Frans Jozef van Beeck, copyright © 1979; *Jesus the Christ* by Walter Kasper, copyright © 1974, 1976; *Jesus the Christ* by Walter Kasper, English translation copyright © 1976 by Burns and Oates, London, England. The Publisher also acknowledges use of the following excerpts: *The Human Face of God* by John Robinson, English translation rights by SCM Press, London, England; *The Myth of God Incarnate* by John Hick, copyright © 1977 by SCM Press, London, England; *Theology of Hope: On the Ground and Implications of a Christian Eschatology* by Jürgen Moltmann, copyright © 1967 by SCM Press, London, United States rights, HarperCollins Publishers; excerpts from *Christians and Religious Pluralism: Patterns in the Christian Theology of Religions* by Alan Race, copyright © 1993 SCM Press, London, England; "Myth in Theology," from *The Myth of God Incarnate* by Maurice Wiles, copyright © 1977, Westminster/John Knox Press; Japanese rights from Japan Uni Agency, Inc.; *Christ: The Christian Experience in the Modern World* by Edward Schillebeeckx, copyright © 1980 by SCM Press, London; *Jesus the Christ* by Walter Kasper, copyright © 1974, English translation copyright © 1976 by Burns and Oates, London, England, and copyright © 1974 by Paulist Press, Mahwah, New Jersey; *The Nature of Doctrine: Religion and Theology in a Postliberal Age* by George Lindbeck, copyright © 1984, London: SPCK, Holy Trinity Church, London; *Memory and Hope: An Inquiry Concerning the Presence of Christ* by Dietrich Ritschl, copyright © 1967 by Collier-Macmillan, London England; *The Crucified God: The Cross of Christ as the Foundation and Criticism of Christian Theology* by Jürgen Moltmann, copyright © 1974 by SCM Press Ltd., London, England; *Theology of Hope: On the Ground and Implications of a Christian Eschatology* by Jürgen Moltmann, copyright © 1965 by SCM Press Ltd., London, England.

THEOLOGICAL INQUIRIES

Serious studies on contemporary questions of Scripture, Systematics and Moral Theology. Also in the series: